I0866545

A Long Essay on the Long Poem

Modern and Contemporary Poetics

A Long Essay on the Long Poem

Modern and Contemporary Poetics and Practices

RACHEL BLAU DuPLESSIS

The University of Alabama Press *Tuscaloosa*

The University of Alabama Press
Tuscaloosa, Alabama 35487-0380
uapress.ua.edu

Typeface: Minion Pro

Cover design: Michele Myatt Quinn

Cataloging-in-Publication data is available from the Library of Congress.
ISBN: 978-0-8173-6068-9
E-ISBN: 978-0-8173-9444-8

What I have noticed in the poetry and poetics of the most important poets is that they are arguing, weaving, and composing a cosmology and an epistemology. Over and over again. [. . .] Repeatedly in the history of poetry, we find ourselves returning to epic structures and the bases of epic in the shape, size and feel of the world, cosmos. I suggest that great poetry is always after the world—it is a spiritual chase—and that it has never been, in the old, outworn sense, simply subjective or personal. [. . .] It is this aspect of poetic experience, its yen for largeness and fullness, that has brought poetry throughout its history into close proximity with the modes of theogony and theology, with science in its deepest concerns, and with philosophies which propose a world.

Robin Blaser, "The Violets," *The Fire*

Contents

Acknowledgments

Acknowledgments: to the anonymous readers of this manuscript for empathetic tough-mindedness; to the University of Alabama Press (Pete Beatty and Dan Waterman) for all encouragement and production; to the editors of the series, Charles Bernstein and Hank Lazer; to students in a number of long-poem courses at Temple and through Temple-Penn Poetics; and especially to all the colleagueship of those poets or critics who welcomed my own long poems and/or at a distance contributed to my critical speculations. These include the series editors and M. A. Bernstein, Ronald Bush, Matthew Carbery, Stephen Collis, Joseph Conte, Michael Davidson, Anne Day Dewey, Margaret Dickie, Andrew Epstein, Bradley Fest, Norman Finkelstein, Stephen Fredman, Susan Stanford Friedman, Jeanne Heuving, Paul Jaussen, Smaro Kamboureli, Lynn Keller, Eric Keenaghan, John Lowney, James Maynard, Brian McHale, Peter Middleton, Adalaide Morris, Fred Moten, Aldon Nielsen, Roy Harvey Pearce, Bob Perelman, Peter Quartermain, Stephen Voyce, and Fred Wah. At least. And to the poets here who answered querying emails with collegial responses—Nathaniel Mackey, Alice Notley, Ron Silliman, Anne Waldman—what can I say but "thanks" and "onward."

To the many people who invited some of these reflections on long poems over many years. I thank you for the conferences, plenary invitations, and lectureships, for invitations into anthologies, and for the intellectual hospitality and the encouragement that propelled these reflections.

Anne Waldman Conference, University of Michigan, March 2002

Processing Pound, Modern Language Association, December 2006

University of Sussex Conference on the Long Poem, Brighton, England, May 2008

Lyric and Long Poem Conference, Grant MacEwan College, Edmonton, Alberta, Canada, May 2009

Long-poem seminars at University of Guelph and Ryerson University (now Toronto Metropolitan University), Canada, October 2010

Charles Olson Centenary Conference, Simon Fraser University, Vancouver, BC, June 2010

John F. Eberhardt Excellence in Writing Lectureship, University of Kansas, March 2011

The Nephie Christodoulides Memorial Lecture, University of Cyprus, November 2011

Green College, University of British Columbia, October 2012

"Short Takes on the Long Poem," University of Auckland, NZ/Aotearoa conference, March 2012

Joseph Duffy Lectureship, Notre Dame University, October 2013

Conference on H.D., Université de Toulouse, France, January 2014

Plenary, Modernist Studies Association, Duquesne University, Pittsburgh, November 2014

The Morag Morris Lectureship, University of Surrey, England, January 2017

Semper Poesia (Seminario permanente di poesia) and Centro Studi interdisciplinary di genere, Università di Trento, Italy, September 2017

Centre for Expanded Poetics, Concordia University, Montreal, October 2017

Passages, Robert Duncan centennial conference, Sorbonne, Paris, June 2019

Rethinking the North American Long Poem, University of Basel, Switzerland, September 2021

Earlier discussions of the concept "nexus" appeared in my essay "Objectivist Poetics, 'Influence,' and Some Contemporary Long Poems," in *Poetics and Praxis "after" Objectivism*, edited by W. Scott Howard and Broc Rossell (Iowa City: University of Iowa Press, 2018). I acknowledge, with thanks to the University of Iowa Press, permission to cite several paragraphs from my essay, first copyright by them.

Several paragraphs from the discussion of Nathaniel Mackey were published in my essay "'The / Whole Was Not The Half of It': Nathaniel Mackey's

Long Poem," in *Nathaniel Mackey "Destination Out": Essays on His Work*, edited by Jeanne Heuving (Iowa City: University of Iowa Press, 2021), and are presented here in a revised format and different context. I acknowledge, with thanks to the University of Iowa Press, permission to cite material from my essay, first copyright by them.

Some paragraphs on Charles Olson are from my essay "Olson and His *Maximus Poems*," in *Contemporary Olson*, edited by David Herd (Manchester: Manchester University Press, 2015); some paragraphs on Robert Duncan are from my essay "Robert Duncan's Long Poem Debates and His Poetics of Grand Collage," *Sillages critiques* 29 (2020); and a smattering of discontinuous sentences are from "After the Long Poem," *Dibur*, no. 4 (2017). I acknowledge their first publication.

A Long Essay on the Long Poem

CHAPTER 1

Length, "Longing," and the Long Poem

WHY DID I write this book? To examine a mode of writing (a poem? an activity? a practice?) involving excessive, hypersaturated, proliferative, and metamorphic works, a mode by which I'd been provoked for decades. I wanted to understand the fascination of the very long poem, so challenging to readers, yet so compelling for their authors, and was particularly interested in how writers use this mode in our time. This book about the modern and contemporary North American Anglophone long poem (with some crucial extras from elsewhere) is the analytic meditation that resulted. Articulating poetics, problems, and solutions for poets in their practices are central goals of this book. It has "essays" in the title, but I don't mean personal, confessional, intimate essays but meditations, essaying a topic.

Being a centaur in this green world—a poet-critic (and a female "centaur" to boot—a horse of another color)—I present a variety of reading modes and taxonomies over five chapters but do not repress artisanal observations about choices and feelings within long-poem *poesis*. Because of the unrolling of my long poems (*Drafts* from 1986 to 2012 and *Traces, with Days* from 2015 onward), some issues in long-poem practices have emerged for me—or at least I see them bifocally. To write critically, I maintain an essayist's attitude throughout: curious, mostly tolerant, positioned, and materialist.

This book is oriented to poetics as a theorizing practice. The dialogues among poems, poets, and poetics (and what or who is instantiated in which) are of constant interest here. Poets think about poetics and purposes in making work, and this implicates thoughts about art, sociality, philosophical issues, historical and political insights, spiritual feelings, and the arcs of their lives in poems. Poetry is a mode of thought fusing evocative meanings within sensuous particulars. Thinking in poetry and poetics is a historical and social practice. These are some of the considerations through which this book takes shape.

For long-poem writers, there is no one single "the Book," but that book is all one is trying to write. That would mean a summary statement of the culture and its society and history as a task of extreme naming and critique—the task of the poetic intellectual offering socio-aesthetic and spiritual analyses. Sometimes this task evokes another accumulative metaphor—for both Anne Waldman and Nathaniel Mackey, this kind of poem might be a Box in which to keep an assemblage of things, the Box in which to send yourself, the Box on which the music of the poems is performed and glossed. These, like Book, are apparently static metaphors (of a metaphoric object), but in this site, performative durations and unrolling observations occur. Whether Book, Box, or accumulative performance, deep cultural processes of addressing "everything" are what these long-poem poets propose—a calling out to a vocation beyond itself. To comprehend these monumental ambitions and lengths, I chose to examine how poets interpret connections to past genres for long works and to reflect on some poets' haunting needs—their longing—to write works on such an unreasonable scale.

Terminology: by "modern long poem," I mean modern and contemporary long poems, twentieth and twenty-first centuries. These generally deploy multiple, interrupted, or discontinuous narrative elements, though on scales and pulses that differ among the poems. I focus on the extremely long but consider some book-length and shorter serial poems along the way whenever their tasks are congruent with that poetic intellectual desire to make a book of socio-cosmological naming. I will discuss the poetics and the practices of modern long poems, but I actually mean Poetics, Practices and Problems.

The seriousness, persistence, and hard-to-describe nature of the task of the public-analytic poet is why I chose to address this topic, grouping different kinds of poets, traditions, and lengths of the long poem. This "longness"/"length" (words that will be bothered throughout) evoke a fundamental desire, a yearning—Peter Middleton has used "longing," a term with serious implications for me—as well as involve actual page counts, years spent, and the frustrating enormousness, with bursts of hope, of facing human enormity (as most of these poets do). Finally, many of these very long poems are virtually endless, with a haunting incompleteness beyond "failure."

This book is divided into five chapters whose middle three concern various poets' interpretations of three genres: epic, quest, and a grouping I call assemblage, with three main branches: Album, *Gesamtkunstwerk*, and the Book. These are chunky chapters, each focusing on contemporary interpretations of those genres based on current issues, perceptions, and needs. The five chapters have subtopics named along the way—some speculative and some on specific texts or comparisons among texts. Genre is considered as a capacious and suggestive cultural practice. I focus on key texts, not treated exhaustively, since many excellent readings discuss contents, themes, and literary histories of these poems.[1] My study is cast as a second-tier, even speculative reading. Because I take for granted some acquaintance with these works, I emphasize their mechanisms and tactics (structures) and the issues, generally with genre and scope, that a given writer was addressing. Discussions of individual poets and texts are often distributed among several chapters. How enormous length gets handled and whether telos occurs are considerations that weave in and out.

This is neither a canon-confirming nor canon-seeking book. The goal is to make tolerant, sometimes odd combinations of texts. An alternative goal would end in an exclusive, somewhat self-confirming club of US long-poem writers with a few intransigent and even cranky members, who are mainly, statistically male-ish and white-ish (if one wants to put things that way): T. S. Eliot, Ezra Pound, William Carlos Williams, Louis Zukofsky, and Charles Olson. A critical discussion of long poems does not have to proceed by self-confirming sets of genealogical patterns, although some known literary genealogies, aside from being patchily patriarchal, are familiar yet reductive of a complex literary practice. In this book I try deliberately to see different intersecting constellations of poets and tasks—pointing to a nexus-based literary history of chosen allegiances and to problems and solutions in poetics as elective affinities, not considered as chained genealogical claims. This grouping of texts is one possibility among many possible interpretations. A nexus model, or an ongoing network of literary formations, allows us to visualize how even very different and sometimes contentious poets can be (or can be presented as) critically and aesthetically connected.

Here, Dante and Stéphane Mallarmé are used as figures of import for long poems, figures who have posed fundamental problems and discussable solutions in their practices.[2] Yet to use the word "influence" wrongly suggests a one-way street. Etymology tells that *influence* is a flowing into—as if the person to be influenced were only an empty pail. The influence model is rather hierarchic, monofocal, and loosely patriarchal ("master" pouring and "descendants" filling). In contrast, as the alternative term "nexus" suggests, a person's analytic agency is engaged in being affected by another poet. The syntheses made in being affected by older/model poets are acts linking humility and mastery. A poet chooses and also shapes the narrative of connectedness or contributes to it. A nexus is horizontal, rolling, dialectical, and accumulative, open to multiple contestations, selected narratives, and strategic links. In a nexus model of literary history, authors perform acts of homage but also of contestation and resistance. The rhetorics, concerns, poetics, goals, distinctive stances, and exemplary elements of another poet get specifically articulated (or challenged or ignored) by you as poet and remixed in your work, your poetics, and poetic career. Critics too enter any nexus (such as "the" long poem) and shape it, continuing or repositioning arguments about connections among works.[3]

Similarly a genre is not like a fixed form (a sestina, say), where you deploy its terms. Every time you evoke a genre, you are interpreting and even extending its characteristics. (Of course, this can be true of fixed forms as well.) The structural mix each poet makes is specific and at least partly deliberate. This is the spirit in which I talk about epic, quest, and assemblage. If three main genres are at stake in three chapters, this means modern and contemporary uses and interpretations of these genres, along with various extensions and fusions. Further, genres have a half-life; even if dormant they may re-emerge. This peg of "genre" to begin discussing long poems that repeatedly prove polygeneric is handled with a brief warmhearted discussion of Derrida.

"Epic" is the word that springs to mind in the literary history of the long poem; yet the usage has now fragmented. One element encompasses the vast historical definitions and applications of this term about heroism, war (battles), and social binding with self-confirming relevance to a dynamic handful of classic poems. Another element acknowledges that now only recognizable episodes rather than the shape of a whole work signal its "epic-ness." Further, modern epics change some fundamental assumptions, such as gender; in the modern period, women writers variously propose "epic" as apt descriptor for their work and decide what rectifications that claim entails. And third, the term "epic" itself repeatedly shifts meanings between a familiar noun for a mature genre and an adjective for large size. With "epic" even Robin Blaser (in the epigraph) uses the term to mean length and cosmic attentiveness, not a particular genre.

In "quest" the general problem is establishing and fulfilling a telos or goal. Dante's long poem of quest proposes that telos with Christian hegemonic answers. His system is both shadowy presence and benchmark for many long socio-cosmological works even among modern and contemporary poets. Yet quest—travel to a goal of vital, even universal importance—will take on revised meanings in a secular world that does not necessarily accept the spiritual specificity of Dante's visualized journey and outcome. In a (semi-)secular world, what is an apt telos? All the writers who use Dante directly and assiduously—from Eliot and H.D. through James Merrill and Blaser—mount reinterpretations of and challenges to a quest and triumph saturated in Christian theology. Interpretations of the spiritual journey in the poems considered here enter scientific, scientistic, and generally cosmological zones. In that synoptic epigraph, Blaser reconciles secular specificity (science, philosophy, analysis) with a still-universalizing spiritual comprehension of the cosmological and social goals of writing a long poem.

The dilemmas of debates with assurance also get staged by Mallarmé, for whom any institutionalized religion or nationalisms and their trimmings were distasteful, and who thereby contributes to long-poem thinking in modernity. His response to the issue of a cosmological sense in the secular leads to his influential (and obscure) proposal of a generally civic but ritualized genre—assemblage—of consequential meaning to the modern long poem. (He is hardly the sole proposer of assemblage; Walt Whitman is another.) In Mallarmé's critical perceptions, assemblage has two related aspects—the *Gesamtkunstwerk* (here interpreted as and in a long poem) and the Book, an endless Book that allows the claim of "everything" to be advanced.

Among the goals of very long poems, according to many poets, are the challenges and frustrations of encompassing "everything"—whole worlds of it—in a single poem, while facing the elusiveness of synthesis. This messy encyclopedism is a serious if startling goal of many long-poem poets. The assemblage of a Book or the performance in the poem of multimedia allusions that also takes responsibility for social critique is the solution of quite different poets to this world-encompassing "everything."

After these explorations in three long chapters, I undertake questions such as, Is ending necessary? Is it possible? How does one get an ending for these "everything" experiences, the plethora of genres, the polymathic subjectivities, the occasionally imperial allusions to cultures and figures? There are three or four approximate choices: a long poem does end (then—how?); a poem flirts endlessly (and seriously) with ending but does not or cannot end; a poet declares that ending such a work is ridiculous/impossible/unnecessary/unidiomatic—stranding that odd, old, unanswerable question of "structure." The fourth choice is rarely invoked currently—the civic performance of the work as a spiritual ritual—but there is one example here. Several poets declare termini to their long poems by deploying arbitrary or meaningful numbers as tools of telos. Others choose a poetics of boundlessness, outlined here in a (posthumous) debate between Olson and Robert Duncan.

The poems discussed are best described with a circus of "poly-" and "multi-" and "a-" prefixes: polylogues, asynthetic, multigeneric, and polyvocal subjectivities (including chronological and social splits in the author), unable to conclude or to confirm an ending (except perhaps by numerologies), heteroglossic, proliferative of tones, and often multiple and nonnormative in the mix of allusions and the mix of dictions that themselves often get figured in those nontraditional page spaces characteristic of poetic-visual texts.

This multiplex I also attribute to the strange mixes of time and space in a long poem, where length somehow equals the attempt to mix poetic times—each moment of shorter ("lyric") or focal time, developed variously, and the extent of multiple temporalities, all occurring in authorial writing time—the time it takes to get "everything" in. Length—in all its evocation of multiples (genres, dictions, times, narratives)—has one key purpose: to satisfy unquenchable authorial longing for such a poem.

A long poem has many parts—perhaps the very same elements that compelled you in a shorter work (intertextualities, semantic play, repetition, findings, imagery, anecdotes, structures, emotional investments, social meanings of textual idioms), but given that there are more of these relationships piled up quantitatively, temporally, and perhaps inexplicably, the reading experience of facing this plethora gets out of hand. There are multiple themes, structures veering upon structure, endless streams of words, shifts of emphasis even in one passage, genre change-ups, alternations of focus, alterations of the poem's purpose over time, questions of what "form" means, is worth, or even what it is. Generally, for the word "form," I use "structure" or "tactics" or "modes" or specific writing practices, hoping to save the specific word "form" for the Ur-realization that compels the work (borrowing from Roland Barthes, to be discussed later). But often the poets cited use the word "form" the ways they want. Conscious shape or shapings of the work at hand would be one definition, but simultaneously long-poem plethora is overwhelming. Does this all have a reason? What is going on?

Further, there is hardly one ideal atemporal reading experience. Reading a long poem involves you in various changing temporalities, as you try to negotiate its extent in space and time, your relative pleasure in it, and even your time for reading it. Finally, a reader cannot read a very long poem or even a long one in one sitting—but plausibly could read a very short, or "nanorific," one. With all this said, what are the functions and values of these very long poems in our time? This essay will offer some terms to consider, speaking variously as a reader/user and as a writer/maker.

As noted, this is hardly a historical survey or a genre genealogy; nor does it claim coverage of everything that "should" be talked about, including the specific findings of many critics and readers. Further, it is almost impossible to write a book about the long poem without lopping off many practitioners as impossible to "cover"—even to mention. This is not a decision about quality, superiority, or canonical power of the texts I've chosen to discuss. To the degree that the texts that I've chosen as examples propel, support, or suggest the interpretations I develop, my observations may be at once informed, willfully self-confirming, and circular. The only proper answer to your forthcoming question "Why is such-and-such a poet [or text] *not* mentioned here?" or "Why did you put that work into *this* category?" is "You're right, of course!" I had also wanted this book to be fully Anglophone in scope but found that only some work from the Caribbean, Australia, and Canada could be included, along with mainly US poems. I do not guarantee that every reader will agree that these poets should be written about in these particular ways.[4] Or that these topics are crucial and necessary. My rubrics are vantages, but they might also be disadvantages, partialities, or accidents of one sort of another. I would like to posit my guideposts as flexible, forgiving and always discussable.

The work published here is revised and recontextualized from any prior in-print thinking, teaching, or talking that I've done on these matters. Being commodious and inclusive about long poems and how to define them at least created a robust and eclectic reading list. In this book the endless cultural acts of the long poem itself and of its readings are creolized, inclusive, errant, omnivorous, palimpsestic, and overwritten.

Responsive, situated, and not definitive, although always trying to define, this book is a cross between a book of speculative essays and an analytic-critical book. In essays you end with mixes of findings and questions, and you articulate your surmises and findings speculatively. As meditative papers essays don't have to insist on one approach, one thesis, or one set of determinants. In a critical book, you come to conclusions (mainly), and you often study the criticism at length (I don't). This book certainly comes to conclusions, but it may not conclude in any definitive way. It is more like a set of pragmatic essays resisting single-focus approaches to the topic. Writing, I am talking as best I can into the space of the works I take up, into the space of this page, and into the space of thinking. I'm conducting the laptop orchestra.

Whereupon: "[. . .] she went bloated into the azure / like a shot."[5]

Alternatively: "Americans like to write big poems, even if people don't read them."[6]

POE, ZUKOFSKY, POUND, AND SO FORTH: CAN THERE BE AN EFFECTIVE *LONG* POEM?

> There is always a book carrying a book
> carrying a book carrying a book [. . .]
>
> Edmond Jabès, interview with Paul Auster, 1978

Very long poems: they may crash and burn on their own rocks—of ambition, impossibility, inability to settle findings, and reader difficulty of encompassing them. Edgar Allan Poe says they don't (or shouldn't) exist, and if they do, you can't call that thing a poem. Louis Zukofsky says they are really "the same" as short poems; excessive length doesn't matter. Some critics want to solve the dilemma by calling the modern long poem by one traditional name like "epic," possibly undercutting, by evoking continuity, any historical specificity of modern/contemporary works and their mélange of genres. *The Waste Land* (1922)—not even very long—made the twentieth-century long poem a challenging desideratum. Yet T. S. Eliot spent the rest of his career backing away from the textures and mechanisms of *The Waste Land*, while his helper-editor Ezra Pound doubled down on those for his own excessive work in time and space. Contemporaneously (1923), long-poem models were pioneered by William Carlos Williams, Marianne Moore, and Mina Loy, in *haibun*, *tenzone* (deploying citation), and serial work, models that did not receive Pound's instantaneous, crucial blessing. There we have it: a long poem doesn't exist; it is no different from a short poem despite length; it's an impossible failure; it's mislabeled; it's suspect and uncomfortable or stupendously useful; and some powerful poems don't count—but the construction of reception does count—a lot. Whatever it is, this is a book about it.

The clash between an overwhelming reading time and a desired emotional impact is why Poe said (in his 1850 "The Poetic Principle") that a long poem "does not exist," being "simply a flat contradiction in terms." If it's long, it can't be a poem because any poetic effect is diluted and erased both by enormous length and by the work's tonal variety. The intensity of "poetry" as an artifact of sublimity—soul-elevating emotion and visceral intensity—cannot occur with any work of larger scale, because that elevated emotion is too "transient" to be sustained during the reading of a *long* work. Any reading experience beyond one half hour (his precise figure) ends in "revulsion," a down after a high, as if poetry resembled an addictive drug. Poe also announced a less-remembered stricture: poems can be too short, too slight and epigrammatic for that uplifting high.[7]

For Poe, "poetry" occurs in an untouchable, sacralized category with a special relationship to "soul." Unlike any other kind of writing, it cannot be thought about much, just experienced. This poetry-purity position still influences readers. The impossibility of the long poem for Poe was based on a particularly rigid (but still evocative) sense of what true poetry means—a work of focused rhythmic song, emotionally and heart-clenchingly intense. Poe's claim of (real) poetry conceptually deliquesces into the longish lyric-pulse of yearning in which idealized female figures play exacting roles, perhaps distant but as often dead. Poe saw no alternative but the lyric, although he invented and used an influential alternative—the prose poem.[8] Yet once "soul" and "beauty" get involved, we are in often-unanswerable zones of ineffable specialness: poetry ideology.

We need not be. It simply seems like common (poetic-common) sense to acknowledge that any long poem has to be built of shorter sections and units generating varieties of feelings in various dictions.[9] It is the negotiation and pulse among these emmeshed units that will give such a poem its distinctiveness and pleasures. The units vary, of course, but any one of them calls on the basic quality of poetry itself. To understand the long poem, one must acknowledge the interaction of disparate segments as central to the genre "poetry."

What is *fundamental* to poetry as a mode of practice? It is not length, intensity, beauty, emotion, lyricism, sound qualities, meter, metrical coherence; neither is it wit, rhyme, imagery, or musicality. Further, the distinction of poetry cannot be found in topics like love, death, nature, vulnerability, loss, grief, evanescence, brevity, passion, uplifting or depressed feelings, transcendence, the personal, the expressive, best thoughts, unity, strong emotions. Nor in song, flow, I/you relations, feminine sensibility (most acceptable when emanating from a male body), epiphany, *condensare*, or vatic tone. Nor is it any one key rhetorical trait (like apostrophe). Any or all of these traits, proffered as definitively distinctive to poetry, may also be found in prose, the novel, and drama/performance. They do not *distinguish* poetry, although any could (and many do) continuously suffuse a given poem.

What, then, does distinguish poetry as a specific practice, besides (at least) the use of words—or wordlike sounds/communicative glyphs?[10] Poetry can be defined as saturated segments in social-sensuous language. Essentially, poetry is that form of writing in *segments* (lines, mainly, sometimes sentences, but also fragments visually strewn on a page) that allows and encourages the largest possible place for excess of meanings and implications to enter any given word or phrase.[11] *Segmentivity* is the central engine of any poetic text—the feature that distinguishes the genre.[12] Poetry is fundamentally the choice and combination by the poet of variously sized word segments—conventionally defined by rhyme, rhythm, repetitions, combinations of syntax and sound, some periodicity and silence (counting beats, syllables, stressed words, sentences); perhaps defined visually, by white spaces holding the lines/segments on a page; perhaps defined syntactically by the relation of specific syntax to line (line break and enjambment name these tactics), or even, in the case of the prose poem, by sentences set as individual units. Conventional definitions for poetry (like using rhyme) exist under the larger category of segmentivity.

Many elements in any poem (rhyme defining units, lines in relation to syntax, stanzas, and sections) create notable segments. Close analysis of shorter poetries reveals these. In much longer poetry, various elements of segmentivity persist, just as in shorter works, but are also scaled up, creating patterns that may overwhelm by being compounded. Still, a great resource for longer poetry is the relationship of any defined section to smaller units of segmentivity (say, a line break), building rhythms, networks, and structures. Various syntactic elements (parataxis, hypotaxis, juxtaposed phrases, the musical and semantic weight of word order) help define the functions and contrasts of segments. And temporalities (timing, pulse, semantic inferences made from shifts in segment) play key roles. But fundamentally the segment and the interplay of defined segments are central to the genre called poetry. The differences and activities among scales of segments become the meanings and activities of duration for poet and poem. When the duration is very long—measured in years—some poets have repetitive patterns in their choices of mode of section, voice or tone of sections, syntaxes, or contrasting assemblages that can be observed, and sometimes linked as a formal feature to specific semantic findings.

Segmentivity is thus scaled into clear structural, sectional, and/or syntactic modes. A long poem is characterized by multiple interlocks of segmentivities, large to small—cantos; sonnet-like section units (Alice Notley); serial work (Langston Hughes); quatrains (Harryette Mullen); constellations of material (Pound's scale of "ideogram"); odic incantations/riffs (Nathaniel Mackey); juxtaposed sentences (Ron Silliman); counted sentences (Lyn Hejinian); visually defined syntactic arrays (Mallarmé), or *haibun*-esque/hybrid combinations of many modes (Williams). A proleptic faith in the expressive authority of that particular unit characterizes the long-poem author. The multiple invention of the serial poem by several poets through the twentieth century applies the tool of segmentivity from shorter (even epigrammatic) sections to the juxtaposed, unrolling, often multivectored argument of a whole poem.

Topical and eclectic dictions that alter the assumption of the uplifting tone proper to poetry also characterize modern poetics (if first accomplished by William Wordsworth, Charles Baudelaire, et al.). Wordsworth's lightly oxymoronic rubric *Lyrical Ballads* announces this crucial genre mix in the Anglophone tradition: the lyric being a poem where, generally, only one figure speaks; while the ballad is a poem that sustains and encourages even stylized dialogue. Any very long poem discussed here tends to have absorbed this lyric/ballad fusion and has massively pluralized those who speak inside the poem; any moments of monovocal subjectivity in a long poem are generally folded into a polyphonic text. Heteroglossia (as in Moore), citation (in Pound), documentary materials (as in Williams), and the depiction of many zones, voices, sounds via page space (as in Anne Waldman, Merrill), and diction glissades and clashes (as in John Ashbery, Kamau Brathwaite) all characterize long-poem polyphony. These expanded options include mixed dictions and hybrid textures in writing; acts defining a continuum between prose, poetry, and performance in "writing"; or acts continuing prose/poetry distinctions for specific goals.

Hence there is nothing overtly wrong with Mikhail Bakhtin's binarist distinction between a dialogic orientation with its "fullest and deepest expression in the novel" and a monologic mode of diction typical of poetry for centuries before. However, the distinction excludes much typical twentieth-century poetry. Particularly long poems have become resolutely dialogic, articulating "social heteroglossia" in dictions, prosodies, and tones, filled with a vernacular "actual life of speech," able to struggle with "socio-ideological contradictions," all terms of high value in Bakhtin's critical framework.[13]

The monologic mode for poetry does undervalue idiomatic layers of voices, social zones, dictions, peopled multiplicities, and their clashing heteroglossias. Hence, Bakhtin sees most poetry as quite limited in comparison to novels, since the highly stylized or conventionalized sublime of poetry (in his view—as in Poe's) deliberately impedes the heteroglot and dialogic. These latter elements are, of course, typical of the modern and contemporary long poem. "Poetic style" is the enemy of a living language, because it cannot allow voices in dialogic "contradictions, conflicts and doubts."[14]

Here, Bakhtin is not entirely "wrong" either; some keen stylization of *something* does mark a text as poetry. However, this defining stylization is not necessarily a tone or diction choice somehow inherently "poetic" (e.g., monoglossia vs. heteroglossia). Choices of elements that make a text count as poetry vary more than that. What Roman Jakobson calls "poeticity" (the stylization characteristic of poetry) is any word taken as word itself, with its own material "weight and value" deployed beyond demands on semantic meaning, that is, reference to something.[15] Poetic stylization might be propelled by the voice assumed in authorship as a self-invented sound or figure "declaiming"/"exploring" this long poem (like Charles Olson's Maximus or Anne Waldman's urgent, sometimes apocalyptic voice). It might be a conglomerate of traits producing the "words felt as words," like overt formal marks, insistent numerologies or metrics; a fragmenting lexicon (as in M. NourbeSe Philip); it could be visible repetitions and cadences, or a palpable surface of language, like rhyme, sound, or aggressively visible line breaks even within a naturalized vernacular diction (A. R. Ammons). It could even be specific uses of uppercase type (in Merrill). *Any* exaggerated mark or even self-invented rule, if used concertedly and repeatedly, no matter what it is or does, may offer effective stylization in poetry. But poetic stylization, *pace* Jakobson, can certainly also evoke social contexts.

All this shows why Bakhtin has difficulty maintaining strong boundaries between the dialogic and the monologic. At the moment of "Discourse in the Novel" (1934–35), these barriers have already fallen and been overridden within modern poetries of all kinds. Modernism in poetry becomes generically and linguistically boundless—it does not necessarily respect poetry's own prior distinctions between tones of poetry and prose or visual cues for "the poem" versus "the poster" (for instance). In such a transitional moment, W. B. Yeats confronted and deemed "satiric" that exact diction shift in the first book of T. S. Eliot with its "stylistic" revolution: its poetry "like" prose, with "no special subject-matter," "no romantic word or sound," "Paddington Railway Station" as "suitable" a topic as "Tristram and Isoult."[16]

However, long-poem scale may be imbued with another kind of poetry ideology—mastery of the difficult—making your success in reading "the opaque prestige object"—a precise reckoning from Bob Perelman—that, say, Pound's *Cantos* presents, be what separates the highly adequate reader from "inferior" ones.[17] To sustain this prestige, reader longing is crucial. Here the intertwined sublimities of bulk, opacity, and yearning displace the sublimity of Poe's lyric climax. Long-poem scale (the automatic monumentality of twenty-odd years and 300–1,000+ pages) may have serious designs on a reader: to awe, to overwhelm, to envelop, to inspire, to persuade, to glorify the commitments to the values depicted—and to exclude, to make you culturally jealous. Sheer heft and difficulty create long-poem prestige.

For long poems we are entitled to ask how, whether, and why an ending may occur, perhaps to give a sense of closure or for other necessities. Any decision to end a work is complicated by that inherent endlessness of writing or *poesis* when a person is inside a long poem's range and its formal propulsion. Hence, ending (as a structural/ideological issue) may become dependent on numbers (a kind of poetic stylization) as a potential guarantee of both shapeliness and some finish even within a poetics of openness. As Clark Coolidge noted about his *A Book Beginning What and Ending Away* (571 pages): "I could never get an overall title for it [. . .] because I worked on it for so long, and I *wanted* it to keep turning and twisting and taking up different subject matter and so on, so that you'd almost have to call it something hopelessly generic like *The Book*."[18] This is a characteristic emotion of the writer of a very long poem—absorptive attitudes toward many topics ("everything"), desire provoking continuance, curiosity about writing into duration itself. This is precisely why numbers—say Zukofsky's twenty-four sections—may both confirm and challenge the question of ending a long poem. Structural or intellectual norms of ending may be in a permanent struggle with emotional or intellectual propulsions to continuance. One's *writerly* judgment often votes (no surprise) in favor of continuance, an authorial act validating one's longing for the poem or for the poem's voice (not even your own, but the voice of language).

At the other extreme from Poe's provoking "impossibility" remark comes Louis Zukofsky's provocation. In comments on *"A"* (826 pages), Zukofsky proposed a seamless continuum between short and long by emphasizing the intensity of multiple verbal resonances interacting everywhere in any poetic work. He's hardly wrong about language (and stylizations) in poetry but is not a help on the impact of scale. Asked to distinguish rather short from really long poems, he said: "A long *poem* is merely more of a good thing."[19] His italicized emphasis falls on the "poeticity" of the work—its poetical, wrought nature; if it's a good *poem*, it's just more of the same kind of pleasure whether short or long. His "merely" is designed to impress. He resists the sense that something large is particularly daunting or takes extended effort by readers. He also claims that there is no excess beyond comprehension, no extreme act no matter how bizarrely such a poem presents itself—a long poem is just a regular good poem, except much, much longer than usual.

Sometimes Zukofsky's remark seems logical. Of course a long poem is just like a short poem; it is made in and of the same full medium, it is fueled by the pulses of its segmentivity, one reads intense word to word, one looks for patterns on several scales, so why even bother to discuss how long it is? Isn't this question a distraction? Why not just read these long works as if they were ongoing poetic "*romans fleuves*," rivers of insight ("flow charts" to evoke the John Ashbery title), things happening, experiences, with or without named characters?[20] At other times it's difficult to believe that Zukofsky did not acknowledge what is concealed by such a statement—authorial choices of complex linguistic-cultural activity; poetic stylization functioning as mannerism; inexplicable or ungainly proportions; too much excess to enjoy; the stalled negotiation between "enough/too much"; cultural ambition—author's "longing"; scaling a literary mountain; making some mark; facing other long-poem makers (in Zukofsky's case, at least Pound); and grappling with literature as a whole and with the ethics of making something so large and knotted that it may overwhelm potential readers. Then, almost an afterthought, there's a question whether the long-poem writer cares to please readers or overwhelm them.[21] Are there no problematics of unevenness or compounded interest, or uninterest? This list is applicable to all long-poem writers.

Certainly witty, Zukofsky's remark is also deliberately disingenuous, because the "length" of "long" is not finally a measurement of space only, linguistic entanglements, or intricate muchness, or of reader or writer patience and commitment.[22] As all long poems require, time is involved, an ongoing investment in such a work for both reader and writer: thus with reading choices and one's own life, and with the energies of thought that provoked the poem and its changes over time.[23] A long poem might not "differ" from a short one, but its greater quantity made over time allows for more dazzling mastery or more inexplicable pile-ups: these displays might themselves become tiresome or tedious, relentlessly in their own long-poem world. Structural poise may never be possible, because the work, too, changes in its time and becomes metamorphic. Its own strategies and their effects may be volatile and unfollowable by readers (even by its writer).

Zukofsky's solution seems to have been to make the sections of "A" so incredibly different in genre allusions and social zones that the work is more like a cultural anthology and set of notable anecdotes mediating public (literary and historical) and private, personal worlds. "A" is both meditative and documentary: to consider one's life and times and to ponder history and culture as one's life's work. Many of Zukofsky's local writing strategies were anthology-based, gathering some enhanced readings: editorial selection and remastering of paraphrased materials from other authors, as Jeffrey Twitchell-Waas has found.[24] His anthology making parallels another sacred book in shared culture; the Hebrew Bible is an anthology, an editorial compendium of prophetic and historically sacred writings about a "people" in formation, in need of a repeated binding together and glossing commentary, then further defined (some say) by a messianic figure whose acts and teachings are anthologized in the newer Testament. Zukofsky aspires to make a twentieth-century counterweight: a *secular* anthology with civic *and* rabbinical (glossing) import. He shows that ambition for a Book about which we will hear more.

The importance of verbal intensity to Zukofsky is borne out again in a response from the 1968 interview. Zukofsky engineers a hermetic-antic escape from L. S. Dembo's serious question "Do you conceive of ["A"] as having an overall structure?" Quite like Bartleby, Zukofsky prefers not to; he turns the question from large to small, and in consequence from structure to word. Dembo is asking about the sheer overall scale of the thing, its daunting scope, quondam opacity, and largeness. Zukofsky answers by insisting (with a nice perversity) on myopia, on the interest to the reader of "the detail."[25] The fact that Zukofsky turns to the smallest local decision, to verbal intricacy, and to the reader's potential fascination with the part, rather than to the question of scope, structure, design, the whole, possibly occurred because he had not yet finished "A," yet the comment is a way of insisting that he has written the long poem with the condensation, verbal focus, and pointed choices of a short work. In Zukofsky's segmentivities, the work is apparently accorded *no* narrative "fill," elaborative rhetorics, or downtime by its author, even though in some sections it is quite discursive.

Yet "A" is hard/difficult because, as a through-composed long poem, it is made like a metaphysical lyric—twisting, as Zukofsky deliberately mis-cited, those "red hot pokers into knots." His allusion is modified, aggressively, from Coleridge's quatrain "On Donne's Poetry" that says, "Wreathe iron pokers into true-love knots."[26] That's an allusive, layered segment—with a defiant "atty-tude"; *"A"* is a poem that will not relax. The intensity of the lyric, the gnomic elegance, the jeweler's sense of every word as faceted, precious, and multiply determined have given Zukofsky's long poem an overall diamond-like and oblique hardness. Both Poe and Zukofsky feared the potential flaccidity of length.

Some people do write their long poems with various local lyric intensity (and other segment types). George Oppen (in much shorter long work) and Ashbery did. Other examples of finesse of each detail are probably Dante, Mallarmé, H.D., Ronald Johnson, and Gwendolyn Brooks; however, these poets all could probably have answered Dembo's question about overall structure, the one that Zukofsky refused, though they might not have wanted to. And various modes and tones of the long poem might vary in their degree of "through composition" and what they deploy to achieve that outcome. Despite reading difficulty, critical tolerance regarding the long-poem array is called for.

We see this tolerance in comments by Alice Notley in her capacity as author of *Descent of Alette*, a work seriously through-composed, and in her capacity as the author of *Disobedience*, which has a much looser structure.[27] Notley is commenting on *Iovis*, the very long poem by Anne Waldman. "Parts of the [Waldman] poem may feel thin; I think that is built into the genre, parts of *Maximus*, *Paterson*, and *The Cantos* feel a little thin to me—as well as garrulous, cornpone, flowery, forced, self-indulgent, pretentious, and impenetrable. The form makes flaws possible; possibly poetry should make room for flaws, being a human form. There are other kinds of flaws in other kinds of poetry: stuffiness, coldness, the omission of nearly everything we think about."[28] To underscore, Notley indicates that one should not necessarily expect a "through-composed" long poem. Further, to discuss very long poems, we must deal with the works we have, not some idealized set, and we must examine what situations and choices produced them, including social worlds and the longing for an ethical *poesis*.

Notley uses humanist/projectivist criteria, just as Pound did when, in the first of the original *Three Cantos* (written 1915, published 1917), he claimed the metaphor of a "rag-bag" as an early genre projection (an array), the first of many.[29] Even when they make art, people are both sloppy and interesting, moving between coherence and "decoherence"; between finish and beginning; between organization and structures of largeness, deployed as authorial largesse.[30]

So both finish and finishing are debated elements. One further consequence, as Allen Fisher powerfully claims, is "that completion cannot be demonstrated, or rather that completion is always in flux."[31] This observation that ending is endlessly debated and never achieved entails the poet's ongoing desire to comment, via the poem's languages and structures, on the socio-cosmological world.

To extend epic or widen epic-only long-poem thinking is what Ezra Pound tried in his early musing on long poems, both in the Ur-cantos and in an early query within poetics. For epic was not his only choice of genre analogy, despite his eventual use of many epic allusions. He seems to have wanted to synthesize Homer and Dante. In his 1916 poetics (and elegiac-memoir) *Gaudier-Brzeska*, as he struggles with his ideas for a prospective long poem, Pound asks himself whether an imagist strategy with its haiku-like condensations (to which he was then committed) could possibly lead to a long "vorticist" poem. The term "vorticist," action-and-energy oriented, may be either Pound's substitute for or bridge out of the genre "epic," which he is testing for its viability.

In his meditation in *Gaudier-Brzeska* (half-concealed in a ruminative footnote), Pound puts three genres besides epic into play: intensely focused "hokku"/haiku, radiant and suggestive, along with the second suggestion, a performance genre "gathered about one image"—thus at least provisionally unified, and, given the Noh example, exotic, allusive and allegorical, itself a vision of a *Gesamtkunstwerk*, "with movement and music" as well as poetry. His third and vaguer model is a vortex, not quite a verbal structure, not quite a poetics, writing filled with the energies generated by decontextualized citation and quick juxtaposition. This is often visualized as a collaged encyclopedic work like his *Cantos*.[32] Yet in the first cantos, his model seems to be a cultural panorama, a phanopoetic montage (like a slideshow) or illustrative anthology of visionary literary-mythic moments. These are like interrupted *tableaux vivants*, animated by Pound's descriptive brilliance, and drawing on the emotional claims made by occult thought in early modernism and by the compelling visualizations in early cinema. This séance calls up an electrical/energy-laden force—Pound's "vortical" yearning ("longing").

This seems like a lot to handle, and to cap off Pound's proleptic and searching remarks, no aspect entails the call for continuous, contextualizing narrative. He wants a postnarrative synthesis of manifold presentational elements, and he says as much in an homage to Browning in an Ur-canto that tries urgently, anxiously to posit the next step: "So you worked out new form, the meditative, / Semi-dramatic, semi-epic story, / And we will say: What's left for me to do?"[33]

The shift from "we" to "me" is ineffably revealing. Note the already multigeneric solution to the long poem. Pound's early answer is to correlate suggestive reminders of epiphanic incidents from culturally eclectic but fundamentally comparable stories not as a continuous or even intricate narrative but as an array of beauties, virtues, and epiphanic realizations. He does not want to "sulk and leave the word to novelists"—an informative statement about the high status of the main twentieth-century genre.[34] Hence, he will appropriate the interiority of consciousness from the modern novel but will make the meditations engage the whole contents of worthy society and culture: culturally significant epiphanic moments of European and Asian mythology, poetry, history, and philosophy: love, honor, political passion, bravery, sacrifice, desire, decisiveness, and productive leadership. These *Cantos*-virtues soon included another—the quick-tempered, often witty, and irascible calling-out critiques of the asinine and the stupid, as he defined these.

One of the challenges of Pound's many challenges in *The Cantos* (and for readers of *The Cantos*) is to track his modifications of schemes over the many years of its composition and his fascinating attempts to bring his palimpsests of poetics and organizing strategies for the poem under one concept, no matter their own metamorphoses. It is a difficult calculus. The constant passage and fluidity between Pound's older and newer organizing ideas and the resulting poem made the construction of his very long poem become a record of its various struggles (as he said), with their conflicts of purpose.[35] In this ambition to correlate and reinspire a sense of nobility from cultural materials, Pound is a model for a public-intellectual poetry; yet despite his inspiring writers as varied in findings as Olson, Waldman, and Duncan to that sense of public purpose, his political adherence to certain fascist solutions (whatever their logics for him) narrows his findings.

Of the two *long* parts of Pound's model in that 1916 *Gaudier-Brzeska* footnote, the Noh depends on a Japanese tradition of mimed-operatic presentation —high moments of ravishing beauty, villainous and heroic power, staged as a dramatic/symbolic array of danced gestures—and is Pound's early model for a *Gesamtkunstwerk*. Yet Pound's alternative description of what could—and did—happen to his canto mode is the daunting "Great bulk, huge mass, thesaurus" that does contradict the impact of the limpid flares of discontinuous beauties and dynamisms that are presented early in the poem.[36] The "thesaurus" will correlate many brisk summaries of heroic activity in culture and politics, making them synonyms for each other. Pound makes quick notes on particular heroes without much context, his and their pure exemplary acts—poet taking up the traditional griot function, singing passions and victories but allusively, as if reminders of stories already known to the culture, or glosses on texts unseen by us as readers. He multiplies his outrage at the malign—a polemical temptation—with explanations becoming sketchier. From panorama to extractable principle becomes the arc of Pound's growing didacticism.

The generative footnote in *Gaudier-Brzeska* that I have been unfurling, as its third point, also suggests achieving a "vorticist" long poem by mixing various contemporaneous techniques to achieve all available presentational possibilities: futurism's *parole in libertà*, cubism's multiple perspectives, filmic montage and jump cuts, all continuously inform the texture of *The Cantos*. Pound's characteristic desire to cover all bases is palpable here. He wanted not to be belated with any strategy for his work yet is already feeling belated both to Browning's long poem and to the modern novel of interiority. Will overload solve belatedness? There could be more said—that goal suggests that my (forthcoming) remark that long poems desire "everything" is casting a shadow, as it will again; here "everything" appears, inter alia, as a grouping of rhetorical strategies in poetics.

More generally, this proleptic footnote of Pound asks what can link the little to the large, the part to whole in a poem of some length; inventing ways, in Daniel Albright's terms, "of extending the poetic image without losing its concentration," a very large challenge solved in part by improvisatory enactments, retaining the freshness of any dramatic moment depicted.[37] How to get from the small units to the large and back is the major question for any long poem—how even to define what the smaller units are, and how flexible they can be. That is, the cut of segmentivity (line, image, anecdote) functions because Pound retells each startling moment as if the reader witnessed it occurring, without having a full context but with a drastic local excitement.

One sees this same aspirational move between the haiku and the synoptic in Roland Barthes—with the same vital question that Pound had asked decades earlier. Haiku and its sense of the allusive real are eulogized as a perfect manifestation of "suchness" and "isness" without the demand for interpretability and a passage to meaning. Then Barthes closes in and pounces on precisely the most mysterious demand of structure—how does a person get that feeling of clarity and instantaneity in any longer work?[38] Shearing off context and gambling on reader inference seems to be Pound's way of retaining epiphanic freshness. The word "instantaneous" is both a lyric criterion and, in these centuries, the shock of the histories alluded to. Relating little to large, segment to structure is an intractable, recurrent, and interesting problem never to be decisively solved because always needing clarification within the granular and (un)/balanced singularity of any given long work and its developing themes and findings.

EVERYTHING, LENGTH, AND "LONGING": FORM AND STRUCTURE

Most books are about something, not everything. Exception—very long poems in modern/contemporary Anglophone literature. These often get characterized by their poets as ways of facing and writing everything (not even "about everything"—something more extreme). "Everything" becomes almost a technical term, used by some poets for their goals. The poets considered here are sophisticated enough to understand, even to theorize, representation (*minimally* entailing meaningful selection from "everything" and then shaping things variously) but seem to put that understanding on hold when they speak about their motives. They also seem to ignore a related issue, whether including "everything" doesn't blur all to nothing via overload. A constant, energetic dialogue between selection and combination actually characterizes art—including the very long poem, but sometimes "everything" looms *as if* beyond this. "Everything" involves a hyperproduction of stimuli—in poetic modes as content. As Charles Olson stated in *Maximus*: "5:30 AM hungry for every thing."[39] That word's open space lets it all come in.

"Everything" shows extreme overstatement, characterizes long-poem sublimity, and declares long-poem assumptions. Why does someone write a long poem? Why such a commitment, even devotion? Committing to "everything" means to a capacious and ever-recomplicating constellation of elements, demanding engagement with a widening "area of resonance and implication."[40] Capacious recomplicating commitment to the poem's development becomes one motivation for sheer length; insight and implication do not end. William Carlos Williams's retrospective remark (on *Paterson*): "To find an image large enough to embody the whole knowable world about me" is an "everything" remark, focusing on a knowable "whole."[41] His "image" focuses on one distinctive city, its waterfall compared to inchoate language, the poet-doctor's encounters with diverse citizens, and his reenactment of local-historical benchmarks. The subjectivity speaking the poem has already been suffused with the many (voices, scenes, histories, potentials) on the terrain of the poem; the poem works this suffusion out in two ways—by an ending (Book IV), and then by continuance: declaring that "ending" cannot contain ongoing poetic activity (Book V).

The same impossible word appears in Pound's 1917 prospective remark: "I have begun an endless poem, of no known category [. . .] all about everything," a comment that delivers proleptic literary pride in conceptualizing *The Cantos*.[42] His early explanations use hortatory words like *big, long, endless, leviathanic*, and (with monumental gleam added to size)—*chryselephantine*.[43] This simply means precious gold and ivory together, but the "elephant" is no accident so far as I'm concerned. Pound's poem remained open to "everything." In a late interview (1962), he notes his *Cantos* creates "a form that wouldn't exclude something merely because it didn't fit."[44] Because *The Cantos* and similar poems are so long, with so many thematic concerns, sources, documents, and speaking/seeking subjectivities over such long time and space, it appears that "everything" in the world is being depicted when, of course, it is not and could not be. "Everything" is an illusion of representation created by the many words of the poem, an illusion via length/extent, and duration, gratifying to the poet and worth claiming. "Everything" is strange synonym for "a lot"—of thoughts, of materials, of pages.

The achievement of "everything" is validated by and dependent on each writer's characteristic choices of segment. Pound validates his everything by juxtapositions of varied examples and by brisk citations of documents, thereby authenticating the thematic decisiveness of historical figures. Williams uses specific short sketches of people or citations of letters as vignettes within the social panorama of *Paterson*—depicting a frustrated urgency confronting blockages. Sentence after sentence, each carefully posing contemporaneous observations but joined without continuity, offers the social "everything" in Ron Silliman.

Even in a shorter long poem, Bernadette Mayer's *Midwinter Day* (1982), "everything" gets indicated with a poetics of the local parallel to Williams's. Her statement "Everywhere there is has everything there is to look at" announces the sensibility in which "Anywhere is everywhere."[45] This stance is rhetorically proven by Mayer's many recurrent lists. Her domestic-scale "shield of Achilles" sections include bits from an available newspaper, summaries of the plots of five toddler's books, a list of stores in Lenox, Massachusetts, an outline of the mental-emotional contents of a three-year-old's tantrum, a catalog of women writers, and more.[46] The lists, interpolations, and associations increase the "everything"; enumerations occur without hierarchic or polarized distinctions—as between adult and child emotions, between dream and waking realities, and between casual and formal dictions, mixing epic, mock epic, and narrative. In long poems no single element is enough.

Declaring a timeframe for the gathering of otherwise endless materials tends to propel closure. Mayer's "day" exemplifies such a choice; Hejinian's sentences counting up to a fixed number parallels this; so too Ammons's numerological choices. A naturalized or arbitrary number-frame allows a poet to stop.

All such poems, barring firm endings, are actually not everything but all "middles"—absorptive, by assemblage and accumulation, an array caused by the endless activity of writing. For Anne Waldman in *Iovis*—structure is activity, structure is energy; her segments often exhort continuance. These are compositions on the run, responsive and situational choices. "Rather than have the poem be an extrapolation, a refined gist of a 'high' moment, I want it to *be* the experience—[. . .] something that would take you in myriad directions simultaneously [. . .] a poem that would include everything and yet dwell in the interstices of imagination and action."[47] Such a long poem is thus an endless performance of ongoing experiences.

Ron Silliman's quasi-autobiographical, pragmatic narrative from 1992 called "I Wanted to Write Sentences: Decision Making in the American Long-poem" parallels this emphasis on an activity creating exact, sentence-length observed experiences. Writing a long poem for Silliman was not a decision about length (or grandeur or the sublime); the length is an "extraneous" factor.[48] If working out a problem ("sentences" for Silliman) was the trigger, then some length is needed to make the point. To treat the length of such a long poem as a side product is a counterintuitive finding. His sentences function as specific acts of naming, presenting the reader with his constructed replication (of thing, of relationship, of action, of oddities of language). Putting something in sentence-statements without narrative continuities frames the absolute "is-ness" of what is. Then accumulation constructs an oddly critical question: all this *is*?—generating an emotion about Being itself from such a massive number of singular decontextualized statements.

Silliman's *The Alphabet*, like Waldman's *Iovis*, is a gigantic book, over a thousand pages long. Both poets claim length is simply an effect of the long-poem writer's chosen activity and its sustaining. That is, the public intellectual in poetry *names*—calls out (in the sense of criticizes), fixes, identifies, designates.[49] This activity is the long-poem poet's work: the writer as cultural laborer makes a time and place visible to itself by constant accumulative naming. In Silliman this articulate naming is the fundamental term; length is a result of producing continuous (not continuities of) accumulation into one's social world, in the tick of time. Waldman's units are larger, events in one episode (as of travel and ritual occasions).

The dialogue between authorial subjectivity and the whole world is potentially as endless and various as very long poems are. Hence a goal (however implausible) or a poetics of including "everything" is simply a motivator to build (write) such poems, a manifesto claim. Because, of course, each writer of very long poems has a different vision of what "everything" consists in. Creating an "everything" occurs in the dialogue on every scale between plethora and selection true of every artistic act, one often omnivorous, risky, and extensive for the very long poem. Since such a poem changes over the many years of writing, the issue of "everything" involves time: changes or elaborations of a poet's opinions, emphases, and interests. The task of constant naming along with normal living suggests that this poem of "everything" startlingly extends one's life, because its presence is like having a second life in the poem, with the poem as companion.

Nathaniel Mackey discusses this "everything," in a 1998 interview, given that Robert Duncan's parallel term "world-poem" had been applied to his work. Mackey demurs. While an attractive and even tempting description, still it "suggests all-inclusiveness and I balk at that." "World" is an overgeneralized category, unnuanced and unspecific, ignoring individual cultural traditions, prone to imperial blind spots and outworn ideological exclusions. "The world-poem is more an aspiration than an accomplishment," joining parallel unlikely goals of being "conclusive and comprehensive"; these kinds of poems are emphatically not "all-inclusive."[50]

"Comprehensive" is the temptation; aspirational nonclosural endlessness in long poems is where the claim of "everything" comes to settle—if never to rest. The necessity for selection, the thematic and structural work of selection conflicts with this longing for everything in poets of long poems. This generates the struggles discussed in this book. Why stop?

However, in a pivoting remark, Mackey allows, "[An artwork is] a selection where one often feels that one has been selected as much as that one has done the selecting."[51] The writer of a very long poem feels like a medium for the project—"selected" by the poem as its maker to channel some "everything" through a sensibility. The forces of desire, ambition, and "longing" posited in the power of an ongoing long poem choose the poet who chooses to write such work. Coping with plethora—"everything"—is part of the bargain. This is the long *poem's* "longing," a very odd feeling to attribute to it. It's as if the poem desires (longs for) its medium—the poet.

How could that occur? Paul Jaussen has argued that long poems create feedback systems, where the ongoing poem informs its writer (as the reader-who-writes) how to respond to its own proliferating ideas, structures, languages, and events. Structures get built up by writers' recognizing and learning from traits that they themselves have invented and deployed. These choices support the poem's own specific continuance, and possibly answer to the sense of a latent form (the Ur-form) at the poem's inception. Poets learn from what has been accomplished in their poems to encourage themselves to continue exploring their individuated creations of "poetic systems" via heuristic ongoingness.[52] They learn to read themselves.

This is an outline that conforms to my experience in the cooperative feedback loop that creates uncanny shared agency between the long poem and the poet. Although it is true that you are writing this poem and that the poem cannot write itself, a poet often finds, after momentum is established, that the poet learns from the poem and might, it appears, have some of its terms and necessities compelled (even dictated), by the *poem* or the poem's literariness as agent. This is one of the most haunting sensations of authorship. It is not even an illusion—or a delusion—but it does mean that the long poem has become a particular/peculiar subjective claim inside its poet, a ghostly force of propulsion, often fueled by this myth of "everything." However, one does not simply create a template and carry on; interruptions, a poet's growth, shifts may occur, activated by the ongoing force of "everything" in time.

Further, one does achieve a feeling of having the language speaking in the poem; one, as author, is a bystander, standing by ready to revise. The poem is coming from a source of language itself, a flood of many-ness. Williams proposed the roaring falls of Paterson, New Jersey, as the real geographical feature that encapsulates the roar of language speaking through the poet. The voice assumed by the poet in writing the long poem can be identified as language itself. When poets hear, feel, and find that sound, it is no wonder that they don't want to stop.

Positing "everything" in a long poem as an ambition, or a physical presentation, says that you see the world's plethora as visual or aural image, as psychic overload, as compelling challenge, and that you need to join it, reveal it, explore it in a long poem written by yourself/by language. Not passively (despite attributing agency to the poem), but as a strange calling, this impossible vocation or electric charge of "everything" demands length or continuance as one dynamic response and a critical naming as one central task.

Another element of "everything" is a muted polemical insistence on serious findings. Often these poems, building piles of evidence, point to paradigm-shattering critical interpretations of one's culture, in both sociohistorical and literary senses. The poems may seek accountability, analysis, resistance, even transformation, and the poets become public intellectuals in their poetic analyses. The epigraph by Robin Blaser evokes all of these: ontology, epistemology, critique, and spiritual quest. The analysis might be mythopoetic, of world-vast scope (as are James Merrill's comic cosmological proliferations), an excoriation of or satiric resistance to social prejudices (as in Gwendolyn Brooks), a critique by accumulation via findings that have to be repeated and refound because the poetics demands nongeneralized specificity (whether called "radiant gist" in Williams or anti-abstraction nodules of meaning in Pound).[53] Sometimes the poems manifest a thaumaturgic function for the central subjectivity—the speaker claims some power of curing, envisioning a future, reinterpreting, mourning, motivating transformation (as in Notley or Philip). Naming "everything" again becomes a goal when the writer—Olson and Silliman are examples—feels conflict between literature/the literary (as convention and containment) and some vision of a "realer" world beyond.

This illusion of everything gets bolstered by long poems' heterodiscursive and heterogeneric qualities. Literally anything can be found in these poems: shifting voices, including vatic, demotic, and multilingual dictions; analytic claims; exorbitant intertextual citation (from other poems but also from treatises, scrapbooks, archives, documents); sometimes visual materials. In the zone of textual plethora created by the goal of "everything," any textual mark, glyph, or sign—even white space—may be a plausible, serious event. A very long poem encourages chains of association that start crossing and recrossing, constructing thematic clusters or collection points (like Williams's metaphor of "rolling up" in *Paterson I*); this accumulation comes in repetition of related elements. The reader often becomes swamped or absorbed.

Still, the goal of "everything" is sometimes expressed by the network metaphor of field, thicket, network—and dark woods, leading to hopes for an epic journey or quest through that thicket and out. This very allusion evokes how much Dante's poem challenges long-poem writers even today—as chapter 3 argues. However, assemblage (as genre, see chapter 4) suggests that the thicket itself is precisely where long poems now begin *and* end.

And incidentally—will any poet have enough time to get this "everything" in? The answer, by definition, is no, no matter how old and productive authors manage to be. If authorship demands always adding *more* to a metamorphic shape, and unless numerologies demand otherwise, any stopping *or* continuing will make the poem "fail." Failure is thus a property actually "constitutive of the long poem" (discussed in chapter 5).[54] One doesn't try for failure; one achieves failure after a very long struggle. I do not want that remark to be misunderstood, of course.

If "everything" is the goal, "always more" will result, always incomplete by virtue of a stubborn but tempting ambition for yet another voyage. Hence Ulysses for Robin Blaser becomes the positive end-beyond-end of Dante's epochal quest (see chapter 3). That figure—evil in Dante—may be the pattern of the long-poem writer—always naming more everything until one falls off the edge of the Earth. Hence, the modern long poem often fails to convince that it has a balanced shape, because it might not care, except to establish a very simple frame or premise (like the original four sections of *Paterson*), and thus rests on local scales of segments and their pulsing and clashing. Perhaps it's more realistic to note that the long poem pretends, sometimes, to a shape, an "as if" for the writer, with endings sometimes becoming the most open (least closed) or most arbitrary part of a long poem.

The term "encyclopedic" is sometimes evoked, yet an encyclopedia, being a selection of the known, organized alphabetically, is thereby more systematic than these extremely long poems. Yet any encyclopedia's naming and defining entry may also, as Wikipedia hyperlinks now show, include many vectoring and suggestive connections to a vast world of endless elaboration. Such a text also may reorganize the library and playbook of what is known. A very long poem may deliberately, nobly, or almost maliciously absorb and transpose Great Works of the past while adding its own reading list, including, of course, itself.[55] "Encyclopedia" and "library" express, however bizarrely, why the term "everything" expresses any long poem's networks of expansive association.

So how can we decode this insistence on everything? And how understand the poly-multi elements of the long poem: multiple genres in one poem (although I've divided this book by genres that are overridden in the works themselves), multiple heterodiscursive tones, many poetic styles and dictions? One plausible finding: the modern long poem is the literary version of the *Gesamtkunstwerk*, a variant approach to this mode, because in such a poem, one may have allusions to or even enactments of other media (performance, visual art, and music), but the way other "media" really appear in a long poem is precisely through the heteronomous multiplicity of verbal/literary means (structures, poetic practices, tones, dictions, genres).

A *Gesamtkunstwerk*, in its more usual version in culture, is an aspirational concept, manifesting itself variously across cultures throughout the late nineteenth century to now, the early twenty-first century, the product of a vague but powerful longing consistent with theorizing a worldview of hope. The "gesamt" part, often taken to mean "totalized" (even totalitarian) is an interpretive translation of a word that also means collection, or assemblage of the disparate, not postulating a forced unity. More is said in chapter 4, but this strange—even disconcerting—"everything" is sometimes noted as the property of a *Gesamtkunstwerk*.

LENGTH

really L O N G, endless, leviathanic

Ezra Pound to John Quinn, 1917

Miles Davis: "Why did you go on so long?"
John Coltrane: "It took that long to get it all in."

Nat Hentoff, "John Coltrane"

Length follows from "everything" by displacing claims of every*thing* to sheer scale—words, extent. How long *is* long for a very long poem? This question does seem to be fundamental and definitional, but it is actually pataphysical and unanswerable. In an absurdist, po-faced conference paper (within "the science of imaginary solutions"), Jacob Edmond deliberately made critical hash of that question of length. In the paper "Long, Wide, Deep, Heavy," Edmond weighed, measured, and counted pages (printed, pdf, and html), according to eight "dimensions," with several statistical graphs of these, leading to many vigorous and absurd comparisons.[56]

Peter Middleton overrides the question by acknowledging that the larger problem of "managing limitless relations" does not encourage stopping a long poem. He finds one justification for variable and exorbitant length by analogy with scientific research and the "ideals of inquiry": "experiment" and "investigation" are a vocation without end (although individual scientific tasks are bounded and defined), and these perspectives infuse the long poem in order to establish "an image of the mighty world."[57] That last phrase, a citation from Tennyson, leads us back to Victorian narrative poetry. Middleton suggests thereby that length or mode per se is not the main concern, which is primarily exploring ongoing patterns of connectedness in extent.

Middleton's suggestive phrase "the longing of the long poem" attributes agency and desire to the long poem itself; it longs for its own length. He did not say the longing *for* the long poem, which can be the desire only of the writer (and possibly of the reader and critic). Middleton glosses the phrase as the "longing of the art work for recognition of its *claims*," meaning "its rights to propose unrolling and endless writing" even if, by excess, it extinguishes (or boringly habituates) its own necessity. All this is reasonably convincing despite the displacement of agency: the claim the artwork makes is exploration *as* an artwork, gesturing toward "ideals of inquiry" themselves.[58]

By "longing," Middleton means in part the longing for definitions that cannot be completed, as we see here and in his essay. He also suggests the "everything" that can never be accomplished. And that further entails that longing for longness to be glossed here.

I would propose several other reasons for length. If one posits that a long-poem writer is called upon to inhabit time by thinking in writing, this is a vocation for creating that responds beyond the composition of any relatively contained artifact. The ambition for that scale of activity really entails *poesis* itself—the longing to be making. The longing of the poem to be written through the poet (that Mackey noted) is a projection of the agency of the writer creating writing to answer to a compelling version of a vision or sound. Such a call to the activity of constant making might be contained by a lucid structure—in some poems treated here, it is—but the more extreme poems just keep going. We may not have a name for a structure in which human proportions disappear, along with (almost) the writer.[59] One could argue that the uncontained ones (like Duncan's overarching Grand Collage) are the Platonic ideal of the contained ones (say, Notley's *Descent of Alette*), or one could argue that the two lengths differ strikingly. But all long poems—because the poetic-analytic intellectual ambition is manifest, tend to the counterpoem or countermap—a critical suspicion of culture and society as they now stand, that in some poets turns to exorbitant length as if to make a sociocultural substitute.[60] The long poem is the "culture" or "society" of itself.

With this in mind, let us be practical, if briefly. Saying "long poem" means two—or three—very different sizes, something well commented upon by Middleton, Silliman, and Nigel Alderman. Suppose I first repeat them, saying that there are two kinds of long poems.[61] One kind is single-book length, generally concluding, taking months or a few years to complete, relatively contained if thematically rich. This kind of work is crafted so that the whole book is a conceptual art object in words, clearer than a very long poem in thematic focus, more bounded in size, with more emphasis on closure. There are many of these—a list includes H.D.'s *Trilogy* and *Helen in Egypt*, Eliot's *Four Quartets*, Hejinian's cluster around *My Life*. Notable recent essay-poems fit here: Caroline Bergvall's trilogy *Meddle English* (2011), *Drift* (2014), *Alisoun Sings* (2019). These are "one-book" long poems (even as trilogies), or a fitted series, books of a particular mastery and intellectual/emotional lens. Some of these works rearrange a relationship to short poems/lyric—even as prose. Often these works have chosen a key rhetorical strategy—sentences with repetition-reminders in Hejinian, *haibun* poems and prose in Bergvall, investigative language dissolution and critique of meaning in Philip. These are book-length long poems, work presented as a single longish book, a related series, or several (with different titles), even with some aura of capital-B Book, but focused as a single cultural intervention and not demanding a near lifetime to write (and perhaps to read).

What is the distinction between long and very long? Mayer's *Midwinter Day* is one book, published as one unit, "written"—at least dictated and documented—on the very same day in 1978 as it was lived, then expanded and completed as a temporally specific *long* poem. With Merrill's *The Changing Light at Sandover*, publication over several years (1976, 1978, 1980, 1982), his reopening the single titled work (in 1992) after apparently ending it, as well as the length (560 pages), suggests that this work be in the next category, *very* long poem. This second type, the very long poem, takes decades to write, has odic, serial, collage, or canto construction (sometimes all of these together, since no one rhetorical choice or scale of segmentivity defines this type), definitely surpasses one book in length, may be published across many widely separated years, and hence appears in and as multiple books yet is often presented under *one* synoptic title (like *"A," The Maximus Poems*, *Drafts*, *A Reading* [Beverly Dahlen], *The Alphabet*, *Paterson*, *Iovis*, *The Cantos*).

For this second sometimes unstoppable category, Silliman's term "longpoem," or the acronym VLP, Middleton's very long poem, may serve.[62] This extreme long poem takes a significant amount of time to write, even decades. There is surprising agreement about this taxonomy (if not about the exact terms used). Shadows of evaluation do appear in this terminology. Middleton's VLP echoes VIP (very important person), something that makes a silent argument, yet he sees a functional continuum between the two types of long. Silliman postulates two different taxonomies for long poems, then uses the same words for both, with only a space to distinguish between "long poem" and "longpoem." In that first descriptive designation (just "long"), Silliman puts anything book-length, anything postulating an ending, a closure (even a loosely "open-ended" one), and taking a fixed amount of time to write—something, one might say, like his *Ketjak* (1974) along with *Tjanting* (1981), the portal poems to *The Alphabet* (2008). For the second order of "longpoem," the one that he has written (*The Alphabet* and *The Age of Huts*, works to be presented together as a super-*Ketjak*) and is writing (*Universe*, begun with *The Revelator* in 2013), Silliman uses "longpoem"—a self-declared, awkward compound word, as if the lack of space separating the component words indicated no brakes on an endless, almost unstoppable work—and if stopped, then not ended.[63] Yet the terms are so similar that it appears Silliman reengages the continuum between the modes that he overtly rejects.

Nigel Alderman calls shorter long poems "pocket epics," and long ones "grandiose projects." The satisfying verbal crunch of "pocket epic" claims closural satisfaction via terminology. "Pocket" plus "epic" "simultaneously suggest[s] an ambitious project of mapping some form of totality and its deliberate restriction." On the other hand, "grandiose" names and resists the ego claims and excesses of the VLP project. Clearly, Alderman does not prefer "unfinished ever-expanding structures." Yet even the literal "everything" poem (as he sensibly implies) is only symbolically everything, and his "deliberate restriction" of a "totality" is a promising compromise for structure and ambition.[64]

However, it remains true that absolutely excessive and capacious poems exist; they are the ones that don't seem to end or want to end. The answer to why such excessive length might be as simple as authorial pleasures of learning what this poem is capable of and how much it can do, and the challenge of pushing the work to go further and further, naming and absorbing more. Such work doesn't actually have to take one's whole life, but it has to take many years, indeed decades, as a career-consuming project, probably published over many years in multiple separate books but contributing to one named Book or one named project. (Here the example of Walt Whitman might be proposed.) This is work done on a daunting scale, the scale of archive, library, midden, churned-up cultural memory, plus the stepwise recording of the life of persons, or places, or times or all of these. These "lifelong poems" tend to be conceptualized (as Middleton said) as investigative or experimental research projects (like a gigantic work in a dormant volcano—this a still-unfinished site sculpture by James Terrell) built in specific, variable, but long-unrolling accumulations and deliberations, tending toward sociocultural critique. Length responds to an author's endless longing.

This kind of work reveals oddities at ending (or the oddities of ending at all, as chapter 5 elaborates): the very long poem ends but does not stop, hence sometimes reopens. It has two endings at least, or several, and none is definitive. We will see this careful choice of both an ending and a non-ending in Mackey's recent three-book continuation of his long poem in *Double Trio*.

So a long poem possibly does not end—on principle. But what is that principle, or the principle generating all oddities at ending? I've said it is *poesis* itself—*making* as a principle and as an activity enacted in the life of the poet. The poet turned inside out into the world, the world turning into the poet all together become the project. It is also a leaping into cosmic time, as if earthly time is not enough. But there are also units of *poesis*—stages of it, certain modes of attention activated at different career moments—this is exemplified in the turn in Olson's *Maximus*. Long poems become magnetic fields of ongoing events and materials in their discourses and commentaries, not isolated items or singular insights. A long poem—thought to be an object and a structure—becomes an ongoing temporal process, even a reading community; this is, in its turn, sometimes unnerving to the reader. Grand Collage (Robert Duncan's term) takes "collage" as a verb, not solely a noun, and then as some omnivorous "grammar" that combines the two.

Long poems may certainly be self-contradictory and oscillatory, dialogic; Olson's dramatic shift from epic-polemic episodes in his first two books of *Maximus* to lyric quest in the third book is an example. And such works may be very intransigent in their changes, not necessarily trying to self-integrate or be ingratiating to a reader—like Zukofsky's *"A,"* with its wide-ranging sampler of genres from full-scale Roman play to four-line lyric.

There are several of these very long and endless or unstably ended works in contemporary North American (and Anglophone) poetry. All are endless in different ways. They are endless first, obviously, by not stopping as of now, in 2021 (Mackey). They are endless by adding and accumulating more "books" to the single named "master" book after it has been announced as closed (Williams, Waldman, Merrill, Hejinian). Third, they are endless by virtue of a constitutional endlessness, perhaps called closed only to open into related long-poem projects (Silliman, DuPlessis). Fourth, some potentially endless works are stopped by death, an abrupt, unpleasant ending. *The Martyrology* got stopped at six volumes plus several posthumous ones because bpNichol died suddenly, in 1988 at age forty. The stop by death also ended *Harlem Gallery*. Melvin Tolson's whole long poem was planned as an epic of the Black man in America mapped on the Exodus story.[65] An ambiguous case may be *The*

Maximus Poems—did death end it prematurely, or was it in fact finished (or pragmatically declared finished) by the author at the time of Olson's death? These are typical situations that might occur after the poem has gotten significantly long with many years invested.

Writing a *very* long poem creates a book that ruptures the book, capitalizes it as Book. Writing this kind of poem extends the book, trails it over time (and works overtime), with purposes that try to be unconstrained—even if, evidently, a sense of selection has to be conceded. The challenges of such works change drastically from a single book-length poem. More is incorporated and (somewhat) mastered. And that is a characteristic of the very long poem—it is circular thinking to say so, but it is also a deep feeling: such a work is dauntingly long (pleasurably so for the author). The scale enlarges. Time and space are investments of an extended sort. This is the endless (mendless?) poem, a work visibly excessive in time and space: a "life's work" symbolically or in actual fact. Endlessness is a reality (in some cases) and an important metaphor in others.

Further, some people writing VLPs (like Anne Waldman, James Merrill, John Ashbery, Ron Silliman, Louis Zukofsky, Charles Olson, Ezra Pound) sometimes also write or have written stand-alone novella-long poems, or serial poems, covering the territory of the long but not in ways outsized and excessive. For Silliman, the longer *Alphabet*, the shorter *Tjanting*; for Ashbery, *Flow Chart* and *Three Poems*; for Waldman, *Iovis* and *Trickster Feminism*, for Zukofsky, *"A"* and *80 Flowers*; for Williams, *Spring and All* and *Paterson*; for Notley, "White Phosphorus" and *Descent of Alette*; for NourbeSe Philip, *Looking for Livingstone* and *Zong!* Nathaniel Mackey has accomplished a parallel very long work—an epistolary *roman fleuve* about a jazz ensemble and its artistic activities, with extraordinary accounts of creative processes. Sometimes these shorter works are portal poems, moving into the long poem; sometimes they are prefaces, parallel works, or postludes; the point is, they are related projects. There are also double poems within the category very long; Mackey makes a transition between two intertwining long-poem projects (from 1985 on), the twins—*Mu* and *Song of the Andoumboulou* then becoming one—with *Double Trio* (2021) as continuation.

If the critical vocabularies that one might use for both book-length long poems and "longpoems" or VLPs are similar, something about their purposes and effects differ. I trouble this question throughout, for the border is ragged and only semiconvincing. As a reminder: a desire for totalizing critical statements (without wholeness or completion), a.k.a. everything, in some way motivates the scale of longer works of any kind. Exemplary focused statements (still with a wide range) are more the property of the smaller long works.

The VLP projects are not (easily) domesticated. They are cross-decade and only vaguely stoppable works. The conditions that govern the continuance of each differ from those of a single book. Writing a very long poem across decades of one's life differs considerably from writing a single named long book, both from the poet's perspective and in the reader's reception. They are also less pedagogically welcoming; often one teaches one section or one canto, or one segment working holographically, as if any part of a VLP could answer for the whole, but any selection will be a sample only, and possibly an unrepresentative one.[66] Even after this discussion, one still cannot easily ascertain just how long is long, and whether "length" defines anything distinctive. No exact cut-off number between extended collaged odes (Moore), novella long (Brooks), and very long (much less "too long") can be definitive. However, time of writing—a few years versus decades—is a definite difference of authorial investment and possibly textual control.[67]

For this unsystematic table, I am counting page numbers, yet pages are themselves of various sizes; fonts of various heft; margins of degrees of breadth. Hence, this table will be fundamentally useless. Evidently the longness of a long poem will not be established in absolute terms. And that was enough of that paragraph.

Counting pages (both statistically rough and obviously ridiculous) is only part of what counts. So why not enumerate "time"—that is, time of composition? But from a quick survey, one finds time doesn't help either, although twenty to twenty-five years seems to be one investment that recurs for the VLP.

The equation becomes activity multiplied by time and factoring genre = "length." Or perhaps that's another meaning of Middleton's "longing," suggesting something is yearned for that cannot be totally satisfied. Which puts desire, yearning, a kind of cultural lust (or hunger) and literary erotics again into the middle of one's ambition. Correctly. To ask how long is a long poem is, then, to answer with another question: how long can the writer desire to sustain it? How long does it still make sense?

What makes this kind of work sustainable at all? Casting oneself into the unknown, risking efforts that might end in a stalemate, keeping discussion open, resisting premature closure. All this is like Retallack's "poethical" attitude or the long poem as essay (in verse), essaying some topics. What, Middleton asks, motivates a writer toward this baggy version of negative capability in sustained and almost optimistic joy at creation? "Longing" is the propulsive sustaining force, the force behind *poesis* on this scale and yearning; I sign on here.

Middleton considers that the "long poem" actually has no limiting rule of form (like a sestina) or one of genre (it is not an epic historically speaking), but in modernity they are heterogeneous and "nonconform[ing]" "wild poems" in

TABLE 1. LENGTH OF SELECTED LONG POEMS

Author	Title	Length (pages)
Nathaniel Mackey	*Song of the Andoumboulou*, *Mu*, and *Double Trio*	1,757
bpNichol	*The Martyrology*	1,403
Ron Silliman	*The Alphabet*	1,054
Rachel Blau DuPlessis	*Drafts*	1,031
Anne Waldman	*Iovis*	1,009
Louis Zukofsky	*"A"*	826
Ezra Pound	*The Cantos*	824
Charles Olson	*The Maximus Poems*	635
Clark Coolidge	*A Book Beginning What and Ending Away*	571
James Merrill	*The Changing Light at Sandover*	560
Caroline Bergvall	*Meddle English; Drift; Alisoun Sings*	483
Kamau Brathwaite	*Ancestors*	468
John Kinsella	*Divine Comedy*	408
Robert Duncan	*Bending the Bow*	436
Alice Notley	*Alma, or the Dead Women*	344
Kamau Brathwaite	*ConVERSations*	315
Ronald Johnson	*Ark*	307
H.D.	*Helen in Egypt*	304
William Carlos Williams	*Paterson*	284
Melvin Tolson	*Harlem Gallery*	262
John Ashbery	*Flow Chart*	216

size, scope, and number of materials in play: they are long in time, long in space, and more undefinable even than the lyric.[68] The core finding in his speculative essay is the compelling force of longing—both of the poem and for the poem, and what that means for authorial ambitions and for the genres that result.

Then, as the table shows, in a debatable and capricious category within this space-time intersection, I'd include honorific/"nanorific" long poems, game-changing interventions that, although rather short, have seemed long because of their explosive and long-term cultural effect. Often they are innocently called long poems by stunned, bemused readers, unused to poems occupying more than a few pages, although they are really not long by "epic-long" standards. It's that their impact crater is quite deep and extensive, a measure in certain cases interchangeable with long.[69] Right now for me, the verifiably nanorific long poems in the long twentieth century include Mallarmé's *Un coup de dés* and Eliot's *The Waste Land*, both discussed here. However, Mina Loy's *Love*

Author	Title	Length (pages)
Lyn Hejinian	*A Border Comedy*	216
Ron Silliman	*Tjanting*	213
M. NourbeSe Philips	*Zong!*	211
A. R. Ammons	*Tape for the Turn of the Year*	205
Lyn Hejinian	*My Life*	203
H.D.	*Trilogy*	171
Alice Notley	*The Descent of Alette*	148
Bernadette Mayer	*Midwinter Day*	119
John Ashbery	*Three Poems*	118
Ron Silliman	*Ketjak*	101
Gwendolyn Brooks	*Annie Allen*	59
Hart Crane	*The Bridge*	56
Melvin Tolson	"Libretto for the Republic of Liberia"	49
Langston Hughes	"Montage of a Dream Deferred"	42
Muriel Ruykeyser	"U.S. 1" (Part I: The Book of the Dead)	38
T. S. Eliot	*Four Quartets*	36
T. S. Eliot	*The Waste Land*	25
George Oppen	"Of Being Numerous"	24
Robin Blaser	"Great Companion: Dante Alighieri"	21
Stéphane Mallarmé	*Un coup de dés*	21

Note: Nichol's *Martyrology* lacks pagination, so page count is DuPlessis's count, some from PDFs.

Songs and Marianne Moore's "An Octopus" and "Marriage," both 1923, have suffered in any agreed-upon account book of impact from the millstone tax on female originality/innovation in these poets' belated receptions. No comment. Or just one: What is literary history anyway?

To "long enough space/time" in a single book-length work of bigness and cultural focus, and then "really long time; really long results" (lifelong, creating a multibook poem done over many years or even decades, excessive)—already two quite unstable measures of the Long—we have to add "currently viewed as culturally necessary in literary history"—whatever that is—and "historically important for some socio-poetic rupture" for capricious category three.

I have almost argued that length does not matter at all—which is a somewhat quixotic, Zukofskian perspective to take, after all. Certainly the reader would like to understand a little more about the formal implications of all those pages piling up, even if the writer just wants to continue. Length, sheer length, as quantity of stuff doesn't matter, but there is a performative dimension to length as elapsed time: time as depicted inside the work (if it is), time as experienced writing the work (sometimes time getting it published or into reception, too), and time as experiencing the unrolling of the work in reading(s). A long poem (like any artwork) is a historically metamorphic set of events in transit—a writing of the work, poetic materials inside the work, and critical narratives of experiencing the work. These events are thoughts that the writer thinks, and that readers tune to, puzzle over, and consider. Each poem has various performance times for its playing out of these elements. Any critical consideration of the poem's goals and shapes in a long space is simply another event in ongoing reception. In the "act of managing limitless relations" in the general absence of plot—a real management problem, in fact—a rereading of any such poem may see new patterns of theme and concern, themselves inflected by the reader's historical time.[70]

FORM AND STRUCTURE: SOME DEFINITIONS

As for definitions of form and structure—and about time, one might say, it appears (perhaps with that pragmatic Platonic trace that might characterize any "theory" here) that *form* is some concept, idea, Ur-thought, a vision of the whole project of the long work as a serious calling or vocation. That visualization of the unwritten idea with its urgencies and demands is, as we will see, what Roland Barthes called "X-ray of the Ur-text" before it is written.[71] It seems often to be a haptic event. For different writers here, this commitment might be a *visualization* (as in Barthes). It might be a *sound*, as in Mackey, the drone or rasp of a Dogon elegy. It might be an almost instantaneous realization of temporal urgency as in Silliman both from a mysterious word ("Ketjak") and from music, Steve Reich's repetitious "layering."[72] It might be the literary intensity and wide suggestiveness of the word "draft" (writing and rewriting), along with the emotional sense of "draft" as a breeze from an opening in DuPlessis.[73] It might be the desire to fill an odd kind of paper—as in Ammons's adding-machine tape. It might be a historical challenge for access: *woman poet* and epic genres. These comments reveal that the desire for the poem is visceral: form speaks as if embodied in you, then you further its embodiment by making (a lot of) words and thoughts to answer that call, a commitment to invention, intertextuality, language, page space, amplification, and poetic development—elaborations of all sorts and modes within the discipline of poetry, or writing. This becomes or leads to structure. The arrival of that sense of Ur-form in any poet is a powerful intuition that, often combined with a related sociocultural urgency, will (can) sustain long-poem writing over many years.

Structure could involve individual acts in time, even ones temporary for a few lines, stanzas, ideas, allusions; structures as expectations also occur when a writer chooses to repeat these in patterns or shapes for a good portion of the whole work. Sometimes ideas in structure emerge continuously throughout the construction of the poem as the drive to write incorporates new stimuli; sometimes the rationale for individual materials included will modulate over decades (as with Pound, who used the same syntactic structures but attributes them to different worldviews). Often, then, the structures do not displace each other but continue to accumulate, marking the poem with its own history of instances as well as incorporating, in the outline of a long poem, an archaeology/assemblage of the poet's changes over time.

Structures are all the ways a poet chooses to carry out that idea—they might change over the years, their justifications might change, and some people might also call this the choice of various *forms*. In order to avoid confusion, *that* word in this book will often be *modes* or *practices*. "Form" is thought of here as an apprehension of the need for Big *Poesis*, the Ur-text, something "relatively" unchangeable—the sheer desire—that propels a poet to keep doing the poem. "Structure" occurs as each poet understands what then might happen with practices and modes—tactics, research to be done, words, events on the page, and shapes to be made in the work.

Both form and structure could be subsumed under the rubric *poesis* (making). Big ambitious making in its inexplicable urgencies and felt drives can motivate a person's longing for forming the long poem—the visceral feeling of that Ur-form and the institution of acts of praxis in time, the patience that it would take to carry out a desire that may be almost instantaneously intuited. Structures (better in the plural) are what happen, what is written, as the outcomes of the sense of—the annunciation of form. Form is like a vision of a project outside of the self whose instantiated making becomes a bargain with the self-in-time.

The longing of and for the long poem has as its basis as a sense of form—an idea. Structures might or might not always live up to that vision. It's difficult to get form-as-idea and structure in a very long poem to coincide, always to match up, to play on the same field, and then (perhaps) to satisfy the writer. It appears as if a very long poem is an endless struggle in structures themselves between the fecundity of *poesis*—sheer making bit by bit in time—and of acts of judgment. An author tries to predict, while inside the poem, how the modes and practices add up to anything like the larger form intuited. This struggle can sometimes explain all these long poems' acts of length: that is, choices whether a given poem will ever end and how, and the question why writing such a poem doesn't simply end up with a *poem* only, but also with questions of poetics.

This statement also tries to indicate (explain?) why endless assemblage itself is, here in the genre discussion, one resolution for structure. That originating apprehension of form demands *poesis* itself—a making at length with some ambitious and relentless drive for bringing more and more together, in larger and larger scope across time. The choices the poets make to give any appropriate design to their own accumulation become "structure." The structures themselves can be so large, or so bricolaged, or so overwhelming that trying to read them demands justifications of form—the originating propulsion. This may be why it's hard to separate structure (the actual poem/text on the ground) and form—the longing that motivates the idea of writing this work, that poem in the distance, forever over the horizon. Sometimes this dilemma provokes the poet to a tactical decision—less length than the monumental can then indicate boundlessness allegorically. That is, the poetics of boundlessness can be indicated by a tactical boundary—a fixed number and then stopping.

However, it also seems—from an unsystematic survey—that most of the poets here use the two terms as synonyms, or even that when they mean specific decisions or choices of mode (like line break, or sentence mode, or white space on a page), the word they use is "form." "Structures" might seem a term that is too "structured"—that implies a sense of system already decided, already organized. Hence, in this book, I try to signal that vocabulary as it appears at specific moments of explanation. Interestingly, as a noun, "forms" seems to suggest a pulse of continuation, where "structures" seems to suggest fixity—a complex entity already interrelated.[74]

THE NANORIFIC "WASTE LAND" AND THE END OF INTRODUCTIONS

If Pound's *Cantos* became the Alps, in Basil Bunting's curtal sonnet of its reception, *The Waste Land* has to be—what?—a confusion and collapse after intermingled unnatural disasters: modernity, urban life, anomie, sexualities, cosmopolitan sensibilities plus a lurking World War I as mingled conditions for shock.[75] Certainly its literary aftermath was powerful. After T. S. Eliot had composed/collaged this work's talismans (materials from at least a decade before 1922), he asked for Pound's edits. By removing several narrative sections and nixing any "imitative" elements, Pound focused attention on its queerish gender ambiguity and haunted revenants, much less on its satires. Thereupon, Eliot chose to control (assess? displace?) some of that ambiguity by adding, without Pound's knowledge or approval (not, of course, required) those distancing, distracting, authority-claiming endnotes, bringing the text from nineteen to twenty-five pages. He thereby placed yet another subjectivity among the poem's many, and another genre into (or onto) the poem. The word "into" implies that the footnotes are a crucial part of the work (my position); "onto" implies they are excrescent.[76] Pound was annoyed by Eliot's addition but always championed the poem, even as he himself was quite challenged by it. Any number of formal and intellectual choices characterize this moment, not to speak of emotionally laden ones concerning authorship and *odi et amo* relations among poets—the eros of *poesis*.[77]

Even before the footnotes, Pound had announced to Eliot that this poem was "let us say, the longest poem in the English langwidge"; my paraphrase would be suppose it is; now what?[78] It was never the longest, of course; Pound's implicit modernist jibes, sidelining at least Chaucer, Spenser, Milton, Pope, Blake, Byron, Wordsworth, Whitman, Tennyson, and Browning, construct one pivot point for my book by insisting on the categories *modern* (proleptically: "a grrrreat littttterary period") and *long poem*—not calling it epic, for instance.[79] Yet its being an anti-epic of an almost hopeless, desiccated quest contributes to the original and still palpable shock of *The Waste Land*. Both genre traces (epic actions and uplifting quest) are played wrong way round; this is part of this poem's cultural staying power and encourages the diagnostic urge in other long poems.

Whether Pound's "longest" is an inside joke, tall tale, or consoling lie, the Anglo-American "modern long poem" as a framed mode of practice and challenge begins with Eliot's poem and Pound's 1921 overstatement.[80] Such a "nan-orific" poem considered *as* long becomes both test and proof of the modern era that ever-impatient Pound was provoking, curating, and advertising. We also see Pound's covert literary-historical competition about what and who is adequately modern—and whose long poem is really long.

The poem also shows, unintentionally, an imperial suffusion. In the period when Eliot had, in his accumulation of shards and citations of Western high and popular cultures, collected, redistributed, and added value to them, he is supported by ethnography and comparative myth studies to find deep (sometimes startling and reductive) connections between Western cultures, other "developed" cultures, and indigenous cultures. This gesture recurs; the modern long poem takes up a fascinated, curious but quite proprietary attitude to a wide range of cultures, gleaning their shards and talismans across many realms, a loosely imperialist *and* comparativist poetics.

The Waste Land practices genre multiplicity throughout and manages its open-ended ending by presenting a sampler of some genres and themes by evoking talismanic citations that have subsequently entranced and frustrated readers for a hundred years. Each signals clusters of genres: nursery rhyme as revelatory apocalypse; spiritual quest and hope of purgation; sexual longing and lyric urgency; melancholy hero without an epic to act in. Further, Tiresias is not a "hero" of one genre—or any—he is a sex-gender transgressor taxed with unifying the poem by Eliot's evocations of this figure's perverse reputation.

A reading strategy should be alert to the multiple genres and allusions in any given longish poem, asking how they function polyphonically. Such a strategy resists reducing a poem to one genre rubric. It's as if a long-poem author is trying to involve and to gloss multiple genres, thus maximizing claims of writerly mastery. Perhaps this is part of that seriocomic accumulative goal, as in Pound's 1917 intention: *The Cantos* as "an endless poem of no known category . . . all about everything."[81] What do we think "no known category" plausibly means except "no known genre"?

The reception of his nanorific *Waste Land* seems to have had a staggering impact on Eliot, leading him eventually to undercut it as "a piece of rhythmical grumbling," and not even "an important bit of social criticism."[82] By 1931 he rejects with distaste the proposition that he was expressing what critics called "the 'disillusionment of a generation'" claiming only to have "expressed their illusion of being disillusioned, but *that* did not form part of *my* intention."[83] This is more than humility; it is the burden of being praised as a spokesman for losses of certainty, not at all what he wanted to profess.[84] He made clear *his* chosen cultural critique in his matching long poem.

Four Quartets dramatizes a penitential pilgrimage renouncing the considerable excitements (and impacts) of his earlier oeuvre. The solemn and deliberate *Four Quartets* was a chance to rectify the hysteria, extreme acts, and cunning prejudices expressed by his significant earlier work (along with his sophomoric racist/pornographic doggerel). Eliot had been trying for a reverent and uplifted, even transformative mode soon after 1922; probably from the Anglo-Catholic conversion of 1927; certainly from *Ash Wednesday* (1930). But singularly motivating (despite *Sweeney Agonistes* [written 1923–24, published 1926–27]) was his desire never to write another *Waste Land*: disjunct, oblique, collaged, exilic, allusive, demanding much reader inference, thrillingly amoral as well as thrillingly anguished—and, finally, *un*resolved. He atoned in *Four Quartets.*

Visible in many very long ("life's work") poems under discussion here, from *The Waste Land* on, is the use of what Theodor Adorno and then Edward Said have discussed as "late style." These intentionally fragmented collage modes do not depend on an artist's being old but on an attitude to the work at hand: born from "a contradictory, alienated relationship" with social and aesthetic orders. This unresolved fragmentation is exilic, resistant, quarreling with time and norm and filled with "unresolved contradiction[s]."[85] However, Eliot tries to fight loose from the "late style" that he pioneered, along with its implicit social critique. Take the citations: *The Waste Land* contains a "mongrel" set from many languages and dictions, quite heteroglossic. In the *Quartets* pious and high literary sources prevail: Julian of Norwich, Herbert, Swift—and, notably, Dante. The fifth sections of each Quartet are "about" language and spiritual struggle, in prayerful tonalities, rectifying any encouragements his work had ever given to a secular culture. His clear enunciation suggests a deliberate renunciation. He thereupon devoted his considerable cultural capital to arguing not only against secularism, thus certainly *not* for any uplifting humanisms or loosely theistic spiritual yearnings, but for one specific Anglo-Catholic version of Christianity as crucial and unimpeachable. His later poem's ending will indicate the only correct path toward individual salvation.

The Waste Land begins this book not for any belief in Pound's literary canonization as the only story, but because its landscape is replete with shards of various broken syntheses, allusions to once-convincing orders, plots, and heroes, in incantatory collage mode and no conclusion. Its late style particularly on the level of the phrasal lines, but also expanded, in the juxtaposition of sections, occurs to jolt recognitions, not to smooth connections. This double segmentivity is characteristic, if not uniform, in many works to be noted here.

Generally a long poem stands in "exile" from unity, having experienced some "catastrophic force" that is, in our time, a refusal of fictitious unities and totality.[86] The catastrophic is a powerful recognition that changes assumptions; it is not (necessarily) an external disaster like war, enslavement, or colonial-imperial relations, but it could be. This is why the motif of "everything," "infinite" numbers, overwhelming (and sometimes unstoppable) scale, multiple genres (always "plus-one" and then another), polyphonic dictions, a social panorama or "mural," and a poetics pledging boundlessness are characteristics I have emphasized to discuss both the long and the *very* long poem.

Whether authorial findings are articulated in the course of writing, or whether findings are preestablished and reaffirmed in the poem, strange splits in reader allegiance result that might be visualized in Charles Olson's very resistant attitude to *Four Quartets*—prestigious when he began writing—for its prosodic repetition of the sections and its cultic affirmations: he saw these as related flaws. In "Projective Verse" Olson proposes that this pre-fixed design conflicts with the heuristic activity of *poesis*. Yet the *Quartets* were also found by some to be consoling and elegant *because* of the general prosodic predictability and sense of return to a pattern, allegorically the assurance of a right path, though actually limiting that path to the Anglo-Catholic.

This question of prior findings simply affirmed, or findings discovered in writing is a major contradiction in the long poem; the test case has been Pound, who did once feel that a fascist political *paradiso* could be celebrated (a fixed conclusion), then found that it could not. Shards of elegiac defensiveness mixed with sub rosa affirmations of that projected paradise trace through *The Pisan Cantos* and beyond. If a pre-fixed conclusion is not desired, but rather the open acts of *poesis*, one understands why a number (perhaps based in numerology) can establish a place to end without negating the ethos of open exploration.

If poems of between two hundred and a thousand pages are the answer—what was "the" question? For some readers, impatience about length and the lack of or instability at ending are the most obvious responses to long-poem authors—why can't they just *stop*? And if some do stop (even constructing viable and satisfying endings), why can't others learn something from that? The points have been made, the instantiations have unrolled—why go on? (I have myself asked this about X, and at times about Y, but never—well, quite rarely—about myself. This should show you the way things can be in the world of the long poem.) This generosity of category for what counts as a long or very long poem has the advantage of creating an expansive field, one responsive to its own expansion, as Matthew Carbery argues, extending into poetics Lynn Keller's title phrase "forms of expansion." Other readings prefer a pedagogic or affirmative payoff, appropriate to the demands on readers made by the poems. Continuing to demand negative capability (suspension and eager incipience) from readers after hundreds of pages asks a lot, particularly if the usual reading segment is jumpy and rapid. Presumably, readers invest in open long-poem poetics because there is poetic pleasure along the way, and ending is not crucial.

What can possibly explain "the poet's enigmatic persistence against all odds toward the impossible poem"?[87] Margaret Dickie sees long poems as sloppy works, with "no principle of generation, no limits to reach or to transgress, no narrative to tell, no hero to tell it."[88] This remark, as conventional and resistant as it now reads, presents an important question in an anguished and emotionally invested tone. Dickie tried but could not make long poems cohere. Her readerly question is haunting.

A poet-centered orientation allows another poetics for the "principle of generation" and the goals of telling, one invested in ongoing processes. There are different initiatory disturbances than Dickie's suggestion to make and carry out a plan. At the inception of the poem, writers might simply wonder how far they can pursue some formal-emotional idea, that yearning for a book of "everything." Another type of initiatory event is revealed in Mackey's 1998 interview with Brent Cunningham, when he traces the provocation to "a Dogon funeral song that I heard on a record in the early 1970s"—"a certain stridency and raspiness" in "the literal sound of the song of the Andoumboulou." His very long poem responds by "discovering the range of things that this figure can apply to [. . .] as it presides over certain areas of my life and work. It [the work] becomes more inclusive and more elastic and, again, vibrates with other traditions and with my own experience."[89] This is a "sound image" in the ways Williams's was "a [visual or conceptual] image large enough to embody the whole knowable world about me."[90] And then Mackey's articulation of the outcome: "It's partly finding out and it's partly making"—research in/as *poesis* itself is the ongoing motivation.[91]

Dickie's annoyed anguish is particularly interesting with *Paterson*—for Williams did make a plan. But then the plan changed. Book V broke through his solid four-square plan; what Williams thought he'd established (the city, the river's run to the sea, the destructive fire/rape as breakthrough to newness, a man's simultaneous birth and death) was untenable—he could not close an experience of writing that had become endless.

This sketchy review of inception and what it provokes brings long poems near the ethos of Joan Retallack's "poethical wager" (Retallack's influential adding of that ethical "h" to poetics): a very long poem built out of changes, without a preplan necessary—maintaining its investigatory curiosity as a "conscious strategic risk."[92] Making (*poesis*) and investigating are intertwined and simultaneous. This combination of making and investigation Retallack contrasts with any congealed values and practices. To examine this tension: a long-poem writer might not begin with a specific or idiomatic "plan" or "goal" at first—but only achieve temporary restaging points in the vicissitudes and vagaries of poetic practice. Or she might have had a plan and later have to modify it or give it up. Or she might keep adding plan (or metaphors for plans) upon plan. Or find that the poem becomes its own "habitus" and becomes rigid, if still long.

In contrast to the concerns of Dickie, Retallack proposes the formal claims of "in *medias* mess," using the pun of "mess" (for *res*) as a key (if shocking—and amiable) technical term, on the wager I borrow here: that long-poem writing—a longing for praxis with poethics—tries "our utmost to understand our contemporary position," bringing the aesthetic and sociopolitical goals of a long poem into mutual interaction.[93] Taking this stance, I see the long poem as the act of a quondam public intellectual in poetry, constructing "experimental thought" and experimental structures via literary-cultural activities, while giving some kind of unusual aesthetic pleasure.

An implicitly commitment-oriented combination of critical social life, political life, and aesthetic life motivates poets' desires for writing. Most writers of the very long poem act as if socio-aesthetic commentary is a vital goal, no matter what their political allegiances are. And some try to incite change itself, or in the tones of their work express the excitement of awaiting transformation—as a permanent ongoing poetic motive. The segmentivities of the long poem engage this pulse of continuance, metamorphic sensibility, and constant making. This leads to a coherence of purpose, not necessarily coherence of structure or plan. Essay-poem thinking transposes events of seeking into states/stages of writing. These may not offer final satisfactions or even agreeable findings.

However, the motives of some long-poem writers might point to grand synopses that resist elements of an open "poethics"; the long poem is hardly a contradiction-free zone. Particularly pedagogic *goals* rather than investigative *processes* undercut the idealized poem-essay that I was limning. According to Ezra Pound (in 1962), "you had six centuries that hadn't been packaged. It was a question of dealing with material that wasn't in the *Divina Commedia*"—meaning, grosso modo, the Renaissance and modernity.[94] Taking your own long poem as the modern extension or crucial continuation of Dante's, as a version of its social and cultural values, and getting "everything" important staged and evaluated ("packaged") inside the poem bespeaks an almost self-sacrificing (and/or self-aggrandizing) ambition, a responsibility to more than the literary—to social and cultural knowledge as well. However, it also suggests a "habitus." "Packaged" is the word keying Pound's authoritarian resistance to ongoing curiosity, while still maintaining his experimental rhetorics with its exploratory jump cuts.

According to some of these poets, your education is their motivation. Pedagogic goals, recognized by Bob Perelman and Alan Golding from the Poundian claim, are a firm property of the long poem.[95] Access to a renewed pedagogy incorporating certain overlooked texts is also inspiration, as in Olson's exhortations to the civic in the voice of Maximus not to speak (I already have) of his "go-get-'em boys" coach-to-his-team, male-inclined rhetorics directed insistently to those he assumed were his knowledge-bearing posse.[96] One of the central (forensic/quasi-institutional) interventions made by any long poem is addressed to its readership: readers do not yet know enough of the world—without this poem (there's the ego or cultural claim), they are not adequately informed; or adequately aroused to the universe of understanding and knowledge, and possibly, if more rarely, to action; or at least roused by a presentation of evidence and perhaps engaged by this worldview. The cultural library has formerly been incomplete; this poem reorganizes and adds to it (including itself). You the reader need some cultural-historical corrective; this long poem serves as rectification.

This rectification may come with a teasing snideness—Pound called universities "the beaneries"; *The Cantos* are Alternative U.[97] It may come with a proud austerity and an intransigent challenge: Melvin Tolson with his intricately footnoted poem *Libretto for the Republic of Liberia* (1953) shows that you (probably) know little to nothing of African cultures and their historic achievements; he will wise you up, as possible. This rectification may come with documentation, leading organically to a changed interpretation of what is seen and known (Olson's *The Maximus Poems*, Williams's *Paterson*, and Muriel Rukeyser's, *U.S. 1*). It may be an investigation of a region and the establishment of new aesthetic goals—"tidialectical" sensibilities understood and appreciated via a renewed vocabulary and a changed history rectifying colonial narratives (in Braithwaite). It may come with a seductive empathy or vatic explorations of the past bringing your consciousness into a new formation (H.D. and *Trilogy*; Hart Crane and *The Bridge*); with exhortation and a manifesto-like energy (Waldman in *Iovis*); with an angry elegiac sorrow, keening over history (*Zong!* by NourbeSe Philip).

Another model of the impact of long poems tends to emphasize the pleasures of making, but not forgetting information or attitude—simply a less fervent or even disinterested emphasis on the pedagogic. The poetry of this set of works does not seek the impact of teaching or exhortation but wants incantation within a goal of witnessing. Their approaching the condition of music will widen the sense of being part of the "everything" or the "world" that the poets offer, a saturation in sensuous meditation. In these poems the reader's experience is the hypnotic one of being simply sung to and thereby immersed in (or seduced by, tempted by, drawn into) a fully spun—and spinning—world, making a rhetorical, sonic cocoon for the reader: the long poems of Ashbery, Beverly Dahlen, Mackey, Notley, myself, and, in a particular way, Silliman have that effect.[98] A related impact for the reader is being thoroughly dazzled by endless formal sprezzatura: Brooks, Johnson, Tolson, Wallace Stevens (as long-poem writer), and Merrill have that effect.

I take long poems to concern things that are too large in relation to things that are too small: the work is an endless negotiation with the scale of an individual and a collectivity (that often gets larger and larger—"everything"). Therefore, a paradigmatic motive is an "I" hardy enough to confront the "everything"—some amalgam of social, historical, and cosmological concerns. (Hardy and Foolhardy—one might say.) It's not so much that such writers have answers as that they have questions and some sense of the crucial formal and rhetorical means each has defined/derived for discovering the scope of that "whole knowable world."

The poetic goal of writing a long or very long poem assumes time, an expansive sense of poetic practice, much stubborn persistence, and some kind of authorial drive to this kind of act. This drive is difficult to decode—a willing immersion in the metamorphic boundlessness that results, some intensity in one's relationship with a number of cultural (and perhaps historical) forces, some primal pride, serious devotion, sometimes devolving into habit. Because of the risks of committing to such a goal over a significant time, long poems are *motivated* cultural responses or addresses to an imagined (but not, let's hope, imaginary) set of readers. The goal of writing a long poem doesn't posit any given "form," system, or structure, or even a single genre (epic, quest, assemblage) or mode (serial, procedural, narrative), but rather posits a drive or ambition, with enough invention to explore *making* (*poesis* and its provisional forms variously solidifying), along with a commitment to the development of meanings (sometimes discovered in or made expansive by this process) both in the extended field of poetry and in a vaster socio-spiritual or historical field. This is why I admired and appropriated the expressive word "longing" for what is at stake.

That is, a long-poem writer is haunted by many and one, haunted by layers of social collectivities and by the vastness of universe and space/time. Given historical effects, the layers of social collectivities create pressure and plethora; the vastness and endlessly deferred furtherness (as of discoveries) and cosmological studies, as in contemporary astrophysics, create wonder on a scale that is overwhelming—and sometimes in contrast with the plethoras of the social and of current political-historical disgraces. This is where a sense of untamed or teeming boundlessness enters and is focused variously, but almost always incompletely, by long-poem poets.

A long poem, by inhabiting duration itself, creates enough space in the unrolling of the poem to deliver the reader to another time—the long durations of reading and sometimes rereading, and the ending of "having done" and of arriving into the future of having read this, after you will have read it. This becomes an extensive space from the beginning of the book to the endless or deferred end. The reading of the book enters duration, and the future, via length.

Some kind of synthesis of knowledge and its stakes, some pile-up of observations via an investigatory individual, demands length and time. That is why the length of these poems, so odd and even disturbing to readers, is fundamental to the analytic poetics of the poets. For many of them, the findings are never enough, or the world as such generates more material, more necessity for the very poem they are writing.

Any work of literature is instantiated in its use of language. Even purely aesthetic literature (is there any, really?) and purely committed literature (to borrow Adorno's terms in the essay "Commitment"[99]) must use all the nuances of language for its "messages." That is, both artful and apparently asocial hermeticism that pretends never to be alert to history and the social as well as a drive for perfect relevance and political engagement must use language, in all its ambiguities of tone and affect. What you say may have hidden corridors to be found and decoded; you might come out with language that undercuts what you think you are saying. Whether intricately or simply chosen, language enacted on a terrain of literature or beyond it, all facts, all forms, all language acts are debatable and mediated—and to be understood as rhetorical risks with the outcome to be read: a long poem.

The result is a work on a scale far beyond any humanist or lyric poetic tempering but containing these poetic processes among others. By "too large" I mean the universe, the Earth, history and politics, the sense of the past, literary history, ethics, and the more febrile, even apocalyptic sense of the future: in short, plethora, hyperstimulation, an overwhelmed feeling to which one responds. Thus, whether you are writing one or reading one, "the long poem is a work of mastery during which you submit to your own powerlessness."[100] The tension between control and out of control is a condition of one's employment in this kind of poem. It is solved (not ever resolved) in a variety of ways.

The artist William Kentridge reminds readers of the end of Dante's *Paradiso* when all the pages of scribble "by the Cumaen Sybil fly through the air and are gathered into one single book, a chaos of knowledge forming itself into a coherence."[101] That his own work as an artist has involved "undoing" the leaves of old books for art projects, the "dismembering of order, a disordering of a coherence," and his "re-inscribing" these pages with his own drawings immediately reminds us of the real activities of art and writing, an endless "dismembering and reordering." This is also a description of a long-poem process. Or, as William Carlos Williams noted in a prose poem of poetics introducing *Paterson* (1946), "by multiplication a reduction to one" and at the same time "a dispersal and a metamorphosis."[102] Of course, these two phrases indicate opposite activities. This contradictory, ongoing activity announces the boundless poetics of long poems.

Williams's hard-won statement in poetics might indicate something about the way this critical book of essays tries to face, inhabit, appreciate, and elaborate on various contradictions in the writing and thinking about a long poem—particularly a very long poem. Such a composition seems to idealize a Book (possibly a dream of coherence, totality) but also to instantiate Kentridge's "revelation of the instability of knowledge in the world, its provisionality. The collage and the reordering becomes the subject itself."[103] The long poem addresses problems idiomatic to its own construction. Writing is a responsive, boundless activity, not a canon. "Literature" is a complex of socioaesthetic judgments along the way.

In attitudes toward the author—who has somehow decided to write such a poem, the reader could simply maintain an alert attitude of tolerant curiosity, perhaps by not reading too much of a given poem at any given time: slow reading. To inspire that tolerant attitude, I offer a wry observation from Gerald L. Bruns, about Lyn Hejinian's *Border Comedy* and by extension about any long poem: "No one wished it longer, but it could have been. Long poems are those one learns to live with."[104]

CHAPTER 2

Deploying Epic

There is really no talking about exact genres—kinds of literary works—as if this term has defined or useful boundaries. Each genre name is a pool of potentiality that has been generalized from a chosen (culturally motivated) selection of extant prior examples and expectations, thereby consolidating the very object they are naming. Genres are vast sociocultural practices and understandings on varied scales. Terms like "epic," "quest," "romance" imply certain motifs, themes, and goals and even specific traditional episodes, while other terms like serial poem, novel, song, essay draw on contingent agreements about a shape and sometimes an attitude toward the material. Others yet, like logbooks, lists, letters, prayers, are often precise and functional in origin but may occur in artworks for broad and decontextualized reasons. Given mixes of attitudes and uses, it's hard to frame "genre"—is it a conventional literary formula? A set of semi-flexible promises for action and outcome? A worthless (or comedic) limit or border? A historically flexible set of expectations? An available practice where you choose what elements to use? One might have a *quest poem* (a trek through incisive particulars to some significant end)—but its mode of writing might be narrative (Notley), serial (Oppen), or procedural (Hejinian). And what if the "end" is undecidable or almost missing when the text gets there?

Genres *are* definable—they could be structures of patterned thinking about motive, motif, and action, and an account of those condensed thoughts. However, these definitions are also situational, institutional, demanding a temporary "as if" agreement, since any categories are both specific historical instances and ideal types. Genres are acts of exploration, category play, choice, and participation/resistance. They certainly are a problem helpfully covered (or at least covered over satisfactorily) by reminding readers of Wittgenstein's "family similarities," as M. A. Bernstein does, briefly, while getting seriously into the question of long poems as epic.[1] We also learn what is supposed to be (or plausible) "in" a genre from literary handbooks, observation, reading and viewing experiences, and some mobile surmises—genre categories are learned (leaned on?) informational clusters or impastos, as much literary convention is. We know we can articulate lists of genres; we know they are frozen versions of practices and prior works; we know variation is as keen a practice as repetition. To use a genre is to remake it.

Genres metamorphose as evidence of authorial thought. Genres—even central ones—are in perpetual motion in long poems (objectively) and from reader vantages (subjectively). They are always interpretations of some not-quite fixed entity. They exist in unresolved dialectical engagements and unresolved availabilities.

Many readers and critics assume that the epic is central to the modern long poem. If by *epic* is meant *only* poems heavily invested in male heroes, warrior-strategists like Odysseus, Aeneas, Beowulf, or Sundiata, depicted with subordinate mates in a cohort (often war), who struggle fiercely through narrated adventures to a goal of sociopolitical value, one might begin questioning, given this description, how one wants *now* to think about the genre. There are also plausible extensions of that definition. Throwing oneself into or against fate in situations of extremis—social aftermaths of anticolonial struggles, or an existential confrontation with chance, for instance, are epic when described this way; the term might then encompass poems by Brathwaite or Mallarmé. Still, to say "epic" now is to have passed through dazzling centuries of social and literary changes filtering and mediating access to any Homer/Virgil (etc.) amalgam with high-born hero and his sociopolitical challenges. Particularly when very long poems are concerned, evoking some exemplary genre or a *single* genre identification is a stance filled with critical troubles. We are so far from tribal or ancient "epic"-ness that the word—while certainly not empty—must be seen in its range of contemporary poetic uses.

Further, a long-poem praxis implies ongoing writing with both social-evocative and aesthetic meanings. Such a practice has many genres in it—possibly as many as one can identify—and then more. Most traditional long poems, even if they have been accorded one genre name, like quest or epic, also have traces of multiple genres in them. A reading strategy alert to these multiplicities and allusions in a longish poem will analyze the functions of narrative polyphony. This situation Hejinian presents in *A Border Comedy* (2001), for she evokes an endless supply of literary categories and tropes and then deploys quirky illustrations that amiably demolish them. She makes clear that we need "An aporia / Which will allow us to go beyond the limits of any one viewpoint / And remain there."[2]

Because of their length and their being written (often) across many years, and more importantly, because of their inclusive ethos, very long poems do tend to have a superabundance of genres. The combination of many genres seems to be characteristic of a long poem, necessitating reader mobility in observations of shifts and combinations of genre, and the ensuing interpretations of a work that roams among genres. Because one purpose of such poems is convincing the reader (against all logic) that "everything" is present, a multiplication of genres will support this illusion.

Hence, modern long poems are often polygeneric. Smaro Kamboureli (for Canadian long poems) and Lynn Keller (for contemporary long poems by US women) have also spoken of the twentieth-century long poem in general as a "multi-coded," flexible and ambitious pooling of many genres.[3] As I will discuss, the polygeneric is also a literary signal of the mode "total artwork."

Anne Day Dewey's condensed survey sees "The Modern American Long Poem" as "intensely dynamic," itself a "genre in crisis and transformation," having at least two genre options: epic and lyric extensions into largeness. Among the epic actions are "a poet-prophet's search through history for mythic forms to revive culture," and lyric actions of presenting a culturally unifying image like the Bridge.[4] She shows, in fact, that few of the distinctive modern and contemporary long poems can be described with "lyric" and "epic" as the *only* genre evocations, and the essay soon becomes a descriptive summary of poetic and critical difficulties in pinning down the modern American long poem. One can only agree.

Indeed, to use the term "epic" at all in discussions of the modern long poem, we also must note that people sometimes shift its meaning midstream in any discussion, just as occurs with the terms "lyric" and "poem." Once the historical basis for the "primary epic" in internecine fighting, real and monster-laden adventures, and their griot-collected narratives is moot, once the "secondary"/tertiary epics of careful imitations or satiric wit are achieved, long poems as quaternary epic-items take an investigative turn. Because they are generic summae, "encyclopedias" of everything the poet considers important, the term "epic" is only partial or honorific. If epic were once foundational as a term and seemed to bring in its wake certain expectations (hero, action, community or tribal affirmations, historical range, geographic intensity, noble exchanges between real and mythological figures), it could no longer innocently be thought to. Now "epic" can also mean large in scope, epic in the ways that poets conceptualized their ambitions, and is even a synonym for a social urgency to investigate epic/large problems—long-poem authors taking on the task of socio-aesthetic critique.

So "epic" may designate a poem with certain traits or markers or simply get used as an enhancing synonym for long and ambitious—or cosmic. This interplay of the two terms—the noun "epic," a culturally vital genre with accumulated literary-historical prestige, along with the adjective "epic" (large, gigantic, big in every dimension, and thereby major)—doubles the impact of that term, so that length itself and the cultural (learned) assumptions about certain important topics combine to impress the reader with claims of major status because of major scope. This gratifying slide may allow for interesting definitional ambiguities and may also be what authors want from the term, connecting their work to the past.

If "epic" means depicting struggles with forces both human and divine/malignant toward social restabilization (not necessarily rectification), whose tasks are adventures and battles (with multiple forces) to win glory, and possibly to reestablish a household-city (*oikos*), start or save a political entity, or show the horrors of war, then only by analogy can modern long poems be thought of as epics. The reading strategy upholding that epic rubric will demand many analogies, many allegories of resemblance: battle equals struggle including research in a library; hero equals central figures of whatever social origin. Such a reading strategy might neglect to see traces of other genres (like romance, quest, lists, account books), other poetic modes (documentary, collage).

However, in loosened definitions, there are works whose epic aura depends on specific episodes as cues inside very long poems, episodes characteristic of the epic, but possibly not insisting on that overarching genre term or narrative arc. Epic as cultural fact, presence, backboard often appears in these long poems only as these notable allusions. These allusions might be such plot points as *katabasis*, or a visit to the underworld; *nekuia*, asking the advice of the dead; *nostos*, long-deferred homecoming, after quests, tests, temptations; *Bildung*, or political-spiritual education producing positive growth, and testing a person in youth or maturity: all are familiar to us. Perhaps the experimental-tending long poems of our era smash "the" epic into intermittent narrative and allusive shards as a social critique precisely of the totalizing ethos of the concept "epic"—substituting partial, metaphoric gestures to epic.

These allusions, not necessarily linked to plot or sequence but free-floating, establish epic genre as a zone, not a narrative arc. As examples: A. R. Ammons's *Tape for the Turn of the Year* evokes "sing, muse," makes an early allusion to Odysseus, and asks exactly how "classical" he can claim to be "without a plan"; answer—classical enough to make this allusion.[5] Bernadette Mayer knowingly begins *Midwinter Day* with "stately," the first word of *Ulysses* by James Joyce, consummate modern user of Homer, and she narrates the action of getting through the day without collapsing, a witty epic of motherhood as a writer with toddlers. Or is this "mock epic" and bathos because the quotidian and motherhood are definitionally nonheroic? There also might be non-epic works that knowingly or by default represent some terms on which epic is based. Oppen's "Of Being Numerous" contains the following elements: two wars—World War II and the Vietnam War; a cohort of men, and the sense of separation between these cofighters and the self; painful political judgments about the nation and war's horrors; a *nostos* of sorts with family figures and nation.

Since it appears in narrative allusions only, one might argue that epic, far from being a central genre, is only residual in these poems, not dominant.[6] In the polyphony of the long poem, certainly some mixture of epic-quest or quest-epic appears to be what many of the modern and contemporary long poems provide. Epic adventures that involve wandering, challenges, losses and anxious suspense prior to the telos or conclusion of the plot get posed in the related genre of quest or investigative exploration. However, these modern, odd quests do not necessarily have a clearly defined goal, a fixed goal (the end might change or be reset), an ennobling (rather than ironized) goal, or even any finishable goal at all.

Another significant shift in some of the "epics" of today occurs in the subjectivities—a fusion between a griot, the teller (or author voice), and the hero. In most ideal-type epic narratives, the writer frames the hero and "narrates" him.[7] Making the teller of the modern "epic" be an investigator on the battle-site of archives, rather than a tribal fighter or tempted strategist, contributes to the meaningful (if slightly paranoid) research energy of some modern scholarly-investigative "epics." Not war but documentation becomes the crucial fight in Olson, Pound, Waldman, even Williams and Brathwaite. The hero-writer struggles to bring certain information back in circulation via the poem to rectify or inspire culture.

A final introductory observation: the epic has cultural and historical aura. Hence an author may, over a long-poem career, both resist and embrace that term. As an example, Nathaniel Mackey has made an endless quest to hear and claim the growth into social justice and spiritual knowledge for his group protagonists in a book that explicitly denies "epic" coherence. The failure, despite fundamental needs, of the quest for racial justice involves setback after setback in the allegorical narrative, while the successes of aesthetic and erotic elements and of questing itself are affirmative. In *Splay Anthem*, Mackey makes a declaration overtly: "It wasn't / an epic we were in." He later elaborates with a comment on epic as socially remembered heroism; while those on another side of history may have evinced heroism, it is "heroic / waste," not highlighted in the hegemonic genre called "epic," even if their acts were both singable and "memorable."[8] Epic, in this view, demands the depiction of social power in a consolidating hero (or perhaps group hero). When there is little or no power, it is not an epic you are in. And if there is no achieved *nostos* in equitable justice, then "not yet" becomes the deferred ending—except for acts of love and art.

Yet, given the plausible mutability of long-poem decisions, in an interview in 2014 with Joseph Donahue, Mackey acknowledges that his poem has come "closer to epic in that sense [its narratives], because it does bring with it elements of story, story and narrative, as the old epics typically did—tell a story—although I never set out to be an epic poet or to be called a writer of epic."[9]

The position I will take here—accounting for the above observations—is that writers use the idea of any specific genre, or the idea of genres, not only as a rich accumulation of narrative conventions, but as a space to think through and a tool to think with, in order to create an apt writing. A modern long poem creates structures of transit among several genres; it tends toward the considerably mobile and metamorphic.[10] To say "I am writing an epic" is to declare you will interpret epic as a tactic of cultural intervention. What each author here does with epic involves social and aesthetic choices about epic (both in general and in quite specific ways). What critics often do is bring that work into conformity with useful definitions of that genre, confirming how each poem exemplifies a generalizing definition. I don't try to do that, as too-respectful attitudes to fixed genre definitions do not help read long poems now.[11] Hence, I enjoy (perversely?) "Save some room / for my epic"—Robert Creeley's tiny poetic mot (given that companions like Olson and Duncan wrote long, long poems, but he didn't).[12] Creeley makes this fond, comic turn into an ineffable wryness about "epic," as a claim of major poetry.

DERRIDA ON GENRE

If ever there were a single named genre for any work, that law of genre has been thrown over—as is true of any genre, according to the seriocomic "law" enunciated in Jacques Derrida's essay "The Law of Genre" (1979/1980; revised 1986). Derrida: "I submit for your consideration the following hypothesis: a text would not belong to any genre. Every text participates in one or several genres, there is no genreless text, there is always a genre and genres, yet such participation never amounts to belonging."[13] It appears that, far from singleness, mobile slides among ascriptions, intertextualities, and interpenetrations among genres are fundamental to literary acts and activities. Derrida's observation is quite idiomatic for the modern long poem.

If genre plethora is the only "law" of genre, then in any long poem a number, even a great number, of genres may be engaged. Then it is a matter of noticing what is on hand, what are authorial priorities, and analyzing impacts, not situating any given poem in one genre spot and holding it there for ease of critical handling. Hence there could be as many generic traces in a long poem as there are genres one might name. For a while, thinking about these issues, I was engaged in fanciful (charming to me) naming: "odic logbooks of continuance";[14] "mythical/musical works"; "grafted or distributed narrative"; "long poem as poetic essay or conceptual text," this last being what Stéphane Mallarmé (in *Divagations*) called the *poème critique*, a tempting mix of poetry and theory. This intricate specificity of naming finally became disqualifying—genre overkill. Further, the nonstop question of category—*should this poem go here or there?*—became tedious. Or comic. Hejinian's *A Border Comedy*, taken as a work of poetics, seems to have been designed to illustrate the comic potential (folly) of trying to place anything, particularly a plethora of potential narratives, into any single genre category. Though epic and quest appear together in many long poems, and seem now to be one amalgamated genre, even here too firm a genre identification could blur or filter out other genre allusions and traces that readers absorb in any reading experience and that contribute to a work's suggestiveness. Thus, talking about exact genres and even designating centers of genre-gravity are only useful literary fictions, pedagogic rubrics. My chapter titles are pragmatic comparativist fictions.

The issues are simpler than this, sort of: to appreciate the polygeneric. Mackey's endless quest still incorporates song, lyric, dialogues, quasi-narratives, essays, or allegorical fables. Waldman's endless epic displays and names a genre plethora (investigatory documentary-odic polemic is just one cluster). The titled cantos of *Drafts* allude to many poetic genres, traditional (epistle, eclogue, *haibun*, dialogue of Self and Soul) and particular (lexicon, interrogation, puppet opera, wall newspaper) in a quirky-serious plethora. Silliman's endless accounting (textual lists) often evoke different genres in any given series of sentences, generating intense local swerves.

The crucial issues involve understanding large categories (such as my chapters naming genre) as mechanisms for articulating and arranging cultural problems. Further, the reading strategy of emphasizing the polygeneric while using three capacious genre "categories" must account for the desire of some writers to *themselves* name a genre for their long poems so their work will be received under this rubric. Should we want to discount their choices? What if authors want the evocation of epic? Then what?

Pound can illustrate, years into *The Cantos*, with his scrap of syllogism "an epic is a poem including history" and the rest of the syllogism implied: *I have included historical snippets and documentary sources in my long poem; hence it is an epic.*[15] It seems perfectly reasonable to foresee a spectrum of genre situations to discuss for any long poem, including splits between poet and critic. A critic might resist a single genre attribution in the functioning of the poem (my tendency) yet accede to what poets declare they want by *their* naming a genre. *Their* choosing to evoke epic as an elective affinity and a genre claim must inflect my analyses. (Should critics override poets?) We need to show what is being thought about via an "epic" designation. Specifically, when any writer says "epic"—what is at stake?

CONSTELLATIONS OF AUTHORIAL CHOICES: THE CONTEMPORARY EPIC

Beam me up, Olson.
Ron Silliman, *Tjanting*

In Pound and Olson, their epics and the society and actions depicted did not include many female figures.[16] Yet that choice and the outcomes occur in striking contrast to their shorter poems. Both Pound and Olson have written provocatively, richly, and subtly in their shorter poetic oeuvre about women and men as complexly gendered figures, and both presented varieties of gender debates seriously and overtly.

There are Pound's "Hugh Selwyn Mauberley" and his contemporaneous poems about sexual *moeurs*; there are Olson's mythic lyrics, the intense poems inspired by his intellectual and sexual connection with Frances Boldereff, as well as "The Lordly and Isolate Satyrs" in which modes of maleness are central.[17] Whatever critical, analytic remarks one might develop in a close-up, granular study of any of these works, there is no doubt that both poets have depicted female figures of great variety, with admiration, annoyance, empathy, idealizing, satire, reverence, off-handedness, bitterness, jealousy, eroticism, appropriative desires (and so forth)—a panoply of purposes and emotions.[18] However, in largest measure, these kinds of depictions of historical and imagined women or debates about their cultural status do not appear at all in *The Maximus Poems*, hardly at all in *The Cantos*. Questions about men, women, and gender are included all the time in their shorter and mid-length works—but very sparsely in their epics. Casual mentions of historical women in Gloucester, a handful of mythic projections and tall tales in Olson are the total; in Pound, certain beset female figures were depicted particularly at the beginning of *The Cantos* when their love, beauty, loyalty, erotic yearning, and willfulness were topics. Yet for both, the epic has been a "manly" genre in twentieth-century writing. These writers construct specific episodes and comparisons of male choices in politics and society, seeing these as essential to epic.

Their choice of stance not only differs strikingly from their own shorter poems but also contrasts with any account of ancient and medieval plots of epic, in which, aside from goddesses, notable females appear: Penelope, Nausicaa,

Odysseus's nurse Eurycleia, his dead mother in underworld *katabasis*, prisoners of war, queens on the losing side of war, Dido, the mother of Sundiata, Grendel's mother—of course, mainly noble or courtly women, socially powerful only within evident norms, manifest in intricate narrative support roles or as singular figures—but all with palpable, if particular agency.[19] Why, then, do modern epics by these two male contemporaries depict such a limited gender zone?[20]

In *Paterson*, Williams emphatically did not exclude female figures; he also did not call his poem an "epic" (though it is a longish poem). In 1951, talking about his ending with Book IV, he names the male figure "Odysseus," who "swims in as man must always do." This allusion to one epic episode evokes but does not necessarily name the poem's genre.[21] He calls it "a long poem" in 1946; "the second of four books on a single theme" in 1948, and he does not vary from this descriptor. We generally call *Paterson* a quest, perhaps quest-assemblage. Apparently, this was Williams's opinion as well: the poem is "the search of the poet for his language."[22]

This does not mean that *Paterson* was not justified in sex-gender terms by Williams, only that he did depict many women within his poem. The very image on which all of *Paterson* rests is traditional complementarity—the man is the city drawing on "that supplying female," the ground sustaining the wandering male figure.[23] And the satiric, tragic dancing male figure of the end (a renewed extension of the poem "Danse Russe") is the leaping phallic figure of closure. At least, one might say, female figures and women exist in the poem and are crucial to Dr. Paterson's *quest*, from "Beautiful Thing" to "Cress."

These examples show, in a stagy fashion, how modern *epics* by male authors seem written within gendered genre boundaries, focusing mainly on one gender only. To understand motives for some of the other twentieth-century works of epic writing, we need to keep this pattern in mind.

In *The Tale of the Tribe* (on Pound, Williams, Olson), M. A. Bernstein offers a well-articulated definition of the core epic task. "The epic presents a narrative of its audience's own cultural, historical, or mythic heritage, providing models of exemplary conduct (both good and bad)."[24] The voice of the poet will not be an individual but a community spokesperson, and the listener is cast as a citizen receiving these "lessons" as part of general education. This didactic "tale of the tribe" (Pound citing Kipling) functions particularly if one accepts the words "the" and "tribe" graciously. Each of those words now seems narrow, with "tribe" being playfully insensitive to changes from tribal society to modernity, to the enriching findings of ethnography, and too hearty about the "tribal" metaphor for nationalist modernity, given some settler land-grabs and imperialist designs on other societies. "Epic" is given a definition of ideologically managed heritage, not built for much dissent. Given this, it seems as if a simpler definition might be less freighted than this stolid agreement about heritage and who defends and defines it.

To say an "epic" has to have metaphoric battles, voyaging, a trip to the underworld; a hero (generally male), and various adventures brings up to scrutiny the cultural assumptions about hierarchy and gender on which epic was, for Pound and Olson, almost invisibly based. Making explicit his gendering of the epic genre was not of concern to Olson (in the war of work and economic and national development done by men) or to Pound in his scatter-shot but intense discussions of male political, artistic, and economic leadership (and other males' obedience) necessary for social order. Both poets apparently assumed the male interests of the genre with no desire to make this assumption overt or visible, yet maleness and the events men generate and suffer *as men* are crucial to their poems. For instance, these wars (real and symbolic) are fought by male figures (inside the representation), and "won" by adherence of men to male leadership and to basic principles. Olson and Pound created these struggles in ways that often side-stepped asking too much about female characters and their social wounds, and whether their values were the same or different from values that motivated male characters.[25] Of course, one might say, *That's just part of their use of the genre. So what?* That's what I am saying—without the "so what." One might instead say, *Now what?*

Olson's epic tracks historical men, often "Seafaring Men" almost so intimately as step by step through Gloucester, mapping them and their doings in this landscape, as if taking a historical census, farm by farm, voyage by voyage, cataloging work challenges, losses, and gains. These historical, documented male figures will lead Olson to, or confirm him in, a poetics and a political vision. They are the makers, and in this telling, Olson is the man who names their primary importance, by "putting things together / which had not previously / fit."[26]

But women, particularly historical ones in this poem, are part of the background, not part of the epic of work, or the epic claim that Gloucester is somehow Phoenician in spirit, or his epic attempt at encompassing all of that history, geography, myth, and local color/folklore to arc between the origin of the United States and the myths of the Mediterranean and Norse worlds.[27] The protest against pejorocracy with "thugs" and "hypocrites" and "nascent capitalism" is carried on by men—and Olson wants to motivate them to pursue this necessary protest by inspiring them now to reclaim their origins in the work relations of Gloucester, and in the animating spirit of autonomy and rebellion, like Toussaint L'Ouverture. Olson is the angel of male annunciation—the power of men to generate more men, announced to men. His poetics is also a wager on inspiring social change. The poetics, as Olson announces in "Letter 9"—"It's the condition in men" acting in tune with nature itself by which the poet defines the ultimate measure of his "song," its "sources," himself, and "my forces," where his exposed rhyme of "sources" and "forces" creates a solid cementing for the strongly affirmed manhood of this poetry.[28] The rectitude of connecting his social urgencies with male natural/mythic forces continues in the lyric notational *The Maximus Poems: Volume Three.*

In Pound's work, aside from early-canto depictions of female figures who have had male lovers (troubadours) so compelling that they die for them (sacrificing all for beauty and love) and the elegiac vision of the disembodied "eyes in the tent" passage in *The Pisan Cantos* memorializing some women whom Pound had loved, the gendered dynamic in Pound's social vision includes a few angry, mocking glimpses of soft, feminized (male) Jews throughout. Jews in general are also associated with swamps, excrement, and economic disaster—truly blocking figures. One can think of Pound's depiction of Semiticized femaleness in men inhibiting progress as part of his work's "feminized" zones, or one can focus only on mentions of his idealized women as inspiring memories.[29] The parallel fighting manhoods of Pound and Mussolini (in the cultural and political realms) are a high point of Pound's affirmation before this winning plot proves elusive to any triumph in real-world history.

Given that these poets have shown women and gender issues (including men and masculinity) in other of their poems with striking success, what has inhibited Olson and Pound from many (if any) depictions beyond passing mentions of women/female figures in their modern epics, poems that claim the goal of bettering society? Let us postulate, however odd this idea, that the force of buried assumptions of genre (as accumulated through cultural history) inhibits them—epic aura is masculine, its tasks are depicting maleness, powerful and subordinate men hierarchically bonded are central to the social world of the epic, and the epic genre is made of topics and plots concerning maleness: war, strategizing to maximize benefits in any situation, certain crucial moments of obedience, growing into manhood, and interior discipline.[30] Epic appears tautologically male. Their genre choice makes aversive any detailed depictions of female figures with historical agency. In this, Pound and Olson are simply uncritically obeying the unspoken and internalized conventions (laws?) of this genre, despite their otherwise high level of verbal and rhetorical experiment. It is just the reigning ideology of the genre to which they conform; they have no reason—or motivation—to question generally traditional gender depictions in their epics.

Observe also that in most epics there is either a literal war; a warlike struggle; a backdrop of war; a displaced war; a postwar aftermath; direct depiction of war in battles, killing, and ferocities of all sorts, as if war were a machine one cannot stop; a warlike contest with nature (sometimes as a monster); strategies about a social war. Epic genre claims and the depiction of war go together. Women are generally not literal armed warriors, so the syllogism's third term (therefore, women are not depicted) supports their epics—if a home front is excluded. There are territorial conquests celebrated, various wars for the soul of a nation; war against invasion; a war against sullying and despoiling forces in society; an economic war against the blockers of social progress (as defined by the poet)—all these epic plot materials reckon with war.

If all this is so, then the question "Can women write an epic?" might not be answered easily.[31] It might best be answered: yes, of course, but those who try might have to construct the "epic" genre as a diagnostic autopsy of war, leadership, and social priorities and to reconfigure the mainly masculine assumptions on which the epic has long rested. Women writers of epic could "celebrate great deeds" (perhaps changing what a *deed* is), and what a *battle* or a *voyage* might mean and how that could be conducted with a female hero or a male hero not absorbed in the ideologies of maleness that (nonetheless) saturate the genre. Such women writers will attend to the home front as well—as Alice Notley clarifies. Women writers could certainly act as griots telling an epic; they could also be the heroes of such an epic. But this would probably necessitate authorial self-consciousness about the epic gesture/genre and its primary gender assumptions concerning manhood, kinds of masculinity, and male tasks, particularly war. This precise cluster of concerns does become fundamental to Brooks's analysis of gender and war in *Annie Allen*, to H.D.'s use in *Helen in Egypt* of familiar Trojan War figures, to Notley's epic materials that culminate in *Descent of Alette*, and to Anne Waldman's *Iovis*.

EPIC AS SOCIAL COMMENT: BROOKS AND OLSON

Gwendolyn Brooks's *Annie Allen*, a mid-length poem from 1949, has an explicit, allusive reference to epic with the section "The Anniad." Charles Olson's *The Maximus Poems* (1950–69) engorges and transcends epic with cosmologies, documents, and social histories, heightened and mythologized. While both began as postwar works, the contrast could not be more dramatic: a white male author maximizing epic beyond itself, a Black female author miniaturizing epic implosively. Both poems highlight ambivalent relationships to the epic. Both poems concern major social clashes in the manner of Olson's remark: "I mean, discords. The discordant. The want of agreement. The want of concord or harmony. Variance, dissension, contention, dissonance. Contest. The *agon* as well as the *pathos* and the *epiphany*."[32]

This discordant social and textual poetics animates each of these poets. Olson made an investigative and meditative poem including/citing documents, where one early settlement of Massachusetts (the fishing port, Gloucester) summarizes the promises and failures of the United States as a settler society. Olson proposes that a great experiment in pragmatism and community work was made in Gloucester but fell under siege by theocratic and neo-aristocratic forces of Puritanism, by developing capitalist economies and now neoliberalism, and by the failure of the men themselves to grasp their existential newness. War is not only conquest or battle: it can involve a social and mythic *agon*. That explains his urgent hortatory tone. This utopian moment of a covenant with "American space" was thus compromised, but such thinking passes into the utopian power of the speaking subject—Olson and this poem—as avatar of polis, inspiring authentic community as struggled for in the poem.[33]

Asking whether Olson's *Maximus Poems* can be read as a "modern verse epic," M. A. Bernstein responds with a remarkable analysis of the first book of *Maximus* only, holding that only there does Olson fulfill the promise of taking real history as the topic of a public work exemplifying socioeconomic values. Bernstein construes "epic discourse" as linking themes of "history and community," "the individual and the polis" by means of exemplary figures and exemplary crises of the community. The figures manifested craft, and abilities to "cooperate with nature" in the deploying of appropriate skills in economic activity to build and enhance community cooperation and existence. This is an epic vision of an interplay between individual men and the new society emerging from their confrontation with a new land and ecology. Bernstein sees a "double plot, an impersonal 'outer epic' which tells the fate of the Dorchester Company's venture, and an inner, subjective quest which unfolds the poet's growing knowledge about his setting and heritage."[34] The outer struggle occurs unevenly between two economic models (the Puritans and the Dorchester Company), between outside ownership and local autonomy, even though an undepicted local/global Atlantic economic interplay was evident even in that early moment of US history. Bernstein argues startlingly that the second and third books of *The Maximus Poems* are not part of Olson's epic.

This critical containment of Olson's poem is a rare—and fascinating—finding. It might be simply that the two definitions of epic collided—epic as a specific genre, what Bernstein allows, and epic as a long poem of extent, scope, ambition, not conforming to any one genre but rather evoking multiple genres—*Maximus* as big, long, and polygeneric. This multiplicity is so challenging to his narrow definition of epic that for Bernstein "the final words of the epic" occur in "April Today Main Street," 470 pages before the actual end of *The Maximus Poems: Volume Three*.[35] This brave cul-de-sac interpretation shows the power of definitional assumptions—must the poem conform to the epic ideal? Or can one investigate alternative practices—epic as part of a polygeneric zone—to encompass the whole poem Olson wrote?

In *Maximus Poems,* Charles Olson visualized what he was doing to expand the epic genre by involving multiple male actor-heroes. "Field"—Charles Olson's notable word for a mix of scale and pulsing on-the-page combinations of analyses, events, and meditations—suggests that the epic poem is centered not by nation only but by action, not just a winning-tribe-and-its-stories but a group of men working individually with a collective ideology (foregrounded by this poem) to achieve an idea of apt economy and civic coherence. His "field of action" (including mythical eros and ancient mythography) will achieve "polis / is this."[36] Thus, *Maximus* becomes the presentation of a social-historical panorama reaching back to the ancient world and its heroisms to prove a political ethos based on the noble (sometimes myth-infused) choices of diverse men. Resolutely social, loosely "mythic," often simply epic only in scale ("large"), but also alluding to epic metaphors or materials (a sense of battles or struggles), highly accumulative, explicitly documentary and epistolary, but filled with loose ends, the epic Olson created was alternately a personal scrapbook and an ambitious patriarchal archive of social instances of care and struggle: "a precis / of land I am shod in, / my father's shoes."[37]

The Maximus Poems: Volume Three is elegiac, notational, lyrical, and ruminative; its genres include epistle, field notes, psycho-geographical diagrams and startling visual texts, archival records, logbooks, conversation poems, and diary—including dates, notebook jottings, expansion of the limits and tones of the "poetic" in every direction. By the end of Book Three, Olson's whole epic is not solely a question of socioeconomic leadership, agency, and male will; it includes metamorphic powers of nature and even death over the speaker. The heroism becomes understanding one's own disappearance into a place as a contribution to one of its epic layers—a lyric elegy and chthonic drama.

The narrating-hero inside the poem (Maximus) is in large measure a conscious projection of the writer outside the poem. He is an epistolary, polemical, prophetic, and exhortatory figure, an omnivorous and emotionally engaging figure whose power depends on the osmotic porousness between writer as griot-hero and presentations of historical figures as quasi-heroes. Olson wants to see epic as jagged anecdotes of local history in collage "as a way around the lyric impasse," this being his own influential critique of the smaller (or too formalist, monofocal) poetry of his time as inadequate *to* that time.[38] This position involved the higher stakes of losing the "lyrical interference of the individual as ego."[39] By this notable phrase, Olson seems to mean the inability of the lyric to exit from a focus on only one particular self as lens, without caring to depict general forces—including myth, history, politics, economics—that, when included, enlarge and more fully explain that self, motivating the urgency of large-scale *poesis*.

Is there an "epic ego" for Olson? I am aware of the traditional gender division of lyric as "feminine" and epic as "masculine"; however, Olson's critique of lyric seems to exceed that point and concern the "interference" of "lyrical" cultural limits and lacks of mythic/archaic range. Given his poetics of projective reach, the "lyrical" lacks any totalizing urgency or gender overrides, not allowing the poet fully to express "the man or woman he is" (an interesting polemical assertion) or to explore that "sister-brother"/ear/mind of the "incest of verse"—all suggestive but not fully worked-out sex-gender radical proposals rarely instantiated by Olson in real life. The poetic act—or the epic ego—is figured as an exciting, taboo androgyny where typically women are absorbed into male voice and do not appear as agents. "Lyrical interference" (of "ego," "individual," or "soul") is not equated with the "feminine," even if such a position would be consistent with his lack of depicted women in *Maximus* and with his general pronoun "he" for poets.[40] It might be wiser to postulate that his epic is an interplay between various versions of the archaic, of male struggle, with many discourses (cited or invented), and the quite undertheorized male/female voice of his *poesis*. It may also be that the final *Maximus* poems enter the chthonic zone of the "lyric-epic"—as, for instance, H.D. did in *Helen in Egypt*.

The grandeur of his unsystematic or intuitive archive-writing makes one discovery lead to another on a world scale and sustains an ego-enlarging correlation of history with myth, particularly for male figures. Olson's polygeneric epic operates like a synoptic proto-history book, an uplifting sweep of time but with the historical still in process, contingent, set down in the hope of inspiring an effective "polis" in future history. The work is a didactic, engaging critical manifesto *in motion* (the anecdotal segmentivity and fragmentation contribute to the verve of constant process), shown in the energy of many shifts of topic and tone and in the riding of the various moments on the page with a fearless/reckless visual-rhetorical sweep. Page-space openness also generally signals scope, reach, multiplicities in continuous transit.[41] This is the way Olson figures the epic "agon" on the page in large contrasting patches of material—the "epic ego" in these poems occurs in the unleashed energies of the multidiscursive page.

Maximus, itself a postwar poem, proposes the war of *work*, workplace struggles, male agency, battles with the elements, and the struggle for the economic and political soul of America from its apparently rebellious beginnings to its callow, reductive compromises in the contemporary period. Olson does not depict war in the sense of battle—but rather work as a social struggle, as well as an economic one with the forces of nature and society, a struggle by male figures to maintain both community and individual action. The poem celebrates the common-people entrepreneurs and workers, their male bonding and loyalty with the virtues of competency and will, the men with *techne*, and those who disappear into near-anonymity and sometimes into the sea.[42] This is a "common man" torque of epic motifs, articulating the popular front ethos that Olson overtly disavowed. In its pictorial variety, showing each male worker and struggler, *The Maximus Poems* loosely resembles the postrevolutionary Mexican murals (as of Diego Rivera) that teem with a panoply of multigendered, multiraced figures celebrating their power to build a new society from historical and mythic materials.

If one redefines epic in the ways that Olson demands—a poem of world-historical mythic-absorptive scale—then emphatically *The Maximus Poems* is epic, but not *an* epic, as he declares this genre category useless. "Words like epic and heroic: typology. Tells nothing" is his terse but clear comment—any summarizing rubrics are useless, categories are useless. For Olson, "any static-ing, any setting up of a pattern except in the instant of the declaration of it" is poetically and intellectually problematic, even craven.[43] If any genre designation is too limited, too literary a framework, what he wants from this poem is a particular attitude toward content, a size, "a dimension," such as Melville and Homer offer, a world scale for writing and its meaning.[44] Olson wants the static noun "epic" to become the descriptive adjective "epic," summarizing a drive in *poesis*.

The act of writing, *poesis*, is the only force behind creation. The only genre is making. Olson demands an epic praxis from himself as the author, not necessarily in epic acts by the quasi-historical characters. The author enters text by making, an action or activity toward any "text" as a demand for "dimensions and dynamics."[45] Praxis in transit is posited as the only way to write (there is therefore no fixed genre "epic," just epic authorial acts). "Making" means, among other things, ongoing projective processes toward an incomplete product. In this sense, as a vatic claim sweeping away mere literature, not to speak of excoriating the pettiness of the literary with its desiccated categories and patterns, and their limited defenders (literary critics), Olson's work in poetry exemplifies a poetics of boundlessness. This "projective" ethos certainly dismisses the normalizing work of "genre." He wants to get somehow under, above, or beyond genre to a primary motive for his synthesizing praxis.

The poet is a griot—he is gathering these stories, these observations, the notations in part because of his griot-heroism: work with exhortatory rhetorics and electrifying research. He cannot act as a physical laborer so much as celebrate those who did act—fishermen whose heritage is powerful and whose struggles must be acknowledged. As a griot, he is evaluating constantly, speaking against the normative culture of the 1950s and early 1960s, and rejecting the complacent leadership earlier in American history, "an example of how wrong you can be and still / run this country."[46]

He enacts the mytho-historical spirit by making a Herodotean collection of folkloric and quasi-historical sources from which the epic itself emerged or whose topics it rearranged. Hence, *The Maximus Poems* might be considered a pre-epic, amassing the materials from which an emergent culture will make another epic thrust/process with a hero in a new historical dispensation (one that Olson also named, as the "postmodern").

For Olson, Homer is vital to the world of the ancient epic, but his hero "Ulysses" projects forward into future history and its archetypal drive farther and farther west, "the central quality of the men to come: search, *the individual responsible to himself*." The characters demanded by Olson have agency beyond the exigencies and limits of history. It is as if Odysseus leaps out of his time into ours—an idealist, transhistorical claim about the exploration archetype for a literary character. In *Call Me Ishmael*, Odysseus predicts the American drive to the Pacific.[47] The essential maleness of agency and will transcend social strictures, limits—or analytic typologies (except archetypes). Such a vision of epic agency contributes to the intense tone of Olson's work, its conviction, its mythologized historicism, and its monogendered array—with the claim of a visionary brother-sister "incest" at the root. The paradox of defining subjectivity in Olson is patent; it seems to be dispersed among the characters but also collected in the writer-griot as an encompassing, heroic Magnus Pater.

Although he wants what I've dubbed an epic ego, the general understanding of "lyrical interference" as translated to "lyric ego" makes this point about "ego" and lyric tricky for Olson readers. As Alice Notley noted with droll understatement, "a male definition of ego/egolessness tends to be a little special."[48] Here one sees Maximus encompassing, as if physically and psychically at once, the whole world to which he has assigned himself—he has "become" all the male characters, identifying with their prowess and dilemmas, taking sublime economic and existential risks for independence from a state or a dominating economic system. Olson tended to interpret the forming nation as having a tabula rasa economic system, although in the historical real, Gloucester's fishing industry was interdependent with an already-established world market. The "world" part in all Olson's *Maximus* work is generally "world myth"; lived historical trends and economics are gestured at somewhat vaguely.

In this polygeneric epic, many searching, pulsing male agents act at various historical times, revealing not just one hero but a plurality of heroic figures. However, there is only one central epitome of male agency: Olson as griot/hero of these synoptic findings. Olson in *The Maximus Poems* engorges the epic itself, by making something larger and less traditional than even that genre attribution but ending firmly in the realm of the adjective "epic."

Gwendolyn Brooks, in her turn, has miniaturized "epic" in the choice of writing an epic of a Black girl-and-woman in a serial poem using very cunning fixed forms and elegant rhyme, and thus raising to poetic nobility an ordinary life in its complex but often overlooked struggles. Her genre allusion to epic occurs as a contained section (eleven pages), a sixth of the whole *Annie Allen* (sixty-two pages). This section's terse, tight verse sets it apart from other modes used by Brooks in this work—ballad, sonnet, and rhymed free verse. "The Anniad," in (generally) royal rhyme, includes a three-page coda ("Appendix to The Anniad") in a modern meditative voice about Annie Allen's life to date.[49] Brooks's one-section use of epic for her characters, within a fine-grained, brilliantly versified sociopoetic study of race-in-America, tracks resigned characters given few consolations by the epic genre or by any other genres and poetic forms in the other sections. There are a number of tonal and perspectival shifts in the work, as both a masked autobiography and the biography of a community. Both attitude and verse forms move from highly constructed distancing to realist and psychological observations about race, gender, and class. The characters Brooks depicts are accorded many subtle recognitions but have little agency even in their historical moment—immediately post–World War II, when, as after World War I, Blacks who fought racist fascism abroad returned to confront deeply rooted racist apartheid at home.

Brooks's "Anniad" hero could not be less maximal—female, African American, working-class, a compromised figure, beginning as a Black girl besotted with the romance plot (another genre zone) and her princess-specialness. She therefore suffers poignant, predictable consequences as she grows up in(to) reality and learns that even this plot (much less any "epic") is not hers to claim by her individual will or agency. The various spaces of closeness and distance between Brooks and the different ages of girl and woman she depicts are destabilizing in their variety—empathy, wariness, judgment, poetic intensities, social ironies, and synoptic summary all are evoked. By the end of the poem, the character is an adult negotiating civic personhood in the fraught world of America's hyper-raced society, with poverty, sexism, and their damages also made visible. Brooks depicts characters staying responsible (or not) under conditions of compromised political and economic agency. Unlike Olson's actors, characters here rarely possess depicted agency; to show this lack, their struggles are tamped into the tight frame of Brooks's language. The whole *Annie Allen* is a formal tour de force with a social analysis.

To propose this social limit in her poem's structure, the epic allusion is sandwiched between other sections, for an almost unreadable, multifaceted comment on Annie—or on epic but, as in Olson's *Maximus*, a deeply meant allusion. Brooks asks who can be considered a heroic protagonist, what is a heroic quest, and she confronts assumptions concerning poetic subjectivity, class, race, and gender to claim an "ordinary" African American's heroism in an extraordinary language. Brooks is explicit about the social limits experienced by all her Black characters—from the soft, compromising parents, to Annie with her hopes and sadness, to the "tan man" who displaces the strictures of race by acts of adultery, to the children raised earnestly but always doomed to have less and be less in a society based systematically on racial barriers.

In the "Appendix to Annie Allen," the effects of war on civilians, set out in "pages from a loose-leaf war diary," show the home front fed up and tired, in angry longing for the life they are missing, and finally in mourning for the men who went away and came back psychologically changed. Annie's husband is "untrue," because now as much enthralled to "Coquettish death" as to living life—but also because this work, as Hortense Spillers argued, concerns the interior color line in the Black community, positing darker women as less desirable, more readily rejected.[50] Particularly in the narration of the "Anniad," the delusions of the childhood Annie, the marriage that changes Annie and the nameless, lighter "tan man" reveal characters irrevocably altered by the war and by continuous experiences of Black and white racisms.

The poem is a system playing with epic nobility and with a wretched romance plot condensing conventional stories of urgent sexuality and male betrayal, intertwined with Brooks's summary of the male figure's point of view—in seduction, war, social impotence, illness. A female hero does not here create the conditions under which her life defines itself. A traditional male epic hero *attempts* with his agency in generally forward-pulsing action, often compromised (as in *The Odyssey*) but depicted in a narrative world arranged to generate the deferred hope of his eventual success. That encouraging narrative world cannot function for Brooks's Black male soldier. Brooks's epic allusions place him in a failed *Iliad* where war is not glory even for the putative "winner," and in a failed *Odyssey* of a blasted homecoming that he himself has ruined. But the female figure lives out her role in that *Anniad* only, a counter-epic, a mini-epic (two words that clash) of war and male power—on the homeland front, where everyone is singularly deprived and resigned, without triumph, but always struggling.

This struggling resignation builds to Brooks's particular nonclosural set of endings of the whole book in several acute poems, one about white characters slumming in an Italian restaurant, Benvenuti's (Italian for *welcome; come on in*), who hope to find Black diners conforming to a distorted vision of inferior, if entertaining, others. That poem is an analytic lyric along with another in which Black friends, driving through a white neighborhood, recognize how drastically they are cheated in every particular of civic life. The latter poems are among the most subtle and devastating in their social comment and their craft.

The final poem enunciates a social challenge to American racism, through and beyond the embedded critical epic. The whole of *Annie Allen* ends with a challenge to any white community for the recognition of Black equity and humanity coupled with the imperative for social recognition: "Admit me to our mutual estate."[51] After an uncaring "whisper" back from the intransigent, dismissive community of whites, this poem negotiates a final turn, calling out white "politeness" and general hypocrisy with an address to the Black community, rejecting, with a critique of one of the trace genres—all racial fairy tales. Without "magics or elves" or fairy "godmothers" to conjure the overthrow of racial prejudice, Blacks must "Wizard" their own "track" to do so. The shift from noun to verb in the use of "wizard" as verb underscores this active necessity.[52] Fairy-tale romances are useless personal—and social—delusions. "Wizard" has at its root the more useful concepts wise, skillful, clever.

Does Brooks similarly reject "epic" as delusion? What are the meanings of her epic allusions? Brooks is notably cagy about her choice. In an interview she says: "Well, the girl's name was Annie and it was my little pompous pleasure to raise her to a weight that she probably did not have. I thought of the Iliad and said, I'll call this 'The Anniad.'"[53] "Little pompous pleasure"? What in the world did Brooks mean with these doubly undercutting words?

Could "pompous," said in 1969 to a particular interviewer, be *The American Heritage Dictionary*'s "an exaggerated show of dignity or self-importance; pretentious"? "Bombastic or self-important in speech or manner"? Is Brooks really undercutting both her hero and her own poetic presentation in one sweeping gesture? What is her attitude to her unimportant main character (minor as girl and woman and "a minority," in that unlovely term)? And is the word "little" self-masking in the extreme? The question of whether Brooks was serious about "epic" and/or ironic remains discussable. She was certainly not naive—not about herself as a Black woman author or about her poignant topic of a *Bildung* for her character inside a powerfully raced system, where this term "epic" abruptly emerges. Nor is Brooks naive about what touching this work with an epic evocation might precipitate.

When the word "pompous" emerges, Brooks is fencing with a critic who responds awkwardly to her recent attention to militant thinking about Black poetry, and he quotes her earlier statement about craft, as if to draw her back twenty years to 1949–50: "The Negro poet's most urgent duty, at present is to polish his technique, his way of presenting his truths and his beauties, that these may be more insinuating and, therefore more overwhelming."[54] (She corrects to the words "Black poet" in her response to him).[55] Brooks, well aware that she is addressing a white male questioner, became a stealth critic, allowing the self-irony of "pompous" to underscore the cultural "pleasure" of her "insinuating" and "overwhelming" epic allusions, for if Annie is "epic"—what then becomes of the Great Tradition of Male Cultural Capital? And of any discrediting of a Black artist? It makes what she had craftily done in her choices even "more insinuating," given the questioner asks with an unsubtle flourish, "is this a classical allusion," as if he could not credit that Brooks did know it was.[56]

Her depicting Annie in "an epic" tale of banal persistent daily life suggests another question: is this, rather, a "mock epic"—a work in a lofty manner so designed to treat a trivial subject to ridicule the pretensions of character, theme, and mode? The "Anniad" part of *Annie Allen* is hardly an innocent use of epic; that's precisely the point.[57] It's a devastating use of epic to show Annie both as a hero and as a character denied even her heroic status *inside* this artwork by already limited social norms outside the artwork that cannot be transcended (even by art . . .). If this is mock epic, it's not mocking the character but mocking the epic for disallowing this character and this community into an epic. That is, the work is not mocking its main character, Annie, but mocking its genre by a tragi-comic scrambling and critique of epic bases and assumptions—who is a hero, who are followers, what are adventures, what are crucial choices, and what are one's powers over fate.

In the other two parts of *Annie Allen*, the subtle arguments, and reasoned perspicacity of such poems as "pygmies are pygmies still" and "First fight. Then fiddle" have an analytical, forensic urgency for which the verbal condensation functions far beyond mockery of anything but the conditions of racialized "civilization" and social inequality. One would further have to remark that the mockery is reversed, judging scales of importance in social assumptions, as if elegant, tight language is inappropriate to outline the trajectory of a life from high hopes to grinding realities, resignations, and the grit of ordinary responses. But still the disjunction between the euphuistic diction and the attitude toward Annie remains almost indescribable when one is brought up as a critic to see "levels" of diction connecting to social hierarchies of appropriate focus. Hence, the satire also turns to confronting the assumptions of readers.

Brooks's interlocking boxes of formal and tonal framing construct an intense literary and social comment. This whole poem is virtually cubist in its depiction of the main character from many angles in several genres and in the distances created by prosody, diction, and tone. The angles, allusively narrative but also hermetic, are structured as a dazzling array of verse forms—so dazzling that Brooks herself later became a little ambivalent to the brilliant skill and the distancing metaphysical wit of this poem. Such articulate condensation is also visible in Brooks's later position on the importance of any Black character in any context: "no concession" and "the quality and legitimacy of our essence."[58] These phrases return me to Brooks's "pleasure" in this gesture of skill at her poetic intensity and poignant aura around Annie. Brooks creates an artful distance between story and author, between story's poignancy and author's witty control.

We do not know where to stand—this "mini-epic" is so large a statement and has pulled the reader in so many directions that any stable viewing position is undermined; this too, for different reasons, resembles Olson's multiple tugging in many directions. What, then, does Brooks mean by "The Anniad" as in some way alluding to the *Aeneid* or *Iliad* as generic entity? There are certainly other genres and poetic forms that appear as both moments and as consistent traces within *Annie Allen*: serial poem, sequence, *Bildungslyrik*, satire, ballad, sonnet all are present. The cultural work undermining one stable view of this section is as complex as Brooks's own multiple genres and subjectivities. This occurs especially because she has put a particular kind of epic (notably in a form very tight, witty, and focused) inside *Annie Allen*, that is, inside the whole poem about a quotidian Black figure, thus playing critically with normal "epic" expansiveness, heroic overreach, and bold adventures. By the end of this *Bildungs* plot carried out as an intermittent history of the Black female experience before, during, and after World War II, a community commentary and pensive satire on white intransigence to social equality are the result; it appears that any Black reach is viewed as overreach by contemporaneous white society. *Annie Allen* is a thoroughly implosive work, and "The Anniad," despite and because of epic allusions, is the most implosive of all.

Given that this work is couched in a startlingly tight penetrating verse, its wealth of language and poetic finesse compared to the normal trajectory of the tale (until the authorial exhortations at the end) suggests that the author is the poetic hero of this work. Perhaps this work is a way of showing her own imploded but dynamic and overwhelming literary elegance—which is itself, given racial attitudes, a proof of fitness with a double-edged sword. The *agon*, or struggle, occurs between the author and the social world she enters as a Black female artist: a griot-hero who herself fights for recognition—in part via intense craft.

In the "Anniad" forty-three stanzas of a difficult, nimble rhyme scheme on an exactingly small scale challenge the amplitude one knows in an epic's hexameter line, or in any expansive telling. Segmentivity and difficult rhyming are used as deep critique built into the form. Brooks's rhyme scheme has been sharpened to a cutting edge—shown in her ability to deploy the ironies of rhyme to simultaneously elevate and undercut her hero Annie. Brooks at the same time proves an intelligence, intransigence, and flair that were almost too much for a good deal of the white and gendered world of literature during most of her career. The defense offered, in 1949 by her craft, remains a good offense.

Given this, is there a point during the reading of this work at which "irony" as a term is inadequate for all the social/poetic electricity charging through this work of honed formalism? Brooks's restrained and elegant language has initiated the reader into the restrained if judgmental tones of "anti-racist intransigence." This is Brooks's version of the "agon" of writing—of discord, "variance, dissension, contention, dissonance" to which the Olson citation at the beginning of this chapter alluded. Formal elegance of exaggerated perfection, especially very tight, restrained, limited line length and intensely calibrated, witty rhyme—almost the rhymes of light verse used to transform that mode of glancing wit—together signal poetic intelligence, distance, and wariness. The very formalisms hold conflicting forces under pressure. That the formalist extreme of the "Anniad" does contrast with the still elegant but less intense forms of other parts of *Annie Allen* underlines this point.[59]

One might suggest that by her diction, as Olson by his poetics, Brooks has called the adequacy of "the literary" and its institutions into question, as resistant to herself and other Black writers (and their topics), treating them as separate and lesser. With both poets resisting the literary for different but equally fierce reasons of social critique, Brooks and Olson turn out to be comparable after all. Both deploy all the cultural baggage and prestige of epic to criticize epic, in one case for its exclusions, in the other case maximally trying to transcend its limitations to become a work of "everything." Both address the limits of epic within literary culture for its social exclusions, and both have generally "common person" politics in the background. Their epics both treat gigantic social and cultural dilemmas. Both works are examples of the political commentary possible in long poems by the evocation—and extension—of the epic as part of genre multiplicity.

THE EPIC, THE "ARCHAIC," AND WOMEN AUTHORS

The Maximus Poems is a meta-epic. Olson's epic task has to do with literary reenactments (and analysis) *of* the genre as much as acts of writing encouraging male will and energy by means of the genre. Olson sought "epic" in ways beyond genre to deny the hegemony of the merely literary in favor of an attempt to connect with the kinds of fundamental, "archaic," "pre-literary" principles that had generated the epic in the first place.[60] These involved a wide variety of sociopolitical fields: economic politics—a critical reading of US neoliberalism (in formation); ethnography—an interest in the presettler societies in North America (Mayan, Native American) as original and authentic; and archival textual presentation—webs and stacks of citations, incipient poetics, letters, et al. as compost for any emerging poems—from which they spring, and into which they dissolve. His research involved intuitive overviews and bold judgments based on close readings of some contextualizing documents, a method that he had successfully negotiated in *Call Me Ishmael*, transformative for Melville studies.

Olson's meta-epic becomes both actively archival and intellectually synthetic, an essay-poem, with the claim in poetics that such a text always exceeds the categories that try to frame it. The influential hybridity of genres in *The Maximus Poems* includes polemic, epistle, summaries, meditations, injunctions, documents, oblique reminders, notations of poetic urgency. It is a maximal midden of materials, functioning both as an epic goad and a performative collection toward that world-synthetic meta-epic.[61]

Olson and his critics are comfortable with the idea that his *Maximus Poems* be seen as an epic because it seems the most noble context in which the work could be set, because it has struggles (analogous to battles), and because it talks of male comradeship, some nation-building, and some historical tests, leadership-education, and the *Bildung* of men, by events, triumphs, and suffering. The work attempts to be analytic and "morphological" (concerned with dynamic structures) as well as political and didactic, yet for all his analysis of the epic, its hopes for a new polis, and his resistance to the merely literary, Olson did not (as we already saw) challenge his vision of the gender arrangements of the genre.[62] Yet for literature—and beyond—Olsonic thinking in general was influential and charismatic in some poetic circles.

After Olson's death in 1970, Jack Clarke continued Olson's announced pedagogic project in community studies, "A Plan for a Curriculum of the Soul," and he assigned essays on Olson's topics to a group of poets.[63] Though most of the twenty-eight pamphlets got written and completed in the 1970s, some essays were long-pending. To complete the set, Clarke reassigned the missing pamphlets, adding a few women authors. This occurred given a slightly embarrassed recognition in that community that no women at all had originally been among the assigned writers, not even for the pamphlet titled "Woman."[64]

Because Alice Notley had become interested in the epic genre and was at that time loosely in the Buffalo milieu, when Jack Clarke asked her to contribute, she chose "Homer's Art" for her commission for the *Curriculum of the Soul*.[65] Her brother's death in 1988, as victim of PTSD after his service in Vietnam, had provoked her thinking "about politics, sexual politics, war, and poetry," and she therefore "became determined to write an epic poem, to create a female protagonist, and to come to terms with the issue of the relation of women to heroic action."[66]

Notley's works in the early 1990s can be critically configured as an "epic cluster": *Homer's Art* (1990), *Closer to Me & Closer . . . (The Language of Heaven)* (written 1991–92) and *Désamère* (written 1992–93), and "White Phosphorus" (1988) (published in the pamphlet *Homer's Art*), with the culmination being the contemporaneous *Descent of Alette* (first appearing in 1992 in *The Scarlet Cabinet*, then from Penguin Books in 1996).[67] "White Phosphorus" is an elegiac choral work mourning her brother and, crucially, inventing a unique line presentation for the voices. *The Descent of Alette* is a "tale of the tribe" whose female quest figure allegorically rectifies the fundamental violence and exclusion that brought gender inequality to the world. Both are haunted meditative poems rich with social critiques of war and of patriarchal power. None of these works is long or overwhelming, but taken together they define renewed epic concerns.[68] Notley always described *The Descent of Alette* as an epic.[69]

Her pamphlet *Homer's Art* defines epic as a public story, swiftly and engagingly written "simple & grand," not just "playing around with words." *Homer's Art* makes efficient critical remarks, implicating Olson, *The Maximus Poems*, and stylistically disjunctive field-poetics.[70] Notley argues that focus on the ongoing discoveries enabled by a unified narrative surpasses the Olsonic mode of disjunction. Instead of "dissolving of the old continuous narrative & lyric coherences & the reconstituting of them into fragments, collage-like entities, & disjunctive & often abstract pieces of language," Notley draws for her epic on mythic evocations, a narrative based on quest stages shadowing the movement of dreams, a female hero, and a visionary drama using a choral measure of pacing insights.[71]

To write an epic, Notley argues, one must find and reenter a primal story, a pursuit indebted to the Olsonic intellectual-spiritual project. Identifying "original mind," or "some sense of what mind was like before Homer" takes up the challenge of finding the "archaic mind," that vital, if ahistorical Olsonic project. This goal had led, in Olson circles, to many Jungian and mythopoetic studies, a yearning to reconstruct or recover this cultural zone (and its underground continuation in hermetic knowledges) with varied ethnographic and rhetorical success in work by Jack Clarke, Charles Stein, and others. Notley does not resist this notable goal, but she reconceptualizes it with a distinct pronoun shift. As the last lines of her manifesto-essay Notley takes the idea of the archaic as contemporary inspiration, not only a recovery of former mind but a heuristic contemporary discovery: "Perhaps someone might discover that original mind inside herself right now, in these times. Anyone might."[72] The pronoun dramatizes her claim.

To participate in the Olson-inflected search for archaic mind, Notley challenges some of that Olsonic context, deftly confronting the gender exclusions as the fundamental assumption of the genre: "perhaps [. . .] there might be recovered some sense of what mind was like before Homer, before the world went haywire & women were denied participation in the design & making of it." That is, some hard-to-define rupture in shared power, ending with males claiming all power is postulated as having occurred in archaic time. (This had also been a general feminist hypothesis about prehistory.) Identifying and narratively extirpating that exclusionary patriarchal power becomes Notley's goal for her epic. Some coequality between humans had preceded an unnarrated catastrophe that imprisoned and "decapitated" the archaic female (and further subjugated both genders to the authoritarian), a crisis engineered by patriarchal tyranny, here depicted as a singular, transhistorical Tyrant; this is the historical myth behind *Descent of Alette*. Notley announces that other epic works have been "generated by war & are male centered—stories for men about a male world"; she wants, in the name of "archaic mind," to undo this epic via a female-world epic.[73] The ambition is uncompromising.

To these motives is added Notley's drastic rage that women seem to have invented absolutely nothing in human culture—probably not true. But since the contributions are hypothesized but unattested, they have no historical credibility: technologies of weaving? cloth itself? rope and string? basketry? use of fire and cooking? agriculture? herbal healing? midwifery? pottery? lyric poetry? song—at least lullabies? Who knows? Notley refuses to point to these—although they were favorite feminist tropes in these years.[74] However, Notley's "How could a woman write an epic?" given the Olsonic challenge to find the "archaic" becomes a culturally exacting dilemma that she intends to solve.[75]

Notley's epic cluster encompasses three works, written almost simultaneously, each taking up her epic topos—the ferocious damage to men, maleness, and society from the world of war, patriarchal tyranny compelling male allegiance, the agony of powerlessness for women after bellicose political decisions were made with no particular input from those who would suffer the consequences, and an "epic" search in spotty archaic and archaeological records for evidence of mutual gender-power before patriarchy.

For this last task, Notley had some ancient literary analogues or at least a satisfying textual indication that at least in the realm of gods and goddesses, power was once shared between the genders. This was the Inanna myth, made available in an influential retelling.[76] This use of the resurrection cycle from Sumer is notable because a female goddess is at the questing center (like Isis, rather than Osiris or Adonis). This myth influenced Notley's archetypal sense of "epic" quest: as lofty, as embodying "life, death, rebirth," as showing characters that "are both women & principles," and of making a story self-consciously "allegorical."[77]

In a curious twist, this is the very same Inanna whom Olson's scholarly finder and intellectual-sexual informant Frances Boldereff had introduced to Olson, based on her own fascinations and her gleanings of scholarship done by Samuel Noah Kramer. Kramer's fundamental research and translations were presented, a generation later, in the Wolkstein retelling that Notley read. Indeed, Olson's relationship with Boldereff is staged at one point as an explosive discussion of male and female power and archaic culture.[78]

Olson knew about the Sumerian epic-mythic characters Gilgamesh and Inanna from May 1949. Boldereff had offered him a précis of Kramer's scholarship and its implications as a topic worthy of his attention and within his intellectual interests, as visible in their subsequent epistolary exchange on "THE MATRIARCHY," and the "patsies" (patriarchal society, his striking term). His letter to Boldereff on Inanna is an enthusiastic burst of Olsonic synthetic power:

> the GREAT GODDESS of the Iranian Plateau
>
> she's the CLUE, she, our SUMER GIRL!

He thereupon encourages Boldereff to use her own (considerable) scholarly skills to make a written synthesis of all she can find out "on WOMAN" before patriarchy.[79]

This is a stunning assignment—a proposal generated inside his poetic furor challenging her (in effect) to synthesize all existing gender materials in the scholarship of the ancient world. However, he assigned this task only to *her*. Had he included himself in a mutual project, Boldereff might have tried to do this along with Olson (and the course of some contemporary literature might have been altered—an unprovable counterfactual comment). Her idea of their bond was to feed ideas to him but not to research these independent of his companionship and needs. Her scholarly outreach, as Sharon Thesen discusses in her introduction, was also a seductive outreach and a desire to live through him as her Great Man creation, a lesser power supporting his Great Authorship. Olson's enthusiasm for tracking a world mythic history intertwining matriarchy, the archaic mind, and gender is patent in their exchange. He imagined the "BEGINNING OF WHAT CAN BE"—a new kind of gender world—yet it quickly becomes a path untaken by either in 1950.[80] This suggestive intellectual and poetic urgency to investigate the archaic and gender relations did not survive their complex, generative, but ultimately lost relationship.[81]

Epic and women writers/interpreters have several moments of emergence through the Second World War and the postwar period. Certainly not all were directly connected to the Olson, or even to the Pound, milieu. Consider that in both *Annie Allen* and *Helen in Egypt*, war and epic are crucially mixed. Gwendolyn Brooks chooses to attend to gender/race, war's moral injuries, and her characters' compromises in a "small" epic, inflected with war.

H.D. renarrates classical-epic war stories and characters until they are displaced from their narrative canonicity into nonnormative outcomes. In *Helen in Egypt*, based upon alternative interpretations of Helen as casus belli, the heroic battles (mixed with yearning) are interior and are "fought" with a psychoanalytic descent into memory to engage in narrative transformations of the concept and claims of war. Almost all the cultural terms have been renegotiated, since H.D.'s characters all emerge into her work from classical epic and mythologies, have traits that began in those epics, and manifest many "epic" elements idiomatic to the genre (battle, heroism, ferocity)—yet all characters and outcomes are seismically shifted by her poetic psychoanalysis. The fascist rage-filled quasi-rapist—Achilles—is one whom H.D. assimilates from Homeric epic into her plot—the psychic quest.

The gender questions in H.D.'s "epic" enter an interior territory of meditation resisting the hegemony and glamour of the epic tale. "Battle" is a struggle —not to win or even to identify what really happened—but how to make the whole epic concept metamorphose, and to ask the dramatic question that undercuts epic plots: "Was War inevitable?" A parallel, but postwar question is "How reconcile Trojan and Greek?" essentially transposing or criticizing enmities as the plot of epic, surpassed dialectically until "only the Quest remains."[82]

These interpretations of epic by women writers differ from each other: Brooks makes epic one notable genre of prestige that undoes her characters; quest and epic are intermingled in *Helen in Egypt* until quest "wins"; Notley and Waldman want to retain epic and perform it with a female hero. All these authors share the desire to question the cultural position of women in the narratives available for epic long poems. And all, in different ways, make their interpretations of epic become critical of traditional epic-ness and of gender.

In Notley epic turns on the consequences of war and loss for men and women—about being used as a soldier and wounded, then as a suffering, addicted veteran. These consequences, subsequently named Post-Traumatic Stress Disorder (PTSD) and "moral injury," have become a serious issue for discussion among doctors, chaplains, and psychiatrists. With great empathy Notley discusses outcomes like the fact that "they [leaders] played with our souls." "Tell details of battle?" "as" "in an epic?" "as" "in lies?" / "We don't want that now."[83]

Buoyed by Inanna, with the poem "White Phosphorus," Notley begins to challenge her sense of cultural elements of epic; that is, a Homeric epic was composed by (postulated) male griots, concerned the glories and struggles of war, and narrated the further struggles of a deferred *nostos*, and the energetic adventures (sexual and voyaging) in which female figures are often present but sidelined. "White Phosphorus"—refusing epic blandishments—is notable for the first "sound" of *Descent of Alette*, the small phrases, sometimes four or five to a line, set off by interior quotation marks, so that every line is multiply segmented, and the whole has a polyvocal air of many contributing voices thinking aloud, and qualifying or extending remarks the others make. This adds up to a communal sound exploring the traumas of war in the choral voices of the socially wounded. Silence between the segments plays a key role in the pensive pacing. "Homeric sacrifice" and "They were sacrificed / for nothing [. . .]" complicate the *nostos* "I've come home [. . .]" "To die."[84]

This unusual and original measure (a notable example of segmentivity), marked visually by the patterned quotation marks, helps the reader accept the narratives (stories and incidents) and motifs (elegiac reassessment, pensive consideration of losses), but particularly helps to create the tone of collective authority that epics often have and to offer an echoing chorale, as if the author were a traditional teller, evoking tales, myths, transformations of time and place, with listeners becoming choral responders. Notley accomplishes this by using the visual marker of "citation," as if this is a "traditional" story and is now simply reevoked, reconfigured. As Notley stated. "I wanted it to sound like it came out of the culture and not out of a single person's very, very interesting head, [. . .] [which is] what Olson is about."[85] This is a use of epic as collective voice to inhibit the "lyrical interference of the individual as ego" different from the one that epistles from "Maximus" proposed (of a collective in one voice). Finding the measure in "White Phosphorus," defining her investigation of epic assumptions, and discovering Inanna all led Notley to *The Descent of Alette*.

At the end of *Alette*, the hero meets her final helper figure, a talismanic didactic owl whose powers she temporarily assumes for her exemplary single act of killing as liberation. The Tyrant, killed and thereby rendered impotent of his many social claims, is Notley's allegorical embodiment of patriarchal authoritarian power that has colonized mind and controlled society. She modeled a single act of violence and no more, that single exemplification as a protest against her brother's obligation to commit much state-sanctioned violence in his wartime service.[86]

Generalizing from wars fought by men to the war of social inequality, *Descent of Alette* depicts a quest for social rectification, demanding an encoded, emotional journey through an infernal purgatorio (subway and caves), in vignettes of both political analysis and personal allusion. Notley creates an always-already narrative quality of fable, allegory, and tale, in a Dantean swift movement of incident to incident. The work is a narrative projection of her political and economic analyses of real historical trends of the 1980s—homelessness, poverty, degradation of the city, erosion of humane values, a shadowy but insistent gentrification, and increasing polarization of the poorer from the richer—as issues visible and crushing, along with endless wars, of which Vietnam was only one example. Reaganomics, a systemic and ideological shift to the denial of social services, produced further economic polarization.

The narrative of *Descent of Alette* combines political allusions and dream logic with psychological *Bildung*. The main character, who, in the many voices of segmented text, is pluralized as well as singular, is given a series of tender tasks. The persistence of the female hero through these quest stages is propelled by her anti-Parcivalian aspect—she is not blank, innocent, and baffled. Instead, even while walking into mysterious places, she asks appropriate questions of her interlocutors, manifests empathy and purpose, and keeps undaunted focus on the goal. With her all-gender feminism, Notley features significant male as well as female helper figures throughout.

The hero finds and binds together the hidden archaic Mother who has been rendered headless by patriarchal relations; this restoration is a benchmark, but it is not the end of the quest, for this act alone will not challenge patriarchy. Notley has no interest either in a "matriarchal" narrative solution in which one gender engineers a compensatory separatist triumph or in any complementary separate-spheres affirmation (traditional, religious, and psychological). Her narrative thereby differs from recoveries of the Mother goddess figure that occur in some mythopoetic feminist plots of the 1970s and 1980s and differs also from Jungian solutions of old wine in new bottles.

Notley argues that if the brutalizing suppression of the archaic female has led to all other brutalities, one must extirpate the force that caused that severing of women from intellect, power, and agency. She therefore proposes that there is no liberation without a full confrontation with male power—in the epic as genre, in recognitions of the exclusion of females (as active agents, perhaps heroes) from that genre, in the costs of war at the root of that genre, in that genre's narrative manipulations and ideological power. The depiction of one exemplary political assassination is the narrative act she chooses to condense her critique.

Notley constructs her female hero to rectify history: to break the ownership of a society by a Tyrant (in oblique reference to *Antigone*), the possession of all ideology and reality by his patriarchal world both inside and out. She narrates Alette's final tests in forensic scenes that involve the Tyrant's subtle temptations to a *female* hero.

The main character abruptly regains her memory and thereupon remembers her name (given before this moment only in Notley's title), her brother's fate ("he died in battle"), her anger, her love for the brother, her hatred of war. The Tyrant counterpunches with a simplistic defense: "Men fight" and the intensity of war "captures/ Many men's" "imaginations." Facing this conflating of archetypal and natural arguments, Alette makes the ethical criticism "Your inspiration" [is] / "drawn from the hardships" "of others." When this grief becomes, in his mocking appreciation, "all" "so beautiful," "so moving," he thereby reveals one tyrannical manipulation.[87] The seductions of art and beauty, the desire to use the emotions of others parasitically as spectacle reveal one strand of patriarchal ideology.

The Tyrant repeatedly attempts to use the clichés of femininity against the female hero, by degrading the Mother, by invoking traditional social arrangements, and by appealing to Alette's caring side. Hence the tricks of the Tyrant, including false empathy, benevolent wisdom, his concern that females should "rest" or eat well, also deny that females witnessed or experienced what they actually did. In Notley's quickly moving narrative/argument, Alette addresses this intense gaslighting by the Tyrant as he reinterprets the archaic Mother—her "soulfulness" "cannot hold [sociopolitical] power"; but she is advantaged because we sing about her as a beloved icon. Alette responds by noting the extirpation in human culture of woman's "power & influence" "equal to" "any man's"—an acknowledgment, in this poem, of Notley's finding that "archaic mind" had been a fusion of male and female powers. In his final ploys, the Tyrant appeals, like a serial abuser, to her kindness, imploring, "Keep me company!"; he finally accuses her of having "no forgiveness?"—that is, losing her very womanliness.[88]

In these scenes Notley depicts several sources of resistance in this totalizing system—the vulnerability of the Tyrant to a figure who can doubt him, who knows or intuits when he is lying, and in allegory by her accepting the tools of the animal: the need to kill but precisely, only to live (again, a comment on war's wanton killing). The narrative tracks Alette's gathering of her will to commit selective violence to root out the last vestiges of the Tyrant's presence. Removing her consent on an individual basis to what seems like an overarching system is depicted as a key act of social intervention and empathy for the unacceptable miseries of all others suffering the Tyrant's power.

Many gory, explicit acts of killing are depicted in an epic such as the *Iliad* and *Beowulf*; there is one only in *Alette*, the act of an avenger in the epic quest for freedom from subjugation. Also notably, Alette's will to power stops there; Notley depicts no explicit suggestions made by the victor for post-Tyrannical society. The multiple people and other life forms emerging from the underground as it cracks open in the social apocalypse of the final section must decide, in the distinctive ungrammatical pronoun use, to exist "between us & I," and to invent a renewed social compact together.[89] Long-poem pronouns often announce renewed versions of "we."

An extrapolated list of the heroic (or necessary) acts of the female hero is powerful but subdued. Watching, empathizing, stripping (for money), dressing, holding (a baby, for example), eating or ingesting something, dreaming and attending to the meanings of dreams, making love, crying, mourning, trusting, persevering, facing danger and fear, continuing into an unknown darkness, listening for voices and meanings, receiving and evaluating (rejecting when appropriate queens and iconic female figures, for instance, also rejecting shame), healing a wound, sleeping, resting, traveling, adorning (and meditating on jewels, cloth, flowers), laughing, thinking, helping others, giving, enduring. And taking responsibility when it is given by fate, accepting the necessity for an act of violence. Aside from the final killing and several defining, "mythic" actions (flying, allegorically uprooting the Tyrant's heart), this is a very mild, even quotidian list of things many people, particularly women, do all the time.

She could, Notley suggests, have written epic to "identify with one of [Homer's] female characters," much like the mythopoetic writing done by many women in the 1970s—telling a female story from a postulated other side. There is nothing intrinsically limiting about such a choice; many wide-ranging works emerged from this reversal. However, for Notley that narrative choice did not answer to her critique and did not, in her view, adequately undermine the fundamental "stupidity" of war, "where tragedy begins & where a story must be told."[90]

Notley's contemporaneous "Women and Poetry" (1991) is a passionate and pivoting essay, inhabiting a double-consciousness argument, by sometimes speaking as a woman exclusively and sometimes as a poet only, while always trying to fuse cultural meanings in a further formation: a humane human. She never concedes any kind of monogendered position (whether taken by men or by women). Notley has always resisted what she saw or thought was feminist intransigence (sometimes embodied in political-cultural separatist movements) but was always in a curious position, as she is feminist in her informed gender critique without wanting to use that word much, if ever. Perhaps for her, this "naming" any one position was inadequately mobile and led to static, repeated assumptions—not open to poetic or, indeed, to processual thinking. The crisis of the world system for Notley does not entail monogendered solutions. This is what is enacted in this cluster of works—being a woman, writing as a woman, and writing toward human transformation. Notley is not a gender-nationalist but a poet using the epic genre for analytic enactment of feminist critique.

With some notable differences, this is a solution also sought by Anne Waldman in a parallel epic text of great length and considerable mutual awareness of and from Notley's and Mayer's works.[91] As Anne Waldman said: "Taking up the long poem was like taking up a gauntlet to challenge the idea that epic was exclusively a male form. What could hold handle transmit incubate resound digress permit transgress more than the long poem? What could demand attention and attempt to deliver apotheosis, new form and language, declare ethos for writing in the first place (a ground zero charnel ground), stay difficult and 'female' yet transcend gender more than the long boundary-less poem?"[92] The double move of being in gender and transcending it will characterize *Iovis*.

In 1998, with two volumes of Anne Waldman's three-volume epic poem *Iovis* published in 1993 and 1997, Alice Notley reviewed it, meditating on epic, women, and formal issues, and also briefly discussed Olson's *Maximus Poems*. Notley (vainly) protests the designation of "epic" for the works of Pound, Olson, and Zukofsky, because they have no story or "continuity of narrative" in distinctive actions but only "continuity of consciousness." As we have seen, Notley also thoroughly resists the disjunctive style for its loss of narrative clarity.[93] She herself had veered decidedly from the accumulative, juxtaposed "collage entity." For Notley, "an epic is by definition a presentation of unity to whatever culture the epic serves"—a definition close to, say, Michael André Bernstein's.[94] Notley clearly presents *her* attitudes toward narrative as a major point of difference from Waldman, and one as well that criticizes the modernist method of collage and fragmentation in favor of a continuous story.

However, Waldman consciously takes Williams, Pound, Zukofsky, and Olson as her models (along with H.D.)—a typical plurality or array, not wanting to leave out even one notable elder. Thus Notley supports Waldman's choices by intransigence about reception categories: if those male "masters" have written what the American poetry community is willing to call "epic" (despite their lack of narratives), then Waldman's work also deserves to be called an epic. Length, "including history," tonal grandeur and scope are now the criteria for epic (even if Notley remains dubious); she rests her argument on equality feminism to defend Waldman's work. Notley also states that Waldman's *Iovis* is "about love and war, just like an epic" in themes. Further, she argues, having a woman hero be her own griot is a cultural rectification, particularly in a culture in which "all is full of Jove." Despite Notley's sub rosa moments of skepticism and resistance to the poem's "irritating aspects," she produces a careful defense of Waldman's ambition and her neo-Olsonic projective practice as epic—even without narrative.[95]

This argument for "equal treatment" in reception is not obsolete, never to be assumed even in "alternative" ("liberated" was the word, once) zones of poetics (projectivist or New York School). A key question about female authorship/authority emerges in one of the many documentary letters that Waldman includes in *Iovis*. In it, K.P. (Kristin Prevallet) had recorded for Waldman a moment in a SUNY-Buffalo course that Robert Creeley gave on Charles Olson. Challenged in class by Creeley to think of people "attempting to write an epic on the scale of Olson," K.P. answered that Anne Waldman was doing just that, only to be told categorically by Creeley that this was absolutely not so, because Waldman had too much "ego" and was "too personal."[96] As K.P. outlines to Waldman in the letter, she found Creeley's riposte unsatisfactory, since Olson himself was not innocent either of ego or of uses of the personal. K.P. outlines for Waldman the instantly chilling effect of Creeley's response on her sense of what a female poetic career is "allowed" to do.[97] Aside from Creeley's unwillingness to concede that Olson's powers could be paralleled by any other poet (or, alternatively, to allow that different poets conducted their grand-scale works in different but pertinent ways), we see graphically the ways that epic (even casually in a classroom exchange) is positioned as a "no women allowed" clubhouse even as late as 1994 or 1996.[98] The letter is of high interest at the very least for seeing patriarchal literary replication and its results right in front of one's eyes. It also supports one thesis of this chapter—that for certain male writers, gender was an invisible problem in the epic genre that, when made visible, was disconcerting, and led to fiat, not discussion.

Confronting gender often does lead to contradiction and dilemma. Waldman and Notley articulate (when necessary, in different situations) both gender-laden and "post-gender" arguments.[99] For example, from Notley's "What would it be like to make a female poetry?" and its confluence with the gynocritical urgencies of the 1980s, she pivots to her antibinarist questioning of that question: "Can there ever be any value in sexual polarization of activity?"[100] Both Notley and Waldman claim and affirm the value of female "sounds" and topics, but both also question whether a "female poetry" is desirable in itself. Is it gender affirmation or post-gender affirmation that is desired? The quandary-laden answer for both poets is—both, situationally, as necessary interventions. However, this pivoting between gender-laden vision and attempts to transcend gender produces double, triple, and contradictory tasks—precisely the ongoing dilemma at least for "epic" and women writers (and often for women writers in general).

Anne Waldman's positions in *Iovis* reveal at least a double bind, a double helix of equality feminism and difference feminism, with queer complicating torques and twists, since she deliberately presents all these positions at various times. *Iovis* is not only intellectually expansive, it replays and retries multiple responses to the dilemmas of gender, with inspirations from powerful mythological females, from many cultures, and from an array of real or documented situations along with a vast rhetorical panoply of spells, charms, analyses, and exhortations. A gender revolution is implied by the propositions undergirding this poem. While Notley's allegory in *Alette* stops just at the promising moment of some different future, Waldman's *Iovis* is a nonstop ritual for continuous struggles and exhortations performing that gender-rich future into being (at least for the duration of the poem).

Waldman's feminism in this "feminist epic" has always been constructed as an unstable mixture of positions, identifying with women but never identifying with victimhood or powerlessness. In her own authorial persona, Waldman is known for exemplary exceptionalist declarations. Waldman's positions shift in thesis-antithesis between equality and difference claims—and the resulting contradictions are familiar and powerful. This undecidability and perpetual debate have also characterized much feminist thinking, where both-both is a useful strategy, or, to say it in theorist Denise Riley's terms, "So feminism must be agile enough to say, 'Now we will be "women"—but now we will be persons, not those "women."'"[101] Often one chooses specific emphases at any given moment, to make specific situational and political-personal choices. This both-both thinking is embedded firmly in Waldman's findings; "both-both" is in fact her coinage.[102] It is complicated by *Iovis*'s dialectical structure, creating a palimpsest of male orientation and female orientation (thesis/antithesis) as if these were self-evident positions, with a third term (gender-queer, yet also relatively female) offering a necessarily unstable synthesis.

The epic genre, however, is the centerpiece of the cultural work of this poem with its complementary gender dialectics. Waldman postulates that patriarchal maleness (most often, but not always, lodged deeply in males), even with its own notable and complex wounds, has caused massive damage in every sphere of life throughout history. This is a more absolutist overview than some of Notley's evocations of male woundedness. Waldman's antithesis displays powerful femaleness, in which female skills in the world can be honored, activated, and appreciated. It does not talk about any damage done by females throughout history, because, for her, females are often too powerless to cause much, if any, damage on a *world* scale. That is her argument. Hence, these are not balanced insights about power and its costs but a defensible framing interpretation of gender and uneven power.

Waldman's depiction of these eclectic activities of power and agency occur both on the realist plane of the quotidian and within spiritual claims and practices from a variety of religions, even those that limit female behavior in real life, or have separate spheres for women. This means that the zone of *Iovis* (All is Full of Jove, male and masculine energy) will be displaced by All is (or perhaps should be) Full of Female, feminine, antipatriarchal, bisexual, and queer energy. All these can be the property of men as well as other genders. Any part of this gender bolus that might be internally contradictory (masculinist *and* queer?) is overridden, talked down, sung away, absorbed, and transcended. The *possible* merging of female, queer, bisexual, and transgender subjectivities is one critical gender assumption in this period; more rarely can queer, the feminine, and maleness seamlessly integrate powers. Contradictions can certainly be imagined in the real world. These idealized aggregates emerge in sex-gender theorizing (and propositions working by utopian hopes) for at least the past forty years, but actually within all of modernity, as in Virginia Woolf's term "androgyny." One does see the gender questions (of masculinity, effeminacy, and femaleness, and of equality, rights for all adult gender-sexuality configurations, laws, sexualities, customs, and resistances) as chronic issues for modernist writers who offer many outcries and outcomes through the long twentieth century.

In *Iovis* often the desired finding of each section is put forth in the several-page essay-evocation heading that section, or in mini-"summaries" situating each canto.[103] Each introductory headnote is not exposition but evocation and sometimes exhortation; we negotiate its political and social outlines because we already know the postulated (male-female-queer) scaffolding of the whole work. Waldman's poem attempts to posit an idealized condition or zone evoked by bardic affirmation in which any power markers would not be linked in any fixed way to any gender. In Book III the finding centers on a neologism: "matriot" (the word "patriot" deturned), not a woman necessarily, but adherence to "feminist mother poetics," a mending but also fierce calling out of the destructive results of patriarchy.[104]

Feminist critique as exemplified in *Iovis* is not only about gender, sexuality, and ethnicity: it is also a challenge to the split between thought and feeling; a critique of values of profitability and wealth as social goods when in fact they create inequality, exploitation, and immiseration; it is a rejection of all the forces that create the many disenfranchised in our world. As with Notley, the task of Waldman's feminist critique in poetry is the pluri-decentering of binarism and the smashing of hierarchy. It is a critique of power in the names of social justice, racial and economic justice, and gender justice. A feminism of critique is based on inquiry, resistance, disobedience, rage, and placing yourself via your poem as if in utopian new time. It is in this enlarged sense that *Iovis* is a poem of conscience, feminist investigation, and critique from "an oppositional poetics" that includes epic as one of many allusions and alliances.[105] Yet the poem does not articulate epic-ness by more than a few key allusions and gigantic scale—except by her claiming to write one as a woman. There is no more epic plot than anything else, except by analogy or in allusions (quest, visiting oracles), but the whole work is realized as a battle on the page.

Waldman makes various but clear claims on traditions that distinguish epic in our time—including writing in the polytonal and fragmented form in which modern epics (Olson, Pound) have appeared. And—particularly in Waldman's case—vociferously and repeatedly compelling culture (as male culture) to admit her. It is not necessarily as "a woman" that she demands this—it is as an exceptional(ist) vessel of energy, when she evokes both "female energy" and "feminine energy" as something that can manifest in any gender—and thereby be genderless (though this does not exactly follow).[106] Both Notley and Waldman work toward naming and inhabiting positions in gender and beyond gender, that both-both position familiar to many women writers. This position is sometimes quite difficult to deploy, since one always has the other (near-opposite) position to accommodate.

Waldman solves for cultural problems of gender binarisms for women by depicting many operational subjectivities. To begin with, her subjectivity is not just female but also male. "Both-both" again. The subjectivity of the work *Iovis* speaks in response to Jove as shape-shifter; she thereupon makes herself a shape-shifter or trickster figure ("Puer, picaresque adventurer," she says).[107] She conjures this figure as one of the mythic investments for this poem. Being a *puer* figure leads her to the incisive command: "rise up paginal," *up* meaning appear, be prominent, increase in intensity, return to, or get erect.[108] This "paginal" evokes a boy as page and is a pun on vaginal, as if the vagina could, with penile panache, erect on the pages of a book. Thus when things rise up paginal, they constitute a male-vaginal apparatus of the book, or a bisexualized, self-inseminating composite. Which is what this book tries for—an active vaginal space in which sperm-words of oneself and others enter and are productive. So there are always two genders (at least) behind any page—a striking extension of Olson's page-space innovations. Even when self-consciously and consistently making the claim of dual genders, Waldman also claims the transcending of gender (which means a queered sensibility is also in play).

Hence, any overviews of *Iovis* proposing the genres or subjectivities of the work via its dialectical scaffolding do not acknowledge the plethora, the tidal waves of social subject positions claimed (shaman, mother, lover, political activist are some), and the polygeneric array that make this a frustrating and startling work, operating on contradictory planes simultaneously—a whirlwind of negative capability. The speaking subjectivity is a master of performances in an "oracular documentary trance dance," for the Waldman-figure identifies with all genders and synthesizes them variously;[109] note the several genres even in that phrase, not to speak of another medium—dance.

Waldman's gender-genre array overrides her own clear dialectical scaffold. Between gender and genre, she is a shape-shifter, a Proteus who can be caught only temporarily (by any hero—or reader). She is "Scheherazade on a whim," though this endless story fabrication is hardly only by whim, but in danger, as a woman storyteller with a world responsibility—keeping the planet alive. To do so, "I will write the new laws of all the land," a gorgeous Shelleyan and king-queenly ambition.[110]

The subjectivity of *Iovis*, the speaking subject, is probably even more omnivorous than Olson's. Her portrait of Olson writing his personal poem as a "salvation for the poet [. . .] surrounded by little scraps of paper and speaking the poem, living the poem" comports with Olson's dynamic of endless writing.[111] Waldman's work also claims multiple spiritual, political, and cultural responsibilities in a veering plenitude.[112] On the quotidian plane, Waldman acts in her speaking subjectivity like a collector of instances or investigator, but (like Pound) she tends to pre-know her general findings. She wants to find out about power, and thus again she must examine men and women, maleness and femaleness, the human, the inhumane and the metaphysical realm of gods and bodhisattvas.

Waldman's investigative poetics of gender—and the shift from three books of *Iovis* to a fourth—is predicted in "FEMINAFESTO" (1994) from *Kill or Cure*. "I'd like here to declare an enlightened poetics, an androgynous poetics, a poetics defined by your primal energy [. . .] a transsexual literature, a hermaphrodite literature, a transvestite literature, and finally a poetics of transformation beyond gender. That just sings its wisdom."[113] The list here passes from query to findings, from gender to being "beyond gender." It also predicts what happens, after a thousand pages, to the idea of only three books of *Iovis*: the fourth "transformation beyond gender" is announced in 1994, way before it occurred.

A second subjectivity beyond investigator in *Iovis* is "Mom," for the poem began as an antipatriarchal document for her son, born 1980. "Mom" is not as much "so random" (in an edgy teasing judgment by Ambrose Bye, cited repeatedly in the poem), as she is flooded with valid, exciting needs, positions, stimuli, demands, thoughts, responses. This is somewhat like an enlarged experience of overwhelmed motherhood in our social spaces. So the subjectivity of the poet is both a real Mom and a Great Mother (Magna Mater), a

Gaia figure who tries to contain all, cure all, unify things in their obdurate plurality.

The use—part of her inclusivity—of letters and of some interview exchanges is a feature of *Iovis* that tends to make subjectivity of the poet/speaker a field site of many vectors. It is polyvocality and pluri-subjectivity as a saturating element, named "epic" because of largeness, not genre. It begins with a photo of herself as a baby with her own father as a soldier and explodes from there. There are a plethora of gender stances inside each of the three sections, and worldwide ranges of examples and allusions. Among these are figures real and mythic; persons Waldman knows; historical figures available only via texts; performative identifications of the poet; attempts to enact and depict rituals involving gender and more. This plethora does make any section unsummarizable—there is always a variation, a qualification, a refusal of cultural hierarchies; another instance or example that raises, changes, reiterates, or confuses the stakes at any given moment. The subjectivity is "decentered," and that sometimes by a "matriot" maternity; that is, a thousand demands pull and tug at her, and she attempts to satisfy all of them in large measure by claiming them within the "just-coming-to-thought" readiness at every moment—a form of the "projective" to encompass plethora.

In genre, then, the poem is hardly only an "epic," and it certainly does not have a focused narrative or a controlled dialectic but creates an ongoing assemblage of events on a texturally jumpy page of collaged materials of many tones and findings, the page as "battlefield"—with experiences, visitations, responses. This page zone is disturbed, displaced, and shocked on a determined scale because so many conflicting elements and their energies are arrayed there. It makes of "writing" a way station or go-between to performance. This has some real cost in word-to-word attentiveness and leaves some questions of sequencing unanswered. The "strands of our existence" in the poem are said to "come together karmically."[114] That is sometimes debatable, but one accepts the monumental results, if not those premises. *Iovis* is also generically hybrid, polyphonic, intertextual, conceptual—a pooling of documents, of analytic findings, and of outcry in an action poetics with a political torque.

Within the stark outline of the tripartite framing, the book explodes with genres, both locally in any one canto and across the time of its making. A catalog of some of them—for new ones are named often, with a prodigious fecundity, might be appropriate in a poem celebrating both plethora and its many avatars. An accumulative or "everything" poem is certainly heterogeneous in genres, large and small; and in reading Waldman one may identify ode, newspaper clipping, epistle, conversation, jeremiad, elegy, interview, document, lyric, reportage, translation, interruption, dream records, diatribes, arias, exhortation, aphorism, invocations, citations, diagrams. prayers, protest letters, exorcisms, maledictions, homages, child-written epistles and stories, visual pages, and a dictionary. These are only some among the genres included.[115] This is, after all, not a poem entirely on the page but a script for a dream film, ritual, private meditation, not even a fully public *poem* but a public performance of a poetic consciousness in time. It is a multi-act opera without single narrative arc, a magical "Bollywood" production, incorporative, absorptive, colorful, dashing. All this is to say that "epic" is overrun by, extended into an unmarked version of a *Gesamtkunstwerk.*

Iovis is keen on its epic necessity, but it is not focused on "being an epic" except in being epic in length (and in general transformative hopes). The work is overall a manifesto-performance-declamation, a scrapbook-travelogue-notebook, and a cinema-ritual-dream experience, crossing spiritual time/actual time. When Waldman talks of genre, the explanations are filled with an exciting overspill and omnivorous plurality. At punctual moments, differently articulated versions of new genres get declared: like "still designing a radical celestial mappemunde."[116]

At what point can Waldman's work be corralled under the rubric of epic (on which she insists) because she uses some epic allusions? And at one point does one say epic is an analogy, one among many, one genre trace among more genres than even the poet can catalog? Even if the poet wants to answer or vary epic, even given her responsiveness to Olson's *The Maximus Poems*, you cannot map *Iovis* on epic particularly (nor can you map Olson's work on epic alone). So, revisiting the genre question, the reader finds that the genres represented in Waldman and in all the poets in this section are as plural as their poems. Whenever Waldman talks about genres, epic is noted as only one among many.[117] The first and clearest genre named is "epic," or at least the "epic analogy," which suddenly becomes less clear—something qualified as "a male form," then with a Promethean vow to "steal some of that power."[118] The cultural status and monumentality of "epic" were Waldman's first goals, simultaneously with a critique—reclaiming "epic for a female imagination with new priorities."[119]

But given Waldman's sheer excess of genre uses, her question "*Why is the* epikos *a repository for your mind out of all the possibilities?*" is answered first by Waldman's Promethean desire simultaneously to deturn and to feminize the epic in one literary act.[120] Just as Notley also insisted, it is culturally necessary to make the epic writable by a woman writer for her gendered critical cultural ambitions (that is, no genre is off-limits). This declaration for both poets entailed the necessity to write such an epic. For Waldman, epic seems to mean monumentally large in order to claim and churn through all that socio-cultural territory, to turn epic to antipatriarchal uses. But besides "epic," two other quite important genres propel *Iovis*. One is quest (the genre also, in my view, infusing *Descent of Alette*), and the other is assemblage, with a visually-dramatic performative "script" for its page space. In Waldman's case assemblage is shown in both its manifestations: Book and *Gesamtkunstwerk*. It is to these other overarching categories, quest and assemblage, that this study now turns.

CHAPTER 3

Interpreting Quest and Dante

NUMEROLOGY, THE SOCIO-COSMOLOGICAL POEM, AND DANTE

IN THE QUEST poem (like Notley's quest-epic), a social vision and a cosmology set clear goals and thus enable an achievable ending with a desirable outcome. Notley's depicts a visionary and realist resurrection. The narrative/emotional satisfactions of such an idiomatic solution with (virtually) no ironies might indicate, if not yet explain, why Dante—from the Italian fourteenth century—has figured prominently for some twentieth- and twenty-first-century Anglophone long-poem writers who correlate their works intertextually with his.[1] On his quest for transformative assurance, Dante witnessed a universe of moral coherence, with detailed, visualized zones for those who are immoral, malicious, criminal, showing posthumous potential, or achieving degrees of grace. In the *Commedia*, Dante constructed an architectural structure to visualize how political, spiritual, and social despoilers would be punished by a Revealed Power higher and more comprehensive than the world as such provides.

However, for modernity such a coherent religious vision and such elegant and lucid allegories toward redemption do not necessarily reflect hegemonic beliefs. One question a modern long poem asks (as this book argues) is how to write quest and cosmology from a generally secular worldview—making a materialist-spiritual fusion, a real if rare combination—when a solidified and socially hegemonic telos (such as Dante's) is suspended, redefined, or uncertain.

Only some of the modern long poems that explicitly evoke Dante do so with a Christian perspective, but spiritual and cosmological explorations—as well as sociopolitical ones—are fundamental. The high seriousness of Dante is often quite individually meaningful to the poets included here, and evoking him becomes an act of homage, an invested stance both solemn and witty, yearning, and fascinated. Yet most of these poets vary something fundamental in their Dantes, whether it is tone, purpose, credibility, or goal. Their works, some infused with diluted Christian materials, become secular if also socio-cosmological, spiritual but neither theistic nor necessarily monotheistic, and even (the most amusing and perverse outcome) Ovidian in metamorphoses and polytheism. Sometimes there is an end postulated, but more often in our general period, any telos is suspended, deferred though still in progress, deconstructed, or refigured as constant, but without finality. This shapes a messianic attitude without a Messiah.

The modern *serial* poem often builds on quest and is a mechanism for it. Seriality is a tactic of segmentivity, a mode of thinking in decidedly sectioned units that themselves join disparate materials along a temporal, metamorphic line of investigation. More modest or contained in scale than cosmic-mythic claims (and their general companion—vatic tones), often presented as individuated soundings in a specific time and place, the subjectivity is the dramatization of thinking scaled to its own intensities rather than animating or validating the rectitude of universalizing belief systems. Unlike narrative quest poems, the teleological goal or a sense of culmination in a serial work is often (deliberately) side-stepped. Hence, the serial poem, of leaps, vectors, and no necessary one-solution argument is often the shape that quest poems take in our time. Seriality allows for loose ends; not all the issues the poem raises are solved. But they are represented in their ambiguities. Seriality is a mini-mode of quest—all middle. Its undecidability or muting of narrative release may frustrate a reader or be deemed plausible expressions of a secular time.

Using the terms "socio-cosmological" or "cosmological" for motives of long-poem writers does feel tautological, given that a long or very long poem is already something of a maximal world unto itself. When Robert Duncan wrote to Robin Blaser (in 1957) proposing that his whole life's work was to be one ongoing poetic act, he foresaw making "large spatial architectures at the edge of chaos."[2] Dealing with order and chaos are ambitious, challenging acts. Our long poems are already (by definition) big, and often ungainly, unwieldy, noncompliant. Perhaps it's only a step from that kind of poetic vision, ambition, and scale to long poems with cosmological aspirations—entering the question how formally and intellectually to organize a universe of order and chaos in a poem, or how to represent a permanent edge, as the psychological and aesthetic condition of "purgatory."[3] Facing such cosmological and structural issues, one understands the many attractions of Dante's synthesis.[4]

A cosmological long poem summarizes the confrontation with a whole—with the cosmos, with the universe, with Earth and beyond. The mystery of our being here. The mystery of our disappearance, death, and then what? The mysteries of time and space and energy as phenomena. And of matter. And, for that matter, of nonmatter: spirit, soul, and other functioning concepts elaborating themselves in worldviews, psychological nuances, and aesthetic choices, all traditionally poetic topics. A socio-cosmological poem also engages historical, social, and political realities as part of its remit. That is, the scope becomes "everything."

Because one wants to find out what all this involves, how these mysteries are adumbrated on the quest, and how order gets certified, a verification tactic in both secular and spiritual cases of these long quest poems deploys the toils and constructs of numerology. The numerological and teleological can match up variously. Long poems may be distinguished by numerology and number schemes, since quests—in part to achieve their endings or their worldviews, may well present confirming numbers, numbers guaranteeing meaningful artifice, or culturally solemn allusions like the number three.

Numbers may even function to assist poeticity, to re-evoke Roman Jakobson's term. The stylization of poetry makes a "special point" of a markable clash between sign and object in order to claim poesis, "the autonomy of the aesthetic function." Any feature of language will do this, so long as "the word is felt as a word," not as a straightforward "representation of the object."[5] Motivated numbers give a paradoxical assist to this goal by not being words but numbers felt as numbers. However, numbers may also suggest vast cultural allusions that allude to scientific, religious, or intellectual systems, allowing a sub rosa, nonautonomous stratum to covertly affect the poem. Purest poeticity is probably impossible. Certain numbers are filled with habituated meanings and can take up the slack for the so-called autonomous word.

One might even quarrel with Jakobson's "autonomy" idea—where does any word-felt-as-word come from; words generally have tonal and historical roots in life as such. A numerological pattern (such as a biblical number allusion) has had plenty of ideological and traditional undergirding. Yet it is also true that numerological patterns are markable artifices, part of the confirmation of the "aesthetic function" by poetic tactics. Numbers in poetry make visible the fact that poeticity in general does deploy this trace aura of the social—without necessarily acknowledging that it does.

Numerology offers whole traditions of cultural meanings, whether religious, hermetic-gnostic, quotidian, or mythical. Dante's elegant, intricate, and coherent numbers are both externally (biblically) and internally (structurally) self-confirming. Number uses in poetry range from the cosmic to the quotidian, from Dante's numerology based on threes and on one hundred, to the twenty-four-hour day divided in six chapters in Mayer's *Midwinter Day*.

Eliot, H.D., and Zukofsky all validate their numbers with either hegemonic or hermetic religious allusions (Christian, Pythagorean, and Hebraic). Many of these modern Dantean homages deploy numerologies to bolster the structures created; this parallels Dante's magisterial numerology but not necessarily its Christian worldview. Number "theories" in poems may be theological and evoke traditions or prophecies, functioning in poetry on many potential scales from the convincingly (or formerly) meaningful, often biblical allusions and structural frameworks, to the personal and contingent.

Many long poems use numerology to shape their matrix although their numerologies are not traditional but based on observed findings, mathematical constants, or invented, procedural patterns. Certain procedural long poems depend on numbers, used in general as a multiplication of patterns for the sake of more evocation of "everything," accounting for (or counting up to) that array. Numbers might also be loosely biographical, like Hejinian's age-allusive number choices in *My Life*. Any numbers may be talismanic for a particular author, offering the private pleasures of finding or enjoying a resemblance for its own sake, linking things deep and decorative; allowing confirmation of a thought by private numerological tinkering, or finding a charming coincidence within the zone of composition.

In the past of our culture, a Christian hegemony intermingled with Platonic-Pythagorean number theory often infuses poetic numbers, but the seasons, the calendar and sequence of the day are also plausible organizing frames, especially when God-based cosmic systems become residual, not dominant.[6] The culturally powerful numbers often evoke known traditions, circularly confirming for people in those traditions. Our year, we say, is 365 days long, and that "is" has allure; a poet alluding instead to the triple cycles of the Mayan calendar year would not evoke immediate agreement but possibly engage exotic fascination. Gematria and various Hebraic number mysticisms offer organizing possibilities untapped in Anglophone poetries; these are of course underknown because the groups generating these methods were once sociopolitically excluded or closed off. However, poets sometimes seek out numerologies not "naturalized" for them (in religion or culture) for poetic challenges or simply from curiosity. Insofar as poetry is a species of understanding and decoding infused with untrackable energies, balanced numbers or numerical allusions can play a serious, perhaps startling role in some of the long poems under discussion here, alluding to past agreements in worldviews or venturing forth in the absence of hegemonic systems.

Long poems work to bring universes and histories together into legibility. Procedural numbers (counting any itemizable textual element) and numerologies (numbers alluding to known philosophical systems or organic patterns) therefore continue to help organize poetry even in our era of various free verses, that is, in an era in which metrical counting per se is of low interest even when general metrical masteries still function.

Numbers once implied an aesthetic principle for poetry: harmony, order, and a higher fittedness of the genre to echo or reflect the universe, itself in the hands of an intentional God. This God even arranged Creation by counting "Measure, number and weight" (Wisdom of Solomon 11:20): such arithmetical assurance that it all adds up or somehow coheres is offered to calm all fears of what the world may actually produce. Discussing the gap between such theological assurances and actual hideous events is certainly out of the realm of this book's competence, but the gap can be motivating for poets toward some order. Poetry, along with ritual, may have even begun as compensatory explanations or placatory moves facing this universe. Any acts of celebrating God's/gods' various arrangements are, however, hardly required of poetry today; various gods and all skepticisms are acceptable, but a vatic, pantheistic, or cosmic aura has generally been part of poetic practice, even when that aura is almost residual.[7] And this vatic aura is certainly part of long-poem practice, as at least Robert Duncan perpetually reminds us in his proposing cosmic architectures against chaos. Indeed, poetry will sometimes get enraptured with a near cousin—prophecy.

The noun "numbers" was (as we know) formerly used as an idiom to indicate poetry itself, when syllable number, meter, and other kinds of textual counting were vital to poetic practice. And these numbers still may make a background hum even when a poet does not evoke them. Numbers constitute an infinite sequence thoroughly cross-hatched and matted by computational properties and cultural allusions; hence, uses of numbers (for poets) have the interest of being finite and markable while deploying the allure of the infinite. By being made finite by pattern but infinite by their nature, numbers can support a poetics of boundlessness.

There are certain studies and treatises (including quasi-religious and mystical ones) that see numbers as somewhat magical features of the universe—perhaps scientifically verifiable ones, perhaps theoretically astonishing ones. Numbers may once have stood for certainty or confirmation of the organization of a material universe, outlined in poetic structure (as in Dante). Numbers now have a variety of different uses (rather than a single hegemonic one) within the same general vision of making links between a material universe and a specific text. Numbers may now be deployed as individual choices for patterning of textual material (as in Merrill's luscious plethora). Number systems in a poem may relate to the organic universe—evoking a specific asterism (in Mallarmé), fractal patterning (in Allen Fisher), or Fibonacci numbers (in several works of Silliman). Culturally traditional number patterns (in the form of allusions and structures) might be reused in a major act of "systems citation" (in Zukofsky) or reinterpreted for our time (in Eliot, in H.D.). No matter: they do stand for something interpretable/discussable and at the same time wonderful and pleasurable. All these traits of numbers, even mixed together, are a pool of possibility for poets. Hence, numbers become a goad/goal within a long poem and plausibly a refined game of necessity—high-minded with unifying stakes.

But finally why all this numerology? And if no fixed numerology, why the invention of a personal one, like counting words, sentences, and sections in procedural practices. It is to gain control of three things: space/poem size (form and formlessness), time/poem commitment, time it takes (threat of death and enough time; setting a boundary for potentially endless elaboration), along with methods to allude to cultural understandings. Numbers can help with all tasks. This numerology may also help solidify an ending, as in Zukofsky's *80 Flowers*, but it does not necessarily propel any.

DANTES IN ELIOT, H.D., ZUKOFSKY, ASHBERY

In what follows I discuss a few long poems making salient uses of Dante. These poems are quests—often precisely a quest to understand how the universe works, with the poets/heroes as specific individuals in the role of discoverer—a quest among a "many" to understand their position as a one, or a quest into the unknown to establish its principles—or more rarely to challenge those principles. If the universe is organized by ultimate numbers, sometimes the poem is cast as an exemplary or teaching model of this organization, making the poem and the universe coincide in goals. In poems that do not hearken to religious worldviews or to ultimates of traditionally upheld order, number can still helpfully suggest adequate order, good-enough order, the order allowing for an aesthetic poise that the universe itself may not fulfill—an advantage, always, of art. Beyond numbers, the general question animating all the examples in this section is what is gotten from Dante by the poets so thoroughly committed to using him that in many cases they have devoted huge poems to his example.

The answers to the question "Why Dante?" differ among the poets. Using that template is an homage to a major work, central to Western culture. Yet is not just the prestige of this choice. Some of the poets want to rehabilitate hegemonic Christianity or to offer modified versions of its spiritual seriousness. Some poets feel the loss of purpose and justice in modernity and attribute this to modernist skepticisms: there should be something to believe in, even as usefully open as "hope" or a better futurity, or humans may collapse. Some poets are fascinated with the intricacy, mechanisms, and sheer integration of the *Commedia* and want to engage with that aura. Some poets believe in the cluster of spiritual feelings, sacred uplift, and cultural evocations that have been one cultural function of poetry—achieved variously but always evocative. Borrowing from or tapping into Dante can satisfy, if not solve, some of these longings. Yet, at the same time, most of the poets discussed here make considerable modifications to his assumptions about the cosmos.

Despite its now significant clash of worldviews with whatever the secular world has unleashed, Dante's *Commedia* (written ca. 1306–21) became a model of Western cosmological ambitions expressed in the long poem, still culturally palpable and definitionally generative, even for Anglophone poetry. It is impossible to overestimate the fine integration of detail, numerological finesse, poetic elegance, and larger worldview of this magisterial work. The individuated nuances of highly specific characters expressing, discussing, defying, excusing, resuffering, sorrowing for the nature of their sins; the acute historical examples; the realistic yet allegorical image of the *contrapasso*[8]; the levels of self-recognition, including by writer Dante of his character Dante—all contribute to its intense finish and fullness. The *Commedia* makes a breathtaking "architecture at the edge of chaos"—the chaos of our experiential reality, the architecture in Dante being exacting and nuanced choices and doctrinal assurance gained.[9] Because of its intellectual and poetic authority, and its synthetic power (handling philosophy, theology, science, politics, society, and personal transformation in one work), contemporary Western socio-cosmological long poems often pay tribute to the vast influence of Dante's spiritual quest with its Christian framework.

Socio-cosmological long poems offer discussions that claim to penetrate the real, historical, cultural, or psycho-social world to some other universal, transformed, or "eternal" world with various properties, fundamentally to clarify the way the cosmos works. Hence, these socio-cosmological long poems tend in a spiritually eclectic, scientific, and secular direction over long modernity. Contemporary poems reframe Dante and his worldview both by spiritual evocations and by cosmological versions of materialist, secular polysemy (multiplicity of meanings), within an ethical compass. The problem becomes how then to construct a cosmological long poem *without* a systematic adhesion to existing theologies or teleologies yet evoking the persistence of such mythographic claims or the shadowy memory of such structures. Dante becomes an exoskeleton for this need, a scaffolding, suggestions of a "mythical method."[10]

An unfriendly critic might say the poets borrow the charisma of Dante's work to bolster the thinner (if earnest) worldviews of long modernity, or to resist "the immense panorama of futility and anarchy which is contemporary history."[11] Given the frayed theology of Logos in long modernity even for the more pious of these poets, evoking Dante becomes the sign or glyph of a relatively intact theology, and therefore Dante's theological-synthetic powers may offer talismans of coherence.[12] Or, conversely, Dante becomes the sign of cosmological poetic ambitions (irrespective of theology), and some of the particular motifs or topoi that he uses can get featured, even when a given modern-contemporary long poem neither manifests a Christian theology nor cares to. Thus, for both the more pious and the more secular twentieth- and twenty-first-century writers, Dante serves as far more than a learned or literary allusion or evocation of the generalized "sacred." He offers a matrix through which the cosmological ambitions of some modern poets get expressed.[13]

Judging from these selected examples, contemporary socio-cosmological long poems generally do not propound institutionalized, normative theologies but "replace" or even moot salvationist theologies with three secular and critical structures: nonbinarist logic (in H.D. and Ashbery), the historical materiality of language (in Louis Zukofsky's response to both Eliot and Dante), or a critique of Christianizing culture (a resistance, passim). Finally, Dante is used in poems of metamorphic fecundity—mythological in James Merrill's case, realistic in John Kinsella's. To make Dante's perfectly outrageous and enabling claim of the cultural work of his long poem took special understanding (via revelation or other interpretive convictions), saturation in theological debates, a serious level of contemporaneous scientific knowledge, and a lot of literary presumption (a.k.a. chutzpah). Given all these serious components and deploying Dante's example, long poems with emphasis on cosmological quest (in a generally Euro-Christian hegemony) become one privileged site to do much cultural work.

In a socio-cosmological poem, an investigative quester (sometimes on a depicted journey or in a vision) travels through the universe of weird geography and remade space and time seeking basic principles. These might involve findings about present, past, future, eternity, sanctified light, stars and other heavenly matter and inhabitants, or science-based light and creatures without heavenly evocations (as the Australian terrain in Kinsella). Eliot's *Four Quartets* is particularly and warily both real and beyond. In some of the poems, poets (and readers) are granted actual permission to enter and walk through this space, carefully guided (as in Dante); given visionary, out-of-time experiences after and during historical events—mainly war (in H.D. and Eliot); or repeatedly wafted into this special space by a bizarre prosthesis, like the Ouija board plus a reflective glass/mirror in Merrill. The space can also be the poem's odd "spatial architectures" entered via verbal construction, as in the secular *locus amoenus* investigated by the etymological dictionary and Linnaean taxonomy of the exemplary garden in Zukofsky's *80 Flowers*.

A socio-cosmological poem is pleasurable for its ambitious claims and for its waywardness as fabulously inventive and meditative. However, these poems generally proffer some ethics with their didactic findings. In Dante and Eliot, here and now are treated as a testing ground in which one makes, with free will, the existential choices that manifest one's adhesion to and one's humility before a definitive doctrinal answer.

The three distinctive zones that Dante visits are rarely replicated in toto in the modern and contemporary poems. Inferno is, for instance, often ruled out of consideration. Eliot is fully purgatorial—our real world is an extension of purgation, with redemptive hope but no sustained paradisiacal vision. Ashbery (in *Three Poems*) plays with evanescent traces of at least two of the three zones, each rapidly changing or blurring into another.[14] Merrill says explicitly there is no Inferno (and that his purgatory is paradisiacal and vice versa). H.D.'s *Helen* occurs in an amoral dream space vaguely purgatorial; in *Trilogy*, bliss (paradise) comes via breakthrough visions of mother goddesses occurring within the everyday that challenge patriarchal religious hegemony. Zukofsky's *80 Flowers* catalogs flowers, plants, and weeds in a real or plausible garden through his complex paradise of language with no question of further redemptive or mythic access to a Beyond. Glory lies in the pile-up of words themselves. Kinsella's work and the much shorter work of Blaser tolerate naming a section of their poems *Inferno*, but both authors remix the three sections in a non-Dantean order.

T. S. Eliot made no secret of his fascination with Dante as a universalizing nonsecular model; he wrote several essays on Dante, and his poetry is saturated with Dantean citations and allusions. The echoes in *Four Quartets* are so well documented that it may be strange again to note some: lucid Dantean similes, the rose and fire imagery; some distinctly knowledgeable citations; and the experiences of a dazzling light—a light much less prevalent in Eliot than in the often dazed and dazzled Dante, but with similarly uplifting goals. Among the few muted citations is an echo (in "East Coker" II) of the evocative "dark wood" beginning the *Commedia* (*Inferno* I). The sections of *Four Quartets* are structurally numerological and match each other formally, with parallel poetic modes and themes in each correspondent section—a repetitious tactic either solemn or oppressive. The poem's balanced "fours" are well known: elements, seasons, humors, Trinity plus Mary, and the paradox of five sections in this fourness (this, an allusion to a Beethoven Quartet). The "fifth" element, some extra or excess, often concerns language in an insistently humble tone, emphasizing Eliot's earnest "trying" (or trying earnestness) to tell the reader what it is like to journey toward "stillness," with salvation only hoped for.

Eliot's worldwide status as a master writer demands his own insistent denials of pride in worldly success in favor of patient attempts to write in a style plain enough to exfoliate the sense of spiritual reverence, or penitential "waiting." The poem's yearning and painful hopes are not concealed, and its satisfactions are low-key, rarely—but strikingly—epiphanic, its style flat, as direct as possible, its diction a traditional ritual or prayerlike sound glossing the right actions for reverence. From this use of Dante, Eliot represents both the humility of tempering his status as a modern master and a penitential yearning beyond modernism. When faced with the Dantean achievement, honored in the last words of the *Quartets* when the flames of purgation are "knotted" into the rose of revelation, Eliot can achieve only the palm of perpetual "exploration."[15]

Eliot's depiction of a confrontation with Dante—Section II of "Little Gidding"—is charged with passionate feeling, recognitions—and authority. In twenty-four unrhymed "terza rima"-style tercets (alternating "unrhymed feminine and masculine terminations"), the figures call to each other in a dim purgatorial urban zone, a "dead patrol,"[16] just after bombardment, for the speaker is a civil defense worker during WWII.[17]

This Dante figure has the downturned face (or brow lowered—[*chinato*, (inf.) *chinare*]), a description (and Italian word) repeated strikingly in the *Commedia*, mainly applied to the character Dante whenever he is ashamed, pensive, or very respectful of others. The word signals Dante's increasing, necessary humility and his intense thoughtfulness about this staggering journey; it also signals his shame at bursts of lust. It is particularly telling that Beatrice, in her strong-minded words to Dante upon their confrontation in *Purgatorio* XXXI, tells him to "lift up his head [beard]," that is, to stop this "humble downward glance"—his gesture is getting to be a crutch; now it is time to look at things full face.[18] By noting, "I fixed upon the down-turned face," Eliot signals his intimate sense of Dante's socio-spiritual struggles.[19]

Eliot's Dante manifests a hard-won humility concerning his "thoughts and theory" and his "last year's words."[20] Yet Dante's long speech, that is, Eliot's to himself in this haunted passage, is strikingly bitter, concerning someone who has outlived his ability to take pleasure in the quirks and vagaries of human existence. This sentiment is quite uncharacteristic of Dante's wonder, curiosity, fear, awe, and empathy. Dante's Dante-character generally observes; he questions, he manifests a patient, courteous (occasionally tentative) approach to the figures whom he confronts; only in *Inferno* must he learn to loathe, judge, and completely reject the sometimes pitiful and plaintive, sometimes assertive and bullying souls.

In Eliot, in contrast, the figure, a "Dante+Swift" amalgam (an accepted identification) experiences severe self-loathing. This passage is like a curse, as if spoken by one of the damned. In the course of this imprecation on "bitter tastelessness" of life and "impotence of rage," the figure talks of shame, harm done to others, and therefore his agony of unworthiness despite his enduring the high regard and respect of others. This is Eliot's striking self-judgment. The speech ends abruptly with acceptance of "that refining fire" of purgation, with neither desire nor yearning but as a fact.[21] However, the Eliot figure is not eager to slip back into this fire but resigned to purgation as a necessary fate, not as an honor and the soul's desire, positive emotions characteristic of Dante's Arnaut Daniel (in a passage in *langue d'oc* that Eliot knew well). Unworthiness is Eliot's motif.

Dantean too is the odd word "sempiternal" in "Little Gidding," in deliberately awkward lines about "Midwinter spring" as "Sempiternal though sodden towards sundown" (the "though" is wonderful).[22] This uncommon word comes right out of Dante; it appears six or seven times in the *Commedia*, mainly in *Paradiso*.[23] Eliot had to be paying serious attention to Dante's text to isolate it. Dante scholar Robert Hollander glosses: "sempiternal"—"having had a beginning in time but lasting ever after" (in the Dartmouth Dante Project); a regular dictionary will simply say "always (semper) eternal," which is hardly as informative. For the pious, the word defines God's fundamental creation and potential human redemption by indicating the intentional continuity between time and eternity. For religions believing in an afterlife, the word "sempiternal" expresses the passage of the soul from time to a timeless zone. Yet with the phoneme "sem" in English encrypting "semi" (rather than "semper"), the word also sums up the strange half-in, half-out pressures of Eliot's poem, the barest glimmers of hope in a relentlessly exacerbated penitence, and it sums up his uncompromising adherence to a Dantean—that is, a Christian—theology.

The Eliot-related *80 Flowers* by Louis Zukofsky shows a world-ranging goal palpable in this statement of array: "To record and elate [*sic*] for all time" in poetry "based on nothing less than the world, the entire humanly known world," another distinctive statement concerning "everything" in long poems.[24] Zukofsky examined Western culture incessantly, determinedly, arrogantly, always vowing to "better the instruction."[25] Hence he drew on Dante, most visibly in the 1934 double "Mantis" based on Dante's sestina "Al poco giorno."[26] More relevant here, he betters the instruction by testing both Dante and the quite Christianizing Eliot, culminating in a late-career socio-cosmological long poem with allusions to Dantean numerology and playing resistantly in this hegemonic, loosely Christian field.

Zukofsky's *80 Flowers*, a longish poem from 1978, is built on a procedural numerology (a "word-count" tactic is its metrics).[27] His goals are consistent with other contemporary uses of numbers, using poetry to examine traditional beliefs and doing so via traditional (but remixed, rearticulated) numerologies.

As H.D. did, Zukofsky absorbed Christian and Pythagorean numbers and at least some uses of the Kabbalah, for a triple-threat synthesis. His own work is indebted to a secular Judaism—an understudied cultural source in modernity.

Syncretic numerological tactics might be likened, as I noted, to "the mythical method" that Eliot proposed from Joyce's *Ulysses*, a scaffolding of sorts, in Joyce constructing a mock epic, a fondly realist, writerly tour de force version of *The Odyssey*. At least in Eliot and H.D., the numerological method and the "mythical method" merge and bolster each other as referring to major cultural mythologies, supporting the outcomes of both poems. The relationship among number and poem begins to shift (change? become interestingly unstable?) in Zukofsky's cunning last work; *80 Flowers* (plus an introductory stanza), is a work of intense numerology based on the number nine.[28]

This partly readable work is written in 81 hermetic poems compressing information on flowers (and a few weeds), as if it were a botanical scrapbook of verbally pressed species. Each stanza contains eight lines made up of exactly five words, without punctuation (except for some hyphenated compound words that drive some actual word counts higher). This is a word-count segmentivity. Thus, "every word occurs with equal intensity."[29] This is an odd effect, generating condensed asyntactic opacity, a democracy, or demos, of words but not a populist one. The intricate richness of the natural elements accurately but *very* thickly described becomes a verbal ecology of materials offering a quasi-scientific, etymological, and folkloric impasto pattern built loosely on Pythagorean and Kabbalistic interpretive encodings.[30] The work's word total is 3,240, which, added up by numerological (lateral, or poet's) arithmetic, gives a Dantean nine, just as the actual number of poems, eighty-one—8+1—does.

Zukofsky deploys traditional numerologies yet separates them from traditions by verbal finesse, creating personal multiplications of their confirming powers. He thereby applies these numbers to himself, as if his life were a collaboration with culture, and his poem a numerological-verbal synthesis of condensed worldviews.[31] Zukofsky's insistent personal-cultural use of numerology is particular and even obtrusive, but it inspires and predicts the procedural numerologies of some contemporary long poems like Silliman's and Hejinian's.

Not trying to replicate the world descriptively but to make its own secular paradise based on the realness of a thing, and of the various words used to refer to that thing, *80 Flowers* is the distilled essence of a hundred books or more, citing from diaries, folklore, encyclopedias of horticulture, dictionaries of several languages, commercial catalogs of Breck's Bulbs from the late 1970s, guides to wildflowers, herbals, classics of English literature (Shakespeare, Milton) and of Greek and Latin literature, including natural histories and poetry.[32]

It reveals poeticity on steroids. The work is a material collage of language bits with their individual origin in the verbal accounts of a real thing.

This work becomes a humanist's kabbalistic playground. It uses decided languages of reference to put together myopically exact words and phonemes so that each poem and the whole work have grid solidity. Specific botanical objects are designated by words one might use—not so much to "describe" them as to conjure their materiality and their accumulated lore. Words are chosen first for their material qualities (their poeticity)—their sound, their syllable count adding up appropriately to the appropriate number. The words do not conjure a picture but give an overload of polysemic qualities and vectors of semantic meanings. In many ways the bounded "thing" (a plant) is swamped by intense excess. The language becomes hypermeaningful—a babbling stanza of words and things, words as things, and words as words, a circus of poeticity and semantic reference. Both individual words and the fixed numbers create a condensed encyclopedism of the segment—each word and the grid of all. This work, antiabstract to the point of abstraction, antispiritual but creating a transcendent materialism, is one apogee of Zukofsky's literary claim on culture.

Zukofsky had maintained a career-long resistance (both antic and bitter) to T. S. Eliot, who, in both the pre- and post-War II period, became the spokesman for (Anglican-brand) Christianity within late modernism. In this status Eliot's *Four Quartets* and its powerful literary popularity play a defining but not exclusive role. Zukofsky's distaste for the hegemony of Eliot's impact on literary culture is visible, though in a typically concealed way. It is the undertone of Zukofsky's dour remarks in 1946 rejecting the then quite prevalent insistence on "myth" and mythic readings encouraged by the New Criticism, as inspired by Eliot's essays, and instead proposes, in Zukofsky's allusive statement, that the littlest, function-filled, ignorable/ignoble words as words (specifically "a" and "the"—the indefinite and definite articles) have epochal and epic (that is, long-poem and cosmic) force. His not-incidental titles of *"A"* and the earlier "Poem Beginning 'The'" become exhibits A and B.[33]

Zukofsky consciously resisted the allegories and symbols of Christianized literary culture propelled in Eliot's later period precisely by the *Quartets* and by Eliot's many heartfelt but insistent essays on "universalizing" redemptive Anglicanism. Thus, in what I am calling his socio-cosmological long poem, Zukofsky read back (to a Dantean Logos), precisely through the incarnation-professing *Four Quartets*, and attempted (quixotically) to pivot culture away from Eliot and to overturn the *Quartets* by a materialist interpretation of incarnation, using Eliot's own images to precipitate transcendent theologies back into matter.

Zukofsky's hermetic *80 Flowers* thus certainly, if obliquely, responded to Eliot's *Four Quartets*, for his poem is infused with Eliotic motifs of time/thyme, fire, the rose, the dance (man-and-woman), and the light. Each famous image in the *Quartets* gets proposed, in some studiedly realist counterpart, in the Zukofsky poem. That is, Zukofsky "encounters" Dante at least via Eliot's Christianized interpretation of culture, and he confronts that cosmos with an antitranscendent, materialist poem, a work—to borrow descriptive terminology from Maria Damon—of "Jewish hyperverbalism."[34] Zukofsky's thematic contribution takes some Dantean numbers and his horticultural knowledge to pinpoint a "liveforever" rose-shaped flower completely non-Christian in its cultural meanings.

The fourth/fifth poem of *80 Flowers*'s grid represents the plant called "liveforever," its name suggesting notions of redemption and an afterlife.[35] It is, in this reading, his way of proposing answers to and uses of both Eliot and Dante—or, to say it otherwise, to answer Eliot (with Dante assumed). Liveforever (the flower "built" in the poem, which is not cited here), is the familiar rosette-like succulent whose Latin name is *Sempervivum tectorum*: the first part of that term meaning "always alive."[36] As early as "A"-2, Zukofsky described liveforever as parallel to the Rose of Paradiso: "leaf around leaf ranged around the center."[37] This is an exact transposition of Dante's climactic Rose to the green succulent. Zukofsky critics Leggott and Scroggins both agree that "liveforever" is an image of secular "paradise" for Zukofsky.[38] Zukofsky knew his Dante—and used Dante for his own ends.

We have seen a version of "sempervivum" before. In *Four Quartets*, Eliot had chosen the word "sempiternal" to indicate finally and endlessly in the eternal, as a way of alluding to redemption and to Dante's Rose of eternity. Extending this dialogue, Zukofsky also paid particular attention to Eliot's use of the Rose, this word, and its meaning. Of the two succulents included in *80 Flowers*, Zukofsky chooses the word "sempiternal" to describe one and *Sempervivum* for the other.[39] In either form the ever-green, multipetaled alternative "rose"/rosette, is his Jewish-secular response to Christian redemptive claims about living forever. Such a life forever occurs in the Christian world only through baptism in Christ and is symbolized by the Rose of the redeemed. Zukofsky replies that only through lettristic art, only through the logos of intractable language-as-matter and the exact verbal evocation of these precise plants that never lose their green do we achieve paradise and (perhaps literary) immortality.

In a tricky literalization of Christian thought, incarnation (small "i") works *for* Zukofsky. He makes this concept into a notable secular claim. The concept of the incarnate holds, in his view, for every single word. That is, no one entity (thing) or word for that entity like Christ/Jesus/redeemer is made flesh any more than any other thing or its word. They are all material flesh and material word, flesh as word. This is Zukofsky's secular Hebraicized interpretation of redemptive logos (word made flesh); his is a historically based, accumulative sense of the force of all words as embodied, as "awe-inspiring" precisely because material and written in letters themselves considered as matter. Indeed, some Hebrew creation stories put the creation of the world and the creation of letters/numbers as simultaneous—both were made as matter by YHWH. In Kabbalah, a Jewish mysticism, the Torah—written in living letters—coexists with God at creation.[40]

That interpretive possibility too points to a cosmology of incipience, not fulfillment. If there is "redemption" in this system, it is via exacting use of the matter of language in endless commentary on its own potential. The Zukofskian mode of socio-spiritual poesis makes "world" cocreated with and coexistent with words. In this contrast the confrontation between a Christian incarnational-transcendent theology and a secular Jewish incarnational-material *poesis* could not be clearer. The cosmic cycle of the seasons in *80 Flowers* is celebrated not as a cycle of redemptive time, as in spiritual calendars, but as a real cycle of gardening and, like language itself in a humanistic and material mode, built of texts about plants through many languages, discourses, and centuries. Each stanza is an intense thicket of matter (that is, of words).

Zukofsky's words are deictic matter pointing at themselves and outward to a matted weave of citation, descriptors, and myths—all textually valid, adequate bits of language without any theological loftiness. And since all humans have language, complex syntax, and verbal traditions, all potentially are already in that kind of materialist "heaven." In contrast, Dante's masterly array of *humilitas* tropes reveals that language becomes inadequate at the moment of the electrifying unrepresentable glory of the end of *Paradiso*.

Zukofsky and John Ashbery as well, in their Dantean forays, offer a sense of cosmic powers via the praxis of language.[41] Ashbery transposes the question "What are the ultimate structures and meanings of the cosmos?" into "What are the human rhetorics for spiritual understandings?"—that is, moving from doctrines or reverence to languages, idioms, and dictions. Zukofsky asks how can the matter of the cosmos be signaled in words. Both offer poetic studies in various pluralist, cultural, philosophic, or linguistic modes to plumb the socio-cosmological—with strongest emphasis on the languages used to create and sustain these questions, without announcing traditional answers.

In Eliot's *Four Quartets* and in both H.D.'s *Trilogy* and *Helen in Egypt*, the geography is a mix of real spaces (called "Egypt" or "London" or "Burnt Norton") and inward spaces of memory and meditation; finally the real is transcended by the visionary and contemplative and/or made *really* real only because of infusions of the sacred. Logos in Eliot is incarnational; in H.D.'s *Helen* it is psychoanalytic but archetypal. In H.D.'s main long poems, Dante is not seen as a character (as he was in Eliot's "Little Gidding"), nor are his hierarchies and geographies alluded to (as in Ezra Pound's Dantesque Hell Cantos), but her major poems are fundamentally socio-cosmological, particularly in their revisions of two key mytho-religious narratives of Western tradition.

The bridge between H.D.'s two long poems is the Beatrice-like figure of the Lady, inspiration to troubadours and other poets, dreamed by H.D., then realized in *Trilogy*, and palpable as the contemplative, sensual hero in *Helen in Egypt*. This emphasis emerges in her manuscript notes on reading *La Vita Nuova*.[42] The works form a double long poem, constructing a counterfactual Western tradition based on a gender critique of magisterial Christian and classical Greek texts. H.D. invents the Western tradition that we don't have (one she felt was articulated secretly, hermetically in Dante), and the one, in her ethical-cultural terms, that we should have.

H.D. focuses on heterodox interpretations that Dante had suggested sub rosa for Beatrice—she is an imitatio Christi, she is a priest and confessor (female roles still forbidden within Catholicism), she is a Dante-canonized saint, and she embodies the spirit of eros—at least for others.[43] In contrast, in Dante's *Commedia*, erotic yearning toward Beatrice is shown as gradually sublimated—that achievement is one goal of his quest. In Dante the key change is clear: he must shift from seeing figures like Beatrice (and Matilda and others—even women in hell) as objects of erotic longing to appreciating Beatrice as a teacher, guide, saint, and Christian priestess. Thus, the force of Love is sublimated and transformed from body to spirit. In contrast H.D. takes this female figure and further enlarges her functions, as sublimely pensive-intellectual *and* sublimely erotic, a critical expansion of her place in Western mythology. The science for both questing journeys is psychoanalysis with its sense of unfixed, mobile genders and desires.

H.D. also produces alternative outcomes for Homeric narratives, in which the classic relationships of mythic characters are loosened and dissolved into a "subtle genealogy" that reexamines the matter of Troy, particularly its representation of male bellicosity, trickster ferocity, and hero-cult behaviors.[44] She turns these epic narrative materials into a constantly metamorphosing meditative quest, thus heavily transforming the founding Western epic of the Trojan War.

H.D.'s work is set in an indeterminate zone of aftermath, the "dead zone" of modern purgatorial poems, in which the characters are both posthumous and living. Helen and Achilles primarily, but also Paris, investigate their long mythic histories and cultural meanings as if they have become readers of their own books. They engage in long, slow-motion changes and transvaluations. Who they were and who they will become differ enormously, as in an idealized psychoanalysis where transformation is propelled by interpretation—whether reading a hieroglyph or recalibrating the stories found both in one's own and in cultural memory. This is how the structure A and not-A works in H.D.'s narrative: each character becomes its own opposite, often a fused contradiction, or a faceted figure of selves, not one fixed "epic" identity. No one of her changed characters has one sole marked trait active in the plot.

A certain narrative ambiguity results—it is hard to tell what is happening, since events will be A and not-A at the same time (a proposition and its exact opposite), and in the present and not, simultaneously. The reader's sense of sometimes stupefying multiplicity (polylogue-style) increases because Achilles, Paris, *and* Theseus, are all said, in one of H.D.'s erotic trifectas, to be former lovers of Helen, each with his pensive story. The work is based on the *topos* of remembering; various stories are told, retold, then told a third time, as the dramatis personae shift their functions (from lover to father; from seductress to priestess). Her characters reinterpret their stories each time the stories are told. There is no villain—love and strife (Eros-Eris in the mythography) are in constant dialogic exchanges.

Similarly, but with a claim of a clear finding, the coequality of the binary genders is her other remaking of Western mythology. The three parts of H.D.'s *Trilogy* construct meditative narratives testing patriarchal or hegemonic cosmogony through which female figures emerge to take their rightful places as goddesses and prophets. A monotheistic God ("Amen") is a guarantor of H.D.'s wondering, wandering universe, but this patriarchal god becomes generally androgynous or feminized. H.D. recalibrates our mythic stories and sacred texts, our theologies, and epics. In her view, we have misinterpreted cosmic meanings in ways neither "feminine"/"female" nor polytheistic enough. For *Trilogy*, the spiritually enriching visions are the Mother-Child composite of care/blessing, and a generously erotic and subtly wise figure of Mary Magdalene.

H.D. also deploys a numerological focus in *Trilogy*, engaging with significant numbers, counting to three times 43 sections in limpid couplets. Her total of 129 sections illustrates poet's multiplication, since 4 × 3 is 12 and 3 × 3 is 9—perhaps thus 129 becomes the number of sections. Numerology also underwrites one section's synthesis, for seven angels, and three emanations of Mary make 10—the godhead number in Pythagoras, here combining revised male figures and fully acknowledged female forces. As with all poet-numerologists, her work with these structuring numbers supports her themes.

Trilogy's second section, "Tribute to the Angels," rests playfully—and with aplomb—on a plot in which seven male angels are celebrated, with a bell tolled from a steeple or campanile, and are carefully presented in this drama with names coming from the three Abrahamic religious traditions. Yet as these hierarchic or patriarchal angels are named, the mother goddess in various guises irrupts, shows herself, and is described as crucial and fundamental. These epiphanic appearances of Mary themselves correspond to the parts of the caduceus, disassembled by H.D., into its three constituent symbols: indicating religion, healing, and art—all powers of females in culture that have been obscured and that this visionary poem makes visible.[45] These *Magna Mater* Mary figures appear in three guises: first as a throbbing breastlike jewel transforming poison alchemically to health, and second as a branch of a tree inexplicably flowering after being burned in a bombing raid. The very striking third "revelation" of this section shows Mary as a gentle, unassuming "psyche" figure—soul or butterfly—holding a "blank book" of future revelations. The book's being blank, ready, and open, not closed makes a very striking proposition religiously, aesthetically, and ethically.

For section 3, "The Flowering of the Rod" presents a new part of the Gospels, an intricate story, biblically based, about two jars of myrrh (one for Christ's birth and the other for his entombment), and about a confrontation between the wise prostitute Mary Magdalene and the magus Kasper, a principled figure of male hieratic authority who is made, in the narrative, to acknowledge, as intellectually and spiritually capable, this formerly despised and sexualized female character. H.D. attends to the analytic-spiritual modernism whose goal is a renovated sense of syncretic Eleusinian Christianity, an expansive comparative-religions or Frazerian perspective proposing a Christian polytheism, a position that also fascinated Pound. Examining stories and seeing resemblances across cultures (Egyptian, Greek, and Mithraic, as well as in the New Testament and Hebrew Scriptures), H.D. will find "oneness" by syncretizing them. This is a poem about the Abrahamic tradition (Judaism-Christianity-Arab [barely, or hardly Islam]) and about the polytheisms that influenced Christianity.

H.D. separates the John of Revelation with his codification of the *closed* book, from Christ's radical, repeated instruction to "make all things new." Pound's modernist axiom in H.D.'s allusion infuses her socio-cosmological engagement. In her probe H.D. finds the historical and ideological contradictions in Christianity, particularly in the split between establishing an antifemale dogma (in John of Revelation and in Paul) and affirming the female parity historically evident in early Christianity and its absorption of Great Mother cults of the ancient world. H.D. argues for a transforming acknowledgment of female spiritual power, with permission given, in her view, by Jesus himself. She has thus considerably extended Dante—and Christianity—to heterodoxy.

Odd as it may seem, the same fundamental A and not-A (both-both) structure as saturates late H.D, especially in *Helen*, is central to a work in which John Ashbery has been magnetized by Dante, among many other spiritual writers. The intense waves of metamorphic meanings as the form of the universe and an uncanny journey to the realization of indeterminacy drive Ashbery's *Three Poems*, three prose works as one mid-length long poem, presenting philosophic meditations without one single philosophic system, but loose bits of many. Socio-cosmological questions abound within a questing pulse of statements always incipient, never settled. With uncanny rhetorical evocations, Ashbery layers together a "pilgrim's progress" (without progress), allusions to historical eras and quests, to famous texts and religious narratives in a mode of metamorphic writing in which the very sentences change, evanesce, and modulate just as soon as they are read—even during the reading. That is, his book mimics these texts in their pious rhetorics but re-creates them as works of *un*certainty.

Yet even without answers at all, the questions treated are fundamental: "what are we to do here and how did we get here [. . .] and the ever-present issue of our eternal salvation." That last is perhaps tongue-in-cheek, even though "the impossibility of reconciling their own ends with those of the cosmos" perplexes those whose purgatorial journeying is the topic—with plenty of Dantean allusions.[46] The work is philosophically porous; although by every allusion—to the dead, to a journey, to a universe of understanding that seems to be around every corner—it is a socio-cosmological poem. Yet the work unfixes that mode of poem by refusing any settled understandings, especially propelled by a characteristic rhetorical floating.

The Ashbery work crosses *La Vita Nuova* and the *Commedia* (with trace cadences of Wordsworth, Shelley, Frost, Eliot, Auden, and many others) in its allegorical journey trying to understand death, the good life, one's sexuality, how to write, the true way, the new spirit. This tricksy work sounds like a firmly religious or spiritual text, particularly when just a few words are cited out of their actual charmingly mobile contexts. *Three Poems* subverts teleologies, single truths, affirmations, and constructions of any system, philosophic or religious. The work is drastically inconclusive and this-worldly, although its genre motifs and its tonality signal a meditative, spiritual realm: psalms, hymns, prayers are palpable. The work achieves a religious resonance without any telos but its own endlessly comic/cosmic unspoolings.

The work perhaps reveals "an event of cosmic beatitude," the author mocks genially. But not, he clearly states, to the protagonist who prefers the "reverse side": "the ability to take up these tattered enigmas again and play with them until something like a solution emerged from them, only to grow dim at once and fade like an ignis fatuus."[47] The human "playing" is the point. In this apparently spiritual work, the protagonist abjures beatitude, finality, and telos in wonderful acts of worldly wit. Ashbery is not so much seeking "the sacred" as teasing its discourses.

Ashbery takes up one of Robert Frost's touching but now banalized poems ("The Road Not Taken") to generate the same A and not-A worldview as H.D. did, where Eros and Eris are not opposing antagonists but shape a continuous, interactive loop. Ashbery's speaker, half-paraphrasing Frost, postulates a fork in the road, and you take "the less promising," then, when "you had a good idea where it led," you come back "to investigate the more tangled way" (a clear allusion to the beginning of *Commedia*), whereupon you discover that "the two branches [of the road] were joined."[48] That binarist opposition of A and not-A, so vital to Frost, is nonexistent for Ashbery's "road," and any absolutist/ultimate choice within quest is irrelevant. While Frost's speaker picks one road and memorably moralizes it, Ashbery's speaker is able to take both roads without distinguishing either or getting any more noble because of a particular choice. Both ways have been explored. Not only are both ways right, the roads are actually the same. (This is certainly not Dante's view—or Frost's.) This has many suggestive ethical implications, including for sexuality.

Further, throughout, Ashbery's sentences are not cumulative and hierarchic, even though many are distinctively hypotactic. He produces a flow of language that never settles on anything and metamorphoses continuously. This metamorphic panache is notable with phrasal tactics of segmentivity that turn quickly within sentences. So any fixed position or finding is dissolved, negated, undone, and then it, or a similar position returns, only to be negated again.

In any binarist, theological, or simply logical worldview, A and not-A (a proposition and its opposite) cannot exist in the same space. In Dante you cannot be both in hell and also in heaven; at the exact post-Apocalyptic end of time, it's one or the other. You cannot be in purgatory, either; post-Apocalypse, that site has been phased out. Either-Or Judgment is final. Yet in Ashbery and H.D.'s *Helen in Egypt*, their antibinarist doubleness, tolerance—even endlessness—provide strong statements about the mysteries of cosmos without such finality.

Both Ashbery, by virtue of his allusions, and certainly H.D., by virtue of her overarching commitments, exist within the expanded field of Christian worldviews. Yet neither affirms anything like an apocalyptic or transcendent ending for their Dantean, mythopoetic works. The ends of H.D.'s works are usually understated, low-key but reverberating and patient epiphanies. Ashbery figures his quite short final section as "The Recital"—a performance ending (at least for the moment) as an audience leaves the hall; it could be a musical performance or some kind of rhetorical elocutionary performance—perhaps even an allusion to Mallarmé's performance notes in "Le Livre"—but it is determinedly secular.

THE DANTES OF MERRILL, KINSELLA, AND BLASER

> Everything in Dante knew its place.
> In this guidebook of yours, how do you tell
> Up from down? [. . .]
>
> James Merrill, *The Changing Light at Sandover*

The poems clustered in this section deploy Dantes bleached of any institutional theology yet invested in the socio-cosmological—seeing our world in relation to the principles of the universe and contemporary ethics. However, in these three poets, Dante's poem does not remain as such; it gets reinterpreted in ways that often undermine Dante's findings. While both James Merrill's mythic-baroque *The Changing Light at Sandover* (1982; coda, 1992) and John Kinsella's realist and eco-intricate *Divine Comedy: Journeys through a Regional Geography* (2008) use Dante as inspiration and model, the metamorphic fecundity of an Ovidian ethos of permanent transformation undergirds these works. This perspective concertedly recuperates (actually, twists) Dante for a worldview opposite to his. Robin Blaser's short essay-poem of 1997 (revised 2006) "Great Companion: Dante Alighieri" celebrates, with another critique, the explorer Odysseus as an ethical touchstone, although he was set, by Dante, deep down in *Inferno* for committing treachery and inciting impious overreach.

All undertake writing midrash (gloss, interpretive commentary) on Dante. In two of these three explicitly Dantean works, readers are repeatedly sent into a naturalized socio-cosmological space, particularly into a poet's meditation, but in Merrill they enter visionary magic in a dramatic format. Kinsella studies (and describes working) his family's acres with their challenging Australian fauna, flora, and social history, and he struggles with the languages in which to render a vulnerable ecology and the depredations wrought on it. Blaser meditates within a lifetime "library" of Dantean questions and contemporary philosophy. In all three works, naturalized, secularized, and reinvested Dantes emerge. Each poem is differently critical, yet each pays homage to the world-ranging scope and ethical transformations that all three find within their now nontheological Dante. For this section, that point of comparability overrides the considerable divergences among these poets in nationality, stylistic traditions, and the tones and modes of their poems. One is comedic-operatic; another complexly plain-spoken yet thickly descriptive; a third anecdotal-meditative. Yet all three poets readdress Dante and bring him into their secular and/or metamorphic universes. These divergent, intensive uses of their talismanic Dantes need to be examined.

Dante's triple canticles are precisely what each uses to turn Dante's findings into their opposite. No matter the tone of these very different works, Dante's structure, the distinctive separation of the postmortem world into three zones with one path to a redemptive outcome is, for these three authors, a cover story for an opposing narrative, a nontheological cosmic confrontation with ethics, materiality, language, and a humane world. In short, these contemporary transformations all recast a world-poem, to (lovingly, admiringly, resistantly) oppose or pivot from what Dante is best known for—exact and only slightly ambiguous placement of all people into three zones of judgment. Two recast him by Ovidian worldviews, and one by reinterpreting Odysseus.

Dante himself had enormous and telling respect for Ovid, probably his main classical source for mythological knowledge, citing him throughout the *Commedia*, and placing Ovid in Limbo (waiting, with other pagan authors, for redemption by fiat). So why does Dante stage a long intertextual scene outdoing Ovid's descriptive powers in a canto that deals with stealing?

To appreciate why Dante goes mano a mano with Ovid for a considerable portion of *Inferno* XXV, we have to understand why he must (and does) win the struggle to subordinate that tempting polytheist whose "science" of creation involves magical, psychologically telling, and verbally dazzling metamorphoses. That Dante combats and bests Ovid's project to engineer and describe transformation is crucial to Dante's worldview of Christian/ethical transformation. This is framed in *Inferno* XXV by Dante's signal to "watch" what is happening—which is rather a signal to appreciate a key passage and his skill both at representing metamorphosis and his crucial resistance to it. Dante then launches into forty-five lines of descriptive brilliance, a long single passage for this poem, in which two robbers have their individual body-shapes stolen by each other, slowly melting into, and each becoming the other, as a just punishment. At the midpoint of this metamorphosis, Dante thereupon challenges: "I do not envy him; [Ovid] never did / transmute two natures, face to face, so that / both forms were ready to exchange their matter"—as Dante himself just showed he could do.[49]

Mandelbaum notes that this is an example of the "literary *topos* of outdoing," affirming that Dante's own "ability to describe it—and, implicitly, to invent it—surpasses" Ovid's.[50] However, since this outdoing *topos* could have been employed at any point in Dante's work, why is it placed deeply down in the sinful levels of *Inferno*? And why is this "outdoing" not simply stealing (taking on Ovid's tempting rhetoric as Dante's act of showing off or display), but an exemplification? Dante is not simply besting Ovid in the jealous jousts of authorship but ridding readers of any attraction to Ovid's considerable charms.

Ovid's skill at propounding transformation as a never-ending generative principle is simply intolerable and must be challenged within the *Commedia*'s Christian teleology. We need to arrive at a beautiful, permanent, and everlasting (untransformable) space to have this whole vision work. Having noted that Ovid "only" changed one creature (say, a nubile nymph) into another item (like a non-rape-able tree), Dante takes another eleven tercets[51] to change the sinners back temporarily, so that the cruel (at least disgusting) process of "stealing" each other's bodies goes on perpetually as a fit punishment.

To what force can creation be attributed? The (proper) answer is God, not prolific, polymorphic nature motivated by gods' (mainly) and sometimes goddesses' peremptory sex-power drives. And when does metamorphosis stop if it is let loose as creative urgency? Dante's horrified answer—*never*—is why metamorphosis gets depicted as a punishment for hubris, a torture, not amusing or helpful in emergencies of sexual threats, or even consoling, but rather a never-ending dreadfulness that no one should desire or admire. Dante's implicit question: Is such transformation to be the basis of the universe in which we are condemned to live? We get persuaded that the answer must be "No!" Metamorphoses—the potential for endless (or naturally dynamic) changes—as fundamental principles of biology and geophysics—are anathema to the universe in which one overriding sin is given one fitting and exemplary punishment (in *Inferno*) or one specific, sin-appropriate penance (in *Purgatorio*). Things must end in justice, not in perpetual change, ambiguities of judgment, or ethical relativism. Ovidian transformation resists a universe of final judgment.

Dante wants every incident to argue for, to propel a "Christianized" universe. Hence, Dante does to Ovid—challenging and displacing him—what these three modern Dantean long-poem writers do to Dante. Merrill, Kinsella, and Blaser use Dante's vision to propose a secular universe of the metamorphic, undoing Dante's worldview while writing significant homages to him. Merrill's homage is particularly striking when he includes, close to the ends of all his three sections, precisely as Dante had, a canto in terza rima (a difficult feat in rhyme-limited English) and closes, as did Dante, on the word "stars" (*stelle*). The last of these (a paradise) takes place in Venice at the poignant viewing of a Maya Deren film, as DJ and JM, with a mockingly ironic shrug, skip out of the hyperturgid theoretical discussion "On the confusing terms: Dance, Gods, Time, Stars."[52] At this moment, "confusing," "luminous," "prolific," "tolerant," and "dazzling"—the whole of Merrill's poem—become synonyms.[53]

These modern long (and nanorific) poems—no matter how playful, earnest, or noble—do center themselves on the *Commedia*, honoring the intense cultural importance of a work whose main premises they reject as either plausible theology or future history. All these poems are overtly, intelligently, and lovingly based on Dante with citation, imitation, deep allusions. But they displace his findings to a secular world, scientific/scientistic, metamorphic, and contingent—and ethical. Their modern attraction to the permanently transforming universe, with natural limits set mainly by matter (or, for Merrill, with no limits because of magic), not by metaphysical miracles arranged by God, wrests Dante from his own theology. And yet their fascinated and respectful acknowledgment of the *Commedia*'s power and prestige fuels their poems. Trying to exist in a socio-cosmological world, mainly a secular world, and yet to feel spiritual urgency and, for Merrill, creative friskiness creates that complex and generative set of contradictions of secular spirituality/spiritual secularity characteristic of our long modernity. For these three poets, Dante's structures of controlled plethora are admirable; Dante's end and rationale are set aside.

What happens if one's cosmological "system" no longer appears to be eternal fixity but involves metamorphosis, shims, and wiggle room, claims of vital structural numbers that then proliferate as in Merrill? The interplay and contradictions between conceptions of the cosmos as a fixed orderly thing and conceptions of the cosmos as wobbling forces in some wondrous but not fully explicable changeable consolidation, and then facing our world wounded by human depredation—these characterize the cosmological poems of long modernity.

Seriocomic, *The Changing Light at Sandover* is sheer proliferation presenting this fundamental conflict between order and chaos layered together, from God B [Bio]—hardly a monotheistic deity—to angels, to the pentagrammic Powerful Five, various prophets, all in a culturally allusive plethora both fabulous and generally unsortable. And sometimes a sense of "science" or a version (accurate, peculiar, or dubious) of "nature" plays in Merrill's poems—for him the natural and the supernatural are bound together in an almost unreadable but joyous zone.

In *Changing Light*, James Merrill writes an engaging baroque opera of special effects with effervescent, reduplicative, undogmatic "theologies" proliferating right through the poem. For a cosmological poem, one needs speculation to how the cosmos is structured, and a way that the form of the poem condenses the form of the universe. With his artful, endlessly generative events, visitors from a postmortem world arriving with their philosophical debates and anecdotes, Merrill's universe is seen as fecund, productive, an overspill of creative forces, many spokespeople with no central authority, but multiple (sometimes conflicting) centers of pulse. The poem barely contains its own fertile, comic excess. Merrill's poem is incredibly rich in specific Dantean verbal/textual and formal allusions, and the whole mechanism of the poem draws on the *Commedia*—for instance, discussions between the living and the dead to understand ethics, afterlives, gods (in the plural), and the challenges of apocalypse. However, in this dazzling show of poetic craft and ingeniousness, Merrill turns Dante inside out, not so much by systematically answering him (the character JM is willfully unsystematic in his poetic persona), but rather by Merrill's taking up central terms of the cosmological poem and undoing the coherent theology, punitive ultimates, and monotheistic frameworks on which Dante rests.

For Dante, apocalypse is theologically important and positive, not negative, a forthcoming result of the creation, fall, and redemptive Christian worldview, but it has not yet happened. It can come only after his poem is over, because only at that last moment do some souls, those who have not yet worked themselves upward penitentially, get to achieve their goal, and only at that point do a few "proto-Christian" ancients (like Virgil, his guide), born before the Christian dispensation and now in Limbo, all get elevated into a Christian Paradiso. After Dante's theological Apocalypse there will just be Inferno and Paradiso, totally separate, no mulligans.

A subtle feature of Dante's heaven—consistent with his interest in human diversity and variation in a universal system, and, it is said (in *Paradiso* IV), his ability to comprehend the power of heaven—are his gradations of various souls' qualities/abilities even in *Paradiso*. This tolerance infuses Merrill.

However, making his structural choice as an interpretive statement, Merrill dismisses Dante's punitive tri-partite canticles in favor of two only—and those two are, finally, metamorphic and mutable in every finding. Merrill even changes his work back and forth between *Purgatorio* and *Paradiso* and undoes Dante by explicitly stating there is no *Inferno*. That "HELL" was a psychological necessity for humankind (not an actual cosmological structure or place) is an extraordinary non-Dantean finding. The "CHALLENGE" of the angelic avatars populating the poem is "ELIMINATE HELL MAKE MAN THE CLONE OF GOD." The tremendous (utopian) hope of this poem is that "EARTH SHALL BE OUR PARADISE," spoken in the capitals that signal the always-emphatic speech from the Beyond.[54]

The fact that access to this knowledge and more is given via the kind of sortilege—the Ouija board—against which all monotheistic religions (fruitlessly) fulminate is part of Merrill's finesse. Note that in *Four Quartets*, Eliot has a (Dantesque, self-citational) passage explicitly criticizing horoscopes, in case an innocent reader mistook Mme Sosostris in *The Waste Land* for the giver of Good Advice. Which, of course, she "accidentally" is.

H.D. had no such textual ironies or astrological qualms. She was thoroughly, compellingly involved in horoscope reading; you can find carefully drawn astrological charts for family and friends in her archive at the Beinecke Library. She eagerly participated in séances to the Beyond, some influencing *Helen in Egypt* but particularly affecting her later novels.

Dante, despite some contemporaneous astrological interests, consigns Diviners, Astrologers, and Magicians to *Inferno* XX for their claims of seeing the future with the impious goal of avoiding God's powers and his choices for you. Thus JM/DJ's very entrance into Merrill's poem, armed with the Ouija board that will generate this very poem and its cosmological findings, is an act (fondly) contra Dante.

DJ and JM work together, one as Ouija's medium for messages, the other as the recorder of DJ's spell-binding spelled-out words. Neither is a Virgilian guide for the other; they come as partners, fresh into this Other world. In his heroes' explorations of this evocative experiment, Merrill develops many cosmological informants throughout who, called up from the Beyond, come to talk; they are a volatile and entertaining community of thinkers and friends, poets and cruisers, real people postmortem and imagined characters from myth and history. That is to say, the poem presents a populous plethora of layered worlds, apparent dogmas and findings, events, and melodramatic trapdoors—all via the Ouija board then "translated" into Merrill's poem.[55] And the work's range of tonalities and dazzling poetic forms (not to speak of the campy visual text with its breathless CAPITALS) makes irresistible the analogy of a baroque ceiling where something swirly, gorgeous, and stagey is happening in every space. In short, Merrill has changed Dante's work by unceasing subversions via plethora and metamorphosis, yet he retains Dante as the sign of this cosmological extravaganza.

This poem consciously claims the influence of certain film genres, where melodramatic confidants, garish pageants, operatic musical numbers, masques, and dramatis personae of the cosmos are played as if on Merrill's private screen. (These *Gesamtkunstwerk* elements of Merrill need to be recalled in my next section.) Merrill achieves something with both significant numbers and with the tsunami of special effects, leading us finally into endlessly transforming plethora, not any ultimate "center." Being gaudy and outrageous in almost every aspect, Merrill's didactic nonchalance (the opposite of Dante's steady, hard-won insistences and theological finesse) makes for a sprezzatura-laden cosmology—with the exception of his own apocalyptic terrors.

The US uses of the atomic bomb on Hiroshima and Nagasaki create a historical-apocalyptic trauma quite significant to Merrill, who processes the impact in the fantasies of his poem.[56] Large-scale versions of death can loom behind other socio-cosmological long poems—often some (possibly forthcoming) apocalyptic event—like the ecological destruction of the Earth or the end of time. Most of the modern poems pull back from that end; hence in even the more religious poems discussed here, apocalypse has been secularized and historicized. Given *Paradiso*'s preview of glories coming to the saved after Christian apocalypse, this pull back is, of course, not true of Dante, who looks forward to what occurs after the completion of Last Days. Indeed, the urgency of Dante's journey is compelled by his desire to complete his own mindful readiness for ultimate Judgment.

For the modern Dantean poets, the Second World War serves apocalyptically in the case of H.D.'s *Trilogy* with her depiction of the aftermaths of the bombing of London, cracking open the rooms of real people's real lives. Under the same bombardment, Eliot tries to transcend the historical war while still in it. He does this mainly by the very shocking section that posits the "trial by fire" of Nazi-fascist incendiary bombing as an act of God's Love, similar to Pentecost.[57] Apocalypse (though not that word) becomes ecological disaster and human brinkmanship in Kinsella's *Divine Comedy*, and it always threatens.

In Blaser last times do not occur, nor does judgment, except in the haunted soul of one individual—Ezra Pound. Blaser makes a point of this choice: "I reject the apocalyptics of modernism and of postmodernism—these are borrowed from Daniel and Revelation. [. . .] Our language has other work to do."[58]

Although the number three is often the structural signal of a cosmological poem (*Trilogy* and *Three Poems* both come to mind, as well as the trinitarian in Dante), still, proliferation and prolixity in the modern long poem may disturb the apparent numerological balance. Merrill does base *Changing Light* on the Ouija board's visual structure of three zones: an alphabet, a set of numbers running from zero to nine, and then two (or three) options for answers to questions posed to it.[59] But this tricksy "three" comes undone by Merrill himself, teasing about his task:

> And so *you*'ll save us from the Tyrant Three,
> Ménage à trois, synthesis, trilogy . . . ?[60]

Attempted allusions to "three" become in Merrill a rococo pulsation of various numbers that simply overrun this familiar numerical allusion. This three has thereupon turned to (at least) five—in the pentagram of leaders, and to four in the final number of sections. Dante's trinitarian "three" is mooted. Or perhaps three has turned into the Ouija board's 26 [letters] plus 10 [numbers] plus 3 [options] which equals 39—divisible by 3, indeed, but giving rise to the charmingly suspect 13. If the form of the cosmological long poem condenses the shape of the cosmos, here one knows only continuous pulsing creation along with a network of new stories and revelations—an Ovidian poetics of plethora.

Merrill's sections have an improvised, helter-skelter "theology" as comparative-religion appreciation, that tries to give bits of many world mythologies some face time on the stage—the nine muses, Buddha, the prophet Mohammed, the highest angels. But the central theology (call it that) is built on the number five, not the trinitarian three. With five avatars Merrill constructs some listlike formalist moves—colors, the five senses: many kaleidoscopic evocations of number play.[61] Merrill's cycle of destruction and rebirth occurs as if in theologies of reincarnation. Most souls eventually recycle back into the world, a few remain in the zone of Beyond, but some are reborn on Earth in drastically different forms—sometimes with serious didactic meaning and intention, but sometimes randomly.[62] Merrill seems to be making a synoptically inclusive total world mythology, no matter if any details are in contradiction with any other.

Merrill postulates that apocalypse has already happened in Earth's (pre)history at least three times—to his horror—in a mix of war and nuclear, ecological disaster, making a mytho-scientific claim that there were worlds on Earth destroyed (by atomic power) before ours (an Atlantis, for example). However, in his imagined universe there is regeneration, and the Ruling Powers (the Five) themselves have promised never to unleash this kind of destruction again. This promise is exacted in part because of the forensic intervention of JM, along with his already-dead friends WHA (Auden) and MM (Maria Mitsotaki) pleading for the life of the whole species in an amazing "judicial scene" arguing for the life of humanity in front of the angels.[63] Merrill has represented an uneasy post-Flood "rainbow" promise exacted from his motley pantheon of angels so that this destruction will never occur again. This scene parallels (differently) Dante's doctoral/doctrinal exam in theology or fundamental Christian principles, conducted by three key saints (in *Paradiso* XXIV–XXVI). That scene shows that Dante has been converted from the temptations of disputation-rich speculative philosophizing into a stalwart, intelligent faith. Dante's scene shows only his appropriately bounded opinions and his humility.

Another feature of the cosmological pretext of the *Commedia* is Dante's depiction of his wonder at being specially chosen by heaven (or Beatrice) to make his journey. Dante publicly struggles with his pride at that fact—particularly when his pride (and why not!) at conceiving and writing the *Commedia* and joining in debates with the visionary company irrupt in front of the reader even as late as *Purgatorio* XXIX. This choice by the universe of Dante to serve as a messenger has some counterpart in Merrill with a provocative central question that at the very least addresses the question of gay male poets parallel to sodomites in *Inferno*. Why was a gay male couple specially chosen to be the recipient of *this* cosmic vision?

For the most startling way in which Merrill responds to Dante occurs in the question: "What part, I'd like to ask Them, does sex play / In this whole set-up? Why did They choose *us*?"[64] "Sex" means sexual preference, also possibly sexual practices. "Us" means homosexuals, who are not "Doters on women" (*pace* the deep affection for Maria Mitsotaki and Maya Deren in this poem).[65] One reason is (as MM later explains) the "CHILDLESSNESS" of this group of souls (MM/WHA) and people (JM/DJ)—keeps them focused "OUTWARD TO THE LESSONS & THE MYSTERIES."[66] Still, JM's friends do constitute a gay family.

After the original question, there follows an explicit, playful, and rather frank evocation of fellatio and passivity as tropes for intellectual tolerance ("We're more the docile takers-in of seed. / No matter what tall tale our friends emit, / Lately—you've noticed?—we just swallow it"). They are receptive, non-macho, and uninterested in their own "Erection of theories." In this, and other statements, Merrill has—dramatically—queered Dante. The revelations go on, but in itself this is a remarkable claim of their gay or queer rightness for a revelation on the scale and elaborateness of this one. Merrill also postulates how JM/DJ are integrated into the metamorphic universe of the Holy Five.[67] Certainly Merrill's defense of gay importance speaks back to the placement of someone like Dante's pederastic teacher in *Inferno*, where his run to catch up with his cohort of tortured souls is seen as if a victory, as if he *almost* plays by his own rules.[68] Merrill's critique of the moral order of Dante (who cannot allow even one gay male in Purgatory) coupled with Merrill's own poetic uses of his gaynesss for this poem makes a keystone of this critique. Merrill engineers a transition from Dantean focus on Platonic/Christian sex-gender sublimation to sexual, gender, and spiritual plethora as part of the general metamorphic euphoria of his universe.

Throughout the work, the name and ambitions of Dante are evoked, and his careful hierarchies are alluded to, but these soon change into the self-interrupting, loopy (in all senses) structures of the cosmos to which the various speakers introduce the awestruck, wary human couple. Yet in ethics all the camp apparatus, catty and charming dialogues, and queer spectacle boil down to one touching precept: There is only one sin—"PAIN. PAIN GIVEN. PAIN

RECEIVED."[69] Kindness and generosity of spirit are the undertone, even with the needling, the spats, the jealousies and preening characteristic of Merrill's array of figures. Mythological excess is coupled with narrative excess in this work, both answering the question of what happens to the dead, particularly to friends and companions. With only two intermingled zones (Purgatorio/Paradiso) in the whole poem—the party goes on and even intensifies.

A postdeath world of great liveliness, pleasure, oddity, wackiness, and intellectual curiosity takes shape. People generally seem to be in a paradise without the Dantean necessity of worship, but rather with visits, relationships, kindness, care, wit, dishing conversations, pouts and a buoyant, empathetic dynamism that is like an improved version of the world.[70] Whether in numbers, characters, lessons, or findings, Merrill creates a changing and allusive prolixity, a "Changing Light" of pleasurable in-jokes and quasi-theological (and theatrical) effervescence. Merrill's order of the cosmos is fundamentally Ovidian, metamorphic, and pulsing with transformation.

Both John Kinsella's and James Merrill's long poems reject the equilibrium and organizational finesse of the original *Commedia*. In both Merrill and Kinsella, plethora and disequilibrium are accepted throughout as part of our precise cosmological universe. In Merrill metamorphosis emerges not as evil (as in Dante's Ovidian episode) but as a playful baroque inventiveness; the poem is trying (and barely able) to track the cosmic fecundity being revealed to JM/DJ. That is, whether these writers retain the trinitarian tripartite zones but place them in an alternative order or reject Inferno outright, the change from Dante's order indicates the impossibility of a stable, progressive teleological universe.

In John Kinsella's *Divine Comedy*, we are entirely in a real geography, a real time, and real ecology, with its three sections in a non-Dantean order: *Purgatorio: Up Close*; *Paradiso: Rupture*; and *Inferno: Leisure Centre*.[71] The work consists of 223 cantos (of a few pages each) in a visual-stanzaic evocation of terza rima. Kinsella renders this stressed geopolitics, an actual time and granular place, with a clear-headed poetic analysis of ecological, material, and economic pressures. This place combines a farming economy (wheat), an extractive economy (uranium, among other minerals), and a touristic economy ("leisurists"), all under an increasing pressure from exploitation and global climate change and from claiming land wrested and expropriated from aboriginal users. The original declaration of Australian settler society comes in this rupture, now a source of permanent struggles.

Although formally he names his books after Dante's three zones, Kinsella has shifted their order, breaking the spell of that necessary telos. He also acknowledges how hard it is to represent anything like "the psychogeography of

Inferno" when faced with the interrelated quiddities of any day. Kinsella rejects Inferno by stating Dante's three zones are one Möbius strip, zones turning endlessly into each other without beginning or end.[72] Using Dante's urgent, committed transcendence to make this opposing point emphatically underscores Kinsella's position: there is no elsewhere, no other space, no end. Or rather—yes, there is the arc of visible sky and the stars, but Kinsella's *Divine Comedy* is a "de-transcendent" mechanism.[73] His subtitle underscores structural proliferation in the plural and real: "Journeys through a Regional Geography."

Kinsella explores the exploitative economic and political depredations characteristic of a particular and exact political moment of local (and world) ecological precarity. He names his findings in uncompromising terms: "This sacred and spiritual place is violated and capitalist cultures drag it into hell (or try to)."[74] That its title says "journeys" makes explicit the Dante allusion to quest, but the poem is generally a georgic secular work in which meditative-observational poems of thick descriptive patterning are written as if a daily report from the field.

This rhetorical presentation shows in the texture of the syntax, in the stanzas, and in the intransigent and unapologetic observations that are more than "clarities" of description—because some are quite matted with apposition. Kinsella's poetic modes and rhetorics are replicas of an intertwined, interfused natural ecology by virtue of his interlaced syntax and unconcessive word choices. This is an "ultra real," where in the verse-sentences things constantly move in inseparable conjuncture with other things. Kinsella's work thereby expresses Dante's "*quia*" (that-ness as such)—perhaps in a more investigative-intransigent way than Dante intended: in *Purgatorio* III, Dante accepts that something *is* (the "it-ness" of it) without being able to track why.[75]

Kinsella's poem is also filled with evocation of metamorphic change, since that is what time and life are: "I am attracted to the infinite possibilities of the mutable and the 'mundane'" is a statement about endless change, not, for Kinsella, as jaunty as the name Ovid would suggest but a definite turn away from a static worldview.[76] His three canticles are "revisitations and reinventions of the same places," but the result is "necessarily always different." This work is a statement about actual mutability, resisting any step into allegorizing the materiality of the Western Australia land.

Kinsella's work does not seek the knowing innocence and pleasant traditions of the literary pastoral but accounts for living in a place and committing to work on the land, while sometimes facing fellow citizens, some of whom are greedy, exploitative, even deliberately despoiling in order to enjoy their versions of the pleasures of modernity—cheap energy (the uranium debates), a casual approach to land, weather, and crop appropriateness, and ecologically careless leisure. John Kinsella offers no theology, but he presents ethical choices of ecological wantonness and profiteering in the "exploiters" and the "leisurists," as opposed to mindful care of the parcel of land that is in one's possession, an ecological ethics that has to be carefully guarded and sustained by recurrent acts of custodianship and often-hard manual labor.[77] The now of his poem recurs to these observations and narrates the work he does to improve or restore his acres.

Kinsella is haunted by the loss of land-use skills for this precarious environment, and the displacement, despising, and near-genocide of Nyungar families, the marginalized aboriginal group to whom the nearby mountain Walwalinj ("Mount Bakewell") is sacred. Nyungar "protected" territory is still subject to encroachment and the hedging or destroying of treaties and commitments. So the sacred—as a compact of respect for other groups and their internal debates—plays a role in this poem, but sacredness functions very differently from the deliberate quest for a wondrous beyond in Dante, Eliot, H.D., and perhaps Merrill. The fact that there is no "beyond" in Kinsella is noted repeatedly; there may be awe at the natural and cosmological world, and respect for the rare fauna and flora in this landscape, but there is no elsewhere, just here. That fact is central to the poem's ethics.

This is why, although the uses and allusions to Dante differ in each of Kinsella's canticles, none is anything but secular. The shift of the order of Dante is not only motivated (Kinsella has brief prose comments on his strategy) but somewhat terrifying—a realist refusal of consolations, a declaration that there is much destruction for the colonists in a settler society still to confront.

The three sections are surprisingly called "distractions"—the tinge of jocular amusement is alarming until the dictionary opens: a distraction "turns away from the original focus of attention" (that would be God or "higher powers," one-point redemption or "grace," or even a turn from Dante's magisterial text itself) to a secular world where Dante's terms become powerful metaphors for Kinsella's real ("for me the world is a purgatory, with hell close at hand"). Yet one still hopes "to move constantly towards the light," of "rectification" of familial, social, and ecological bonds—an in-world set of shifts—in which "diversity, pluralism, even weirdness" may be celebrated. This is human work: "We have made our own purgatory and have to unmake it to survive."[78]

In Kinsella's "Purgatorio," a number of cantos begin with an epigraph cited from Dante, whose strictly rendered images and subtle observations from nature (something for which Dante is well noted) have led to an allegorical reading or suggestion in each individual canto. In Kinsella, the same image is rearticulated entirely within the natural world. Dante externalizes a smoky cloud as punishment for Wrath, but smoke and fire occur in Kinsella because of a gigantic ecological error made by settlers—planting eucalyptus—a flammable and invasive species, prone to cause fires and to displace other species (as also in California), originally planted in sailing days to have quick-growing tall, straight masts. In *Inferno* XIII, the briar-filled field of the suicides in Dante becomes de-allegorized in Kinsella as the task of clearing barbed wire from a dump for "rusty coils, / sprigs of jags" where trees have been clear-cut—a difficult task that must be done to allow the land a chance for regrowth and regeneration.[79]

Dante's images or citations are tools or reminders for triggering Kinsella's own associations, memories, or ideas. Dante is rearranged, glossed, extended, varied, used to provoke Kinsella's meditations. Kinsella uses Dante as a source text from which to begin his writing; it is about as unpious a use as possible.

Many of Kinsella's cantos confront the intense moral ambiguity of his own *Divine Comedy*—where right, wrong, pain, remediation, suffering are not presented with any of the moral clarity of Dante's proposed punishments for sin. In Dante this is *contrapasso*—any depicted punishment has allegorical appropriateness to illustrate, to correspond to, and suffer a literalization of the sin until the time of complete penance has been achieved. In a fundamental resistance to Dante, Kinsella finds *contrapasso* inadequate. He is "haunted" by the patness of its concept—its final lack of hope for change or revaluation in *Inferno* in which sinners are punished without the prospect of any penitence—although the *contrapasso* works in Dante's *Purgatorio*.[80]

In case we miss this judgment, he underlines it in his introductory remarks: *Inferno* is "a smug work." Kinsella's whole text has been written to denounce any separation of an "us" from our complicity in all these sins and crimes. Even the worst of the crimes—cruelty to animals, killing the gravid kangaroo, manipulating and touching her joey, and then discarding the baby animal—even the worst exploitations he catalogs belong to us all—to each individual and to the collective. "The small crimes we all commit, amplified, ultimately connected by degrees of separation to the crimes that rightly horrify us."[81] The ethics of Kinsella's work shows we are complicit and need to choose to change behaviors at every conscious moment, practically and existentially. His is a didactic text.

The struggle, moving across his *Purgatorio*, is with climate change, causing severe drought, with his dilemma "ploughing dry land"—a punishing fate, in which one is a prisoner of one's own fields, "atmosphere heating up like safe-cook Teflon." When, as in Dante's *Purgatorio* XX, 91–93, there is finally some rain, in Kinsella's version, there is little relief, knowing the compromised Earth is still endangered. Thus the famous "rainbow" in the Dante passage becomes a "short, sharp / emotional quagmire," because in the real universe depicted in this poem, there will be forty-four more pages of struggle, ending with the grim recognition of drought: "There'll be little harvesting // this year. [. . .] All will be scarcer."[82]

Kinsella is articulate about his goals, his planning. For each canticle, he has written a short preface of explanation. This background from an interview:

> When it came to considering a "take" (some critics have called it a "riff") on *The Divine Comedy*, I felt that I didn't want to create a dialogue, I didn't want to use it simply as a "model," but rather wanted to take on the fundamental notions of what we consider to be "good" or "bad" in any given place at any given time and to set up a way of comparing personal response to place with historic and cultural tropes. I wanted to "distract" readers from their knowledge of the original texts but encourage them to reinvest their interpretations in the place and time of their reading.[83]

To gloss Dante's quest is, as with all the uses of genre in this book, to remake and reinterpret him. "Templating" (Kinsella's name for his practice of rewriting culturally foundational texts) reliteralizes Dante in order to turn him inside out and show secular regional precarity.[84] Torquing texts, riffing on texts, revisioning texts are vital acts in literary culture that gain in intensity and meaning when a social crisis or sense of possibility occurs. This use of classic texts via critique and revision occurs concertedly in later modernity as both homage to and resistance to the worlds of our cultural heritage. The same is true of uses of genre itself. Many gender-related and African diasporic sets of texts testify to the intensity with which such "torquing" is used—not playfully but with tremendous emotional investments—political and personal. This desire is not limited to long poems—but the scope of long poems makes torquing texts or other parallel modes of critique particularly powerful precisely because of length. This use of a classic text by allusion or rearticulation tries to create a cultural pivot. This impact and attempts at a pivot are also visible both in Olson's extended "epic" and in the uses of the epic genre by modern and contemporary women writers (as in chapter 2).

Ecological fears for the Earth itself motivate both Merrill's apocalyptic narratives and Kinsella's dogged account of an actual place. Cosmology does, after all include the Earth itself, not simply as a point from which one looks out, but as the only ground we have as a collective heritage. The socio-cosmological quests here have shown the insistence on a worldly, secular, human universe through a text whose original meanings included the theological and redemptive. *Divine* in Kinsella's title means the real world.

All three Dantean authors (now including Blaser) agree that one cannot now "have" their Dantes in the traditional order of the canticles, as a quest of ascent in theological (and rather glorious) terms, beyond natural experience yet rooted in exact time frames for the journey and lucid descriptions of natural phenomena. In these contemporary long poems, fundamental interpretive statements are made by the numerical structure of tripartite Dante. Both *Inferno* and *Paradiso* make implausible demands on contemporary authors—a proof of the insistence on the secular world in modernity. Merrill skips *Inferno* without apologies. Both Kinsella and Blaser place *Inferno* last in structural order, and at vastly different lengths. Both of them touch on all three zones but also braid those zones throughout, and in ways that ceaselessly argue that those zones are interconnected. Seen from a secular worldview, the wonder is that Dante was able to separate out into three zones what we experience every day as a world of endlessly mixed motives and strange consequences. Dante's unambiguous lucidity on that point is one of the pleasures of reading his quest narrative, particularly when mixed with the telling selection of the individuated inhabitants of the three nuanced but exact worlds.

In Kinsella the three sections are in the "wrong" order, and the first two sections are intermingled; all three are worldly positions and have no status in any existing beyond, except in the imagination. In Robin Blaser's order of the canticles, *Inferno* is last; the others weave together in the body of the work.[85] Blaser's *Inferno* concerns the suffering of a problematic, important long-poem writer—the twentieth-century poet Ezra Pound, who (in an encounter with an Italian journalist, cited at length in English by Blaser) is revealed to have found hell in his own heart.[86] This is an image psychological, political, and aesthetic all at once, actualizing Pound's suffering and perhaps self-condemnation emerging from his personal history and social vision. The passage leaves Blaser's work poised on an open-ended question about a key American modernist (one with some serious credibility in the Italy where he had lived for fifty years).

When one begins with long poems, dark woods are never far away. In an interview with John Sakkis, Robin Blaser comments on the "thicket" metaphor with which he titles his collected poems:

> *The Holy Forest*, what I had in mind there when I pulled that title was Dante and the whole sense of being in a forest, wandering in a forest, lost in a forest, finding yourself in a forest, or other people finding you and all that. [. . .] *The Holy Forest* itself is an *imagery* in which you really are lost in a forest, of thought, of people, of things, and I have continued to work it all these years because it allows me my conversation with everything I can think of. I use quotation, I want them there in their own voices, I want my voice there with them so the interchange is a constant folding, I think of reality as a constant folding, and *The Holy Forest* is my way of folding tree after tree. I can wander through the forest, but I'm actually folding whatever reality I can find.[87]

In his words, "the real business of poetry is cosmology, and I'm claiming my own stake in this." One of the magisterial late works of Blaser, "Great Companion: Dante Alighieri," is a philosophical essay that becomes a poetics. This prose meditation contains memories, juxtaposed summaries, philosophical arguments, personal passions, and two long citations. Taking a porous and tolerant tone in his rhetoric, Blaser's very meditation seems random, acts of associative ongoingness, as he speaks apparently casually yet with the most serious intention, using talismanic citations meaningful to him and suggestive responses to Dante's "great, vulnerable poem" in his own allusive, vulnerable prose.[88] The work presents itself as a chain of associations, an argument by indirection, errant, wandering, and a "*randonnée*" of ethical considerations, built like a serial quest-in-thought.

This is a text concerning a revisionary/revised Dante who, by the end of Blaser's meditation, is presented as a poet of interrogation, Odysseyan (exploratory) desire, and critical thinking. This piece metamorphoses Dante because it indicates latent but, to Blaser, palpable critical moments in Dante's thinking that need to be highlighted in the contemporary world. Blaser's work further presents a Dante of situational evaluations, not of fixed judgments—a distinct reinterpretation.

In this version of a Dantean poem, neither Ovid nor the Ovidian is in any way central, nor is nature alternately discussed or glamorized as in the Kinsella and Merrill. However, as Merrill and Kinsella do, Blaser pivots Dante into an interpretation not Dantean. He does so by resisting—actually challenging—what Dante does with the character Odysseus (Ulysses).

In Dante's *Inferno* there are areas, "circles," apt punishments, and so on, but the whole is sometimes more destabilizing, more chaotic, more threatening than most other canticles, particularly in the Malebolge area, where Virgil is at a loss and both characters are melodramatically threatened by devils. As in a cowboy western, you know the cavalry (or Calvary) will come in time, but it is very difficult to contain the chaos of evil, and the suspicions that it brings in its wake—will justice and our permission to visit hell save us, or will we fall between the cracks? The chaos and disequilibrium of the complex system of Earth's uneven ethics have been squeezed together.

Ulysses is placed in this *Inferno* zone (in Canto XXVI). Why? With his mate Diomedes, Ulysses is a "fraudulent counselor," tricking the Trojans—who were ancestors, after all, of Virgil's people, the Romans—to open the gates of Troy for the gift of the gigantic Horse. This ploy Ulysses himself invented (the *Iliad* tells us), since the horse was sacred to the Trojans and seemed to be a monumental offering to the city, but it contained a Greek advance force that took the city from within by this act of fraud. This episode ended in the fall of Troy.

Dante's canto celebrates but suspects Ulysses's further adventures—product of his ceaselessly restless mind: "I had to gain experience of the world." No family/social appeal to temperate responsibility would stop his fated exploration. Rowing through the Gates of Hercules, he and his implicated crew, "followers of worth and knowledge" with a lust for cosmos and geography not to be denied, are swept into a whirlpool near Mt. Purgatory, having passed the boundaries of the world itself and challenged God's limits for human exploration and research.[89] So they die.

However, Blaser will rescue Odysseus/Ulysses—in another deturning of the Dante narrative. But why again? There is no limit for human exploration—let's say, although one might think otherwise, and much ethical second-guessing (of human subjects in medical research, and extractive exploitation) might be devoted to these considerations. But Blaser makes a different, formal argument for continuous seeking in the matrix of quest. Here and elsewhere he validates the serial poem as a particular nonteleological mode for the quest poem central to modern long poems precisely because of the continuous open questioning of any finding. In a discussion of this work in 1997 at the Università d'Annuzio, he speaks of Odysseus as embodying a valuable "poetics of interrogation."[90]

Blaser's appreciative discussion makes of Dante less an icon than a correspondent to fundamental questions of civic life, ethics, and spiritual meaning that are also tracked in his citations through the thinking of Agamben and Nancy, among others. Blaser takes "il poema sacro" to demand acts "daring" a journey to intellectual complexity and entanglement.[91] In this Odysseus is a hero—a figure of poet-philosopher-searcher. For if "the poetic is the language of the mapless," Odysseus is the figure willing to enter where there is no map, simply for love of knowing as a constant seeking-in-language: "*The attempt to lift the topos* [of Love] *itself, the event of language* [language as an exploratory tool] *as a fundamental amorous and poetic experience*—the *loved experience* is found in the poetic of unmapped territory."[92] Thus, Blaser constructs an image of Odysseus as a figure embodying Dantean values.

Poetry and philosophy are brought forward by Blaser as Dante's field—not poetry and the sacred. We saw how un-Dantean this position is from Dante's final exam—where he stands against philosophical speculation and for belief. In part paraphrasing Philippe Sollers on Dante, Blaser affirms "*The Purgatory* [. . .] *is a continuous image of the poetic condition*—Dante walks and questions —perhaps the poetic condition is a matter of interrogation—certainly, it is for us, as it was for him."[93] This is not a Dantean Dante, but Blaser's contemporary reinterpretation of him.

Blaser uses, in this meditation, the tactics of a serial work moved into essay mode. In interviews collected in *The Astonishment Tapes*, Blaser recalls to us that seriality emphasizes concentration on instances of insight and interrogation rather than the pursuit of one clear argument or one narrative sequence. Blaser talks of seriality as a perpetual rebeginning, a move back repeatedly to an epiphanic realization, not to the past as a flashback, but rather an endless return to the moments of beginning in order to go forward. He frames "what it means to be in serial form—that it's not one truth, because after you're through with it it's bigger than it is in each of its parts, but that literally it is the narration of its reopening the real each time."[94] Any one-truth totalizing Blaser resists as based fundamentally in intellectual (and political) terrorism.

Serial work is where quest reemerges in certain contemporary long poems, as in their characteristic tendency to "begin again and again" (a poetics from Stein's "Composition as Explanation"). Seriality for Blaser is not a quest with a telos so much as a mode (and structure) of extending questions. It is interchange as folding, points touching, diverging, conversations without resolution and therefore not Dantean in direction toward telos, but thoroughly Dantean in exploring meaning and ethics in a cosmological site. Folding over and rebeginning become a metamorphic and plausibly cosmological structure for seriality in poetry. In poetic acts evoking "a cosmology and an epistemology," Blaser insists on an ethics of interrogation as the central purpose of his writing, bringing it in confluence with "theogony and theology, with science in its deepest concerns," and with a continuous and synoptic philosophical propulsion.[95] This is where Blaser connects his intellectual ethics to Dante's worldview but will transpose and extend Dante. And the serial (episodes without exemplary narrative telos) and rich Dantean allusions are how both Kinsella's and Merrill's much longer works are built: of struggle, not resolution.

Blaser's image of his meditative essay, and his connection to the spiritual adventure he sees in Dante, is the initiation into a thicket of serious thought, or what Blaser calls the Holy Forest. This central Dantean metaphor for poetic thinking became the title of his collected poems. Not "holy" in any theological sense but the celebration of a secularized spiritual yearning; holy as consecrated by the acts of speculating, listening, conversing, and considering illustrated *in* this essay and *as* this essay. Blaser thinks of thoughts not in hierarchies but as recursive, the continuous folding of "pleats" of poems and essays, and of argument within this work. Blaser invites Dante out of his gorgeous (fixed) cosmology into lateral, Odyssean, exploratory activities of responsive thinking.

Odysseus appears in Dante's *Inferno* only eight cantos away from the Satanic bottom of things. Blaser ends his meditation with Ezra Pound admitting to being in his own hell. Decades before, Pound had begun his *Cantos* with the

Dantean hundred Cantos as one goal in view. He also began it in the middle of Western culture with a palimpsest of the *Seafarer*, Odysseus in the *katabasis* section seeking the advice of the dead, and a Renaissance translation of *The Odyssey*.[96] Thus, Pound and an Odyssean stance have been associated with his (potentially Dantean) ambition of making a long-poem synthesis. This ambition is clearly fixed on exploration, investigation, and a desire to know more, to correlate as much of Western and some Eastern knowledge as Pound could manage. Without an explicit statement preferring Pound's early-career interrogatory explorations, Blaser has judged as inadequate Pound's midcareer fixation on one politics.

Blaser leaves quite ambiguous whether Pound, in his whispered "Here is hell," pointing to his heart, is repenting his fascism with its murderous absolutisms; whether Pound is still baffled that Mussolini (and his political terrors) did not become a political hero in the historical world; whether Pound felt like a Dantean sufferer; or whether (because of—or despite—his absolutist modernity) Pound could not "complete" *The Cantos* in a successful Dantean closure with appropriate fulfillments. What Blaser makes clear (as does Kinsella) is that we live with our Infernos—they are not segregated in a special place apart from us.

But for Blaser, any part of Dante—and any part of Pound—that appeared as a fixed system celebrating an always potential rigidity and dogmatism in religion or an absolutism and hierarchy in politics is "corrupt." "To what are you faithful?" and not "What is your faith?" becomes the only viable question—this from Agamben.[97] Blaser's socio-cosmological work, enters a continuous search for ethical meaning and does not seek an establishment of certainty.

This is the Odyssean transformative yearning that Blaser eulogizes, and that he announces as an argument for the productive "dangers of language traveling, Odyssean, eager, and infinite." He talks about the "Odyssean language of the *Paradiso*," sailing "*in waters that have never been sailed before*," taking Dante's noted metaphor of going into unknown seas, used for his entrance to *Paradiso*, and transposing it to claim passionate curiosity as the poetic condition, and cosmic love as the condition of writing. That "Odyssean language" is no longer doomed with the Ulysses figure in *Inferno* XXVI but escapes as an ideal "of human liberty through oppositional writing—of the stake in desire of any one of us—" The last lines of this essay-poem show that for Blaser's remaking of Dante "the *Paradiso* is Ulyssean. Although Dante did not know *The Odyssey* except through Virgil, Odysseus haunts him even in his dreams."[98] The endlessly exploratory interrogation of certainties, via language and ethical understanding, are what Blaser proposes for his rearticulated Dante—precisely a critical revision, via Odysseus, of the fixed Dantean theology. Further, Blaser does enact, in this poetics, the fantasy of centuries of disgruntled readers to release the ever-questing Odysseus from *Inferno*.

By his incorporative use of citation and anecdote, Blaser slowly tracks an argument for a faithfulness to a transtemporal community of fellow travelers who think about community and language, are committed to debate, and to renewals of understanding via language. We "rebel at the theological imprisonment and abandonment—and suspect that Dante now and then does so too" is Blaser's radical proposition, although Dante's rebellion is well hidden. The former cosmology, in which totality is valued and language is a closed meaning, Blaser describes as "gone in the teeth." This very phrase alludes to Pound's "Hugh Selwyn Mauberley," in lines about the cruel, war-prone "botched civilization" seen in WWI, the beginning of the twentieth century. This is a civilization that Blaser is committed to displace, because it serves those too "enamoured of an absolute."[99] Religion in its depleted forms as piety and religiosity and (elsewhere) rigid political systems that organize humanity for spiritual and material deaths are other elements of the systems Blaser excoriates. "The cost of these Totalities—of Christianism, of Marxisms, of Capitalism—are on the public record—forgiving themselves again and again for the terror of this century."[100]

Blaser has used his 1997 lecture in the land of Dante to present "the task of our ongoing departure from the *totality* [that Dante] *confronted*"; this totality is the theological system that he was illustrating and elaborating in the *Commedia*. Blaser finds his Dante underneath this canonical, normative figure. The whole tone of Blaser's essay, incorporating words of others, makes its communitarian points in a lambent inquisitive meditation among morning coffee and what he sees in Dante—"the ever changing polyphony of amorous thought."[101] Stylistically, Blaser offers an example of both absorptive tolerance and an inquisitive stance. The mystery to pursue is human life, ethics, and language—this is hardly a theology or set of dogmas—whose rigidity and destructive certainties are anathema to Blaser.[102]

Dante's beginning and end, *Inferno* and *Paradiso*, are now shorn by Blaser of theological (and sociopolitical) certitude; and the Dantean position toward systematizing dogma has the corrective of Blaser's call—this is his "eros"—for a tolerant, investigative, secular modern world, rejecting all absolutes in favor of tracing and depicting entanglement and a "human freedom" of speculation and community.[103] This is at least an indirect notice that a spiritual infusion into a secular world is again seen as the task of some poets in the contemporary world—precisely the vocation of a socio-cosmological poem (not a sacred poem or a purely secular one.)

All three Dantean long poems produce an ethics, but none with a theology.

To be more exact, Merrill deliberately has too much theology, and some seems invented, spun out on the spot, the charming opposite of Dantean theological precision. Merrill's endless fecundity and metamorphic inventions are here called "Ovidian." Both Merrill and Kinsella employ Dante's *Commedia* to the utmost and at length, but as permission for what looks like an opposing ethical aesthetics: both settle on versions of an Ovidian transformational universe, whether magical or ecological. Merrill seeks the beyond with baroque, proliferative excess, and Kinsella seeks the real world's ecology with an overloaded verbal sense of the actual matted ground. Saturated allusions to Dante's overarching structure, verse forms, and cultural meanings abound in both works, both being full-length, full-scale Dantean explorations. In Merrill this pivot is visible in the energetic plethora of trying to keep up with cosmic-comic fecundity. In Kinsella the pivoting disruption of the poem occurs by "distracting" readers from pious adhesion to literary tradition, transposing Dante to investigate historical ecologies and potential rectification, a vulnerable place, and problematic politics.

In parallel critical ways, also idiomatic to Dante's socio-cosmological universe, Blaser uses Odysseus to rearticulate what he wants from Dante—even if Dante has to be turned upside down and thoroughly reinterpreted for Blaser to get it. This third response to Dante treats the traces of a tripartite theological structure as a palimpsest of ethical realities. In contrast to Dante's *mesura*, in both Merrill and Kinsella chaos and disequilibrium are accepted, because these are the ways the Ovidian universe of metamorphosis declares itself, in an endless process-oriented mutability; Blaser's recursive "folding" structures mean that philosophical evocations are never settled, and that interrogative empathy is a functioning ethics.

CHAPTER 4

Assemblage, Book, Total Artwork

BARTHES ON MALLARMÉ AND HIS POETICS

SO FAR, THIS essay has treated long-twentieth-century interpretations of traditional long-poem genres concerning the concept epic, and who can be an epic hero-griot, and has asked what becomes of the telos of cosmological and spiritual quests in the secular world. Chapter 4 explores genre mixtures under the rubric assemblage: among them the Whitmanic album but particularly the Mallarméan Book as combined with a totalizing and inclusive long-poem-performance of "all" the arts in a *Gesamtkunstwerk*. These modes are strikingly relevant to the anarrative Anglophone long poem.[1] These genres make a nexus of secular-spiritual concerns for a performative book of assemblage with an ethical dimension for textual choices.

In his 1895 essay "The Book as Spiritual Instrument," Stéphane Mallarmé begins with the provoking, provocative claim: "That everything in the world exists to end up *as* a book," and in another translation, "that everything in the world exists to end up *in* a book."[2] This sense of a Book—and everything (whether or not Mallarmé is explicitly attached)—has galvanized many writers of the long poem.

The longing for this kind of long work is patent in *The Preparation of the Novel*, Roland Barthes's speculative lecture/essays on writing from 1978 to 1980, with its nuanced accounts of authors trying to shape largest-scale works.[3] He presents the poetics and appeal of the Book in his own analytic-seductive way, hoping that Mallarmé's essay and fragmented meditations on "Le Livre" will inspire his own newest projects, a large literary work (probably a novel); thus, he was investigating how authors prepared themselves for a major effort.[4]

Barthes reminds us what Mallarmé wanted: "architectural and premeditated"; "a book that really would be a book"; "*the Book* [. . .] there is only one."[5]

He is further eloquent on "fantasized form," that projection not of content but of a purposeful object that the writer envisions, whose exact contours are not palpable, but (in my view as a long-poem writer) offers an interior standard of evaluation and a network of feelings concerning what this book could be, what it wants from its author, and what its structural elements entail. Barthes particularly visualizes some emphatically grasped "X-ray of the Ur-text." Barthes: "To write—according to my desire and in my experience, at least—is to *see* the book, to visualize the book: *On the horizon, the book.*" I can only concur. This moment can come instantaneously or be renewed periodically; the "Ur-text" (a sense of form as such) may announce itself haptically or in sound as well as sight. Always in this process of the "Projected Work to its Fabrication," the imagined work remains a palpable presence and even a partner.[6] The book to be written becomes the inspiration for the struggle for that book, which is held like a secret self in its incipient author.

"The writer 'sacralizes' the Work [. . .] and by putting himself in its service, by becoming a 'convert' to the work," the writer is changed. The biographical "person" has been absorbed by the boundlessness of the work while devoting the limits of one lifetime toward service in its realization. These vocational attitudes—irrespective of poetics—propel the long-poem authors of the extreme works discussed here. The Book is "homologous to the world" (to a worldview, really), as with Dante, "the totality of reality and history from the perspective of Transcendence."[7] In a secular world this is difficult, for this formulation does not postulate contradiction or debate, but it plays among past, present, and uplift (possibly future).

Barthes's fail-safe, postulating an alternative for such a gluttonous, absorptive, impossible Book, might help rescue authors from such absolutist temptations —if not from the use of this rhetoric. After noting his own longing for such a single ultimate Book, Barthes also offers the album, also derived from Mallarmé, a genre that tempers or even dissolves the uncomfortable absolutism of that Mallarméan concept of the Book as ideal.[8] The album is more "scattered, a pure interweaving of contingencies, with no transcendence."[9] It may be laden with debate and contradictions. With this, in Anglophone poetries we are in vastly familiar territory, because this major overarching category—assemblage, serial work, accumulation seen as Album—is as idiomatic to our long poem as is the longing for a Book. In fact, they intermingle interestingly—as they do in Barthes, although he reserves transcendence only for the Book.

If a Book is "a 'structure founded on the nature of things'"—this is presumably an agreed-upon sense, a social-intellectual hegemony such as Dante used (or postulated).[10] The mode of assemblage (album, array) questions that unlikely agreement in our societies, much less its instantiation in a poetic structure, by the pluralized recognition of multiple systems, not one hegemonic zone. Thus, assemblage/album is at once what is left of the Book and an actual long-poem mode, an ethical *poesis* encompassing—not unifying—a social and textual "many."

So this album-Book continuum or (in Barthes) "dialectic" seems to rest on the question of whether masses of material can create a sense of transcendence—possibly without unity. Let's say that album is a work that does not postulate a specific ending as climactic, but that the Book does work toward transcendence. One is contented, in an album, with the notational, the contingent, investigative fragments of a research process, the work as diarylike, in "dayforms," a "scrapbook" or a serial poem that is not a quest, with things in no absolute order, yet set in a work that has social-secular necessity.[11] "Endings" ("cadence") might also be displaced in a long work or compounded.

Everything to end up in a Book? Still, that enraptured Mallarméan ambition has bearing on the poetics of the long poem, since some long-poem writers seem, with a fascinated yet self-critical literalness, to be attempting just this feat. With all nuance burned off, what would long-poem poets posit as their goals if all the world (or everything in the world) were *not* intended to end up—probably in their Book.

So the Book is inescapable once its voracity is named. Although in Mallarmé, album and Book are opposites, they are "dialectical" ones, presumably a binary without resolution. Barthes wants this album to soften the ideal of the Book in Mallarmé, but sometimes this mode is a version of that Book. What we see in many Anglophone long poems is a simultaneous embrace of album/assemblage and a critical idealization of the ultimate uplifted Book. Hence, I postulate that in assemblage one can sometimes mark a trace of the Book as ideal.

Assemblage as a genre addresses the poetic desire for an overarching long-poem work encompassing "everything" necessary to show society to itself; as in the other genres, this is the work of a poet acting as public intellectual. "Assemblage," "array," "accumulation," "album," "compendium," and "collection" are related, flexible terms that characterize this genre. Some long poems construct this large-scale cultural and social address, making a portrait of the force of a varied "many"—many people, many voices, many observations. Listings, transformed or untransformed (as in Charles Reznikoff); careful modules of shaped related elements (Crane's vignettes); collections of specified units (cantos as temporal clusters in Waldman); accumulation itself propelling recognition of mass (in Silliman)—all these are baselines for the overwhelming and implacable feelings of "suchness" and "manyness" that characterize assemblage.

In discussing Silliman, Pound, Mackey, Brathwaite and NourbeSe Philip and the sense of assemblage and book in the long poem, I am *not* stating that Mallarmé (or Whitman) is explicitly evoked, but that an album-to-Book poetics helps illuminate these assemblages. Only Pound can be said to evoke Mallarmé, if indirectly.[12] Even as album or assemblage, the book's bulk and quantity will tend to transcendent claims—social, political, performative, aesthetic. In a long and additive poem committed to paratactic ongoingness, the notion of a Book emerges in allusion, in theme, and in structure.

Assemblage/album is a way of accumulating related moments of response, a range of social vignettes held in a set or series. Hart Crane's *The Bridge*, with picturesque, lush, and baroquely intertwined syntaxes characterizing a nation's citizens and geographic plethora, are almost unified in their disparity by one transcendent poetic evocation. This is the trace of the Book: the Brooklyn Bridge as singing harp, at the beginning and end, spanning these individuated moments, as if between two covers. Assemblage, perhaps looking like too undistinctive a genre, might provide intellectual and aesthetic flexibility, given its acceptance of disparate, even "awkward, ponderous" characters and situations together.[13]

Assemblage provides for a "category of multiplicity" in poems of social investigations, to think about the many and then represent that array formally in a poem.[14] One can multiply anything into an assemblage poem: smaller units (like sentences), notational *aperçus*, stages of a jump-cut argument, modular vignettes. Telos or climactic ending is hard to achieve, though a sublime transcendence may be built (as in Crane). However, any ending, no matter how suspended, is sometimes discouraged by the additive power of accumulation itself (there's more! more!) that may push back against the poet's (apparent) wish to end or to bring the poem to a unifying image.

A defined group of observations, like the notational poems in Robert Creeley's *Pieces*, or a serial set of varied observations recurring through an oeuvre (Blaser's "Image-Nation" poems), or a landscape of briskly changing fragments (in Pound), or any narrative sequence collected in a fixed time (in Mayer) or by fixed sentence number (Hejinian)—all these shapes and patterns of the long poem are differently scaled serial assemblages: that is, compendia of related instances. This is a loose mode of the serial, without pressure on conclusions, which are sometimes suspended or evanescent.

Seriality as a mode for poetic organization might certainly be seen as a mode of assemblage (as well as being a quest among particulars), with both social bearing and an evolving pulse of thought. Seriality assembles linked political/personal instances and recognitions of array or (using Oppen's word) the numerous. Any intentional grouping or set to highlight civic questions or specific communities, including community as protagonist could be expressed in a serial album. The book-length work *In the Mecca* by Gwendolyn Brooks presents implacable narrative vignettes of the Chicago apartment complex. The granular observations of social/racial inequality in Hughes's *Montage of a Dream Deferred*, the events in Reznikoff's *Testimony* that itemize industrial accidents in flat but devastating reportage are works of album assemblage both descriptive and allegorically didactic. The serial in its assemblage mode may have less sense of terminus than a quest poem; it may manifest the Brechtian poetics of confronting the reader with insoluble contradictions, not resolving them in the artwork. An array or an album of instances may suspend chronology or firm telos so that the whole structure presents materials to contemplate together in mutual interactive bearing.[15]

In this genre of assemblage, its main speaker might combine traits of the other two genres discussed here: as a cultural fighter, griot, or researcher (as in the epic) or as a seeker, traveler, pilgrim, rereader (as in quest poems). The speaker of an assemblage may assume those roles in a collectivity or in dialogue, using a pronoun like "we" or, citing Brathwaite's first-person combination, a "mwe" or (in "Bermudas") a color-word pun for "our," "ozure." The speaker is a collector and cicerone of instances, a participant in an ensemble of questers and discussants, one voice ventriloquizing dialects and citing multiple texts, all tactics for projects embodying social array and tracking its implications. One question assemblage broaches is how the poet formally presents a "we" when the "I" is writing.

In their roles of participant-observers of these massed instances and evolving assemblages, both Silliman (as recorder) and Mackey (as singer) compose their ongoing works—a *many* as the topics and subject matters of the poem into which themselves or their writing-selves are absorbed as sentence-making and long-song participants. In the assemblage genre, the long-poem claim of "everything" may modulate to a writing voice including "everyone." A writer-character or performing-recorder of thought or song is a figure showing "adhesive" ambitions both to participate in and to hold all this together with the glue of longing. Whitman is one sign of this ambitious longing to depict an erotic or yearning sociality: "My hand / in yours, / Walt Whitman— / so—"[16]

WHITMAN

Whitman, a maker of assemblages, thus becomes a figure of interest for long-twentieth-century long poems. The grouped poems in *Leaves of Grass* celebrate a nation by describing various citizens in their typical specificities, affirming them bound together in a spiritual-political community as one adhesive body, sung through the poet's inclusive, polymorphous voice. This Whitmanic array has both social scope and the aesthetic potential for adding more poems in paratactic formal units (as he did through his life with different editions). *Leaves of Grass* has an affirmative furor, making a catalog of upliftingness, plethora, and multiplicity, bringing together all those generously described smaller units into a freely modular, long-line list exposition. In its several editions, *Leaves of Grass* is an ever-mutable Book with poems continuously multiplying occasions, catalogs, arrays—the many, all present in a sublime community that evokes national hope.

His 1855 preface argues for this endless recurrent plenitude (as of grass itself). His poetics of the long poem depends on additive (and adhesive) assemblage condensing a whole national body into his poet's body ("Copious as you are I absorb you all in myself") and will thereupon be expressed through himself; poem and poet become a secular and national "incarnation" of political and cosmic import.[17] Adhesion is compelled by rhetorics of repetition and recurrence. The voice is insistent, prolific, and inclusive, creating a paratactically increasing omnivorous collectivity embodied in this expansive poet/poem and *poesis*. The poem unrolls as assemblage, a poem expanding by addition of line segments and units dynamically and continuously performing plenitude.

Whitman's "true use" of poetry "give[s] ultimate vivification to facts, to science, and to common lives"—a secular-spiritual, populist, somewhat masculine, and modern proposal.[18] This poem precisely incorporates an extensive "everything"; the sometimes daunting, ever-increasing descriptive paeons of scope in modular units of both specificity and fullness—birds, land masses, peoples, crafts. This exposition values commerce, science, work, openly expressed emotion, and descriptive exactness tending to affirmation.

Whitman's whole work as corporeal entity is designed to be the emphatic physical (beyond literary) expression of the United States itself, as spoken through the poet who incarnates the nation. The whole is his secular testament, or Book of that poetic incarnation.[19] In its biblically inflected and sublime versets of perpetual apostrophes, this work has origins in political speeches, sermons, and collective prayers, deployed here for secular spirituality and collective national self-recognition and uplift: precisely *Chants Democratic*.

In the name of the "longing" for the poem and its meanings that is characteristic of long-poem ambition, Whitman commits to personable erotic frankness and to the secular incarnation of the poet in the nation, given people's "general ardor and friendliness and enterprise," all operating with the unifying pulse of "large amativeness"—a political eros directed to the nation. His special words "adhesiveness" and "amativeness" suggest materials accumulated together by the power of their own / his own political-erotic yearning—amativeness is both a theme and a mode of assemblage.[20] This emotional, intellectual, and spiritual "adhesiveness" emerges in other long poems as a compelling glue: Whitman's term[21] is a version of the imperative, subjunctive demand of long-poem authorship that this array *be joined* by long-poem longing.

SILLIMAN AND THE ALBUM

A movement between assemblage as Album and the Book, accumulation and the quasi-monument transformed by accumulation itself, characterizes Ron Silliman's secular array of long-poem works. These are the super-*Ketjak*, itself a totalizing assemblage of works including *The Alphabet* and *The Age of Huts*, and including *Universe*, more recently begun, turning 360 degrees around a particular world. I emphasize *The Alphabet*, along with his two portal works to long-poem projects, *Ketjak* (the "short" book-length version, written 1974) and *Tjanting* (written 1981). The materiality of language, reality, and the Book itself make the title *The Alphabet* a witty indicator of album, with its twenty-six very long cantos, each with one key letter and sometimes numerological schemes. This doubly evokes materiality—in ABCs and in sentences cataloging the real—lists becoming, in their bulk and range, the Book of everything.

Counting, accumulating, negotiating with length—poem-time and life-time—are familiar acts for those involved in long poems. Silliman's obsession for assemblage of this array exemplifies the ethos of "everything": to name every detail of the world in language, no matter how banal, normal, minimal, taboo, apparently excrescent, shameful, cast off, silly, unnoticeable, and nonliterary. The work has no master narrative, and there are few or no markers of spatial/temporal mappings of events and of the connections/relations (of causality or expectation) among events/statements. There is little sense of foreground and background as conventionally positioned or as indicators of importance. This writing declares an iterative poetics of endless middle.

The work depicts writing as if it is occurring continuously. Each unit written, generally a syntactic sentence, occasionally a fragment or defined line, is a singularity set in a vast network. Silliman does not draw explicit links among them (this mightily frustrates literary conventions of reading and its satisfactions) but assembles an array, a social scan seen, thought, and composed in each specific time and space. There is little emphasis on memory, further contexts for statements, anticipation, or foreshadowing, but the scan and array made by meditative-descriptive statements extend out to an infinity of everything.[22] *Everything* is on the manifest.

Silliman's version of the writer of assemblage is the poet as worker. The author writes an account of what is, in the world and in language, tallying moments and thoughts in an ever-increasing now, constructing an album of individual instances. It is an account of "this this this this," showing assiduous patience and ambition at once, a patience with depicting what is seen (experienced or remembered), and an ambition to offer it up by making precise words in lucid syntax, without hierarchy or flurries of affect, but simply as a deictic presentation.[23]

Silliman also made a life's-work commitment to labor on specific projects in time, one after another—a bargain with himself about accumulation. The final pages of *The Alphabet* detail some of the projects—"one paragraph a day, one section per week, for a year." Other such tasks are "Every day for one year I looked at the sky & noted what I saw."[24] Accumulation and deliberate projects faithfully and habitually carried out in have built this oeuvre, one statement and one project at a time. Sometimes the calculus of intention within the labor of writing demands self-referential accountability: "Today I wrote eight pages" or "This sentence has five words."[25] Silliman has found a way into a perpetual, absolutized middle, as if recording "everything" in time (today) or space (on the page).

Reading Silliman, one registers the constant materiality and physicality of writing—his hand, a specific pen, the page, the places the author sits. He alludes to the colors of notebook covers, to colors of pages inside notebooks: "A sentence begun on the green page is completed on the yellow," is a typical pertinacity to see and record what is often overlooked.[26] Losses of hierarchy and of any filters of importance/significance are his principles.

Using the alphabet in unit titles as the basis for a contingent array does not appeal to traditional cosmogonies but constitutes their opposite; alphabets are culturally arbitrary, materialist, and sociohistorical, thus a pointed intervention against transcendence. Not all extant alphabets have all the letters familiar to us from ours or in the same order; not all writing systems are alphabetic, but alphabets are culturally supported nonhierarchic series that close but do not end. The letters are equal—A is no "better" than M or Z, except for its frequency, which is not absolute (universal) but language-dependent. Twenty-six works in *The Alphabet* are arranged by those album principles, not chronological, teleological, or narrative.

Silliman's work in the mode of the middle derives from one key instruction in Stein's 1925 "Composition as Explanation": use everything.[27] Silliman's motives are less like Stein's language experiments (themselves often *semi*semantic) than political experiments with extent, with the numerous, with social depiction and observation of an existing actuality to create an intentional array of sentences, as if a tracking shot taken with a pen. The ethical dimension of his textual structures evokes pluralism, curiosity, tolerance. And he further allows:

"It is not that / there is no narrative / here (each sentence / is a narrative, / each line moves) / but that there is / no hierarchy / of narratives (not even / the story of the / poem), no sentence / to which the others / (all the others) defer / and are ranked."[28] "No hierarchy" is what he is after, not the suggestion of one single narrative but a (daunting) array of many latent or intermittent narratives at once, where sequence and consequence matter far less than constructing a plethora of observations in this procedural space. This is a closely rendered social catalog of items in no institutional, single narrative or political ranking—as if the poem itself constituted a disparate community of multiplicities themselves.

Tallying and telling are not far apart. If one does not "tell," as overarching development and change, motives and rationales, social functions of the speakers and the pressures upon them, how, then, does one "tell"? Silliman's way is tallying; the one plus one plus one statements in their paratactic relation structure the arrangement of his varied, often hypotactic sentences. Sentences and fragments in any syntactic mode are set in a tallying (paratactic) context with a deictic purpose, pointing. Particularly compelling about parataxis, an additive rhetoric with imaginary plus signs joining the elements, is its appeal to temporality as ongoing, not completed. An album (like a collection of photographs or any set of similar things) can always absorb more. Further, an album format can emphasize defining distinctions, as in a stamp collection. Thus, in Silliman the whole becomes the listlike extent of a paratactic form, while within that, one may get a plethora of mininarrative vignettes (whether hypotactic sentences, intricately subordinated or two-word fragments). These individual statements, themselves placed as an album-array, are not made into a sequence but often monitored by specific numerological choices. It is fundamental activity composed as oeuvre: "What I am writing is writing."[29]

That array (in whatever writing procedure) sometimes works by exfoliating existing sentences or groups of sentences by *tmesis*, not here a rhetorical turn but expanded to a structural procedure: opening and adding whatever quantity of statements is demanded by numerology. "This to me is tmesis," stated with punning wit, is a prod toward additional writing, a method for more assemblage.[30] Tmesis could be exemplified by one colloquial rhetorical instance—"Jesus H. Christ"—the insertion of an unexpected element between words of the expected phrase. These acts of opening and adding without connecting (separation, insertion, rejoining) construct amplification without demanding development, as in the tmetic changes from freestanding *Ketjak* and "Ketjak 2" in which sections are inserted.[31] Silliman also increases his writing by additive strategies like the Fibonacci number series for accelerating numerical expansion of extent and bulk. The additive also involves his use of a disjunctive "New Sentence" jump cut, not for the sake of creating any plausible continuities or temporal-causal logic (as in Sergei Eisenstein) but for contrasting two implied contexts.[32] Silliman is not trying to depict what is actually "out there" as a descriptive scene; rather, his mix of sentences from different contexts creates denaturalized jolts in the final work for a characteristic texture of bumpiness amid listlike plethoras.

Though readers do not easily find emotion in this writing, it is present in the passion for fabrication and in the social emotion of living in a city, being one observer among a multitude. Silliman's work is not predicated on emotional responses to events; it emphasizes strict noticing, description, without emphatic judgment—except a kind of observational, deictic wonder: that *this* is, and that *that* is. Most of the emotional and passional energy is put into lucid noticing and exact rendering. Silliman's works are "like" a populace or a demos in the Whitmanic sense—arrays of people and events copiously assembled, plus thoughts on the poetics of making this array, but without the incarnational mystique.

Thus, "everything," in his hands, is precisely antilyric. This is not true in other hands—most long-poem poetics treated here envelop the lyric in some form (even as notational fragments), rather than resisting it; some try both. Silliman's argument is precise. For Silliman, "the longpoem is never innocent."[33] Especially in his assemblage mode, long poems critique the romantic lyric. They can never claim to be a unique overflow of feeling, an emotionally authentic entrance into language crystalizing in that instant, because their extent in space and time trips up that instantaneous temporal urgency (which is why Poe rejected the very existence of the long poem). Silliman argues that the lyric typically wants time to be contained, arrested, held, universalized, summed up, to become "timeless"—which is ahistorical. The long poem, in contrast, has the goal of saturating in temporal and historical ongoingness. It is inflected not so much by the summing up of a historical era with its lessons for the future, but by an insistent confrontation with time itself as matter, each sentence—personal, messy, with intimate events and one's observations of them—becoming an album of particulars, not an intersubjective study of relationships.

Silliman's work is engaged in scanning the time/space coordinates of *now*, artfully packing much contingent informative and descriptive observation into one sentence and then another, then sometimes also in gnomic, punning, and theoretical language observations. Each individual freeze-time moment of syntactic intensity and presentation occurs as a statement, whose untranscendent accumulation becomes a long poem (often, as noted, by a numerological, exponential calculus). He does not necessarily produce statements that record sequential time as it occurred, but discrete, juxtaposed observational summaries of something occurring or that occurred, either in the world, or in the language about the world, or in the mind making up that language. Anything stated can come between anything else that is stated without establishing a thematic, imagistic, temporal, or causal connection. It is an infinite network.

The glut of any "now" is not rendered as linkages, interruptions, causes and effects, logical connections, plots of events or surprises, conventions of sequencing, remembering, and reflecting afterward, nostalgia, build-ups to an insight, or hierarchies of emphasis. In Silliman there is much "time," and one senses the weight and fullness of any moment but no particular organization of time by chronology or consequence; there's a lot of "time" but few explicit markers. Past and future, historical events, dates and hours are sparse (though one might infer these from some allusive residue in the writing). The work constructs a totalizing right here, right now. The clock ticks, and another sentence or phrase occurs. Each moment of time added to another eventually becomes an assemblage of times or a bulk in space.

Yet *The Alphabet*, as well as the works in *The Age of Huts*, despite being more than a thousand pages of text are, in their sentence-based texture, as if simultaneously present. Wherever you open this book, there is a right here, right now, and lots of it. He provides, sentence by sentence, a proliferation of narrative bits (implied, completed, partial, incomplete, suggestive, never-ending, unfinished) but no developed stories—except "writing" as the network of itself.

The obsession for the long poem in Silliman is naming, seeing, elaborating, describing, discovering, investigating—in any order, and with the object being world or word and the endlessly interesting seam that one can make between them. His "Crazy to do this" means both nutty and desirous.[34] Despite little dramatic emotion expressed *in* the work, a good deal of emotion is ascribed to *doing* this work, to the relationship between this person and his writing, as a sustaining process toward the Book, a project of tallying the world in exponential numerological expansions without closures. His commitment to the materiality and practices of writing are where, paradoxically, one sees the muted spirituality of this work. Silliman, as much as Reznikoff, embodies the position of recording angel, the implacable watcher of what is and how it gets said.

For the reader, the small but palpable observations made in language concerning the accretion of detailed, granular perceptions about the world, and the saturation in that surround of detail, read second by second, all make an unusually challenging experience by demanding (as much Stein does) minute nonextractive attention. The reader is (re-)trained not to ask for Grand Narrative, Grand Theory—and yet is given a Book.

The work creates a fantastic zone in which one is (as if) experientially inside the life of another. In this Silliman does something to time that is characteristic of time given to, that is, chosen by, the writer of a long poem. The writer of a long poem doubles time. Silliman doubles the time given to him first by noticing, then by recording the details and syntaxes of apprehension within a certain space and time, generally impersonal. In Silliman sentences (each its own mininarration, aphorism, description) are the central writing strategy, rather than a continuous linked story or suggestively juxtaposed fragments.

For him, the continuities and logics of narrative necessarily legitimate social order. If one desires a critique of social order, one may choose to resist modes and conventional satisfactions of narrative as being an active and solidifying agent confirming worldviews that need to be questioned and displaced. This resistance occurs in language writing but also, with various strategies, in such other critique-laden contemporaneous poetics as feminist writing and anticolonial writing, visible in this chapter. Therefore, a debate, in these practices, between accessibility and deconstruction of conventions is a permanent feature, solved by different writers in different ways, often by choices of social dimensions of meaning in page space. The general meaning of Silliman's page space makes accretive time turn into a solid space that registers the presence of the many.

In Silliman statements create documentary lists, an account book, serial vignettes, a tallying as telling. He asks of his notebook writing: "In what sense is this a ledger?" for a ledger has both numbers and possible accounts in small accumulated units.[35] The works of *The Alphabet* make the ultimate, or fundamental realist move: they are an indexical anatomy—both a display of catalogs, lists, enumerations, and a diagnostic display of cutting up, dissection, analysis, minute examination, along with the sense that quotidian time is discontinuous to a fault. This is the long poem as Assemblage/Album that turns into an untranscendent Book by sheer material bulk and temporal persistence.

Interiority has little value for most of Silliman's writing. It is a stream of observation, not a stream of interior consciousness. Silliman exercises the will to scan and record "it" (anything, all the world, everything in the world) as it goes by. Whatever is happening at this minute can be recorded. Yet the material artifact is both being made now and eulogized for its future form. "'No,' I say to the man who asks, 'Is that your diary?' 'it's a book.'"[36] This moment is the acknowledged trace of the Book. Mallarmé's world ending up in a Book has found another champion in Silliman.

WHY MALLARMÉ'S POETICS? BOOK AND *GESAMTKUNSTWERK*

This genre of assemblage has, besides Whitman, another serious source in poetics and literary history in Stéphane Mallarmé's essays and unrealized projects. There are two notable manifestations of assemblage announced, and both are palpably expressed in and connected to the Anglophone long poem—the Book and The Total Artwork (*Gesamtkunstwerk*). Both modes propose poetic contributions to social, civic, and cultural knowledge in this gathered plurality. Writers of twentieth- and twenty-first-century long poems manifest a desire for an ideal synthesis of the arts and perhaps a celebration of civic coherence—or civic critique, not only in a performative *Gesamtkunstwerk* but in their compilations of and addresses to the most pertinent social and cultural knowledge in The Book. The two concepts are intertwined in this chapter in fascinating and meaningful ways for the Anglophone long poems—particularly by the presence in long poems of heteroglossic diction, citation/polyvocality, and visually and texturally dynamic page space. Versions of these projects became crucial to the Anglophone modern long poem's poethical concerns.

MALLARMÉ'S "BOOK"

> . . . the Great Work. What would it be? It's hard to say: a book, quite simply, in several volumes, a book that would be a real book, architectural and premeditated, and not a collection of chance inspirations, however wonderful. . . . I would go further and say *the* Book, convinced as I am that in the final analysis there's only one.
>
> Mallarmé to Paul Verlaine, November 15, 1885[37]

Mallarmé's contributions to a vision of poetic possibility in the twentieth century emerge in Mallarmé's essays and his sketchy work called "Le Livre." These first envision a great synthetic Book, a transformative, culturally penetrating work representing (symbolizing and exemplifying) "everything." He saw this book also enacted in poetic performances with civic bearing, combining many media, tending to a secular ritual with deliberate mystique, and published as modular texts of these performances. This was *apparently* to be a serious theatrical event—an assemblage of yearly cycles of ceremonial performances written in exchangeable, aleatory scripts that were (then?) the Book.

The Anglophone long poems discussed forthwith manifest or reinvent a parallel poetics of cultural intervention by means of an assemblage in performance and/or book. Potential socio-spiritual grandeur and the presentation of political-aesthetic structures explain (or at least suggest) why for the modern long poem, the capital-B Book becomes a goal and goad—even without explicit allusions to Mallarmé. A Book is culminating, redemptive enough, showing an ethical *poesis* of the many, and offering a world-scope assemblage, a completeness of address to the "everything" of large issues with an alleged wisdom.[38] The concept of a Book might mediate the very long poem's omnivorous concept of scale and assist the active dialogue between universalizing and particularizing elements. The metaphor of Book might sweeten the unbearable ambition or unspeakable desire for making something beyond declared terminus, reasonable narrative arc, or anyone's ability to encompass the materials. The temptation inherent in long-poem ambitions of culturally encompassing works is the idea of making (one) total Book—of everything.

The Book as an idea and ideal has a particular aura for writers of the long poem. Dante's book held to a single point redemptive perspective focused on the Bible as the book guaranteeing his—yet his work also deftly assimilates and chooses among conflicting contemporaneous debates in theology. Using a biblical numerology and the best that science then offered, Dante's cosmological work became a great synthesizing Book of the knowledge worth knowing and named the crucial spiritual telos. Mallarmé secularized that idea of cultural synthesis while retaining its civic-spiritual aura. Mallarmé resisted both institutionalized religion and affirmative and mythologized nationalisms as essential, necessary social bonds. He postulated that inventing a substitute intellectual and aesthetic formation was crucial for a functioning social/spiritual plurality in society. Poetry was to provide that great synthesis. In the twentieth century, the Book realized in a very long poem becomes a metaphor and a drive, an object and an imagined goal concerning ultimate processes toward poetic vocation and cultural meanings.

Mallarmé's provocative absolutist claim (everything in the world held in a Book) is affirmed in his 1895 essay. He teases, in this impressionist feuilleton, about the open folds of a newspaper and the closed, in-folded pages of the book, needing to be cut with a knife. This then commonplace *intonso* publication of a book—in library terminology, uncut quires—made it mysterious; in apparent contrast a newspaper has advertising, varieties of stories, dailiness, availability, a spectacle of everything—as assemblage. Yet the newspaper (open, popular, and quotidian) is on a continuum with the apparently more secretive book, he argues, because each practice is one site of the inky miracle of language, allowing this miracle to be made visible every single day to everyone. Newspaper and Book are on a popular-to-elite continuum. "Making typographic composition approach a rite" infuses the look of a page (its page space) with a sacred, awe-filled experience.[39]

Mallarmé asks why can't a book be more like a newspaper; and why can't a poem be arranged in an open-page (collaged?) format as a newspaper is? Why can't a poem also be simultaneously as in-folded and ex-folded as a Book of a new kind of News. A book, in short, could stop being the way it is "now" (in late nineteenth-century France)—*intonso* and closed in its uncut quires—yet remain as open to ambiguous readings and mystery as the once-uncut book had been before being cut open.[40] Here is the zone of the nanorific *Un coup de dés* (1897)—with its "headlines," and collection of *faits divers in extremis* as a new kind of book, open and hermetic at once, never making a statement that is unqualified and finished, and exhibiting an enfolded, nested syntax on its wide-open pages. The best of both worlds, the newspaper and the Book, real and idealized are, arguably, combined in such a model.

However, even tactics of citation, documentation, using reports, archives, and legal cases, making poetry from history and the news, deployed regularly in Anglophone long poems do not change the impact on modernism and modern long poems of the initial proposition of this essay, perhaps its greatest temptation. That "everything in the world exists to end up in a book" remains a scandalous goal. Even if one recognizes the political, ontological, and social shock of this statement, its intentional displacement of established religion, its scientific ridiculousness, its reductive superiority, and its conflicting appeal both to secular documents and to cosmic mystery, some writers are seemingly motivated by this claim.

This idea seems to have come into Anglophone literature as a hint of summation, a breakthrough, a vision both utopian and revelatory: the Book. Our long-poem writers recognize and embrace the dialogue between the Book as a fundamental gathering of all importance and a secular and quotidian mode of writing and its presentation like the newspaper.

The Book, with its capital letter, imbibes grandeur from historically spiritual zones, transferring this to secular writing, claiming that accumulation, by sheer obsessive density, becomes self-sacralizing. A traditional sacred book rests on cultural claims as closed, finished, sealed to further revelations. Hence, this metaphor freezes or solidifies the processual, additive, and ongoing poetics of many long poems, which are thereupon unfrozen by the secular ideology of album-assemblages. The sacred metaphor (tending toward one book) does conflict with the secular poetics of many of these long poems, particularly in continuous making versus ending. The tensions or contradictions between metamorphosis and the monument, fragmentation and finish, fixed ideas and the pulse of the "projective," exact procedure and ongoing process are part of long-poem ethos—and problematics.

MALLARMÉ'S *GESAMTKUNSTWERK*

A *Gesamtkunstwerk* (multimedia syncretic artwork of uplifting force; the German means "total artwork") was, in Mallarmé's era, exemplified by Richard Wagner's operas, performances with political, mythic, aesthetic, and spiritual goals. A *Gesamtkunstwerk*, in its opera format, would have music, dramatic structures like ritual and heightened melodrama, performance strategies, dance, costumes, special effects, lighting, and scenery, engaging most of the senses in spectacle.

Propelled by Wagner's poetics and works, this fusion artwork was slightly suspect first for the translation of "gesamt" as "total," bringing in the unpleasant potential of totalitarian unity rather than "aesthetic integration," an alternative translation, though "integration" is also aesthetically loaded as a criterion. The total artwork is, as Koepnick proposes, "a constitutive element of modernist aesthetic practice in all its multivalence and ambiguity."[41] Yet Wagner's nationalist myths and deeply embedded anti-Semitism in certain opera plots belied the neutral triumphs of his integrative, composite art, given the problematic implications of their actual arguments. This is like Pound's passages evoking Italian fascism and anti-Semitism in polemical groundswells in his *Cantos* beginning in the 1920s. Thus, while evoking *Gesamtkunstwerk* (composite artwork) can be disconcerting, I argue that its influential poetics (putatively including "every" art) and its suggestive syntheses enter the Anglophone long poem.

The surface reason that these two ideas (Book and total artwork) are linked in Mallarmé's poetics is that in the notes called "Le Livre," or the Book, he talks about his never-realized plan for a large-scale performance cycle. These plans for his unwritten performance work mainly describe a *Gesamtkunstwerk*, while his ideas of the Book come in essays. Essentially, for Mallarmé, these two ideas of an "Ur-form" are double and the same, two prongs of a single overarching ambition. Mallarmé's concerted response to Wagner—whose work he resisted—declared a total artwork separated from Wagner's bombastic insistences. Challenged by such mytho-spiritual opera cycles as the Ring Cycle (still a Mt. Everest for performance), Mallarmé fantasized making a different version of a *Gesamtkunstwerk* in a *poetry* that suggested many media in coordination.

Mallarmé proposed this kind of *Gesamtkunstwerk* perhaps twice, although one is unrealized, only in manuscript notes, and the other is debatable as being such a work.[42] These are The Book/"Le Livre" and what we have of it, the extremely unfinished manuscript. This work spottily postulates schemes for a secular but mythic dramatic cycle intended for performance, with the bold goal of replacing theistic religions with a tempting if intellectual atheism filled with elegant ritualized enactments (possibly of traditional tales?) and civic uplift. (The work also contains many practical notes about pricing strategies and shape of the book.) This would be given in public performances like theater-based poetry readings, available as (chapbook) scripts.

The other proposal could be (and sometimes is) seen as the short hermetic poem *Un coup de dés*. Mallarmé had claimed that a poem of sufficient sublimity could—because of the power of poetry as a medium itself, unify, reintegrate, or entwine many art media by linking them together in an immersive experience: intellectual, dramatic, visual, rhythmic, haptic, and mysterious. This is the "polymorphous" promise of poetry—linked to the aesthetic potential of free verse as a formal breakthrough.[43]

In making these double proposals in the essay "Crisis of Verse," Mallarmé claimed the "essential" fundamental language of poetry: "an art of achieving the transposition into the Book of the symphony, or merely [a way] to take back what is ours [belonging to *poets*]: for it is not through the elementary [e.g., simplistic, Wagnerian] sounds of brasses, strings, or woods [woodwinds], but undeniably through the intellectual word at its height that there should result, with plenitude and obviousness, as the totality of relations existing in everything, the system otherwise known as Music."[44] As Mallarmé says concessively, this "totality" does indeed exist in the system called Music, but it is too melodramatic and "elementary"—crowd-pleasing? not adequately subtle? uplifting but coarse? However, there is a much better medium. He is about to claim these spiritual excitements, discoveries, and commitments to unify media as the property, the sole, or most appropriate property of poetry.[45] Poetry is, thus, a higher idealized Music. Hence, Mallarmé's missing long performance cycle of a Total Artwork (in notes called "Le Livre") was projected as a rich pageant and set of ritualized readings, celebrating the socio-cosmological universe with poetry.

The critic Danielle Follett extrapolates from Mallarmé's hermetic, incomplete, and messy notes a sketch of performative theatrical works: "a series of readings" with a script of "many loose pages" that can be read in "interchangeable" order by an "operator" (an aloof, priestly master of ceremonies) during a "ceremonial in multiple sessions," tolerating a symbolically important "limited dose of indeterminacy," and accomplished with a "latent redemptive function in its [Catholic] masslike event." Mallarmé wanted to replace religious ceremonies and nationalist mythologies with repeated performances of abstract cosmological awe. Follett views this (unrealized) work as "being perhaps the first alternative theater project that intentionally incorporates chance procedures," like certain happenings.[46] This accurate extrapolation, however, sheers away from any corresponding sense of the work as also a Book.

A parallel reconstruction from Mallarmé's notes is Trevor Stark's: this performance would have been a recurrent civic ritual honoring chance (in random choices of recombined readings from a set of fixed poetic scripts) and entering a collectively evoked Void—the Mallarméan opposite of Christianity's personalized salvationist teleology. In addition, those recombined pages suggest that their sum makes up (would have made up) the Book, which seems to have been a multibook assemblage of writings, constructed with foldouts and back-front reversals—like a set of artist's book as well as a text, making some ideal all-encompassing statement.[47] Reminder: All these daunting ideas and projections were made in sketchy notes, existing only as a set of thoughts unrealized by Mallarmé, and thus appear only as postulates in poetics extrapolated (as here) by critics.

UN COUP DE DÉS

Un coup de dés (1897) is one of the more obscure, hermetic, abstract, and baffling poems in the twentieth century. Because this is such a difficult text, because it deals with issues of chance and the universe, because its position in Mallarmé's canon arguably assumes the cultural space prepared for "Le Livre" but never filled, the aura of this work is considerable, and it may refract, or involve, claims of the "book as spiritual instrument" *and* of a *Gesamtkunstwerk*. Perhaps it is a blueprint, but it always remains a mystery: a secular performative evocation of strange events via page space, as an essayistic long poem with absolutist axioms. This nanorific poem is a syntactic assemblage of nested hypotheticals concerning social-mythic figures and cosmological forces. The sculpting of syntax by typography, not to speak of the evocativeness of the mysterious words, the choreographed performance of statement against the white background, alluding to dance and sculpture, and making shapes in page space, the sizes of the words in typography, the poem's musical "arrangement of fragments with alternations and confrontations, adding up to a total rhythm," all together suggest that *Un coup de dés* is an intensive condensed version of a *Gesamtkunstwerk*.[48]

Un coup de dés offers three poetic/thematic innovations and challenges. While there are prior shaped poems, poems as amulets or magical formulae, and poems visually palpable in illustrated books, as in William Blake, this is (apparently) the first influential Euro-cultural poem whose operation rests consistently on its original, intentional, and drastic page space.[49] Mallarmé made a visual text, extending the statements of each poetic line across the fold, into the space of the double page. This "across the gutter" placement transcends the normal book by a design for the words integrating semantic meanings with syntactic ambiguities. Challenging the normative organization of a poem's page, this work has no poetic peer, only polemical peers in just-later modernist manifestos as page-space posters.

Exaggerating the impact of the nonmetrical line to poetry, the poem's second innovation, is addressed to free-verse controversies, sweeping aside traditionally elegant but stodgy French prosody. And its third innovation involves thematic allusions to sacralized, scientific, and mythic materials and characters freed from religiously inflected stories and plots of redemption or tragedy, thereby reducing/elevating the whole narrative and actual universe to acts of chance, with human spiritual meanings always in question. The poem thereby absolutizes itself; it is only and finally itself—intransigent and resistant. Because the status of "event" in this poem (what happens? really?) is so oddly allegorized even as anything has the status of occurring, the poem seems always to be at one remove from itself.

Most of the poem talks of things that only might or may or could happen, not things that clearly did happen. The text gives and takes away at the same time. The page-space clusters tend to overwhelm, with syntactic modification, the headline thesis-bearing semantic statement distributed throughout the work. "A throw [or toss] of dice does not abolish [nullify, eliminate] chance" is the broken-up topic sentence or proposition.

You can repeat this "Throw of the Dice" mantra until you are transfixed, but a deeper uncertainty emerges about what has just "happened." Finally "nothing will have taken place" in the poem except the place or site *of* the poem with its visual text sculpting thoroughly ambiguous events. However—that dice toss has thrown up, into this universe of chance, one event forming part of a constellation, but we don't know much from this asterism (our "Big Dipper"), its existence or numerology, except that contingency will always rule the next throw. As an evocation of the constant further-beyond complexities uncovered by contemporary astrophysics, the poem is suggestive. As a satisfactory "answer" to what spiritual consolations could occur in any modern book, it is neutral or indifferent. Nonetheless, this work is one inspiration for the gathering of sociocultural and performative visions in many long poems in the absence of fixed and formerly settled spiritual understandings. Moreover, this poem traffics in awe itself.

The medium for this argument is its unique page space. This page is experienced as a glyph or graph of the lobes of thought from a hypotactic, deeply modified sentence or two. The pockets of parenthetic modifying clauses and phrases disperse the grammar across the double page (visualized as a canvas or performance space). The poem has a high degree of white space, yet it is not only a page considered as white background for inked words that is at stake, but the page as sky or stage for cosmic questions. The relative sizes of the typography are actors in this space, for the sizes of the one font indicate the syntax of the main clause and its modifiers and interruptions, which are pockets of conditional, suppositive, subjunctive, and modifying hypotheticals, nested inside each other.

Page space is the zone where Mallarmé's proposed "gesamt"-ness occurs, poetry's nonnormative page designs become the symbolic act of including all the arts—that "Wagnerian" combination of all-in-one-place—music, costumes, poetry, performance (and so on): The Opera of It All. With evocative words and with page-space acts alluding to different arts, Mallarmé makes the counterintuitive claim that all the resources of all (many) of the arts collude and combine in their agglomeration under the rubric of Poetry, not operatic performance.

The meanings of *Un coup de dés* within Mallarmé's career and its poetics are much debated. However, this book is about Anglophone literature, and I will regard the poem as a major instantiation of page-space innovations in poetry, done with grand intellectual and poetic authority, one plausible precursor of page-space use in Anglophone long poems.

In a transnational extension, the Mallarméan idealizing poetics of a special book of performances both civic and spiritual becomes a material goal within Anglo-American poetries. This is the aesthetic-political Book assembling knowledge, its histories and uses. Pound was, as with much else, at the inception of this strange fusion in Anglophone poetries, and in *The Cantos*, he synthesized the spiritual-documentary, the mythological-political, the hetero-discursive, and visual text as a peculiarly dynamic Book of epochal, encyclopedic "everything."

The interlocked ideas of the "Book as spiritual instrument" and social/civic consolidation in a total artwork seem to have entered Anglophone poetry via Arthur Symons's short essay on Mallarmé in *The Symbolist Movement in Literature* (1899, reprinted for at least two decades), and the contemporaneous enthusiasms of Yeats and Pound for this poetics. The relevant passage is a defense of a "new art, more than a new religion," whose precise form in the world could not be settled. This passage seems to take hold of the considerable occultism and spiritualist experiments of the nineteenth century and pre–First World War years and to reform these practices into a new art, "a spiritualizing of the word," a way to displace religion by an even purer aesthetic-spiritual affirmation. Symons inspires this revolt against exteriority, against rhetoric (except his), against a materialistic tradition: "in this endeavor to disengage the ultimate essence, the soul, of whatever exists and can now be realized by the consciousness," and these became the hint of a new fused artwork with a spiritual or sacred aura.[50]

Symons's version of Mallarmé came into Anglophone letters with Yeats and Pound catching this propulsion toward synthesis, possibly in their mutual interaction between 1913 and 1916. Both were fascinated by Pound's (Fenollosan) work with the Noh as a synthetized artwork (in fact a *Gesamtkunstwerk*), a hieratic drama involving dance, masks, music, and ritualized actions.[51] Yeats's attraction to what he had assimilated of Mallarmé intrigued Ezra Pound, who became a consolidator and important spokesman for the modern long poem as culturally influential Book, and (with its heteroglossic social sounds and socio-cosmological poetics) a *Gesamtkunstwerk* in Anglophone cultures.

However, at the time of this dialogue with Pound, for Yeats—as for Symons, the nonspiritual was "an imprisonment." "Spiritualising of the word" was the only good outcome of these matters, with a "confidence in the eternal correspondences between the visible and the invisible universe"—an articulation of the occultist and symbolist poetics of "correspondences."[52]

One sees this tension in the work of Pound, who intermingled a secularized *Cantos* with history and a mythologized set of sacred-spiritual affirmations. His poetics came from a phrase that Pound *said* was said by Yeats: "new sacred book of the arts," consonant with a poetics from Mallarmé. In my transmission narrative around "the Book," Pound evoked this in 1932, in one of his several recastings of the question of *The Cantos*'s structure(s) and purpose(s). He declared "an imperative need of a BASIS, i.e., what ole Unc. Wm. Yeats called 'new sacred book of the arts.'"[53] Pound also said Yeats "prayed for" the "new sacred book" in *Polite Essays*.[54] He clearly employs the Mallarméan lexicon for a political-aesthetic statement, this visible because he fused, into his (and/or Yeats's?) complex phrase, the two aspects of Mallarmé's project discussed here. One is a book of all the arts (the *Gesamtkunstwerk*), and the other is a new "sacred" Book, a book that can bear that capital B for its purposes of transforming "everything"—including politics. In another late summary of his project, Pound explains this Book as a presentation of universals. That "sacred book of the arts" is, then, Pound's polemical and poetical homage to Mallarmé. The finality of "BASIS" has other sources.

Pound's multiple schemes of documentation and arrangements of granular, cited, and summarized details in *The Cantos* presented permanent sacred principles of aesthetic-political leadership and order under the play of all historical contingencies, exactingly and obscurely arrayed. All events and leadership successes were undergirded by his implicit argument that *The Cantos* would reveal itself as the culminating Book of political-mythological knowledge, the condensed and intense outline of forces behind history that put a particular leader, laws, and a regime in tune with the elemental underpinnings of everything vital in nature and culture. Hence, Pound in the 1930s wanted *The Cantos* to become a version of The Book with a special political and cosmological status as a work that diagnosed a world and summed up that world system of fascist nationalism that he wanted his book to celebrate and affirm.

HETEROGLOSSIA, PAGE SPACE, AND ASSEMBLAGE

In *Anglophone* long poems, the sense of assemblage is achieved not solely by theorizing a total artwork, or simply by allusions to mixed media or various art forms, or only by the idea of a Book with distinctive page space. In Anglophone modernisms the language ranges of extensive heteroglossia are a vital component. Much more than a *stylistic* trait in Anglophone poems, heteroglossia centrally underlies the purposes and social meanings of assemblage as a long poem genre and supports both Mallarméan ideas of a Book and a *Gesamtkunstwerk* as a totalizing array. It also tries to answer, in diction, how a poem can say "we."

Defining heteroglossia, Bakhtin observes that traditionally poetic "poetry" (as actually in hermetic Mallarmé) "is suspended from any mutual interaction" with the jostle and cacophony of discourses. However, in the modern period, possibly drawing on both novel and newspaper, poets negotiate their degrees of closeness to and distance from socially inclusive dictions. Some poets remain generally "monologic," some even sublime and poetic (using special tones, topics, and diction for poetry), while others embrace "the influence of extraliterary social dialects" including learnèd hypervocabularies, technical jargons, ethnic nuance, foreign-language phrases, nonnormative language cadences, local idioms, regional vocabularies, immigrant crossovers, plural Englishes, popular allusions, and aural orthographies. Some poets toggle (freely and heteroglossically) among these possibilities, constructing musical, visual, and socially allusive mixes of language.[55]

Heteroglossia, the pluralized dictions of language use, a linguistic cosmopolitanism, is crucial to the Anglophone modern long poem, underscoring its social range. Heteroglossia in poetry insists on socially evocative sets or civic arrays of dictions, lexicons, and orthographies. With tactics of heteroglossia, poetry and its page spaces fill with dialects, jargons, bureaucratic and poetic sounds, languages of social and professional groups, slang from different generations and marginalized groups, as well as citations from socially diverse texts and several languages.[56] This wide language use gives the Anglophone modern long poem its power as a gathering or assemblage of social allusions in language itself. Heteroglossia offers the equivalent in language of both the "everything" of a long poem and, with its diction varieties, even the multimedia mode of a *Gesamtkunstwerk*, *as if* different arts emerged in the self-different aural and social idioms. This is an argument by analogy, making different social sounds as if parallel to different artistic mediums. Heteroglossic diction thereby may allegorically or metaphorically encapsulate "all" the arts.

The visual text of these long poems, much more palpable than the normative page look from prior poetic centuries, further characterizes Anglophone long poems. Whenever poets use a multiplicity of social languages or bring various voices into their texts (sometimes by citation/quotation), a nonrectangular poem or a presentational page space may further dramatize this diction choice. The material look of the text thereby supports the multiple dictions and social vectors with the poem's evocation of array or extent suggested via the dramatic potential of the posterlike platform—the page itself or more-contained local modifications of that page. This generally differentiates a poem from a novel, which, though often heteroglossic in dictions and social depictions, has, for the most part, a conventional squared-off page space with no fancy or provocative visual text.

The socially lively sounds of heteroglossic dictions are demonstrated on the page of long poems in collage visual strategies (typographies, white-space uses, indentations, fragmenting pulses of syntax). The effects of page space are also visible in the open layout of serial works, in emphases on arrays of cited materials that are visually marked (as in Williams, Waldman, or Olson), in juxtapositions supporting a poem's performative qualities (*The Waste Land* like a radio play performing distinct voices), as well as in any possibility for typographic variety, signage, and unusual white spaces on the page of any of these book-works. Poetry need no longer adhere at all times to a rectangular (conventional) visual appearance. This is dramatized in Kamau Brathwaite's striking choice to alter his conventional page space in the reconceptualized version of *Ancestors*, making social array palpable on his reconfigured page.

These heteroglossic dictions and collaged pages as dramatic, presentational, and typographically lively have the potential visually and semantically to signal a polyphonic assemblage. You *see* the text dramatically; you don't only read it. Heteroglossia and diction glissades, citation, and nonnormative, inventive pages in modern long poems indicate their social array and suggest both a socially inclusive artwork and versions of the synoptic Book within the genre assemblage.

Taken generally, tendencies to heteroglossic diction and to nonnormative page spaces may interlock, but either will dramatize aural language ranges and social reach as well as intensities of aesthetic performance. These multiples of diction align with the trace of the *Gesamtkunstwerk* (multiples of arts) that emerge in Anglophone long poems. Any nontraditional page spaces with visual emphases and heteroglossia support a Book as a poetic performance of social assemblage, assembly, or arrays of multiply voiced peoples. Hence, heteroglossic dictions of all sorts plus active page space are crucial underpinnings of long poems considered as assemblages.

POUND'S BOOK

The problem or issue that assemblage, album, or array addresses is organizing the many: multitudes, peoples, their languages, their histories, acknowledging multiple societies, accounting for array when hierarchy or telos is under scrutiny or unstable. In this general long-poem practice of assemblage, poets put concerted pressure on various modes of segmentivity—often on different scales in the same poem: fragments, sentences, cited units of many tones, odic sections, serially organized aphoristic vignettes. Just as epic-quest is a good description of some long poems, quest-assemblage works as an overview descriptor—both formulations revealing genre polysemy. Both epic and quest evocations together in a canto array are characteristics of Pound's Book.

Pound pushed forward with *The Cantos* at a moment (1922) when two other Anglophone writer-friends had already published significant works. Eliot's *Waste Land* had some of the traits of scope, heteroglossia, mythic and social explorations, and something evocative and "new" that seemed to offer a cultural summation. Of course, it's too short to be anything like a speculative world-encompassing work, that ideal form of the Book, but it remained a long-poem challenge for Pound. In the case of Joyce, Pound had brokered early appearances of *Ulysses*. Like his own early cantos, it had epic goals; for Joyce, that "world in a day" sense of everything, a heteroglossic multigeneric tour de force in its range of tones, styles, genres, and manners that has made it a particular summation within twentieth-century literature of city, day, outsider hero, wanderer, and Homeric allusions and scope in a miniworld.

The year 1922, the publication date of each, begins the long-reverberating receptions of these major works. All through the teens, Pound felt the pressure, as well as the pleasure, of being intimately involved with both these authors and their distinctive works. His sense of being belated irked him through his whole career and was a continuous motivation. For Pound, the existence of *The Waste Land* and of *Ulysses* cleared the way for—and provoked—the work he wanted to make both to rival and to become the equal of theirs. These works challenged him to live up to their examples, to continue his own big Book, and to join the modernism they had exemplified—and that he had encouraged.

He had said to Joyce in 1917 that he'd already started "an endless poem, of no known category. Phanopoeia or something or other, all about everything."[57] If editor Forrest Read is correct that Phanopoeia (casting images, like a slideshow, via light) was the work's provisional title, we can think of Pound's desire to make this book not only about "everything" in multiple heteroglossic voices but to collect exemplary moments of illuminated knowledge. This fortified his desire for a book of synthesis and wisdom, continuing his imagist presentational principles of lucid graspable units but using that tactic toward his intensifying interests in summarizing societal potential and its failures.

In early *Cantos*, Pound was trying to synthesize Homer and Dante, as if saying he could bring both major long-poem writers in the West together under the rubric of his work. Then he was trying to synthesize ancient cultures with a political economy that also attempted to get to the root of productivity and distribution—combining the "sacred book" of ritualized fertility-potency evocations with the political "secular book." He was trying to synthesize the poetic text with knowledge, so that poetry became a way of learning and following condensed historical principles, particularly about leadership. These goals led to scintillating heteroglossias of diction, quick squibs of multiple times, and a lively page space to present this assemblage.

Further, from the beginning of his career, he had hoped for "our American Risorgimento."[58] Then Pound thought he had the conditions for the renaissance in England with the artistic friends whose work he had supported in the teens and early twenties; however, WWI had destroyed this incipient new era. By 1919–20 he had begun his idiosyncratic but serious and sincere involvement with a reactionary politics that he hoped could fuse an elite of artists and political leaders toward a renewed version of that renaissance. By 1928 this became "Quite simply, I want a new civilization."[59]

Ten years later (1937–38), his goal for *The Cantos* was a "new synthesis, the totalitarian"—a formulation emerging from the realms of total artwork intermingled with Book, both condensing the materials of the "new civilization." The final developmental phase and the 1938 "new synthesis, the totalitarian" show Pound's culminating poetic hopes in a severely binarist universe that takes all his intellectual, economic, and aesthetic findings before the early and midtwenties and reshapes them under the fascist compact that he was proud to support.[60] This goal is no longer a cultural-political totalizing "Book" but something far more drastic, a totalitarian (authoritarian) civilization with that Book as centerpiece and encyclopedia.

Meanings of "totalitarian" for Pound range from a benign "totalizing" (or "everything") to a full-scale fascination with monolithic cultural-social unity using authoritarian means, a temptation for Pound because it was speedy and cut through blockages (i.e., institutional constraints). He had offered this stance as a calling card in *Guide to Kulchur*, a belligerent, tendentious, and polemical book of cultural provocations, necessary, in Poundean terms, to attack hegemonic structures preventing political-cultural transformations.

From about 1924 Pound was in a big hurry, the urgency exacerbated by his intense attempts to transform and save (salvage) cultural good but also to savage "usurious," bourgeois, and complacent culture. He defended his condensed insights and notations in *The Cantos*, formerly the epiphanic, imagistic fragment, with a newly politicized justification. This "detached phrase," once imagist precision, is now praised as "the most rapid means of communication," leaping over the tedium of argument and potential difficulties of convincing others directly into essential knowledge that would bring instantaneous political results.[61] Often these were tiny (i.e., speedy) bits of citation selected from historical and archival documents, decontextualized but talismanic.

This sense of the Book defined in Pound's Italian period resembles an urgent manifesto, calling people into political action. The telegraphic style of his essays, and more, of his long poem recall the electricities of spiritual vibrations supposedly present in occult communication and evoke slogans in advertising and political activities. Speed was of the essence; instantaneity underwrote comprehension and credibility. Yet the reader was continuously faced with flashes of assertion and insistence without any social context.

His *Cantos* as Sacred Book and totalitarian (secular/political) synthesis operate in tandem, always offering slightly different emphases or poetic goals at different moments. This is also assemblage—groups of poems making *The Cantos* the sum of its own shifts of materials (different plans) and emphases (different historical source texts). There are the nine units of *The Cantos*, some with intense bouts of allusive documentation from published materials and archives. His various *Cantos*-plans are repeatedly announced, as in the 1927 letter describing a "fugue"—"subject," "counter-subject," and transformation.[62] Or in the very loose but compelling tripartite allusions to Dante's canticles. Or in a descriptor "the permanent, the recurrent, the casual."[63] Does it matter particularly that Pound could not settle among these (and other) recorded structural schemes? It is part of the generativity of *The Cantos* as assemblage—a forgiving mode of collection—that he has invented so many schemes and still others.

In the bounce of heteroglossic juxtaposition, Pound gives the sense that a great discovery from this assemblage is imminent, around the next corner of the poem. Further the pages are exorbitant with provocative self-differences of discourse and tones. The impacts of juxtaposition (on many scales) as texture and as structure are fundamental to Pound's exciting sound and visuality. Yet for him, the "heteroclite" variety of the "modern mind" was a problem that he wanted to solve by accumulation of "answers"—not interpretations but universals.[64] This meant that the textures of *The Cantos*, fiercely heterodiscursive with rich middens of social languages and accents, are seen at least by late-career Pound as a symptom, a "heteroclite" (irregular, abnormal) swerve from necessary discourses of absolute certainty. Does the texture of *The Cantos* as poetry stands in fundamental conflict—at least in unstable contradiction—with the goal of *The Cantos*: to find and embrace the "BASIS" that never changes? If so, the poem is self-divided at the core, but Pound tries in his central period to assert that its rhetoric is confluent with fascist "basis."[65]

If the texture of his poetry (its heteroglossia) pulls in the direction of sociality and array, its politics, a belief in a strong and hierarchic social and economic order and a set of dogmas invested in Mussolini's leadership, goes the opposite way, in a totalitarian direction. The contradiction does not resolve but simply stands *as* the poem in at least a ten-year sweep, possibly more, certainly from Canto 41 (dated 1933) to 1945/1948 with the elegy for Mussolini as sacrificed god (Canto 74). Pound's fascism may be enacted in quixotic or self-canceling gestures, but he did attempt, among his various shifts for this assemblage structure of *The Cantos*, to reinterpret this poetic text as contributing to a fascist culture.

In the 1920s Pound had called his economic and political findings a third way (between communism and capitalism). His one-member "Party of Intelligence" had its own program. However, that renaming calls attention only to his own self-assumed, self-assured singularity. He worked for the fascist movement in the Italian political context and did not repudiate that allegiance in his public actions until the very end of his life. Or perhaps he didn't.[66]

Another way to explore Pound's intellectual and poetic presentation in *The Cantos* is to track Pound's taut pedagogic *mot* on the epic, one of the central genres of the whole poem. His aphorism defines an epic as a poem "including history."[67] "Include" states clearly that historical materials are one constituent part or aspect of an epic. But by "history" Pound seems to mean verifiable accurate descriptions (like the wounds described by Homer[68]), anecdotes or materials from the past, freshly described or presented (via "phanopoeia"), as if the writer were an eyewitness, registering impacts anew. He also means citations from documents, treated as clues to mysteries and conspiracies about responsibility that he is trying to solve to make "the *Cantos* historic [. . .] but not fiction."[69] That is, the text exists to tell the truth. This means his book can be used as a textbook of *exempla* for historic leaders to learn from; the poem is no longer a fiction, though it is fictive (made). By "history" Pound does not mean analysis and interpretation of the past but functional declarative precepts.

The Poundean version of historical truth constructs exemplifications. What this attitude led to, as Truth becomes the de facto muse of *The Cantos* in Canto 8, is a wayward but intense, purpose-urgent gathering of materials from archives and various kinds of historical sources; then Pound "wrote from" this accumulated material, citing it with a self-declared intuitive grasp. He considered the gritty details and instances that he chose to be significant manifestations of necessary truth without any impediments such as hypotheses to be discussed, debates on the relevance of certain documents, or methodologies of interpretation. The ideogrammic method of juxtaposition would guarantee that lines of intellectual force would be successfully extrapolated by the reader, by-passing interpretative categories. Those able to penetrate these vital gists would get the Truth.

This is an exciting but incomplete notion of cognition and a fundamentalist stance toward knowledge, as any number of Pound's readers have shown; Bob Perelman's account is particularly compelling.[70] Pound's findings have that latent authoritarian focus on right and natural categories that undercuts his surface scintillation and arrays of material; plethora is really occulted "BASIS." Pound did not evaluate his analytic processes of selection, or any historical hypothesis from the evidence collected, or offer serious historiographic debates about interpretation of extracted fact or anecdote. What he included were, in his view, not simply selections of detail but the eternally salient ones; they were "real history" or its instantly decodable clues showing true patterns, not interpretive readings.

Pound's axiom is that presenting one truth is the core reason for writing. "History" gets identified by Pound as if it were a physical science, with basic principles (like gravity, magnetism) undergirding everything, but he takes an incomplete view even of science as having no discussion of these principles, no debates about their functioning under various conditions, or links among these basics. Yet no intellectual field is constructed without interpretation, debates of and about assumptions, data, and findings; Pound, however, thought the search through raw fact for universal principles was history's goal—a timeless, unchanging synthesis perpetually reaffirmed, not contingent or discussable. His model of heteroglossic long-poem texture was to provide encoded information.

The two kinds of books he wrote—his essays/handbooks and the long poem—merge or fuse into one circular book, a closed system of identifications and associations. Pound's essays are needed to read his variously condensed phrases; his data are eased, often by repetition, into being truths and then the only truths, building the lexicon of allusions that will decode *The Cantos* by a detour through Pound's own gloss.

The Party of Intelligence rested finally on conspiracy theory. In certain essays Pound had continuously speculated about conspiracies that blocked new culture, new society, and the knowledge eventually to emanate from his Book. Particularly after the debacle of World War I, those he thought were responsible were cursed in the Hell Cantos. Then moving well into the 1930s, Pound came to identify "ONE ENEMY," though multipronged.[71] The amalgamated list would include ideologues such as publishers, journalists, monopolists of money (bankers), war profiteers, gun sellers, financiers, "usurers," failed or debased leaders, politicians in general, and by the late thirties specific political figures whom Pound excoriates as almost personal enemies. To top it off, there were the Jews.[72] These act as "one" force, as if unified. Pound's perpetual question is "*who*" did this—not *what* complex of forces and interests, *what* struggles among groups, or *why* things coalesced, or *how* consequences unfurled.[73] As a result of this personalized "one enemy," "whole beams and ropes of real history have been shelved, overclouded, and buried."[74]

If, as Pound postulated, this was the work of a conspiracy, his undertaking *The Cantos* becomes his desperate, heroic attempt single-handedly to throw enough "facts" and historical information into play to befuddle and paralyze this conspiracy and to construct new cultural and social benchmarks for his readers. The Pound "character" is a warrior-griot; his enemy is repressed information, and his battlefield is the archive. True fact guarantees that the "one enemy" has been defeated at least temporarily when Pound unburies what he calls history (signal flares from cited documents). Pound did probably feel he was a self-elected savior of modernity from itself: he would, in *The Cantos*, thwart the work of the conspiracy by giving access to rectifying information. The poem thereby assumes a polemical task, an instrumental purpose, and a historical role.

Given Pound's lifelong quest for the renaissance aborted by WWI and for the triumph of his Party of Intelligence, he longed to find its potential in real time and had decreasing motivation to evaluate what his historical moment had generated. He was convinced that the renaissance of the teens did not happen *because* of the First World War, although he and the time had been ready. Hence Pound would not let the opportunity for the next renaissance pass him by. He saw it in Italian fascism.

His position drew in part on fascism's cultural self-propaganda, which confirmed his hopes. Just after the rise of fascism in 1922, with Mussolini's March on Rome, Pound arrived permanently in Italy (1924) and became galvanized by the struggles of "*mussolinismo*." This was the political vision idealizing the power of a strongman hero toward this renaissance of cultural restoration and social projects—via political repression. Pound's own sense of art, politics, and history became confluent with the "regenerative myth" in fascist thought claiming its *romanità*—Roman "imperial glory" revived in the present day. This evocation of the "idea of Rome" contributed to Pound's sense that Mussolini was the actualization of a leader for whom he had long been waiting, a leader whose ideological appeals included that resurgence or renaissance.[75] Pound became convinced that Mussolini would lead that renaissance come to "redeem" modernity and modernism.[76] Hence, Pound became an enthusiastic and unapologetic supporter of *mussolinismo*.

In a telling personal moment in 1923, his hotelier in Rimini, a committed fascist, helped Pound gain access to the library/archive where the Malatesta papers were kept, solidifying Pound's thrilled commitment. The activist/fascist forcefulness (and possibly threats) of his hotelier, cutting through bureaucratic blockage (the librarian)—along with the new direction for *The Cantos* achieved through his access to the Malatesta materials—were significant proof, for Pound's leaping mind, of the intellectual, artistic, and political necessity of a coup using force majeure to renew Italy. This close-grained biographical anecdote from Lawrence Rainey is suggestive. This reading connects Pound's general fascination with *mussolinismo* to his own compelling personal and poetic benefit from a specific intervention that had a direct impact on *him*. Pound's attempts to reach Mussolini personally to discuss cultural programs with him then began around 1924.[77]

Thinking that here the vortices of artistic and political power touched in the very place he was now living and in the ideologies and actions generated by fascist leadership fulfilled Pound's deep desire to be at the center of a major cultural and political shift in his lifetime. The polemical memoir *Jefferson and/or Mussolini* offers Pound's richest exposition of this idealized superimposition of artist and leader, sub rosa, himself and Mussolini. He centers on their mutual "passion for construction." "Treat [Mussolini] as *artifex* [skilled maker] and all the details fall into place. Take him as anything save the artist and you will get muddled with contradictions." That last word meant any complexity, mixed motives, illegal and murderous tactics, any set of problematics that Pound always drastically disavowed in this period, in part by quite deliberately looking away. Pound thought Mussolini was his parallel, the artist-figure, politically sculpting a new society. In *Jefferson and/or Mussolini*, he revisualized his "Make It New" ideogram, now retranslated as "the fascist axe for the clearing away of rubbish."[78] Pound had always liked to imagine a tabula rasa sweep of cleansing.

Indeed, in a full act of identification, the essay "Murder by Capital" proposed that he and Mussolini had come to the same recognitions, albeit by different routes.[79] Pound felt that Mussolini was his secret sharer, his doppelgänger. They were both "artists," and they were both political figures: both made a totalitarian work (Pound, interpreting his *Cantos*).

In 1933, to actualize or reaffirm in the twentieth century, the patron-artist formation of Renaissance Italy, Pound repositioned his *Cantos* as if the book had had a "patron"—a leader who celebrated the work of artists by commissioning works from skilled craftsmen (one key theme of the Malatesta cantos). Pound believed he had found his Malatesta. How else to explain the yearning, motivated visit to Mussolini in 1933 so Pound could present the leader with the book, *The Cantos*, in effect redefined as Mussolini's Book, the leadership book. He tried to show Mussolini its potential importance as a catalog of excellent leadership and exemplary acts and to suggest that he/Pound was the man for a high-level cultural appointment to help the regime. He thereupon received that off-handed accolade of "divertente" ("amusing," Canto 41) from Mussolini himself. Because Pound viewed Mussolini as the fulfillment of the political, social, and aesthetic desires that had long been his own goals, his individualist one-person "Party of Intelligence" had allied with that regime and wanted the regime to reciprocate.

Thus appreciated, even anointed in this fantasy structure of feeling, Pound could see himself as an independent cultural contractor, trying to support fascist Italy for what he claimed, aided by the regime's propaganda, as its cultural and economic promise. He thereby politicized his own art, casting himself in a role even beyond the warrior-griot who constructed a representation (a fiction) of multiple cultural and political heroes in an assemblage. Again to cite the 1962 interview, he tried to make his *Cantos* "historic [. . .] but not fiction."[80] As a culmination of his poem in its vocation of salvaging the leadership necessary for our time via assemblage of many instances, Pound more and more assumed the historical role of political actor in the real as he perceived it, a subject in real time about whom newspaper headlines could be written (and eventually were). The Poundean motifs go into hyperdrive, including the lack of time, the impatience with art alone (its slowness to make an impact), the desire to make words that lead directly to action, the urgency that this poem, at this time, must enter this historical space. Pound cast himself as an actor in what he saw as a real historical epic, beyond the literary that was impotent alone. Hence he became a low-level cultural activist on the radio and a polemical journalist for Mussolini's Italy.[81]

At all times Pound used *The Cantos* as an assemblage pointing to a synthetizing Book, a collection point for necessary documents and an archive, a library, a research midden, almost, perhaps not quite, taking his poetic tactics instrumentally, habitually, or for granted. *The Cantos* had always been Pound's synthesizing Book of society and culture because he selected, glossed, and polemicized documents and materials that he presented as the truth of history. In this period the goal of this assemblage, always mercurial, always in play, got redefined as a new sacred book of Mussolini's regime in Italy—its answer and Pound's to failed modernity.

This goal was thwarted by actual historical events. When fascist Italy was defeated, *The Cantos* lost the raison d'être that Pound's convictions had provided for a decade or more. After his arrest for treason for his radio broadcasts paid for by Mussolini's regime, and when he was imprisoned in the Pisan

Disciplinary Training Camp (before incarceration in Washington, DC, from 1946 to 1958), he again reframed his goal by writing a book (*The Pisan Cantos*) constructed as an album of memoirs and notational observations, eulogizing his past, rearticulating a self, returning to some of his principles about art and beauty and preserving cultural heritage but also offering shadowy ways of justifying his continuing political values. There are both bibliographic debates and interpretive discussions about ambiguous passages in *The Pisan Cantos* being indicative of muted support for, or nostalgia for, fascism.[82]

This phase of his Book (true of all synthetic Books, as Barthes argued) is linked with the autobiography of the impetus to write this Book and to fulfill the claims it made on the author. This fact is acute when one faces Pound's oeuvre. His commitment to fascism as a renaissance is not in doubt; this conviction has been somewhat repressed, muted, and refocused during the postwar period, but it never disappears.

However, *The Cantos* as a whole "wanted" to become a Book whose culmination was knowledge: a Sacred Book, not only of a regime, but of a world's worth of wisdom, fusing the arts with knowledge. Having made the link between Pound's poetics and politics in this key era clear enough, here I want to focus further on the fate of the book as an assemblage. The final cantos become sketches of these goals of wisdom; they are the fragments galvanized by Pound's hopes for that book of wisdom. He returns to a defensive, searching tone on the topics of light and the Book.

His 1938 statements in *Guide to Kulchur* prefigure a loosely engineered Dantean connection of Book and light in the last cantos.

> Properly, we shd. read for power. Man reading shd. be man intensely alive. The book shd. be a ball of light in one's hand.[83]

He means to understand reading as discovering defining principles for exemplary leadership. How does this book as light—his last vision of assemblage—illuminate the Book he wanted *The Cantos* to become? In "that great acorn of light," the Book is viewed as a seed for the future. The whole of *Thrones* is an accumulation, like a list, of instances of the good: good fertility, good laws, good leaders, good practices that bring insight, and many presentational beauties. *Thrones* is an astonishing reading experience, as if Pound were simply adding one line to the other (an ultimate array) until they become an asyntactic river of light, using a Dante metaphor from *Paradiso* to help solidify (adhesively) what he needed to claim.[84]

And so too one of the final metaphors and challenges ending the last canto, 116. This oft-cited apologia is packed with challenges—the challenge to others to lift "the great ball of crystal" is prime, but there are other metaphors of generative light. Pound's phrase "errors and wrecks" is much cited as a self-recognition. The proud humility of these statements and their beautiful poignancy need not make us reluctant to clarify his stance. This crystal ball as book as "acorn of light" gets constructed as a metonymic chain among natural seed, a crystal (transparent and lucid), and is a version of the Mallarméan ideal of one book, a further expression of the desire for transcendent visionary clarity.

Wherever and whatever this imagined zone of illumination is, this crystal has been brought to this zone by Pound, poetically and metaphorically. The rhetorical question posed to others about lifting this crystal implies that, as a feat, Pound already did lift it (to get it "there") and thus already had revealed his strength and fortitude. He has proven himself heroically adequate for this intellectual/spiritual labor and has "entered" its aura.[85] This is a self-eulogy. The ball of crystal becomes a challenge of strength and poetic nobility for the next person. But who indeed can lift it (or define its necessity) besides the man who already did? Pound remains proud and heroic enough, claiming this light as a zone he had once dominated.

Could this crystal ball allude to the phrase in common parlance—a device for seeing or predicting the future? Such claims of predictive powers made crystal balls quite popular. If so, Pound then affirms that he was prescient in his political-cultural hopes for fascist Italy. His crystal ball prophesied Mussolini as an exemplar of leadership with eternal values; this would not be an untoward reading of the image, if an unsettling one. Pound has shown us this insight but was compelled to set down the crystal where he stood, because—there are several reasons. One is that Pound ran out of time. Another is that the poem could not end in the triumph that Pound had worked for.

In Pound's long poem, a large quantity of eclectic material has been "included" and arrayed; he struggles to make sense of it, to make it "cohere," but then realizes he cannot or did not because: "I am not a demigod."[86] The newly introduced term "demigod" is striking in its defensive revelation. This word is unique in the poem. It alludes to a hero born of a god and a mortal, protected from death in all particulars but with one vulnerability. A hero in an epic was sometimes a demigod (as Achilles was, with his Olympian genealogy). The testy fantasy of not being a "demigod" is hard to admit to, yet it is an interesting justification. Failure is excusable as part of Pound's "epic" fate; he was not a god or even a demigod. This is a heightened version of what is generally true for many reasons: the "failure" of the very long poem.

Yet Pound still insists "it"—a solid finding—is still there, some revelation, some pattern, some basis with the claim that something coheres, but that his poem (now become "notes") does not.[87] The introduction of the simple genre "notes" for all that effort is striking. The verb "cohere" can be transitive or intransitive. Intransitive "cohere" means "to stick or hold together; to be logically connected." That is: something out there, in the world coheres (adhesively). The transitive "cohere" means: "to cause to form a united or orderly whole." That is: the poet cannot make it cohere; the ending of the poem (or even the whole poem) becomes notes toward the poem that do not fuse. Given Pound's investment both in the pattern and in his aptitude for seeing and communicating it, this is a devastating moment. The poignancy of these lines in the genre apologia is that he still claims without a doubt that some single pattern is out there to be revealed, and he is still loyally working to achieve it. It is a natural pattern galvanized by some electricity or adhesion, and it involves major political leadership in tune with a fixed universe. Yet the actual poem presents a splayed and even conflicting assemblage of hopes for that pattern—not the pattern itself.

In these words of self-judging unworthiness, Pound still insists that this coherence exists not only in scientific findings (like his ready evocation of the "rose in steel dust"—a visible magnetism) but in sociopolitical findings, taken as basic, fixed, and never contingent or debatable. "Truth is not untrue'd by reason of our failing to fix it on paper" is Pound's justification.[88] The crystal ball metaphor presents the trace of that future Book of truth.

Pound projected various structures for *The Cantos* during their more than half-century of composition. These constitute one aspect of his assemblage. While fascinating to track, none is ever final (definitive), and the real interest becomes their creative plethora and variety supported by heteroglossia and Pound's world-ranging array of materials. Simultaneously with Pound's multiple schemes, he also claimed permanent (sacred) principles of order under the play of these particulars. Their solidity amid contingency contributed to his implicit argument that *The Cantos* would reveal itself as the culminating ideal of Book of political-mythological knowledge and its reenactments, the condensed (boiled down) outline of forces behind history that put a leader, laws, and a regime in tune with the elemental underpinnings of everything in nature itself and the best in culture. Pound wanted *The Cantos* to become a version of some all-encompassing Book with a special socio-cosmological status as a work that politically diagnosed a world and summed up avatars of a world system that this book would celebrate and perpetuate.

Is this exactly Mallarméan? Probably not. It appears that Mallarmé wanted a sense of chance, contingency, a mix of allegorized narrative elements, and awe of cosmology and mathematics, not of political certainty in his Book. It is certainly Pound's version of a summary "sacred book" of secular histories—his interpretive use of the genre of assemblage and the notion of the Book.

Pound's work has mixed the key genres discussed here—epic and quest, along with traces of many other genres—documentary, citation, gloss and oblique commentary, aphorism, notes, lyric, making this a polygeneric assemblage ending in frustration because he is not able to consolidate its own main genres, achieving neither an epic completion nor the completion of a quest. It could not be a fulfilled epic for its writer, because the hero (whether Pound or Mussolini or both) had not accomplished his historical mission. It could not be an investigative quest, because by about 1924 Pound felt he already had a political-cultural truth revealed and was insistently presenting its reiterative claims as nonnegotiable answers. Readers, in contrast, may feel it is a constant quest for clarity with an elusive, suspended goal. However, it remains one most—possibly *the* most—startling assemblage in the modern long poem, not only by its heteroglossic textures, arrays of cultures, figures, and multiple versions of its structural plans but by the fact that Pound did not want to end with assemblage alone as the default genre of this work and so engineered an abrupt return to Dante. At the very end, in the image of book as light and crystal ball, Pound, repositions the book more as a "sacred" enterprise than overtly political, with himself as prime mover of that crystal ball/book. Both, he thinks, have seen the future.

MACKEY'S BOOK

> the long song's
> longing to go on.
>
> Nathaniel Mackey, *So's Notice*

In 1985 Nathaniel Mackey began publishing his "unending book," a long poem creolized, dialogic, filled with musical allusions, and intermingling spiritual and political themes in ongoing cantos.[89] Mackey committed to his capacious and ever-recomplicating long poem, having found "individual poems as always incomplete," "installments" only, and necessitating a larger "area of resonance and implication."[90] This work is infused with a socio-cosmological poetics involving gnosis, myth, and music worked through "creative incorporation" of the "disruptive or even catastrophic" in both general and African diasporic social experiences. The work became an "eclectic" and "ecumeni-/cal" quest-assemblage, with Mackey, exploring his several cultures within a community of varied voices, in a poetry of sublime pulse with the task of investigation, reconsideration, variation, thematic modification, and rebeginning. It's "the everything was."[91]

This assemblage complex buoying the questing pilgrimage unrolls in long serial sections (each a differently titled book) celebrating political struggles, dilatoriness, lingering, reflection, dialogue, responsive music, and intense appreciative sexualities. This whole work, meditative and recursive, has a loose narrative trajectory, presenting recurrent travels/quests of a "band" (a musical and "earthical" community), quests that frustrate and fascinate by never quite achieving their goal—repeatedly thwarted by forces not in their control. A recurrent motif is a "soon come" arrival, always delayed. The mixture of longing, struggle, and hope is characteristic, and the yearning for an achieved social and aesthetic coequality is the goal of pilgrimage after pilgrimage. When this hope is rebuffed, lost, broken, and compromised, some band slowly regathers, affirms its longing through memories and discussions, and reclaims its metamorphic community through shared music, eros, and a battered idealism. After another failure (often a "crash"), sometimes after crablike sidesteps, another beginning is painfully and hopefully affirmed, and the pilgrimage begins anew. The band reboards "box, book, break, boat, bus" for a continuing quest.[92] The boat image evokes the Middle Passage, among other journeys.

Two modes of transport (box and break) allude to musical performances that inspire; book is this whole poem, a sacred secular journey, a long song that must be written, of a world-historical necessity. "Begin-again begun again / everything set off" and "for the muleteenth time," that pun combining the belated liberation news of Juneteenth and stubborn affirmation.[93] The accumulative trajectory of assemblage becomes both a thematic and formal framework for long swaths of Mackey's serial poetry, set inside Afro-diasporic historical experiences, depicting many social networks, each quest a haptic, affective, and historical sweep with unrolling consequences.

The transport of "book" shows that this long work of several books has become, in the extended Mallarméan and Whitmanic senses, a culminating Book. In Mackey the making of the work becomes the theme of the work; the product or object of all this work is simultaneously the career-culminating "boxed set" of musical performance, in keeping with the genre of assemblage and the mixture of Book and *Gesamtkunstwerk* defining what "we" or community is plausible.

Both quest (with its taxing pilgrimages without reachable termini) described as physical, imagined, dreamed, and performed (in playlists) and assemblage in serial cantos are the doubled genre modes the poem deploys. Simply put, all the books tell almost the "same" story and hopes but are differently configured, newly inspired, and necessary in particular contexts. The paradoxical advance, retreat, and mutability of Mackey's formulations (both structural and poetic-syntactic), and the debates among characters, are part of his work's uncanny power; the unrolling variety of occasions enhance the poem's pluralisms. The variations among the books tell the same story differently—pilgrimages on various vehicles, a sense of abandonment (sometimes leading to powerful aesthetic or erotic abandon), articulate characters facing each other in couples, as friends, or in groupings, confrontations with myth, place, music, sexuality, companionship, allegories of real events. Altogether the poem searches for and tries to create the post-Andoumboulous "we."

Mackey's discovery (in 1971) of the Dogon myth of the Andoumboulou represented a major moment in the original conception of this poem, opening its possibility and compelling its necessity.[94] The Andoumboulou are "rough draft" liminal figures, our twin selves, striving endlessly (as most of us are) to become reasonably human.[95] The Dogon funeral "Song of the Andoumboulou" becomes a thematic allusion redeployed with intellectual rigor across the work. The chant makes a droning, heaving sound of struggle, a blued "rasp," underwriting the poem's call into its own existence.

Mackey's critique of narrow poetry (pretty-only, bounded, or "phanopoetic snapshot") led him to value the "growl" or "rasp" of his initiatory call into long-poem ambition and its encyclopedic practices of "everything."[96] Mackey's books offer intense identification with these wounded, striving, struggling, not-fully-human subjectivities. The underlying premise (straightforward and direct, as in many long poems) is that they/we are sketches or drafts, not fully developed, making various forays (as in performances of music) to achieve or find the humanity to which they/we aspire. Full humanity in general also means full personhood in the historical Black context and the end of Nubbishness (macro-catastrophes and micro-aggressions) in other political contexts. A further finding: that acts of "mu"—myth, story, "restorative" and "elegiac" song, and rich sexuality—help transform these partially human drafts.[97] With this myth we are delivered into the ecstatic, striving poetic space of a quest to depict Andoumboulou incompleteness perhaps changing to human possibility. This pilgrimage rides on the lyric sublimities of music with the song of itself arousing humanness.

The whole work to date, adding *Double Trio*, is a quest-assemblage. It is an example of a contemporary "gathered" or assemblage work with a *Gesamtkunstwerk* flair, alluding to jazz and other music as its main "art," and, as the books continue, the work increasingly emphasizes an assembled Book. The total work to date (in 2021) has two main stages—the sections of "Song of the Andoumboulou" integrated with "Mu," under a thousand pages (titled only in individual books), and then the work *Double Trio* (in three separately titled volumes and a thousand pages), with a similarly allegorical attitude to the arc of repeated quests discovering endless impediments and crushing blockages.

This 2021 work makes explicit political allegories of the Trump era and its belligerent dangers to others in the country here called Nub.

The quests, voyages, and pilgrimages in Mackey's books do not stop or terminate; they intensify spiritual, sexual, and political elements, allegories of real events, and real events as allegories. Seriality of organization, Mackey's main formal strategy, is a beginning again and again of the quest poem, of the social struggles, of varied characters in communities, making new assemblages of each journey. The length of the work now seems to replicate the long, circuitous paths of the quest.

In *School of Udhra* (1993), Mackey writes in two different groupings of cantos: "Song of the Andoumboulou" and "mu" poems, differently titled and numbered. He continued this double mode in *Whatsaid Serif* (1998), and then, in a significant change, he intertwined the two categories as twin sounds inside *Splay Anthem* (2006). Instead of alternation, there is a network with implications for purpose and genre.[98] The preface to *Splay Anthem*, a notable document in poetics, discusses this, including a midcareer narrative fitting his past works and their intuitions into this long-come long poem.

That is, after the original commitment to the poem, the work makes a "quantum leap" when the author discovers that the two poem-modes ("Song" and "mu") were always intertwined, and that one *could* be in two places at the same time via these acts of poetry. One is henceforward in "mu" and in "Song of the Andoumboulou" sections at the same time, co-entangled; this insight is cast as a hermetic finding of generative doubleness.[99] The recognition of twinned modes allows Mackey's renewed propulsion into the poem and its ambitions. Characteristically, a long poem develops by rethinking its strategies and rationales as it is written. In general, for any long poem, a completed "Plan" might be available only in retrospect.

Splay Anthem laid out some purposes and genres of this work. Despite many of the mythic allusions in his earliest books to the African god Legba and his "liminal, intersectional unrest" limping through crossroads, and to the genie-muse Erzulie, or the erotic—with intense, sensual passages—Mackey's depicted quests were never solely in the zone of myth but certainly political.[100] "A / political trek we'd have said it was" and "nothing / wasn't / politics we'd say," makes this clear, in riposte to "everything was mystical / they'd say."[101] Hence, "socio-cosmological" seems an apt term for his quest-assemblage.

Although in some long poems, quest and *epic* can occur on a continuum (instances discussed in chapter 2), Mackey has explicitly resisted "epic" genre designations, except as loosely telling stories in song. Disrespected, undercredited Black life and art having been viewed as negligible by culture in general, the poet could sing only "heroic / waste" not the heroic fulfillment characteristic of epics.[102] This waste alludes to lost potentials in the history and politics of the contemporary world. There are hints in Mackey's chapbooks (from 2014 to 2018, now in *Double Trio*) that, for the whole work, a presumptive *nostos* (or home—an epic allusion) might be a Book, or a Boxed Set—not a fixed place or abode/house. Yet with ever-multiplying genres (into the polygeneric, as in many other long poems), Mackey will now concede, in the trilogy *Double Trio*, the paradoxical (im)possibility of "a new epic, no epic, unsure which," or a "distended epic," making the genres of the work even more inclusive and multiple.[103]

Mackey constructs quest as an odic logbook of continuance. "Odic" alludes to the lavish pulse of sublime diction and syntactic recursions that characterize the work, never narrowing or crimping what "the poetic" engages or indulges. One of Mackey's most distinctive features is his ability to riff, to amplify (in the rhetorical sense of *amplificatio*), to elaborate, to follow through with arabesque after arabesque, gloss after gloss. This produces sustained investigative and serial meditations, saturated in poetic turns. Sometimes this trait or ability leads into the semicomic, semitranscendent, touching moments of endless appositive phrases in his work—a local assemblage of segments. Apposition becomes elaboration and repetition via these riffs; the differences among the appositives then get used to open more narrative development; all these elements then have an allegorical *and* a metonymic relationship.

The *logbook* (as if from a voyage, but also as book) is an articulate and minutely detailed record of changes of place, weather, washes of feeling, and subtle shifts among characters, an attentiveness that only increases from the earlier works into a community's self-examination under pressure in *Double Trio*. Mackey's series of books incorporate refined and nuanced travel-travails and doubled sets of experiences that, no matter how repetitive, are always individuated and particularized to *that* crossroads, that song, that space, that time.[104] And *continuance* is postulated by the openings provided in the idea of the serial, material growing from itself, if sometimes vectored and disjunct. Hence seriality is the main idiom and vehicle of Mackey's mercurial and testing sensibility.[105] The additive assemblages created by seriality are both thematic, proposing reflexive meditations, and structural, derived from a vision for (and pleasures of) a poem expanding in scope and implications.

With any long poem, both the means and the poet's justifications may shift during the life of the poem. The discussion in *Blue Fasa* suggests that "long song" uncramps and uncrimps aesthetic limits, parallel to Duke Ellington's moving from shorter works to jazz suites. Mackey's statement "The long song, the long poem particularly the serial poem, the extended lyric, is one in which carol and qualm, carol and qualification, carol and caveat run as one" notes a rhetorical and attitudinal array—an assemblage of statement and qualification.[106] This points to the formal and political narrative of one step forward, two back. He describes his characteristic use of serial structure: by always beginning again, the poem "moves forward and backward both."[107]

This is echoed in a distinctive line and line break in which Mackey uses a hanging word as a syncopated marker or hovering off beat, a hinge hovering between forward and recursive motion, in which visual text signals performance, hesitation, a catch of breath. There are also syncopated syntactic turns: "The / life whose allegory our wandering / was was ours again."[108] That awkward doubled verb makes syntax reaffirm an endless recursive questing. Such syntactic riffs are like "solos" propelling development—and more recursions.

A further distinctive formal invention of Mackey's assemblages will put forth a long ode section, then draw a line, after which shorter sections are appended—are these glosses, extensions, qualifications, offers of alternative perspectives? Yes, and more. The formal tactic produces arrays of thought from a single statement or event. These sections are perpetually plural as various pendants or paths.

"Recursiveness" comes from filling up "a sense of deprivation fostered by failed advance," but this itself depends on maintaining a "large appetite" and social alertness for the possible—an inflected "blutopic appetite," the neologism from Duke Ellington. Empty orphaned losses and potential plethora move together. Mackey here joins method, theme, impact, and tone: "Seriality's mix of utopic ongoingness and recursive constraint is blutopic, an idealism shaped or shaded by blue, in-between foreboding, blue, dystopic apprehension of the way the world is."[109] This paradoxical seriality is therefore a mode for investigating ambiguities of ethics, politics, history, and for articulating one's individual responses in extended lyric riffs or sections.

Serial pilgrimages under these worldly conditions create the endlessness of the quest. The poem is a "world-poem," among other universalizing pilgrimages of humankind's growth (and failures). Robert Duncan's concept, discussed in Mackey's essay "Gassire's Lute," concerns "a global, multiphasic work in which various times and places interpenetrate," a description applicable to his own long poem, and to other works noted here.[110] His taking of radical agency, enough time, adequate space, and his investments in world-cultural materials place Mackey's poetry within a Duncan-Olsonic nexus, with its endless "going on" creating "meaning enough," a poetics of entanglement in which all and any directions/topics are possible, any connection is justified, and nothing does not, potentially, enter the poem—including paradoxes unsettling the settled.[111] His materials include ethnographic studies; mythic tales and rituals; explorations of Black Atlantic, African and Black diasporic cultures; prior cosmopolitan and global artists, particularly US jazz and blues, Moorish, African, and Caribbean world-music innovators; socio-aesthetic debates within contemporaneous African American artistic communities, including the theorizing of jazz masters. Increasingly, after about 2000, he makes explicit allusions to political and contemporary crises. I'd surmise that as he acknowledged the cumulative power of these multiple materials, they collectively propelled him to declare the continuing challenge of this long poem as a large (and enlargeable) site for poetic and social research; the thinking that emerges as the poet claims further projective range for the poem.

However, this hyperuniversalizing vision is modified in recent work with its historically diagnostic cast, tracking the great pain of Trump's assaultive presidency. In general the diasporic zone of Mackey's poem deuniversalizes West-only culture and claims some world-poem status (whatever his demurrals). The poem then inclusively reuniversalizes (a meaningful paradox), by presentation of the knowledges coming from various zones of the world—usually through informed musical allusions and eclectic references to cosmogonies and spiritual practices.

A writing subjectivity is dialogic, consisting of the writer and (perhaps curiously for those readers who are not poets) a speaking ear. Deep in any long-poem author is a capacious, voracious, and suspicious ear, another self-other.[112] With this figure poets achieve their own interior listeners and develop their ear for their work. Mackey names his version of self-ear subjectivity the "whatsaid serif"—one example of the poet's phrase-making panache in condensed syntactic kennings.[113] Mackey's "What-sayer" as serif (mark of the listening maker) offers questions inviting elaboration, if not finality. The "whatsaid" subjectivity here, as often in Mackey's work, is a "lyric we," an "Ourkestra" or band that might incorporate solo performances, since *we* is a contentious grouping, not simply an agreeable collective *I*.[114]

The choral voices will allow for many tones and openness—global pluralities, various dictions and multiple musical allusions, abrasions, ranges of experience from the intense eroticism throughout ("loin-musk" to the rage about the "Governing / beast" and "Butchers / in black tie").[115] This Whatsayer will certainly complicate any narrative or finding, initially by inviting the story in the first place and then by insistence on development and clarifications that, as with anything, can lead anywhere and track anything or disturb things, too.

In *Whatsaid Serif* (1998), Mackey articulated the "whatsaid book of undoing the / book"—both a powerful claim (overwriting the inadequate books of history, culture, and society by alternative writing/music) and also something once again (full citizenship, aesthetic multiplicity, and racial justice) that cannot yet be achieved.[116] Some long poems do question themselves as they go;

this self-consciousness (what *did* serif say in this "whatsaid"-ness?) is consistent with the forward and recursive (and to the side) motion of Mackey's quest.[117] The poem explores the persistence of "Whatsaid remanence. Whatsaid / remit." Thus again, final closure is unlikely, as the work revisits recurrent "Andoumboulous trauma."[118]

However, "Whatsaid serif" is not the final speaking subjectivity of this ever-evolving work. With the modification "What was said / mattered only so much, what-sayer, so- / what-sayer so much, no way to say / what / was what."[119] The "so" is a question of measurement, truth, and consequence—one of those daringly grand little words in Mackey. With "so," in *Nod House* and *Blue Fasa*, another speaking subjectivity emerges from "Whatsaid serif," sign of the crisis of falling and being hurt, and the deep crisis of recognizing one's death.

Hence the poem's speaker "took / now a new name, I, Insofar."[120] When "I, Insofar" emerges, a change in the attitude of the author is felt. This is the subjectivity making a quest without progress that emerges at the very end of *Nod House* and continues to haunt *Blue Fasa*.[121] "Whatsaid" probes and challenges—why this, why that; go here, go there, find out. In contrast "insofar" is a concessive, meaning *as far as we have gotten*. "Insofar" is a bit tireder, it appears, understanding some limits, whether the legalese of "insofar as" we know or can postulate, or whether soul-making has led to the painful thought, *All this, and I've only gotten in so far*. Mackey eulogizes "the book of not getting there / yet," managing a painful, tempered insofar as recommitment to the quest with a painful hope as lifeline.[122]

Then this subjectivity modulates in *Double Trio* to a third subjectivity, the less concessive, if still pained "So." And this subjectivity has made a large turn, always latent in Mackey, to the declaration that this long work of several books has become, not only a unique lexicon but a Book. With a *So there*, the fullest Book ambition has been instantiated.

In this study of assemblage as a genre, we have seen the Book emerge several times as a long-poem goal. In Mackey the making of the book becomes the theme of the work; the product or object of all this work is simultaneously the career-culminating "boxed set" of musical performance. This concern is reaffirmed in the short preface to *Double Trio*, with its crisp list of modern long-poem writers and the allusions to the "box set" in the extensive, "capacious" and "extended" projects of such distinctive theorists and instrumentalists of free jazz as Antony Braxton, Cecil Taylor, Ornette Coleman, named as companion artists.[123]

This (doubled) goal, boxed set [Box] and Book, is affirmed from the very beginning of *Double Trio* in a struggle with personal vocation. Thereupon, in an H.D.-like turn (familiar in spiritual quests), the reader-writer remembers a much earlier, first-book moment after a dream, his being handed a book by an angel, announces the project of Book itself.[124] Thereupon emerges a thrilling and daunting multiplication of potential books set forth in the Udhra "school": "Book of / sound, book of sand, book of / water . . . Book of glint, book / of glimmer, book of then . . ." setting up the hope that this book will be actualized (if not finalized) in the works to come.[125]

In the much later *Double Trio*, the declared emphasis on doubling and self-parsing is quite in keeping with the genre of assemblage and the mixture of Book and *Gesamtkunstwerk*. For the Book is not the only goal but always intertwined with music, as in a passage at the ending of *Nerve Church*, evoking "the sound of words / on a page." Mackey claims both assemblage as Book and the *Gesamtkunstwerk* trace within talk of the ultimate Book, which has the synaesthetic traits of a merging of many arts.[126]

Assemblage as Book being written in and as this book, books in the plural that also aim at intense sociocultural summations clearly face the force of religious culture and scripture. The Bible gets alluded to tangentially, as in H.D.'s resistant vow to an anti-Johannine blank book, for Mackey also writes of resisting "the binding of the book," which connects both to the serial as mode and to that H.D. book in *Trilogy*.[127] Still, books perpetually to be written are one of the main repeated motifs of *Double Trio*.

Mackey sees the book, capital letter or not, first in *Splay Anthem* as one of the evanescent elements of the impossible fullness sought on complex journeys—the book of the travelers in the plural. This quest instantly modulates to something subjunctively titled: "Had it been a book *Book / of Opening the Book* it / would've been called, // kept // under lock and key."[128] This passage has conditionals, questions, suspicions, and paradoxes (the locked book of Opening) yet announces a Book-related longing. Writing a book as an "unbound" assemblage, while talking intermittently about the longing for that Book, allows many elusive enactments of the book, always incipient, but ineffable.

In *Double Trio*, Mackey comes closer to naming a Book. There are many pages of *Double Trio* with book titles and allusions. *The Book of About*; "the book of burnt pages"; *The First and Second Book of So*.[129] These titles suggest the range from realist/secular to spiritual, if interpretive (not absolutist). The word *So* has enough definitions and ambiguities to constitute a title that slips between realism and speculation. This Book seems to be a single title grasped but evanescent and escaping at the same time, whose extensive contents no one can pin down.

This dilemma of finding the Book is articulated in a passage in *Tej Bet* (the first volume of *Double Trio*). This is in italics, so the question of who is speaking gets complicated: "*All my life I plotted the one book of so, no / clue there'd be others, the book of a better / life 'like so' such the one I drafted.*"[130] But whoever that speaker is, a Book (precisely with that capital letter) is treated by Mackey as more and more the desideratum of this poem. As Mackey's *Double Trio* unrolls, *The Book of So* may still be the title and is always available to read against Nub's book of US politics and society.

However, not only does Mackey repeatedly locate *The Book of So* as what has been accomplished here, he qualifies it in his "Author's Note" as the "equanimous *Book of So*." Why in the world is this "equanimous" (serene and calm), given the disruptions, the pain and blockage of quest and political suspicions even unto despair that are revealed and have been always part of what Mackey has been stating in this work? It is certainly a hard-won equilibrium and involves facing death, but it is also ever conditional. Mackey says this work would be "versed in amative and spiritual resolve" were it not for Nub's "appetite for diminution and mistruth."[131] Yet it also is filled with that spiritual resolve, linked to the distinctive Whitmanic word "amativeness"—an accepting and generous inclusivity. Despite the monumentality of Mackey's whole long poem as a project of poetic thought, the perpetual restlessness is not resolved. With no period at the exact end word, we are left inside "dislocated / this, dislocated that ramified forever."[132]

So, what does "so" mean/signify to Mackey? Mackey likes the unassuming word turning intense and semantically rich and undecidable, especially as "so" is a conjunction, an adverb, and an adjective, hence operating in hypotactic syntax and with verbs and nouns. Tonally, the word can be used to affirm the veridical (this is *so*) or to indicate sarcastic doubt or astonishment (*so*, you really think *so*?). There is a "so," in consequence/result, something already joining act and effect in a linked (fixed) chain. "So" can point to limiting conditions—*so* long as this or that happens or, even more interestingly, how far any action gets: *so* far *so* good. "So" puts simultaneous options in play; it says truth and doubt. And any act and both consequence and/or limiting conditions. Everything in the world seems to be ending up as a book, again, with Mackey provisionally titling it *The Book of So*.

"So" is one of those devastating have-it-several-ways words that Freud points to when he names a property of language as "the antithetical meaning of primal words." This double, opposite set of meanings is at root an indication, to cite DuPlessis, of poetry's "intricate bottomless tangibility," quite fitting for Mackey's doubled, paradoxical quests and narrative assemblages.[133] I have proposed elsewhere that poetry as a mode of thought has the effect of (and the impulse to) make many of its words behave like these multimeaning antithetical primal words. In Mackey the word "so" is dizzyingly suggestive in purely semantic terms, and his poetry compounds this in its own intensifications. Is

The Book of So the book of truth? The book of doubt? The book of causes? The book of consequences? The book of Thus It Is (and don't you forget it)? The book of *so* What, *so* How, *so* Why—that is, something like a book of questions? Al*so* of some certainties—in Mackey community connection, genial debate/sparring, music (and verbal arts), sexualities, and the senses of pleasurable community are all certainties, returned to repeatedly as ground tones of rightness: the "so" that is veridical or at least satisfying is a term "versed in amative and spiritual resolve."[134]

The more so as all this must take shape and abide as a "pledge"—the final word of his "Author's Note."[135] It's worth noting that the varieties of "so" are not proposed in an either-or form—"so" is too weird for that. Further, such absolutist claims are uncharacteristic of this work's curiosity and poethics.

Understanding that all the *Books of So* as provisional titles emerge in different contexts would involve entering the allegorical narratives in Mackey, given this work's big tent of characters, with various couples taking up positions (spiritual, analytic, and sexual) that seem to become overviews of Mackey's readings of US and Black history, and African diasporic history. These Books of So all will reckon with alternative experiences of "polis" and pleasure. Given there's enough trickster material and elaborative sprezzatura to spin many possibilities, at root, Mackey declares and performs a spiritual and a political long poem with a multifaceted book as one goal. Among many other activities and insights in *Double Trio*, we will see Mackey pursue *The Book*—and plural *Books of So* will be part of the strands of the quests. The whole second book here is, after all, called *So's Notice*, and it begins with three citations: "So that:" from Pound's first canto, "So What" from Miles Davis, and "Like so" from P.D., with consequence, doubting challenge, and affirmation triply presented.

At the end of *Double Trio*, given several factors, including the age of the author, the work's intense recurrent meditations on illness and mortality, and the extraordinary poetic indictment of "Nublicans" of a regime (2016–20) generating fear and loathing among many civic communities and particularly the communities of Black and other people of color shaped throughout the final book, it is quite a serious choice that Mackey provides double passages that, read one way, could stand as an ending and, read another way, could be a bridge to further continuance, in a projected work called *Double Quartet*.

The 2021 ending occurs in two parts, one pertaining particularly to Mackey. This is a fantasy of his playing the oud, a Middle Eastern plucked instrument with a broken neck (a trace reminder of lynching), a resonant lutelike instrument with a very large "belly" or buttocks (sexually interesting throughout) but imagined as a wooden boat (as from the Middle Passage, deturned now into painful and then affirmative acknowledgment).[136] Mackey has stated in interviews that he has never played a musical instrument, so it is particularly satisfying that the trio he imagines playing with includes John Coltrane (soprano sax) and Leroy Jenkins (violin)—and that he can keep up inside that music, in a section with the unique title "Untitled Original 11386i," from the John Coltrane "Lost Album."[137]

In the second part of the ending, the oud is imagined gathering people up in its boat-belly to continue the endless pilgrimage still being made. The second ending is a doubling of many events in this poem, where the band rides together in a bus//boat/book, a general gathering of all the prior characters in this work who have been actively sought and exfoliated in the whole of *Double Trio*. Of these two endings, one is a personal culminating fantasy of highest adequacy to the art of free jazz improvisation (this an allusion to a total artwork incorporating music).[138] The second ending is a call to continuance and rebeginning, a book of traveling in what he calls "a distended epic" (note the pun on *end*). For the Book in Mackey is not the only goal but always intertwined with music and community, as in a passage at the ending of *Nerve Church*, as noted, proposing "an imaginal sound no sound could / equal," which is simultaneously "the sound we were driven by." Mackey evokes both assemblage as Book and the *Gesamtkunstwerk* trace ("syn-/aesthetic") within talk of the ultimate Book.[139]

In most long poems, and certainly in Mackey, "myth" (the spiritual/cosmological) and "history" (social/political thinking) are hardly opposites—they are interactive and mutually transformative. Sometimes long-poem poets engage with ritual and the performative staging of myths, sometimes with documents and historical analyses to achieve thinking and critique beyond centrist (contained? decorative? urbane?) definitions of poetry as a practice. The term "socio-cosmological" proposes that social elements, here spoken of through travel and geography, music in concerts, churches and clubs, allegories based on real events, plural subjectivities, and political ferocity join up with a yearning wonder occasioned by sexuality, the pulse of endless rumination, myths, oracles, dreams, visitations, cosmologies, and gnostic (or dia-gnostic) systems. However, the double ending may or may not be the absolutely final section. The bus as "a boat of longing" is still on the watery road for more forthcoming disappointments and adventures.[140] The Book continues to be written.

THE BOOKS OF NOURBESE PHILIP AND KAMAU BRATHWAITE

The intellectual-conceptual, even polemical nuance of the long poem as an extended site delivers a large-scale cultural address. That is, long-poem authorship often involves a buried role as messenger of a consuming idea or structural feeling. These ethical-aesthetic goals of speaking into a culture with a total artwork as a Book are visible in Brathwaite and Philip, in works of Anglophone Caribbean and Canadian-Caribbean writing. For these two authors, explorations of the textual visuality and the embodied materiality of the book have a particular status—in one case as a major revision of authorial attitudes toward his poetry's purposes and audiences, and in the other a notable critical-poetic exploration and ceremony mourning an unassimilable historical tragedy. Sometimes these acts of implacable visuality resemble artist-book strategies, particularly considering the book as "auretic object" with a compelling meaning to multiple communities.[141] Sometimes the strategies represent community and personal pain—social and historical—written but also embodied by the author in the page in versions of the book as performance and total artwork.

A serious culturally vital Book (like the Bible, the Koran, the Torah) is sometimes "performed"—adorned, illustrated, embellished—by coverings outside the book, honored unique spaces for it, and special rubrics, sometimes pictures, and calligraphies inside the book. In our more secular era, long-poem books express their content in visual and physical embodiments, the poem as extended site, presenting ethical and social meanings via aesthetic choices. Some books emphasize visual and written text—a "form" that becomes content or a content that becomes form. *Zong!* by NourbeSe Philip and *Ancestors* by Brathwaite (plus his *ConVERSations*) claim that zone of material text. The designs of the pages, the typography, and visual elements of both construct each as the embodied artwork of its semantic content. Both works elaborate critical, historically focused resistances to the uses and abuses of Africans and their descendants in the settler and slave-built societies of the New World.

In *Zong!* (2008) Philip claims the ethical meanings of page space and both political and spiritual purposes for the shape of her book. She enacts the shocking act presented and countered within her book, an act at the violent core of enslavement itself. Philip has made this work from a story that she insists cannot be told but must urgently be told: the failure of a historically significant slave-ship voyage, based on a court case from 1783 concerning the deliberate murder, by throwing overboard to drown, of about 150 living people, Africans taken in enslavement. The offloading of this human "cargo" occurred to finesse a later insurance claim. (About a hundred other deaths from thirst had preceded these.) The surface causes of this historically attested event were the captain's poor planning of supplies (particularly water) and failed navigational skills, whereupon the crisis of lacking good water became desperate. The deeper cause is the systemic and definitional status of the Africans as nonhuman or nonpersons, destroyed to save the remaining crew and "cargo," and to recoup losses.

The law of the time debated only whether the institutional entity that would be financially indemnified was Gregson, slave-trading company and owner of the ship, judged by some as liable for the captain's negligence, or Gilbert, the insurers of the human "cargo," since the jettisoning was, in their view, necessitated by "perils of the sea."[142] Because of the way the law case "misses" the point that people were deliberately murdered (our point, not its), the case seen now becomes a political-economic statement both ironic and shocking. It wouldn't be the first time in history or the last that an enshrined legal text as the enabling document, bureaucratically defended, overlooked something ethically essential.

The "law" is treated here as one gigantic socially revelatory blind spot. Hence, the author tears it to shreds, literally, deliberately destroying, breaking, and fragmenting its words, as she clearly states, elaborating various strategies of enactment to fragment the "whole" and smash the text, so rational, and yet more deeply irrational. Philip then sutures the fragmented elements for what she calls "a recombinant antinarrative" of bizarre "contortions" on the border between sense (order) and non-sense (chaos) that this case represents.[143]

The first section of poetry dramatizes the gasping for good water in letters and phonemes of the words g-o-o-d w-a-t-e-r, whose lack was killing. This whole section is accompanied by a paratextual running footer of Yoruba proper names. An actual slave ship's manifest would have had no such names; the names of the people enslaved were unrecorded, a tactic that shifted them from socially embedded persons with sociocultural existences to chattel in the trauma of the Middle Passage crossing. The Africans may not have been accorded names, but they did have market value (30 pounds sterling each); this is what the law case concerns.

This section (Os [bone]) takes some key words from the document of *Gregson v. Gilbert*, reprinted on the last two pages of this book, and breaks, fragments and recombines them. The legalese and other careful phrases rendered as decontextualized words sometimes make a little sense in their new phrases but more "often do not"; the effect is "another submerged meaning" that sounds variously ashamed, self-justifying, and subverted—showing the deeper "chaos" of the system of explanations.[144]

The term "paratext" alludes to the whole possible apparatus of any book as composed by the author, aside from the actual text: its title, author's name, prefaces, introductions and dedications, chapter titles, inserts or illustrations, perhaps authorial oddities of punctuation, and then toward the book's end, afterwords, appendixes, indexes, footnotes—anything an author put there that is not the core text. Paratexts are hardly extraneous, although they may be innocently overlooked as content-laden; in contrast, if something author-generated is centrally located inside a book, one understands it is the book's text. Philip uses the distinction between text and its "extras" (glossaries, manifest). She places all the mechanisms of a book—an author's afterword on making the book, documentation, all informational and analytic essayistic texts as paratexts. Meditations on the emotional impact of this event intermingling with her scrupulous readings of (and motivated resistance to) the documents are central to Philip's chapter "Notanda" on the difficulty and necessity of this writing, along with her sense of spiritual responsibility, and her questions of knowing, representing, and ethics along with grief.[145]

In two of the paratextual sections, there is a somewhat useful glossary of the mix of languages on board, everything imperfectly cataloged, and incomplete (deliberately so), but useful for understanding some of the dissolving phonemes in the text's center, particularly words for water in Yoruba. That deliberate incompleteness continues in the "Manifest," normally an account of what a ship is carrying, with a list of languages, a list of animals, including "lion"—probably not on board, and probably not others like "owl" and "stag." The list of food and drink is even more deliberately curious, being rather the foods of rich ship owners and merchants on land than vittles of men at sea. Certainly "éclairs" or "rose water" are not served to the crew. In the category "Nature," a ship could not carry "bog," "dale," "fen," or "garden" (though "sea," "mist," and "ocean" are palpable surroundings).[146] It is suddenly clear that these are concepts, memories, words as words that the ship is also carrying.

So this "Manifest" not only lists items *on* the ship (an incomplete list, like the whole incompetent voyage) but suddenly transposes itself into what is carried *in* the ship and *by* the ship, in the minds of those on board, and what is manifested or shown by this unstrung language. The "Manifest" contains the weight of ideology, privilege (or not), class, status, race, material realities, stories, and memories that this ship carries as some of the dying speak their unstrung suffering and as a crew member confesses to his absent beloved a garbled and shamefaced confession of the rape of one of the African women on board.[147] Words and memories are part of the "baggage" itemized on the "Manifest," and they become broken streams of interrupted consciousness and phonemic irruptions of pain.

A strange visual section bridges from central text to the "Glossary," "Manifest," "Notanda" (an essay in poetics and analysis), and the legal brief. These pages are composed by the computer and printer together itself, a rogue overprinting of words and phrases in grayscale, a fading text, demanded by "Ebora," name of underwater spirits in Yoruba and the section title. This section depicts layers of the mourning central to *Zong!* An "electronic device" can sometimes become possessed. This book is as well.

To hold and mourn this act central to the *Zong*'s voyage, Philip creates the central pages of *Zong!* as the fractured imprint of a book, by a visual and semisemantic text of persuasive power. This textual center of this book can be only partly read but must be seen, mouthed, felt in its brokenness. This consists of dissolved languages in phonemes and syllables in which bits of words and stories can occasionally be picked out but float unjoined in white space, disperse, disappear without being fully "grasped." The page space is *open* to this float of phonemes, arranged in such a way that none is on top of another; all accorded a space to honor their nonbeing/being.[148] This presentation creates an ethical meaning within page space. It is a gripping and emotionally fierce visual text.

On the stressed central pages (the majority of *Zong!*[149]), in a mix of European and African languages, phonemes split, and untoward spaces challenge the reader, whose meaning-making brain function is more and more "at sea" and faces awe-ful information, with feelings of horror. These fragmented, suggestive, half- or barely readable phonemes constituting the bulk of the book have used the alphabetic letters from *Gregson v. Gilbert*'s words (and some of the ship's "Manifest" and languages), then repeatedly broken them to bits, sometimes forming words accidentally, recombining, undoing, slipping like the understory, the social unconscious, or the ghosts of words palpable in the law document and on the voyage.[150] The words have come apart, and the story barely exists except in shards, fragments, and suggestions, often outcries or enacted drownings or vestiges of bone. Readers witness this drowning. It is a haptic embodiment, a trace or pooling of the remains of the major commerce and trade in enslaved peoples in the Atlantic Basin in the eighteenth century.

The middle part is, then, a middle passage and a monument for the drowned, taking place as if water itself, ungraspable and fluid. This is the Book of the dissolution of what a regular book might undertake. To say this is uncanny hardly begins to acknowledge the impact of this use of page space and of the dissolution of the book itself. The mechanisms of the Book have been used against the reason, argument, rationality that documents and legal accounts are conventionally thought to chart. Such a Book undercuts the book's rectitude and authority, making the solidity of law and its arguments, all economic justifications, and the splendors of Western culture (allusions to Venice, Shakespeare, confessions of sin, epics as of Troy, love lyrics) disintegrate in a more and more agonized page space of drowning people and disorienting phonemes.

The locus of authority has shifted. The book itself becomes an indictment. And the book, by being turned inside out, becomes its own understory. When Philip unwrites the writing, she thus makes the book into a ritual of mourning with a unique visual text. All together *Zong!* is a total artwork with striking social and ceremonial meanings. The phonemes floating in the middle section of the book are a manifest in its other sense: a manifestation, the word often used for spirits or ghosts. And the end of the book—usually a summation of some sort—is that court case brief, a document that has been shorn of its former authority yet retaining (by its effects) a haunting afterlife. *Zong!* reframes the book as a visual and performative entity, a speaking, haunted Total Book. The visual form as an assemblage and *Gesamtkunstwerk* creates an embodied, ethical content.

The non-Book of these sounds, undercutting the specious authority of the law document (that to us seems to miss the point of mass murder) has elicited from some of its readers an act of mourning so great that Philip has offered ceremonies from the work *Zong!* that make a ritual of grief.[151] Not "poetry readings," these are group performances that enact a ceremony for the dead by reading *Zong!* This book thereby passes from a secular judgment on the past (and the author's judgment on the present that has benefited from societies built on past enslavements) to a ritual Total Artwork, her own "Ceremony of Souls," analogous to Caribbean spiritual practices.

The ethical-aesthetic goals of speaking into a culture with a Total Artwork as a Book are visible in a different fashion in a career-arching revision undertaken by Kamau Brathwaite from poems to Book. These poems, originally published by Oxford University Press as *Mother Poem* (1977), *Sun Poem* (1982), and *X/Self* (1987), constitute Brathwaite's trilogy, received as a significant contribution to postcolonial writing.[152] Years after, in a major act of self-assessment and historical intervention, Brathwaite transformed these into a long-poem Book called *Ancestors*, a conceptual and visual remaking of the poems with a "videolect," and in a further extension into a poetics of the Book-in-society in *ConVERSations*.[153]

That is, Brathwaite fully altered the original poem sequences with major textual and conceptual bibliographic shifts into the retitled *Ancestors* (2001). This trilogy, drastically remade and reimagined, is not only a verbal revision or refreshing but "A Reinvention."[154] Brathwaite changed at one and the same time specific granular elements of the poetry (line break, certain words, orthographies, punctuation, some sections cut or added, and some spaces altered) and also changed the whole visual text and compositional presentation—page space, font sizes and modes, the margins, with additions of glyphs and page illustration, and allusions to newspapers, to posters, to nonbook pages. His refabrication of visual manner and meanings uses the "'Sycorax video style' type[face] as developed by the Author."[155] Brathwaite takes normative typography as colonizing of the social meanings of these works and declares Sycorax, mother of Caliban in Shakespeare's *Tempest* and a symbol of indigenous peoples, as his new compositor, inventing her voice and its visual articulation as the center of his text. The whole bearing and address of the work changes to a confrontative presence. The former sequence of poems is thereby transformed into a long-poem Book of Caribbean culture. It is a Book as a social and spiritual instrument.

The trilogy had from its original books emphatically presented "nation-language" on the page with a resistance to Standard English so that voice, cadence, and sound occurred in a dialect-orthography (but in normal fonts and sizes). The reframed *Ancestors* goes further into physicality to emphasize the non-neutral material invasiveness of page-space interpretive shifts on the normative look of the first (Oxford-published) poetic text. What happens in the changed typography is that embodiment and a fleshy thickness of boldface (sometimes with jagged pixilation, like early videogame fonts) are a textually confrontative presence embodying Bookness, vernacular diction, and Blackness. The heft and large headlines of a newspaper, a poster, a handout all combine as a poetry, newly set on the page with visual and temporal-art allusions such as sculpture and dance. *Ancestors* is not just a more dramatic rendering of "nation-language" but an embodiment in printing modes, including font size and mixed patchworks of font types, of a fullness and physicality of the culture—its NAM-ness—rendered as page presentation.[156]

Soundings in *Mother Poem* (1977) and in the "Reinvention" done in *Ancestors* (2001) reveal that the first publication presents an already quite brave and nonstandard poem in some of its diction and some of its orthography, but the work on the page is normal-looking poetry, a rectangular window looking onto the culture Brathwaite depicts. Exemplary ethnographic commitments suffuse the original work, but the "poetry rectangle" regularizes the text. Such distancing and framing effects have been altered in Brathwaite's *Ancestors*; its *parole* have claimed *libertà* (as in a Marinetti poster). The page space is bolder, larger, darker (literally), and more immersive for the reader than the Oxford edition. The "videogame style" (Atari font) looks as if it is active, in motion; the Sycorax allusion to the mother of Caliban claims (at least) power and looming presence. Most words of the poems in general have not changed (some have—see below), but by precise, particular, and distinctive changes idiomatic to the visual mechanisms of poetry as a medium, Brathwaite has made the intellectual and emotional claims and the poetics and social study of Caribbean culture stand as paramount. A new form becomes a new content: a Total Artwork as Book.

Formerly regularized as poetry (even as the content was unusually rich in "nation-language"), after the change into *Ancestors*, a lavish use of boldface, of italics, of very dark and enlarged words have remade the poem into a whole environment or milieu of argument.[157] The shifts of poetic detail are many. Already dramatic orthographies, sounding the cadences of dialect, are bolstered and enhanced in *Ancestors* by line breaks that often shift the odic and incantatory lines of *Mother Poem* to shorter, more percussive lines.[158] This change in segmentivity is sometimes also supported by the removal of commas (as between items in a series) and their replacement by periods after phrases.[159] Other presentational shifts emphasize dialogues more emphatically with antiphonal presentation and alternating font modes (bold/bold italic) on the page. Brathwaite's changes often involve relineation. He deliberately centers many of these lines (away from left margin), which is conventionally a nonnormative presentation for poetry. Other pages emphasize poster format or different textures by varieties of fonts and weights. To read the poem now, one must integrate the visual presentation with the semantic and thematic elements. In Brathwaite the text dramatizes itself as social arrays of characters, tones, moods, all in mercurial shifts and intensities; the poet has invented an enriched visual page.

With this tactic among others, the pages of *Ancestors* claim more physical space than in the Oxford book, with an allegorical impact, and the darkening and saturating of fonts (not built for clarity of line but for weight) claiming a parallel cultural impact. Every page is loosened, opened, and often centered, calling attention to the deliberate ruminations in the text. In many of these works, Brathwaite has removed section numbers, allowing formerly delimited interior units to stream as one, so there is no stopping. All in all, Brathwaite wanted to produce a quite different page of poetry from the usual for a set of different attitudes, and a more dramatic sense of a dynamic, encompassing book of a whole culture and history, with specific figures (the mother) becoming enlarged and exemplary—an argument always palpable in the 1977 iteration but not there advanced with such visual drama.

Two other changes to *Mother Poem* also suggest enlarged cultural directions. In the first instance, a new section called "Pixie" inserts a set of news stories, social worker reports, headlines, letters, and a transcribed radio interview concerning a runaway girl who became a prostitute. These materials are given in boxed sections like a set of posters, wall newspapers, or framed snapshots of the salient points of her life—a performative page about a woman lost. The vignettes are devastating and end with a peroration to poets to account for this "dancer" in this "dance"—a challenge from the Caribbean to a version of modernist idealizing with that citation from Yeats.[160] This section also incorporates the visual textualities of newspapers, posters, and "wall newspapers" into the total artwork Book.

A second change removes four pages of explanatory endnotes from *Mother Poem*. These notes, of real benefit to at least one reader, may have had the whiff of the schoolroom (and/or of *The Waste Land*—a significant model poem), emphasizing the reader as outsider appreciating and consuming this culture as a visitor. The removal of the notes centers the work on a different readership, marginalizing the tourist (however well-meaning) and centering on readers as near participants in this Caribbean proto-operatic text.

Here we appreciate the complex pun Brathwaite made when he changed a subtitle "Nametracks" to "Nam(e)tracks."[161] Without changing the poem—though thickening and darkening its pages, name/nam dramatizes "the heart of our *nation-language* which comes into conflict with the cultural imperial authority of Prospero" (renamed O'Grady, the villain in a Caribbean-centered interpretation). Brathwaite spells this out in the metonymic chain set out in this now-cut note: "*nam*: secret nam, soul-source, connected with *nyam* (eat), *yam* (root food), *nyame* (name of god)" along with "*nomminit*," the "nation-language sound/word for 'cultural domination,' literally 'the gobbling up of the (other's) name.'"[162] "Nam" is also the outside of normative society (colonial power) enacted in *maronage*.[163] It is a condensed powerful concept that demanded serious exploration by the poet in his poetics, a task more encompassing and saturating for him presumably than the helpful gesture of information sharing in the note.

Nam-ness implicates the explosion of visual poetics in *Ancestors*. What seems to have happened was that the crystallization, via this note, of the concept of Nam became too vital to be buried in that note.[164] Brathwaite seems to ask—why this note? for whom am I writing? It is a moment in which the shift into visual text and page space is exposed, the beginning of a textual and book-immersed poetics of speech visually palpable along with a social space on the page. Making the *Ancestors* text immersive, interventionist, and inferential shifts his discussion of poetics out of the mode of illustrative information and into continuous cultural enactment.

Brathwaite's changes underscore what I argue in this chapter: that in Anglophone poetries, heteroglossic languages plus a unique and emphatic page space become (variously in different poets) an *engagé* mode of *Gesamtkunstwerk* propelling these long poems and underwriting their cultural-social stance of Book. With Brathwaite not only his own personal autobiography but a syncretic mythography and dynamic presentation of a Caribbean ethos occur as poem and poetics. The new presentation has "liberated" him from "the School" of only British and European models for writing.[165]

This change is further discussed and analyzed in his metabook of Caribbean poetics, recharging his prior books as material objects for social and poetic engagement: *ConVERSations* (1999).[166] In effect, Brathwaite has made a doubled Book, the renewed *Ancestors* and a network of conversation and poetics evoked in this interview—a work summarizing and extending the rationale behind his trilogy *Ancestors*. The argument for a Caribbean poetics, its elaboration and justification, occurs in the design and content of *ConVERSations*.

The book begins as a 1993 interview at Poets House, New York (conducted by Nathaniel Mackey—who is a significant respondent and an encouraging creator of the occasion in which this poetics is discussed). Brathwaite's work is structured as an album, primarily a dialogue-interview, with poems by others sometimes inserted, some surveying of Caribbean literary history, a memoir in Q&A, a self-study of the motives and contexts of the poems in *Ancestors*—and more. In this almost indescribable work, Brathwaite presents a poetics, an apologia, a research-based elaboration of scholarship, brief highlights of anticolonial resistance in Barbados, and political cautionary tales of realignments post-emancipation, when historical forces of further oppressions come into play. The book presents family memories (framing *Ancestors*) so that his "personal" life is taken to exemplify the political and economic forces that work on and around life choices of individuals in a colonized society, limiting them, modifying them, narrowing possibility. The book cites news reports of often-merciless events. It includes audience participation, extending the dialogue outward in a "call-and-re/sponse kinesis."[167] And this list does not complete even the genres of information, visuality, poetics, and poetry that are in play.

Amid this polygeneric and scrapbook range—and the work is about one-third poetry, two-thirds prose—Brathwaite explores his major redesign of the visual elements of the book, a statement concerning a Book made, in its material texture of presentation, to summarize Caribbean cultures, their sea-inflected aesthetic and their struggles. As the *VERS* of the title indicates, the turning of verse (vers) toward (vers) a turn in poetry involves the dialogism of conversation—not only toward others but toward a radical turning of the Book itself.[168]

ConVERSations becomes a poetics manifesto of this nonnormative material "Book-ness" paralleling *Ancestors*—its typeface, page layout, confrontive articulations in total design. The work is a polygeneric scrapbook-assemblage. Brathwaite presents his motivations for reconstructing his work into a Book of political and cultural synthesis, using his startling, invented typeface for presentation. Each page is like an analytic poster, a way of speaking that quite knowingly casts away the normative look and feel of a book and a poem, substituting an Afro-Caribbean historical analysis and artifact presentation that refuses visual decorums. Brathwaite's boldly presentational fonts, layouts, sizes, and inking are again attributed to his "Caribbean" computer, Sycorax, with her "Sycorax Format."[169]

This book creates rupturing insistences. Every page has a unique design, many printed in a pixel-pointy, thick, boldface type. Sometimes words almost bleed together—an intentional effect that delivers allegorical impact, saying both "power" and the "rush" to tell this story. Occasionally another typeface is used where individual letters have had spaces cut in them, a device now prominent in encryption, making those letters difficult to decode by machines, so only humans can access what is said.[170] The work is printed in a variety of fonts—visualizing voices and a social play of statement and tones. When the work is printed, for instance, in Courier, it has the impact of typewriter urgencies or the epistolary, a work not separated from its origins in the visible labor and emphases of the writer. There are also many boldface glyphs, recalling pictographs; certain material is boxed for emphasis. Headings and divisions of the text are boldface and varied. The text is focused and purposeful but visually jumpy in its attempts to join many separate "fields"—autobiography, social history, reportage, scholarship on the Caribbean, poetry, and more—with presentational panache, as a Book of multiplicity in assemblage.

Further this book, along with *Ancestors*, is not only visual text, but an inventive, bidialectal oral book with pronunciation-oriented spellings to match. It is in island English, or "nation-language," but word choices and respellings also make creole critique of a "regular" lexicon by modified and philosophically telling new words inventively indicting a reseen reality. "Migration" as "nigration"; "skeletons" as "skeletones"; "we" and "mwe" as first persons; "migraint" and "migrained"; "perdict" (with a hellish "perdition") from "predict"—every such formation offers condensation, crypt words suggesting other words, often a critical analysis embedded in a transfigured vocabulary formed by double-sighting words shadowed by their critical neologisms.[171] "Mwe" is quite important for its mix of "me" and "we," answering the unspoken question—how to say *we* (communities) when an *I* is writing, an issue that haunts the poems of assemblage here.

Brathwaite's typographic and page-space ruptures, added to the generic boldness of the assemblage, makes this, like NourbeSe Philip's Book, an intervention with the scope of Mallarmé's predictive and unrealized postulate of a new kind of Book and visual performance. All these page-space works are in the nexus my analysis has created by evoking Book and total artwork, concepts linked historically to Mallarmé but newly applicable here for works expressing and articulating other crucial cultural and political contexts. This shift in presentation by Brathwaite not only is a rupture with main-cultural

Euro-American book presentation strategies but seals the multicultural promise with a typeface named for Caliban's mother, Sycorax, and a diction replete with "Calibanisms"—beginning a critical retelling of colonialism by repositioning Shakespeare.[172]

ConVERSations is close to an artist's book, a significant text of "writing the *visual*," and it evokes "intermedia" work, for Brathwaite postulates numerous visual genres: "video-poetry," "a mural," "cinema-painting," even "graffiti"—the whole functions as a "wall of memory."[173] Brathwaite's term is "transboundary" from music to orality to the word and into "gesture, dance/drama."[174] From his Book, then, a *Gesamtkunstwerk* is postulated, again within the logic of such projects in writing, a social and ethical dimension made by forms of typography and page space. It is solidly and defiantly a Book as a dramatic enactment of multimedia social and cultural histories.

Brathwaite assembles a necessary, formerly unseen archive—as if reconstructing the archive that he lost tragically when a hurricane struck and destroyed his house. A new archive becomes visible, palpable, and audible through inventions of page presentation that are confrontative and attention claiming. The difficulty of getting the silent or effaced part of a historical record to "speak," to be recognized/seen and acknowledged, gets faced in Brathwaite's Book—as it is differently, in NourbeSe Philip's work.[175]

The Mallarméan version of the Book began this discussion, rather than the Whitmanic aspects of this grouping of long poems. Yet assemblage in a Book also draws on Whitmanic poetics, as Mackey's "amative" allusion reveals, and the Book most familiar to those in the US would be Whitman's civic collection, suffused with a spiritual yearning, and taking shape as a great, and endlessly added-to Book speaking from and to a nation to celebrate and inspire inclusiveness, openness, and insistence. With a nation-Book/world-Book of everything, a Whitman and Mallarmé fusion (with its contradictions) begins to seem like a reasonable rubric for the idealized Books and their further *Gesamtkunstwerk* impulses of Pound, Mackey, Philip, and Brathwaite, and for any modern long poem in its particularity with the ambition to name social-historical and secular zones intermingled with degrees of spiritual striving.

It's clear that the long poems of assemblage in this chapter tend to mix album and Book/*Gesamtkunstwerk*, and are all engaged in some sort of fundamental critical acts as social understanding using the medium of language and visuality. The context from which much long-poem work emerges is critique of narrative, poetry, and literature, the critique of official history and its losses, and of the construction of ideology by and in language. The "normal" entities—poem, findings, centrist elements of culture—are never enough, never adequate to the world.

That's why the literary is never only literary. The literary is not only at the service of literature—indeed, it is sometimes motivated precisely and exactly in a shift away from the felt limits of that institution and a rejection of it. In short, literature as ideology, the sentence (in two senses), the normative book, and sometimes a government of failed social justice are made visible in these poems. These long poems, by the accumulations of length as evidence, and by their visual presentation, make striking interventions into poetry and what it can achieve, using this literary mode—the long poem—as the site of struggles for knowledge and perception. Writers of modern long poems often enter this practice with a sense of historical crises or issues that they can and must address. The crises differ; their observations differ; their means differ; some crises are more convincing than others. Proposing a Book as an album/assemblage will often sum up the crisis; the book can mark it, annotate it, depict it in texts with visual flair—up to page-space dramas of enactment and texts of ritual and ceremonial embodiment.

CHAPTER 5

Meditations on Ending Very Long Poems

closure is an inevitability of anything you can identify as an act
a   performance or even a process   because the tendency of
a process is to play itself out in a certain direction and either
to arrive at an ending or imply one as you walk away from
it   so even if you walk away from it   still feels closed

David Antin, *John Cage Uncaged Is Still Cagey*

ONE OF THE best innocent unanswerable questions that people ask artists and poets is "How did you know when to end?" The question is ineffable. And the answer is often "I just did." Is there more to say?

Yes—because many writers of long poems in modernism don't end their poems, even if they say they've tried to. Ending a modern long poem does not happen easily, if it happens at all. As Middleton notes, with that charmed slippage of agency, "These poems don't want to end. They long for more."[1] The idealized "beginning-middle-end" mantra about form seems pat, untenable, or excrescent, although some poems discussed here—Notley's epic-quest, Eliot's Dante-laden quest—are choice exceptions. Long poems may offer several portals for beginnings; multiple middles; abrupt, apparently eroded, or hovering endings; or even several closures. Further, if you call your work a *life*-poem, it behooves you to keep it going. "How did you know when to end" is a question in method and in time; one answer is feeling a consolidation, a fullness, or a sense of enough. Or even—enough of *that*. These responses displace the question. Another answer is the pert "Right before I did end" (aside from revisions and rewritings). Another answer might be "Before I die"—this does not necessarily work out as planned, nor is it particularly consoling. This chapter acknowledges that an endless (or ambitiously long) literary work of all-over writing, many processes, one event after another will inevitably stop—but how?

If nothing else, death is a terminus. Death stopped Tolson's unfinished long poem with its striking first book, *Harlem Gallery*. This work is a study of artists, curators, and manipulators attending a museum (gallery) opening. He produces their intersecting stories: intellectual rivalries, jealous positionings, alternative interpretations of Africa and diasporic ideologies, sexy sordidness, all wrapped up in a main character white enough to pass, a Janus and trickster figure. The gallery of satiric portraits of Harlem's denizens is, in a blaze of irony, structured with the plot of a noir. Even this dazzling book's murder mystery is not solved, exactly (so much for plot leading to conclusion). Tolson's work is fiercely poised, as an array of stances, not endless, but intensely closural from line, to stanza, rhyme to rhyme. His taut epigrammatic poetic focus offers a finished tightness even when the planned full work could not be accomplished.

At another extreme is Olson's abrupt finishing line recognizing losses by listing them ("my wife   my car   my color   and   myself") amid a complex editing job left undone at his death, and a plausibly endless poem declared finished in order to achieve some control over both the poem and his final illness.[2] These two authors illustrate the "Atropos" principle, named after the Fate with the Scissors, whose name means "no more turning," or, interpreted, both *no more time* and *no more verse*.

Whether or not a very long poem is or could possibly be defined by some specific cantos of ending (as Dante's is), all long poems seem to play with ending, the question of ending, the meanings of ending. Perhaps every long poem demands its own individualized foray into ending. Hence questions of form (general), structure (specific), and their poetics abound.

To construct an adequate ending, do you have to understand what will give satisfaction (and to whom) or simply what might allow stoppage? How can the emotional and aesthetic effects of endings on readers be agreed upon for long poems, given that so much has transpired? Endings often seem sudden, inadequate, understated—light in weight—given the abundance and complexity, the oversaturation of what went before. How far back in a long poem does an ending have to start? A long poem's heft and length mean that you might not ever be able to "sum it up," so perhaps it is more strategic just to close and produce some "finissage"—a word for the closing of art shows analogous to the word "vernissage" for art openings. Is such closing a poignant party, a celebratory one—or simply a benchmark?

The habits of reading for the sheer experience of a work suggest that wherever a work simply stops necessarily deploys the weight of silence, or nothing-after-something thrown back upon it—so even if not intended as a closural moment, simply stopping will have a significance attributed to it or accruing to it because the writer halted. This effect is similar to the scrutiny of a "last poem" or "last words" before death, as if these were fully comprehended *as* their Last Word by the moribund speaker or poet—with some aura of special message. It's hard to avoid a just-stopping (accidental closure) or a deliberate but random stopping from accruing the special status of an ending. This paraphrases "Antin's Law" in my epigraph.

Yet couldn't stopping be just one incident that occurs—a pause? A consideration before another beginning? This is certainly true of cantos by poets fascinated by the vectored movement possible in serial writing while they think through the next directions for the poem. Ending by going to another beginning might be a recognition of the goal of "everything." And this "everything" will have multiple processes and stages that a poet is trying to examine, constructing a network of implications with plausibly different temporalities. How can that conclude? This is the difference between the one declared and controlled temporality with telos of Dante's journey and the plethora of processes and meditations in most modern poems.

Strange to say, ending a very long poem especially *at* its end begins to seem a less and less likely outcome. Perhaps endings occur elsewhere in the poem. NourbeSe Philip ends, perhaps, in *Zong!*'s floating middle of mourning; or alternatively, she ends ironically, critically with the original legal document. She generates at least two endings. Given that many of the long poems discussed in this book tend to the endless (only semiplotted) middle as their totality, perhaps terms should shift from ending to elsewhere. Forms of continuation are characteristic of long-poem writers; multiple endings might be plausible. To negotiate any ending may conjure so many loose ends that satisfaction is provisional, a sop, or another "as if" for the reader.

The question "how to end"—what ending satisfies and how does *that* work—can also be asked as "why" end. If endings are tied to conventions within relatively fixed and single-minded genres, or to ideologies demanding assent and belief, readers will have convictions about the emotional contents and ideologies of form instantiated in structure, for instance at the end of a ballad, the end of a sestina, the end of an ode or of an epic—yet even these convictions may become ambiguous or unsettled. When is an ending not ambiguous, anyway, even involving monofocal genres? Sometimes, although a work is closural, such ambiguities, reverberations (or even ironies) are sought deliberately. In contrast, an unfixed and pluri-generic poem, a poem with a small proportion of "plot" trajectory to a large proportion of exploration within that trajectory, presents a further challenge.

Silliman states that the "sense of closure is one of the defining problems of modernism."[3] His solution is to commit his work to anticlosural endlessness. Because his writing is mainly procedural, the door to writing is always open by the choice of yet another procedure, often temporal, sometimes numerical. But even more: "Being unfinished is for me the norm—I am in fact always in the middle, rarely in a position to take a step back and say that this (or this) is the final shape of something, only building blocks toward an emergent *thing* that I call a poem principally because poetry is the art of language, and hence for me the category that contains all others at least implicitly within."[4] In-folded and out-folded processes propel these (and other works treated here) to a far receding horizon.

For works organized in multiple individuated genres, like "A," one might argue that each section represents a closure. But once Zukofsky's projected number twenty-four is fulfilled, we see that he has (in my view) included three endings: the alphabetic climax of "A"-23 that he composed—from A to Z; the compiled cantata of "A"-24 selected from his prior oeuvre and combined by Celia Zukofsky; and an index as genre, as antic and incomplete as it is unconventional in poems. While Zukofsky always exceeds by his intransigent defiance, it is also arguable that there are extra endings of "A" because, in a long poem, one ending is never enough. Say this is a long-poem condition—or temptation.

The DuPlessis long poem called *Drafts* is also distinguished by many genres, seen in specific canto titles. Each canto, generally closural in semantic ways, opens to yet another canto, linked to the priors by some repetition, or textual déjà vu, making the whole work a weave of allusions, imagery, and social array. The trope of "drafts" proposes that all the poems are only rough drafts of an ideal or comprehensive statement—attempts toward "everything." (The poems, of course, are complete and concertedly revised.) I temporized for a couple of years wondering whether an exact, closural ending would be possible for the whole work, but the poem's deliberately chosen number pattern (a grid of 114 poems, with one unnumbered poem, the 115th) and its open-ended title *Drafts* impelled an incomplete stopping or pivot point that I never called an ending. That point called for turning again and again—the last words of *Draft* 114 are "Volta! volta!"[5] "Turning" from one poem to another makes ending into beginning.

If, as I've argued, modern long poems are multigeneric repositories, then insofar as endings confirm or are comfortable with specific genres, pluralizing the genres will necessarily create a dilemma about how to end. No matter whether a long poem is set out as an ongoing practice, as a conceptual/fulfillable set of strictures, and as a grouping of themes, any single ending might seem arbitrary or inadequate given the range of materials and meanings let loose in the work. Or an ending might just release us from the spell—of the poem. The sense of relief at finishing or just stopping for writer and for reader might substitute for a sense of completion at closure.

Yet poets could become quite fond of the sound, mechanisms, pleasures, and unrolling formal strategies of their own poems and not want to stop writing them or stop living in those worlds. One's investment in that poem has been so hard-won and so absorbing (perhaps even gratifying) that one doesn't want to leave that zone. Poets might get habituated inside the extents and fields they are now in—by the pleasures these give and even for choices of career strategy. Because—what happens afterward? This can worry poets. James Merrill's operatic tour de force, *Changing Light*, was articulated and, in its baroque fashion, "finished," but wait—after it was published, Merrill added a lengthy coda. Inside the enormous party, inventiveness, and formal sprezzatura of his long poem, the poet had trouble saying that last word on the Ouija board—goodbye.

The discontent with finishing (or even stopping) in the life-poem/long-poem mode is visible in several other poets who declared finis but then reopened the poem. Writers might first have chosen endings for the works but then discovered this choice no longer felt right or was not an adequate rendering of their experiences of the poem's processes. This changed outcome occurs in *Paterson* (as I've noted), with Williams's two endings, the first (of Book IV) whose last word is "the end," and the second performing the endless dance of erotic *poesis* in Book V. And Book IV even has doubled instances for that ending—a Paterson figure coming ashore like Odysseus in the Nausicaa section (girls playing ball nearby), sleeping, finding a dog, eating a sea plum, and (always vital in Williams) spitting out its seed. The second, the negative of this, is the public hanging of a man, a spectacle that always ends with an ejaculation ("the blast").[6] In Williams life is continuance with seed, and death also comes with seed.

Multiple thoughts about ending are part of Williams's reflections on his three decades of writing *Paterson*. He says in 1951 that he has "no recollection" of when he thought about *beginning* the poem, but somewhere between 1925 and 1927, he made a deliberate choice of significant city, using it strategically as an allegorical image of national promise and destruction. Further, he "decided" [that] the poem would be four books long, with analogies between a local topography—a notable falls, the course of a river, and the life of a person—along with a touch of old-style "humors" (air [perhaps], earth, fire, and water are present, deliberately paralleling *Four Quartets*). He postulated generalized ends to these thematic images of the city in its geography. But then "there were a hundred modifications" as the theme deepened metaphorically into a search for language—a language of the social-poetic realms he was depicting—a heteroglossic language and poetic structure of collage adequate to his sense of layered realities of place and time.[7]

Thereupon, "I had to think hard as to how I was going to end the poem." He had originally mentioned a few possible tropes (the Odysseus figure, the hanged man, the seeds), used in *Paterson* IV. Yet several years later, in 1958, after Williams had added *Paterson* V, he explained to the New Directions editor, "I have been forced to recognize that there can be no end to such a story [as] I have envisioned with the terms which I had laid down for myself."[8] That is, writing the poem changed the poet's plans, an honest statement (and hardly a surprise, after all).

Williams's "forced" means the poet has been confronted with the poem, and by the poem, as if the poem had its own force or agency, and the poet learned to read what was spelled by that sibyl's leaves. Poetic flexibility and curiosity in that situation, rather than obedience to the former plan is valued; it is an ethical-aesthetic attitude to the work, not a formalist insistence. An ending, if the poem has not been fixedly preplanned or prepostulated, necessarily entails a good deal of reading (self-reading and realization), and a curious retrospective prolepsis considering the many years of composition, past and (even) to come.[9]

With *Paterson*, if the poem goes into another key, "a new dimension," what does this adjustment mean? For Williams, the choice was a passage from tidy (and sentimentalized?) thoughts at ending to an open-ended, ongoing dance, precisely framing the question of this chapter: to end? or not? And how are endings decided? He chose a dance of accumulation and evokes the erotic and aesthetic powers of the processes, with that other medium—dance—and two genre evocations, satire and tragedy, with goats: "Satyrically, the tragic foot."[10]

This thought necessarily involves an author's judgment in the course of the poem about major themes, repetitions, recurrences, genres, and purposes, which further may involve slow modulations as certain elements grow more important, some less during the multiple decades of writing. For the writer is (as Williams says) "drawn on" by the poem, both moved forward, down into the roaring sound of Paterson Falls as a thrilling, primal "language," into that river to the ocean, perhaps written on (inscribed) by the poem, and further challenged by what he himself has made.[11] He is propelled by the poem, as if the poet himself is a resource for the poem to claim so it can get itself written.

Similarly, when Anne Waldman began her epic *Iovis* in the mid-1980s, she had a plan to end it with a gender-synthesis as affirmation. However, when she got to that end point, about twenty to twenty-five years and 1,013 pages later, she changed from that plan into another, with two cantos (published in 2018) from an as-yet-untitled "fourth book" to rupture any declaration of the final moment.[12] This move is characteristic of the dilemmas for long-poem writers. With the large scale of this work, Waldman presents a changing case of the debate and intellectual-structural question in this chapter—can one end a very long poem or not? Waldman first felt extrinsic reasons to end the poem but was discontented with that choice. "She didn't want to close it down, resistant to pressure of 'finish book, finish book' maintenance of identity."[13] Thus her own relationship to this work shifted; its ongoingness became her chronicle of loyalty in the vocation "to become more conscious," continuing the poem's absorptive energies.[14] And so despite the tripartite structure promised—and even given a "good-enough" ending in her original "Coda" (my metaphor draws on Winnecott's phrase "good-enough mother")—Waldman stated in 2018 that *Iovis* had not been finished. This suggests that the poet, while clear about her scheme and the postulated synthesis, could not actually find any specific end point or useful knot to be tied and had no plausible culmination (climactic sections). The satisfaction of *Iovis* is only in continuing in the same mode of evocation, imprecation, spiritual striving, and absorptive shamanism. In her work's becoming an endless poem, an ongoing network, Waldman fulfilled or recognized one formal destiny of such long poems—unstoppable.

There are also interesting tactics in some of these poems for what happens on the last pages. Any ending of a long poem might have to be at least double in idiom to account for different themes (we saw this with Mackey's provisional double "ends" to *Double Trio*). Multiple voices and an open or ambiguous ending are characteristics of even nanorific "long" poems. *The Waste Land* is polyphonic; Eliot chose a set of citations that arguably alluded to some of the genres/feelings that emerge in that work, talismanic citations from a personal zone of naming and of need. In these citations the despair, narratives of compromised and blasted relationships, sexual-spiritual yearning, alienation, and exacerbated suffering do not work in closural fashion but make suggestive reverberations back to the whole poem and outward.

Citation strategies at an ending send the poem sailing back into the culture. So the ending of Oppen's "Of Being Numerous" cites from a letter by Whitman about the construction of the US Capitol Building, then in process, expressing a hopeful wonder that the nation built of so various a many and a one can long endure. Aphorism will also work—as in Hughes's *Montage*—but it's a complex moment, for the axiomatic summary of the "dream deferred" occurs in "Harlem [2]," the seventh section *before* the last poem. Hughes has offered a varied middle that extends over the whole poem gathered in the pensive knots at the beginning (the title) and the summary (final stanzas). It appears, from the touch of circularity at ending, that the dreadful, barely breakable cycle of deferred social justice is beginning to repeat again, and that the several voices at the end are beginning to articulate the thwarted frustrations of "deferred" once again, in Hughes's polyphonic coda of comments sharing this news.

Mallarmé offers a definitive "end style" finding (or was that his thesis?), but it is startlingly distributed throughout the work; "DICE THROWN / NEVER [. . .] / WILL ANNUL / [. . .] CHANCE," because chance will never cease operations. However, this distributed-thesis axiom rests uneasily with the conclusion: "All Thought utters Dice Thrown."[15] Taking this as syllogism suggests that all writing and thinking occur via chance; endless "throws" and thereby endless numbers of statement are possible; and agency is displaced, coming from dice and universe, not "poet." What, then, is authorship but being a vessel for chance? Given that this is proposed within a nanorific "long" poem, a reader doesn't know quite what to believe: containment of ending by poetic agency or endless possibilities of statement in a secular, intransigent universe. But these two axioms are so multifaceted in implication that their apparent definitiveness leads to polyphonic reverberations. The relationship of central axiom, distributed throughout the poem, and axiomatic ending are the polyphonic mise en abyme of the poem.

There are also some "excessive" modern long poems that do end, but few. Ronald Johnson's *Ark*, concluding and carefully architectonic, and published seriatim over twenty years, is a rare instance of a lifelong long poem that ends; Johnson wanted to insist on this, as we will soon see. His ending (in my view, his whole final section) might be an exaggerated version of the same language and number play that have been happening all along. When the final rocket takes off, sending the whole poem into the cosmos, we have definitively *exited.*

Ancestors, the historical-personal encyclopedic work of Kamau Brathwaite, also has a terminus. The ending is an elegant short poem (all of section IV of the third work, *X/Self*) called "Carab," a pun on "crab" and on "Caribbean," and taking a long overview of witnessing: "my hand following the crabs poem / stalks the inheriting ghosts." It is a long view drawing from the course of the poem as the haunted course of Caribbean island history and a list of the elements of the poem, mingling place, event, peoples, beauties, losses. His "cramp hand [. . .] xplores" what he and the ancestors have endured—and survived.[16] The lyric list, in ending, evokes sleep, memory, and the stars—classic reverberations for endings. However, the later metabook *ConVERSations* extends this whole long poem, breaking beyond the elegant lyric listlike ending to acknowledge the many more forces, ideas, experiences, and language uses that generated the whole book of *Ancestors*. *ConVERSations*, by genre plethora and by a visual text that underscores the changed look of *Ancestors*, is an enveloping extension that tidally overrides the poise of the crab conclusion.

Many examples in this section show that perhaps a poet can end, but for a very long poem, it is harder to complete the conclusion. If poets develop a shape or terminus during the writing, it is from thinking with the discoveries and generally giving allegiance and attention to the findings generated in writing in one's time. And the poet responds to formulations that the poem generates, which offers these (back?) to the poet who of course originally wrote them. There are always real moments when the poem delivers such material to its maker; it is the maker's task to recognize them (right away or eventually). This is a moment in ongoing praxis that intrigues me, summed up once by painter Helen Frankenthaler: "You tell it, then it tells you."[17] Writing a long poem is a process of thought—thinking as if aloud onto a page, incorporating materials, writing to find how and why the assemblage, quest, or epic will move, and move forward—into its own field. A Book as an entity can be visualized as a thing (an object) and a goal to fulfill (a temporal goal for the writer) but may also be summarized as ongoing events of making, of *poesis*. Events in the world at large keep the book open. You can see that sometimes art has a startling side ("then it tells you") crucial for both the ego and the humility of that artist.

The tendency toward "resisting containment" that Mackey speaks of in poetics is generally shared by all the poets discussed in this book. As he says, "In the context of an open poetics, [there's] something that wants to if not resist closure, which is impossible, at least be tentative about closure, or be provisional or become self-conscious about closure in ways that leave open the possibility to continue."[18]

Yet the stranger question with a *very* long poem is why bother to end it. Granted, the poet might run out of energy for that poem and its accumulation of materials and want to stop.[19] Yet can the "everything" or maximally heterogeneous work have any plausible natural/logical/thematic terminus? After all, all long-poem poets perpetually negotiate a zone "between," between a sense of form and structure, along with focus, selection, combination—as against the temptation of (the pulse of) the ongoing. Another way of asking why bother to end: can a tendency to endlessness be an aesthetic and structural decision, rather than a case of bad judgment? The answer seems to be yes, sort of—but only when displacing throughout the work the urge to create one ending by structuring multiple termini across it. Perhaps these stages will build to one final finality. But by then perhaps we don't need one.

The issue of structure (some say "form") in the large poem is a large problem, however, particularly since a poem conducted over many years' time is bound to change or modulate. Hence, structure is not only a "simple" aesthetic problem but an issue of how the poem grows and changes, given a poet's responsiveness to the poem's modulations within its—and our—world. A paraphrase—how the poet grows in responding to the work she does. That makes ending a personal and social problem about adequacy or at least a triangulated negotiation—poem, world, poet.

This involves mobility, reinterpreting one's own work. Or knowing how to extend it, how to follow its own formal paths, its desires, and paths of thought (there's the poem's "agency" again), how the writer absorbs multiple stimuli without being overwhelmed by them. One's fortitude might flag or (in compensation?) become overly defiant or stubborn. In talking about processes, and decisions or choices, temporary or permanent, one may be further unsettled by an observation of Robert Duncan: "The imperative in form isn't always understood."[20] (It's an even more intense sentence if he is talking about "Urform," but let's say he means structure.) I take this to claim that the artist herself does not necessarily know how to credit her own structural choices or to evaluate their structural satisfactions but has to live with them and track their implications as concertedly as possible. This takes time, and that time might create more "long poem." So much for ending.

If the imperative to structure is not understood by its maker, it also may not be by its readers. Long-poem writers, especially of the VLP variety, have a drive, a drive to *poesis*, to choices, observations, rhetorics and shapings both within traditions that one recognizes as producing "poetry" and beyond them. Writing a long poem is a large risk, possibly a large risk that points toward failure (too long to be read; too many parts to keep together), yet there is some need for the reader to acknowledge both the drive and the risk. Hence, this book.

But by the time one gets to failure on that scale, the word is meaningless, because the drive to make, in terms of matter and form, has been fulfilled. What allows us to think we can understand it? Respecting that mystery, this section has simply specified a few pragmatic observations about different writers' choices. Failure in the long poem? One does not begin by assuming failure. One achieves failure, importantly and fully, only after great effort. The terms of long-poem failure are significant to understanding its practice. The poem fails because it's never enough and then (of course) because it's too much. Such failure is a topic for the serious, invested student of the long poem, but it is, after all, a somewhat creepy idea if the critic sits as jury and judge and awards points or stars. ("Fail better"?)[21] It is not so much the deliberate making of failure as the composition of ongoing responsive thought in time. Here, I've focused generally on the praxis and its rationales.

It appears that almost any ending of a very long poem variously manifests a resistance to ending it. Perhaps as a poem gets longer and even longer, ending is impossible or implausible. Or unnecessary, because if you just stop a very long work, that moment will be retrofitted in the mind of the reader as an ending. "Antin's Law" seems to work.[22] Or closure as such becomes irrelevant. If keen closure and summary satisfaction are impossible, then perhaps simply stopping is the only way to get out of what you are in. That act might just suffice.

NUMEROLOGIES AND PARTICULAR ENDINGS

If, in long poems, "no decision seems more fraught with tension, even fear, or is more apt to be stumbled over or canceled after the fact, than determining when and how to stop," then the interaction of numbers and endings needs to be examined.[23] Number, fulfillment, and solidity of findings have tried to coincide in prior eras but are vulnerable in a period, like ours, which tends to see dispersed arrays interacting, rather than one monolithic or hegemonic system whose discipline one accepts. Number becomes independent of plot and findings in many cases of the modern long poem, uncomfortable even with the elegant patterns of "Euro-Christian" (Dantean) work by Eliot and H.D., sometimes losing or fraying any numerically monocultural symbolism or theme.[24]

In the citation above, Silliman mentions only "stopping"—not concluding or ending. Given a potential lexicon in ascending order evaluating the endings of poems, mine would be stopping, closing, ending, finishing, concluding. Further, given the scale of "everything" as the very long poem's quixotic challenge, it is no surprise that numbers become a useful intervention from outside or from some system, used to control or corral that dream of "everything."

Numerologies do function in some modern long poems, but they are not confirmed by one culturally sacred book. The numerological poem is sometimes built from mathematical wonders (like the Fibonacci numbers, or the multiplication of nine); sometimes numbers play with general cultural associations or naturalized ones (twenty-four hours, seven days, twelve months). They may signal private systems, not drawing on shared ideological or cosmological agreements—except by claiming a method of creating some shape, given the disparate "everything" that the poets desire. A numerical goal depends on whatever procedure the poet chooses. Any private number mandates stopping for an abstraction, not necessarily visible to or meaningful for the reader, but a satisfactory fulfillment of a contract between writer and poem.

How is the universe organized, after all, and how do we know? It appears that multiverses are the cosmological hypothesis in our time. Can *any* long poem now give the illusion of a total sense of things, a picture of the world's fundamental knowledge and of its fundamental organization? Can any very long poem make order out of chaos—indeed, even out of its own chaos, that uncontainable sheer length or a temptation to that length? The aesthetic and ideological problems are almost intractable. But they are, for that reason, a notable challenge filled with gleeful possibilities.

Numbers become part of a poem's "cumulative nature," and they have a "performative function as active mapping of otherwise massive, astonishing, and irremediably cryptic material," as Hélène Aji noted in an introduction to the long and very long poem work of Hejinian and DuPlessis.[25] Some allusive numerological patterns may be used by many (though not all) long poems. These numbers might be backed up by culturally saturating ideologies, make scientific allusions, be the ludic result of a lust for pattern, or have emerged from individuated, even quirky, choices. And—the point here—these numbers get used to declare or prepare for some ending to a longish or very long work. Numbers become a fulfillment not of a vision claimed for the cosmological universe but of the patterns chosen by a particular poet.

Here is a personal narrative of decisions, since a series of numerical thoughts, arriving over several years, were part of my twenty-five-year construction of *Drafts*. First, the happy accident of nineteen poems in the first set of *Drafts* propelled me to establish a patterned recurrence of nineteen for each book, as in "why not"—following the original accident of that many poems even before a "set" was thought of. Then the challenge/temptation of Pound's (unused) Dantean "one hundred" and his several more cantos became a number that I wanted to swerve from but to hover near. So given what happens if you multiply nineteen by various numbers, I decided on six turns of nineteen sets, or 114 poems as a potential terminus of the poem. This seemed an impossible number of poems (I had written perhaps twenty-one Drafts by that time), but it postulated a desirable scope. However, going on endlessly struck me as a tax on the poem, and on the reader, so not an advantage—another structural decision that emerged from several intuitions.

Sometime during the writing of *Drafts*, I also decided that while one number kept the poem "stable," yet another number would destabilize it—another fitting choice. Having two final numbers was in keeping with my sense of the poem negotiating among various outcomes for its own structures. There were several reasons for this "closural" but open benchmark. Hence, I wrote a so-called unnumbered poem in the middle of the 114 (placed after Draft 57 and before Draft 58). This work, "Précis," consisted of fifty-seven sonnet-like objects that repeated, in miniature, each of fifty-seven Drafts motifs to date. This choice happily made my total number of poems both even (114) and odd (115). The thought of making minipoems inside a rather large work, and of saying "summary" when any poem is essentially unsummarizable, also had its charms.

These thoughts occurred as challenges to myself and real pondering of structure, not game playing, but interesting things to be done to express the emerging nature of my long poem and its social and cosmological perceptions. These choices also allowed the shape of a grid to occur as a way of expressing the array that my Ur-form moment had intuited—both infinite (in concept, as grids are) and bounded (in the work's instantiation). All of these decisions came one by one, sometimes painfully, in some cases over years, negotiating with my longing and with elements of the poem talking back, telling me things (as Frankenthaler said) even when I almost didn't believe what it was saying (particularly about projected length—115 poems, really?—and about adding the unnumbered Draft in the middle).

Silliman makes large-scale uses of specific numerologies, with some variants. He yearns to deploy generative strategies that are number based, all involving modes based on exponential growth: something gigantic and enormous starting from a very small seed. There are only general, not systemic cosmological implications—the exponentially enlarging numbers help "prove" the way matter and its organization in a poem fix one other and fit with the encyclopedic breadth. Among those are tricky number properties where you get rapidly multiplied amounts that are outsized, off the charts, out of scale. Silliman used these in two early, portal works, probably as a way of claiming the praxis—an invitation coming from number to the poet's goal of *poesis*. The Fibonacci number series as one series is an organic and arithmetic progression, an endless, infinite series, unlike the closed-system numerologies of small poetic forms like the sestina. It is often found in natural objects (as in a head of Romanesco broccoli) and is the basis of *Tjanting*.

Another numerology provokes exponential growth, like compounded interest, but more quickly. In Silliman's words: "The game in *Ketjak* is the old one of doubling the pennies on each square of the chessboard. Start with a penny & you will need more than a million dollars to cover that last square."[26] A work like *Lit*, based on multiple sets and factors of the number 12, takes a third tack: Silliman claims the uses of 12 for the twelfth letter of the alphabet ("L"), a number with many properties, especially when its square (12^2) gets to the number 144, while in a Fibonacci series the number 144 is also achieved (uncannily) at the twelfth turn. These become confirming properties in the poem; that is, as the numerical properties are revealed, the numbers confirm the rightness of the poem's structure. In all cases the terminus of any poem comes by a choice made at the poem's inception—an organic fiat—organic because these numbers exist in nature, and fiat by the will of the poet.

Most of Silliman's works, grosso modo, are *not* systematically numerological, once the habit of writing had begun after the first two works (*Tjanting* and *Ketjak*), but most depend on time (another number)—the poet's declaring a fixed period for writing and filling the space with elements that have the same kind of all-over surface. The word patterning is given structural terminus in all cases by a number pattern of enumeration, compounding the rationale for the segments. Silliman is not trying to translate numbers into words, as in gematria; he deploys numbers as a goad to building the poem's extent with statements.

Three contemporary works besides Silliman's, each from rather different poetic allegiances, can signal numerical or spatial instantiations of ending a long poem via numerological mechanisms.[27] They have in common only an individual evenness of text: all have one key visual practice for all the poems. In Ammons, a thin line; in Johnson, completely centered sections; in Hejinian each poem is a small square or rectangular shape, often accompanied by a smaller boxed aphorism. The examples of A. R. Ammons, Ronald Johnson, and Lyn Hejinian, with a discussion focused almost entirely on their numbers, shapes, and endings, suggest that numbers are important for keeping control of a longish work as a proof of some poetic rectitude (poeticity) via freestanding pattern itself, sought for its own sake, and expressive of content.[28] This outcome occurs whether or not the patterns have any larger cultural or ideological meanings. In Ammons the line is like a vein or life line; in Johnson the numbers create a humanist shapeliness even from mosaic bricolage; in Hejinian the boxes are like a calendar—day by day, month by month—"my life." Even with an unnerving poem-extent, the poetics of boundlessness can be indicated by a tactical or arbitrary boundary of a number or time frame.

All three poets considered in the next sections want to declare a terminus to their poems, and all may be said *to* end by using the numbers (including measures of space/time) that they have declared. These shorter number-based works allow us to examine some outcomes within this set of poetic demands or goals.

A. R. AMMONS

Ammons's poem *Tape for the Turn of the Year* is a procedural work beginning and ending within an allusive time—December holidays to the New Year.[29] In late November 1963, Ammons bought a sizable roll of adding-machine tape, tempted by its look and perhaps by its intended use—tallying, accounting—to help incite a purely additive poem. He vowed to write every day (or almost) until the tape got used up.[30] The visceral attraction to that, or any particular paper as a support and temptation, should never be underestimated as a spur to writing. Here a mysterious size and format of paper functions as a zone of interest, with the additional fascination that the roll of tape (narrow, just a few words possible per line) is quite unusual for poems.

Yet unlike fixed procedures that have predefined numbers for endings, this end number is unknown both in the amount of time it will take and in size—how many poem-pages will be written. Even if the package gave the buyer a size and length of paper, and even if this measurement in inches is known, it is unknown how much can be/will be written on it, and how many days will be involved. A red line preprinted toward the end of the tape indicates when it will run out ("time to reorder"), yet still the moment of ending was unpredictable, mechanical, not organic. This situation offers a maximum of unknowns to the poet—time and space, effect of size, not to speak of pertinence, or "now what will I say?" This arbitrary size of paper became invested with poetic challenge.

It appears that Ammons published what he wrote in *Tape* with a "first thought, best thought" ethos (paralleling Allen Ginsberg, and similarly derived from Williams's notational work), words without edits, rewrites, rearrangements, or exclusions. He said "[I wrote it] straight out of the well—good, bad, indifferent," in an unsent 1964 letter to Denise Levertov.[31] The fixed flexibility became an experiment for the poet in exploring elements of his vocation. The poem is unshaped tonally, deploying sententious, quotidian, and clowning dictions for its heteroglossic effects, sketching without follow-through, presenting insights uneven as any day itself.

The poet sometimes pursues painful meditations—self-ironizing (the uselessness of poets), self-questioning (is this the right poem to be writing?), self-judging (am I good enough, or even any good, as a poet?). It becomes clear that the long narrow space of the tape is a nervously available symbol of the lifetime that any individual may "write on," in any poetic pilgrim's progress. There is an allegorical connection between the unknown "numbers" that the tape will generate and all the unknowns of a poetic career and a life span.

The poetics of chance associations and a commitment to daily writing produce unease throughout. The flat, disparate, unintegrated elements create a visibly vulnerable poem in its committed but somewhat dazed imperfections. The topos of adding, counting up, and worrying how good are the results become further generators for writing. In this case the anxiety is relieved by simply stopping; the experiment gets finished thirty-six days after it begins. Indeed, as a long poem, *Tape* is rather short, from a formalist comic-stagey "prologue" and invocation of the Muse to the anticlimactic, self-commenting "so long." The poetics may be documentary, a resistance to metaphor and imagery, reportage filled with "commonplace" appeals. Also, more strikingly, is sheer "tallying," as the number marks "1 1 1 1 1" set down eighty times show by literal gesture how many lives were lost in a tragic lightning-struck airplane crash that is mentioned early in the poem.[32] In many ways the poem is the tallying of a life as lived—one's own spotty diary, other lives noted in the quotidian ordinary, the fears of inadequacy and of loss.

The tape is also an intermittently deployed (charming? cartoonish?) reminder of male potency. Ammons deploys an unselfconscious masculine affirmation, such as a (self-mocking, yet self-amused) comparison of the rising tape to an erection, a sophomoric (or simply familiar) discussion of sex, sublimation, impulse control, and a comparison of writing to semen. There are also intermittent, explicit comparisons of male sexual desire to writing, and the intense teasing adultery he imagines with the Muse at the end of the poem.[33] These are frank thoughts, confirming a loosely realist (masculine-inflected) confessional mode. *L'homme moyen sensuel* writes a poem.

The imagined Muse-female is capricious throughout and may not inspire when he wants her to; he may not be pleasing to her; she may deny him what he wants; he may not be man enough for her—in that, the root anxiety and "show" of this poem emerges. The poet-speaker wants to get to the end of the procedural invention, visualized as an intense bout of sex with a metaphoric mix of woman and Muse, where the tape has been worked until it finishes, gets smaller and smaller, and pulls out of the typewriter platen.[34]

At the ending, when the tape runs out and "the roll lifts" from the typewriter, the writing is abruptly finished. Ammons is home, safe with his goal accomplished; the explicit finding is "self-acceptance" and "do the best you can"—remarks on writing and on relationships. The reader is saluted: "thank you" and "so long." That last comment seems like a joke about how long the in-process writing stint was. Maintaining the negative capability to wait for the unknown moment where the tape runs out becomes an awkward vigil for the reader as well as the poet. Ammons's commitment to his own strategy conflicts with his enduring of "my / emptiness" and his contemporaneous preference for a short aphoristic (focused) poem.[35] His whole experiment may have self-tested his choice of allegiance in poetics, trying out an open-form strategy.

Concerning Phyllis Ammons, readers may have to endure dated (informative, presumably well-meaning, and shopworn yet uxorious) passages. The second passage toward the end of the poem—the uncritical affirmation in the possessive case that "a man's center is his / woman, / the dark, warm hole"—manifests an unease signaled by Ammons instantly, and immediately after, by his moving into both country-local and then fake German dialect.[36] Such a "warm hole" is a normative sentiment, hard otherwise to decode except as a free-floating bit of ideology. The Muse (not the wife) is the female figure more powerful and useful in terms of the poem, despite the wife's well-alluded-to meals.

Further, "his" woman might be the man's center, but the actual center of this poem in its structure, and even in terms of a painful empathy, is the memory of a mule named Kate when, after his rural childhood with that animal companion, Kate is abruptly trucked away as the payment for a serious family debt.[37] This has a semiconcealed parallel to (and displacement of) the very traumatic death of Ammons's younger brother. Even the next mule eventually acquired does not compensate for this fundamental loss; his recollection (characterization) of Kate's befuddlement at departure is a startling moment. The emotional clarity of these painful passages falls (coincidentally but eerily) close to the numerical center of the poem.

In 1996, thirty years after writing this work, Ammons produces the ex post facto idea that the tape itself is the hero of the poem. This would explain the refusal to push on certain themes by the writer at the time of writing: "Soon after I started the tape, I noticed resemblances between it and a novel. The point, like and unlike a novel, was to get to the other end; an arbitrary end would also be an 'organic' end. The tape itself became the hero, beginning somewhere, taking on aspects and complications, coming to a kind of impasse, then finding some way to conclude."[38] The topics talked about were secondary; the words were there to be "occupying space." The important act is getting through, concluding. This is a singularly embarrassed way of describing his experiment in notational process writing.

Ammons's ending is thus a given by virtue of certain measurements and numbers but not a given in terms of themes, except that the poem will loosely be day work—a risky investigation of time, season, and chance thoughts. The writer can only decide to write without flinching whatever occurs to him during his stint and without any more than short-term shaping to achieve the poem. That is, despite the passage about the plane crash, about Kate the mule, ecological meditations, about his wife and his Muse and a sexual hum, and other openings that the poem offers, the only recursive repetitions that seem to deepen across the poem are the intensity of looking at nature, and its sense of *salience* (ecological fittedness), an important materialist concept for Ammons. This poem is deliberately awkward and not comfortable with what happens; it does not weave its stated themes and insights allusively across the whole as these develop (as in Williams's writing tactic of "rolling up," incorporating things that went before) but produces starts and stops. The task at times seems dutiful only, a stint, not a surrender to a notational poetics, and without an ease either of linking the thematic development that is sometimes achieved by poets working in quotidian collaged associations or of producing incisive epigrams condensing his moods.

The charm is to allow that quotidian unrolling to occur as a project both self-conscious and "natural" (unselfconscious). The end is a stoppage when the paper runs out, based on a mode of procedural organicism—a measure of the paper, and an irregular amount of event, memory, now-time observation at his disposal when he sits to write, an awkward flow of consciousness registering thought in the now. The split is clear between the writer who has self-agreed to these rules (including the rule *I will end wherever it ends and be satisfied by the experiment*) and the writer who is made uncomfortable by the loose ends generated by this notational praxis. In this sense the numbers (measurement of the tape) and the ending (thematic elements) quarrel. Was the tape long enough to work out the themes? Do the themes develop along with accumulating numbers (of days) or on the arbitrary size of the paper? This poem uses a physical extent to define its structure—when the tape stops, it does too.

RONALD JOHNSON

> [. . .] the poet's prayer at starting a long poem—Lord, let me finish.
>
> Ronald Johnson, "Take a Chisel to Write"

Another poem fervent in its commitment to number and ending is Ronald Johnson's twenty-year work *Ark* (written 1970–90; published 1996) using numbers to establish and shape both ending and closure. Johnson's general structural and numerical goals have been carefully preestablished with a desire to make "a poem with a vast structure."[39] That vatic architectural ambition occurs with each succinct individual section, written as odes or ecstatic shorter poems. Each section is like a holograph of the whole.

Ark is built in three sections, with an exacting numerology. The terms used for its shape are part-whole architectural metaphors, although the title also has spiritual meaning as containing a sacred text (The Ark of the Covenant) and housing a start-up remnant to be rescued from YHWH's wrath (Noah's Ark). There are three book-units of thirty-three canto-sections each. First unit, The Foundations (whose sections are Beams—of wood and of light), deploys the visuality of the alphabet in witty/winning work drawing on concrete poetry. Second unit, The Spires (whose sections are named Arks but are strongly vertical in look), is almost comically rocket- and fountain-like.[40] Third, The Ramparts, is a fervently static unit (as if "surrounding" Foundations and Spires) and, unlike the other two, deploys one single stanza size and line number for all its thirty-three sections. It is the most fixed and invariable numerological section.

There are thus ninety-nine sections total, but only the first two book-units feature sections of fluctuating lengths. The ending moment is imagined as a joyous launch of the space shuttle carrying this whole architectural and numerological vision and its meaning as a seed pack of spermatic efflorescence into space. A science-fiction, male orgasmic fulfillment, a Fourth of July fireworks rocket, an American optimist's vision fuse at the ending of this poem, in which the poem "building a time capsule of everything that I've heard and seen, [goes] out to the dark, to the stars"—a visionary cosmological closure with the long poem's characteristic "everything" ambition.[41] Johnson's *Ark* is a taut and scintillating but very closed poem whose telos is a humanist sublime: wonder, awe, a sense of intense Being, man as the container of all nature and cosmos, with language/alphabet as the path to these spiritual findings, a fittedness affirmed by number.

Every single canto of the whole 307-page text is centered on the page, an unusual look offering very striking bilateral balance for its visual text (like a person's bilaterality).[42] The poem was built with minute, shardlike phases, similar to the elements of Zukofsky's more citational compositional strategy, and with a mosaic-musical "gluing" together of lines in the numerical orders he designated. "I write lines," and those lines make "an architecture."[43] This intense segmentivity along with the intense counting characterizes Johnson's visionary poetic practice. The earlier two sections sometimes have a concrete poem's alphabetic and glyphic playfulness that offer in their riddling word choices an almost kabbalistic intensity, as if the lines were coded translations of secrets of the universe.

Blissful, excessive sound and intricate visual signs mark the first two book-units. One bold section consists solely of Johnson's own handprint, reminding the reader of the marks of hands in cave art across the world and of the urgency of *poesis* itself—making a mark and continuing to do so.[44] Another consists solely of recordings of birdsongs: "Ark 38: Ariel's Songs to Prospero" ("constructed out of recordings of songs of birds of eastern United States").[45] This long poem has distinct "total artwork" elements and is, overall, both visual and aural.

Johnson's theories of the universe show the links of all scales and modes of the creaturely—how echological is ecological, and how alphabetic-etymological puns play the text like a visual song from alpha to omega. Shape and number are fused as one. There are traces throughout presenting a celebratory use of religious (also patriotic and artistic) texts: an intense remixing of lines from hymns, and an important section under the rubric of Orpheus that reorganizes the Psalms by tactics of erasure. In these cases (as in his related work erasing some Books of *Paradise Lost* into *RADI OS* [1977]), he seeks to distill words to their highest or most essential inspiration.[46] This is a poem representing, again and again, that "all sounding bodies [—all objects shown or shone via all words—] are in a state of stationary vibration."[47] The claim of a brilliant stasis of resonant visual-aural vibrations is marked. Any line, stanza, or small visual unit has been turned/tuned in the sight-sound-intellection equation, so each bit is a faceted sounded gem.[48]

Johnson admires three distinctive outsider artists who made ambitious architectural structures parallel to his poetic ambition. Their obsessions for *poesis* provoked their major works. These aesthetic models are three socio-spiritual bricolaged constructions (intransigent, individuated, quirky, and radical) made over decades. Johnson celebrates the Watts Towers of Simon Rodia (1879–1965) in Los Angeles, balanced mosaic-studded loops of wire coated with cement, the tallest at just over ninety-nine feet.[49] *The Throne of the Third Heaven of the Nation's Millennium General Assembly* by James Hampton (1909–64) is a brilliant room-sized installation of wood and old furniture with used lightbulbs, all covered with silver and gold foil, now housed in the Smithsonian Museum, Washington, DC. Then in southeastern France, the Ideal Palace is a few acres of multiple temple-like building constructions and sculptures of pebbles, rocks, and cement, hand-built by Ferdinand Cheval (1836–1924, postman [Facteur] of Hauterives, a village in the Drôme). Johnson's deep identification with outsider artists helps define but cannot sum up his literary path; he is a very knowing and literary poet with a fundamental stance of naive and awestruck wonder. He summarizes that outcast heritage in his defiantly Melvillean declaration of outsider leverage: "CALL ME / ARTISAN."[50]

Johnson identifies with poets and naive obsessed artisans of continuous practices who became *makirs* of the persistent production of wonderful objects, installations filled with awe and passion, made as stubborn acts of worship from and to the creative force in the universe itself. Fundamentally, Johnson celebrates *poesis*—making, and language is his glistening medium.

Johnson is also one poet who seriously discusses ending the long poem and always projected a precise ending to this work. He "didn't know [he] was going to" choose "exactly *that* ending," because "I get ends as I go along," but he was strongly motivated to listen for them. Therefore, he recognized the satisfying ending ("I don't need to add anymore [*sic*] to it") and, with numerology as an architecture also satisfied, "that's when you quit."[51]

He contrasts his choice proudly and exactingly to fellow long-poem practitioners of a slightly older generation, marking his distinctive resistance even within his own poetic genealogy/nexus by constructing a serious ending where they had not. For Johnson's intensely built verbal-visual structure precisely *differed* in one key particular from other long-poem models of the recent past. Because his poem ends, Johnson's work is odder than even the large-scale works by Duncan, Olson, and Pound; he achieved deliberately balanced form. Further, Williams, Pound, Zukofsky, and Olson all use collage, in larger chunks than what Johnson selects, and with a striking degree of vatic, historical, or intellectual observation and comment, and in some cases a didactic claim or interpretive freight.[52] These are all poems evoking process, not finish, and in Johnson's view do not end effectively. Johnson even casts a suspicious eye on Zukofsky's "A," though like his, it's a long poem that *does* conclude.

So Zukofsky, with whom Johnson struggles, is a half-exception. And while "A" is filled with an extensive stylistic variety and range of tones, in fact, this long poem does end.[53] Being a user parallel to Johnson of citation and of the multiplicities buried in words, Zukofsky is, of course, a special case of the long-poem writer. Hence, Johnson wavers as to where and how to place Zukofsky's achievement. Johnson sets him near enough to his own distinction, but Zukofsky is definitely kept at arm's length. Johnson is inspired by the cluster sight-sound-intellection—the aim of poetry theorized by Zukofsky for the lyric or shorter poem. These "objectively perfect" criteria become Johnson's ideal, and he acts as if his quest and test are to engage and surpass that model (a very Zukofskian motivation). Yet Johnson half dismisses Zukofsky's lifelong poem (his work's closest analogue in verbal density) with a respectful raillery: "A" does end—but is altogether too obscure. "I think Louis maybe had gotten it all there; if you can ever figure out what's there" is an interestingly dismissive as well as witty remark.[54]

Other long-poem works are notably resisted. "They stand before me, great obstacles" is his rather unforgiving statement. Johnson, hardly a bit *un*informed about his major predecessors, wanted the Zukofskian trinity in poetics: "its cornerstones the eye, the ear, the mind."[55] Johnson is quite proud that *his* long poem is "finished," and quite rare for that fact, compared to his "confrères."[56] Although an "equivalent" in intensity and years spent, Johnson claimed decisively that *Ark*, while "comparable to epic Modernist poems," was the opposite in mode. Johnson wanted a poem rejecting the "with history" model of Olson and Pound. He wanted it to "be without history," a startling thought.[57] "If my confrères wanted to write a work with all history in its maw, I wished, from the beginning, to start all over again, attempting to know nothing but a will to create, and matter at hand": sheer *poesis* proudly affirmed.[58] Note, however, in both, "everything" is still the desired outcome, whether from the old clutter of "history" or as a new invention from whatever "matter" is at hand.

Johnson has thus presented himself as a singularity because of his rare choice in the long-poem world of a closed, final ending and because of his "non-historical" poetics. What does it mean deliberately to write a poem without history and yet "constructed of things in my time."[59] Johnson resists the illustrative theorizing of Pound and Olson, the engorging of documents as provocations to polemics made in their work, and their tendentious or suggestive sociohistorical analyses.[60]

The original title of *Ark* was *Wor(l)ds*; the evident pun presented an "everything" poem (often a type that automatically "includes history") but also a signal of the mechanism of making those worlds: words.[61] One cannot regret the loss of the unpronounceable title—which was Guy Davenport's telling objection, whereupon Johnson changed it. However, that former "concrete" title showed that an "everything" ethos was always on Johnson's agenda as well as the permanent kabbalistic sense of worlds within words (and words inside words). So the poet is no longer the exploratory and performative gatherer and disperser of the plethora of "everything," but a builder of a work out of various bits, rejecting the hierarchical sorting of important and unimportant in favor of the simple "things in my time," composed in an overriding elegant structure, poised and sonically scintillating: a spiritually focused affirmation of permanent wonder.[62]

This claim of "no history" means, apparently, that you think spiritual ecstasy has no actual aesthetic, patriotic, or philosophical history of its own. Languages (however smashed into shards) do remain social and historical—a word is not just a piece of tile set in a structure, and even in a mosaic mode, contains traces of syntaxes. The fact that languages and their words have histories—of etymology, of usage, of orthographies and tones—is studiedly ignored, although not as much in the first two sections of *Ark*. Many mosaic bits for his bricolage do point to past processes, technologies, and economies—all the histories buried inside them. Yet Johnson elides the histories he in fact deploys and evokes.

Given the amount of material and the length of time invested, it takes a certain amount of time to "stop" or end a long poem (as to stop or change any large-scale ongoing event). Ending a long poem is often not a matter of a few lines but several sections and might even begin far back in the poem. *Ark* displays a striking instance of that situation, since the whole third section is arguably a path to ending. The poem literally lifts language to its own glory via an insistent numerology. Given that 33 + 33 sections (irregular and varied in shape, look, feel and tonality) are the sum of the first two parts of this poem, one wonders why the final section (at the same 33 number) is not similar (or similarly playful) in its tonal and formal variety. The total number of sections is ninety-nine. The "hundredth" canto, Dante's number, is a ghost presence. Perhaps the "night of the soul" that he alludes to makes any "paradiso" of endless illumination difficult.[63] A second might be the wall-like warding of an extrinsic element in "history" that lies in the background of "The Ramparts": the devastating AIDS crisis of endless death with President Reagan's refusal to recognize the crisis and thereby begin supporting research protocols to alleviate the medical and social devastation in the gay—Johnson's—community.

Still, the reader wonders why the poem does not somewhere have the thirty-fourth canto, thereby paralleling Dante. We saw that *RADI OS* was rejected for that task and must surmise that the startling presence of even an erased Christian allusion (to Milton) at the end of Johnson's poem (the hundredth canto) would have opened many speculations about a quest to faith at the poem's end. *RADI OS* is not only an erasure of Milton but a way of naming glories and beauties without theology (or much syntax). In any event, this (now freestanding) work does not appear in *Ark*.

Is this avoidance of a one hundredth poem a mark of a deliberately chosen "flaw" for a cosmological poem, although ninety-nine is a perfectly desirable numerical goal in its own right? Johnson's explicit refusal to allude to Dante's hundred-canto work is revealed in a wonderful exchange. Peter O'Leary pointedly comments about the number ninety-nine, saying, "That brings up Dante." Deadpan, Johnson replies, "Not for me."[64]

Yet both are quite aware that even if constructed in threes and not achieving one hundred but only ninety-nine units, and even if Johnson is "only" an American "home-grown" poet, Dante does hover a bit, at least enough to be swatted away.[65] Johnson has made things work in these threes. Yet the ninety-nine—a thoroughly mystical and exciting structural number in a cosmological work—cannot help but "recall Dante" to everyone who reads this poem—except (he avers) to the poet himself. Still, as an elegant case of a numerical conclusion, Johnson's closure is indeed conclusive—a rare outcome in this period.

LYN HEJINIAN

> It seemed that we had never begun and we would never be there. [. . .] And we've known that—that changing of endlessness, since endlessness is right in front of us.
>
> Lyn Hejinian, *My Life in the Nineties*

The proceduralism of Hejinian's *My Life* and its elaborations sum up a realist-inflected poetics facing contradictions felt in thinking about representation itself. "Actual life" (all the potential minutes and days in a year) and the art of making sentences considering some of these in a procedurally exact number of sentences per section create an antiorganic, only loosely sequential framework. And while there really is closure everywhere (in every sentence) in the three "Lives," there is not any plotted event followed from beginning to end, but, as in Silliman, virtually every sentence is an arc of "plot." Things have happened, and in Hejinian's telling and invention of what happens, she puts words that happen on the page, thereby making new events happen now, as well as (only sometimes) recording some events having happened "then." Events pass into words, which are another event. Mainly these individual sentences *are* the event. While claiming to represent something, Hejinian also shows how representation happens, continuously laying bare the device.

Hejinian's two semiarbitrary numerologies for the first two "lives" of *My Life* are sometimes discussed as if the nature of this artifice (poetic form, numerology, and the organic body) with this title has a particular fascination in the work of a woman writer because of Hejinian's structural panache around (apparent) biography. The several iterations of *My Life* are built, neatly and compellingly, on an organic-procedural system. A general parataxis generates a gap between every sentence, building on change-ups that have no particular code or logic. Even though the prose-poem sections are manageable looking (Silliman's in contrast often get exponentially large), a lot of the gaps are associative or fond jump cuts concerning interior observations, external events, and writing. Being organic and procedural together creates a synthesis of near-opposite tactics, here involving arbitrary versions of Hejinian's age at composition and chronologically evoking (but not really tracking) elements of her "life"—really her thinking—year by year in the sections. No sections are "official" biography, designed to account for important events of each lived year, but all sections allude to events or quotidian observations from each year, as if memories remade or refabricated.[66] This is not the work of "description" but "scrutiny."[67]

Hejinian's stopping or finishing any section and defining the whole were accomplished by an arbitrarily chosen number, a procedure based on the age of the poet when she wrote the first *My Life*—something not attributed a heuristic meaning (with any dramatic revelations about that year grandly revealed by the text).[68] However, it appears that she began writing *My Life* at age thirty-seven, making the choice of that number a full claim of and on vocation. One can see a discussion of poetics obliquely alluded to in three sentences in section 37. First we read the refusal: "If there is a story at all, accounted for, a settled thing to have experienced, it's nothing of the kind"—I take *it* to be the sense of the work to come (and "now" completed), the Ur-sense of form as Barthes evoked it. Then, "The obvious analogy is with music as with words"—at the very least, this means that recording and reporting the true thing, like journalism, is not the motivation, but rather a pulse, rhythm and sound—ruminating wonder. And then the positive poetics: "A sense of definition [. . .]

develops as one's sense of possibility, of the range of what one might do or experience, closes with the years." That this is immediately followed by "So I gave it away" does suggest that here a plan is adumbrated, but we won't learn more than this sketch here.[69]

In section 38 (of *My Life* II), the "rhythm of cognition" is well under way, and "My life is as permeable constructedness." This is where the narrator wonders at her lack of frissons of memory, although she lives just blocks from her childhood home.[70] Memory or remembering is absolutely not the point of the work, especially not reconstructing any "I"—given that "I" is in process as a subject, not as a finished topic (or subject/matter) to be written about. However, constructions of memory in language made now are absolutely the point of the sentences. This work thinks new memories as an act of *poesis*. Fragments of making are the point; even if images come from the past, they are shaped in the now of presentation. A particular age becomes just a number to be deployed, not a teleology or culmination or notable plateau; specific events, trauma, reasons for these numerical choices are invisible or semivisible; reconstructions of feelings are not the point. Because of the strict prose-poem containment, the elegantly managed stylistic elements, and the ironic pleasures of the title/genre and allusions to several other genres, the work presents a deft interplay between lived time and time of composition.[71] The work has an amused, courtly subjectivity, as if inviting the reader into this pleasurable space of meditation.

Both the words "My" and "Life" are (in effect) used unconventionally, offering meaningfully mischievous and misleading information. As fact-telling autobiography or a set of dramatic occasions, the work is wanting—with almost no sense of World War II and postwar atmospheres in the eyes of a child, of the fairly early death of the father, of moving cross-country, of the all-too-perky 1950s for a young woman, of leaving home for college, of child-raising or a working life, of becoming a poet and publisher within a still rather male universe—all plausibly memorable events and situations.[72] As *female* autobiography, the work is even less informative, resisting, by clear choice, the conventional (feminine) "personal," and thus barely mentioning and rarely elaborating moments considered distinctive for women—menarche, marriage, childbirth (though child care is noted), domesticity, divorce, remarriage, Hejinian's serious plural vocations (writing and publishing), responses to one's femaleness, friendships, and the feminisms and gender debates emergent and influential in those years of writing.[73] Hejinian veers from any commonplace conceptions of personal "life" or commentary on politicized life in her sentences. Her work is rather constructing "spots of time" and flashes of insight (like "my love for these kids").[74] Her tasks in poetics are reconstructing/

inventing memories and making observations as externalized aphorisms, engineering leaps within notation, as consciousness continues at work on itself by the very acts of writing.[75] There is so little Sturm und Drang in *My Life* that, in the second version, Hejinian stated that many of the sentences she needed to add were "darker" than materials in the first iteration, now including anger and rage, given her now "Permanent constructedness."[76] "Permanent" and "permeable" are two key substitutable words.

Once the second *My Life* is made, this concept of regulated additions could have offered a mechanism for a very controlled "endlessness." With the relationship between the 1980 and the 1987 *My Life*, Hejinian showed that hypothetically the addition of interior sentences to that matrix could be produced successfully even again, had Hejinian wanted to (basing later sections on another root number of her age). However, with *My Life in the Nineties*, she alluded to those prior "*Lives*" but altered their formalist premises; this book is no longer a "My Life" in the same terms. This apparently final iteration, in another pattern, contains ten sections (each representing a decade) of sixty sentences, each representing her decade-age at this time span (going from fifty to sixty years). Hejinian's invention of structural patterns and modular procedures suggests a prodigality of invention—the meaning is *poesis* itself: "My life is as permeable constructedness," to cite this again.[77]

Given that Hejinian's are hardly gigantic long poems, the sense of the length and breadth of this "Life" series is a strong illusion created by a set of tactics. Hejinian composes a nanorific cluster of work with a strict number of numbered units per section but flexibility of tone, observation, sentence structure, and temporality. Each sentence generally constructs a statement, finding, or aphorism made in the time of writing (not of living), facilitating both quick insight and retrospective rumination as a steady, placid assemblage. The "Lives" seem to be written in the now of composition, although she drew on real and constructed memories. And her order of sentence sequence does not represent any single arc of real time for one year of age, but her ruminations within the writing "now" about each particular age.

"My Life" is "My meta-life." There is no cumulation. Even in an anecdote that suggests something did occur (some of the longer sentences are built this way), there is a scan of a variety of moments—serious, fun, intense, epiphanic, ordinary, intelligent, meditative—a set of details of the quotidian that is not trying to get anywhere or be anything more than a statement that contains (embodies) itself. While these works are based on accumulation (assemblage), Hejinian resists the potential drama of the cumulative for a rangy network of linked findings. In the second two "Lives," there is a special recognition of continuance—of being the person who wrote *My Life*.[78] That moment of vocational grasp is something one sees in other long-poem writers—Mackey is one, Waldman is another. The question what to do with what one *has* done provokes many realizations.

The ideological commitment of her oeuvre both to endlessness and to dailiness is here achieved by short prose-poem sections that house precise moments of ending all over that work—sentence by sentence and unit by unit. These endings close only to open. A second tactic of endlessness—really of affirmation—comes from the repetition of statements that Hejinian makes almost proverbial as indicating the whole work (like "we who love to be astonished"), a very striking and focused use of repetition. These axioms thread through—and act, as she notes, to "postpone completion" of any particular train of thought, by disruption and mysterious reminders, setting up a reverberation without one referent.[79] Instead of ending, one might say, Hejinian substitutes recognition, often based on the repetition of these minititles or glosses to the side of a main prose poem, set in a box to the side or as reminders in the text. The effect is a magnetic attention to a focal spot-of-time in the Wordsworthean sense, no matter where it is placed. These tactics reclaim some issues within early modernism: clock time, conventional chronologies, and the expansive time of thought (consciousness), all in contrasting interplay.

Lyn Hejinian has stated that she "rejects closure"—that very phrase emerges as one of her striking principles in a notable essay in poetics—so what is her work doing in this discussion of endings? It is to state that numbers do not guarantee closure—in fact, in Hejinian's hands, quite exacting numbers have been deployed almost to taunt closure (to tease it might be more tonally just), taking one of the guarantors of formal solidity in poetry (numbers) and altering their effect. The "My Life" series needles formalist artifice in striking ways, mainly by providing closural circumstances but absolutely no ending. A. R. Ammons finds his chance moment of ending from the measurement of a spool of paper. Ronald Johnson insists on a numerology to support the end moments of his long work. Hejinian produces procedural numerologies to *avoid* closure and to offer an endless process of *poesis*; it is a wickedly witty playing with structures.

Closure emphatically does not finish if one depends on "exoskeletal formal elements" like arbitrary numbers of sentences.[80] It does not finish if one writes streams of crafted observed meditations, observed thoughts. So in this case, numbers, the guarantor of form in one poetics (by counting up to the end and making themes hold together with numbers) instead deliver a sense of a plurality of other possibilities, other plausible insights, other observations. The numbers become porous, not solid. Something may end by counting to a fixed number, but it won't finish, and it won't close. The lexicon of ways to define a terminus picks up resonance with these works.

In addition, "Antin's Law" (wherever an author stops feels, to a reader, like an ending) helps define Hejinian's works as ending but not necessarily closing or finishing. This is how an arbitrary limit can signal a poetics of boundlessness. These structures, invented in and for the work, particularly counting, repetition, and sentence construction, do not create a fixed zone, but encourage an ongoing activity of making.[81] This is a poetics of boundlessness in the guise of a play with limits.

"PASSAGES," GRAND COLLAGE, AND THE NEVER-ENDING POEM: ROBERT DUNCAN

> We see in every part signs of the formlessness of the whole;
> the formlessness of the work then is a significant form.
>
> Duncan, *A Selected Prose*

Robert Duncan had many encouragements and poetic contexts for writing a long poem. He maintained a challenging friendship with Charles Olson, a long-poem writer in the canto-like multigenre arc out of Ezra Pound and William Carlos Williams, through Louis Zukofsky—to offer that particular genealogy. He was close to Jack Spicer, arguably one of the inventor-users of the serial long poem, along with Mina Loy, George Oppen, Langston Hughes, Lorine Niedecker. He was greatly fascinated by Dante, the writer of the consummate long poem in one of our several collective cultures. Duncan also made remarkable statements essentially concerning visions of form and hints of structure at the same time. Form (an Ur-vision) and structure (the instantiations of form) he twists together, as a double helix under the larger rubric *poesis*.

His wide-ranging claims for and in poetics permanently propel his vastness of purpose, and such visions of scope could have produced long-poem ambitions. Further, some of Duncan's statements do have the tone of someone about to embark on a long poem, such as his desire (cited before) to make "large spatial architectures at the edge of chaos."[82] The prospectus in "The Poet and Poetry" symposium (published a year before Olson's 1950 "Projective Verse") could constitute a program for the long poem as well as for his oeuvre. "How to increase the complexity of interpenetration of parts; how to make the poem go on as long as possible—that is to contain the maximum quantity of moving parts so that the final performance of choreography and design will keep me intrigued intellectually and emotionally."[83] Both statements even have *Gesamtkunstwerk* allusions to other arts. These dramatic and continuous suggestions that *poesis*, even endless *poesis*, was his goal could surely have issued in a long poem, acknowledged as such.

Around 1960 Duncan even began a long incorporative and perpetually unfinished work—in prose. *The H.D. Book* just grew and grew as an assemblage of essays; it was shaped into a reading copy only by editorial interventions after Duncan's death. That prose work resembles some long poems discussed here: its accumulative bricolage of meditations; the claim of "everything" going into this Book—those encyclopedic and polyphonic criteria; a wide range of authors discussed in their relationships to an enlarged modernism, with the author's history of his vocation all drawn into the assemblage of the "occulted." *The H.D. Book* was a life's work intended as a culture-shaping intervention.

Given his poetics and this endless prose-essay, what prevented Duncan from defining a very long poem within his poetry? Without oversimplifying, it seems to have been the problem of ending, the structural idea of finishing that fundamentally conflicted with his articulation of form as a proliferative, never-ending *poesis*. Duncan's debate with Olson on *Maximus* illustrates these concerns about ending. He felt that Olson did not rightfully claim, in the last, hard moments of his life, what Olson himself had enunciated: the open-ended nature of "composition by field." Duncan enacted this disagreement in an essay delivered in 1979, discussing (among other things) Olson's ending to *The Maximus Poems*. In addition, Duncan refused to frame, as long separable serial poems, his own titles "Passages" and "The Structure of Rime." These are sections of poetry and prose poems recurring throughout his *Collected Later Poems*.

In his 1979 essay, Duncan reports that Olson used the Greek term "temenos"—a temple enclosure, the site of particular divinity that infuses us, taking this as a metaphor through which Olson "heard the *space* in which he could take place [as a poet]."[84] It's the place where suddenly *Maximus* is "*fully* out of bounds."[85] The admiration is patent. Duncan's definition of Olson's *temenos* (and what Olson's poem achieved in Duncan's view) is the whole Earth, the enlarged everything of everything, a "world mind" or "world-mind-image."[86] Or, in an alternative metaphor, "the incomparable Book or Vision."[87]

This is Duncan's ideal—and describes his sense of what he had achieved. Sometimes dubbed Grand Collage, sometimes "symposium of the whole," this oeuvre-level writing, always plural, polysemous, inclusive, excessive, and endless becomes a metabook of collected poetries.[88] Grand Collage is Duncan's fulfillment of the Mallarméan prophecy: that everything in the world exists to end up in a book.[89] With this ghostly evocation of a Book in its grandeur, as well as collage as its combinatory motor, we are firmly in long-poem territory.

Something that began as a sacred enclosure, for the Olson remade in Duncan's hands, becomes completely without enclosure or boundary. This multiphasic endless entity is not only the goal of scope for Duncan, it is a central goal in the modern and contemporary eras for many extremely long, or simply very long, poems by other poets. Within the context of a debate about ending a long poem, Duncan's unapologetic move of claiming Olson's *The Maximus Poems* as "endless" gets foregrounded.

Duncan's insistence on boundarilessness instantly raises the question of Olson's own opinion, given that Olson had assured Duncan that *The Maximus Poems* did end. Here, Duncan's witness testimony is fraught with ambivalence: "Charles's statement to me at the last was that he had finished his work."[90] Then, given that single elegiac ending line (at top of the last page of Olson's work), "my wife my car my color and myself," it is difficult say whether Olson meant "finished," in the sense of "ended," "closed up," or "completed" or whether he meant "end" as "come to an adequate (and elegiac) stopping point."[91] George Butterick, one of the coeditors of *The Maximus Poems: Volume Three*, considers that ambiguity. That *final* line, designated as such explicitly by Olson, dictated to Charles Boer (the other editor), was in place. The issue is what comes before.

Olson told people who visited him in the hospital that he had "'finished'" the long poem, but the rest of *The Maximus Poems: Volume Three* was still disorganized, not fully sequenced, not clearly final in some details. Butterick does not flinch from this discussion. What does "last" mean: a true finality? Or "a shrug in the face of fate" considering that there "was no grand design" to the whole and that, generally speaking, the work was heuristic and "unplanned."[92] These questions haunt Olson scholarship, but they also signal any long poem's difficulty around concluding. And around theorizing what such long-poem ending actually might be.

This Olsonic pulse of making without (necessarily) thinking of ultimate structures or of anything but ongoing writing as a praxis was, for Duncan, precisely a triumphant parallel to his own poetics. Hence, he struggled to allow to Olson (now, of course, dead) Olson's own thoughts on the subject. If there is an ending to a long poem or perhaps to any poem, according to Duncan, there will be nothing left over. "You can't have that business, coming to the end," or "coming in and finding that there's a leftover."[93]

So ending is a space in which there is no "leftover," no more event or experience, no more "continuous process" of picking things up—no more themes added, no more movement, no more thinking inside more and more poetry.[94] It is almost a picture of the death of the poet, for ending something fecund and inventive becomes the equivalent of death. With things left over (still to write, still to explore), you instead enter Duncan's sense of open space—the ultimate paradox of unenclosed enclosure, a perpetual passage to more passages.

In both the transcribed lecture on Olson (here as "Charles Olson") and the final form of the essay in "The World Felt as Presence," Duncan tried to blur and obfuscate what Olson felt he had achieved—some ending for *Maximus*.

The difference between Duncan's ideas about the *never*-ending poem and Olson's testimony about ending *Maximus* is so fraught that Duncan at first denies Olson's stated position. In the pamphlet he says that he and Olson discussed the ending of *Maximus as* an ending, but Duncan is *sure* that "the end declared proves not to be the intent," double guessing the now-dead Olson.[95]

Yet Duncan concedes—and immediately tells his listeners—that his finding is incorrect; he is willfully *not* honoring what Olson thought about his major work. The "underlying figure here is exactly the circular one that I [Duncan] said it was *not* going to turn out to be."[96] Duncan acknowledges that Olson ended *Maximus* with a circular "world returning into itself" image. On the surface this is inaccurate to all of *Maximus*, which began with an image of a city on water and a magisterial voice, and ends with that line of personal ebbing, of things lost. More deeply it points to the potential of a single image cluster that might *close* a long poem—as it does in *Trilogy*, *Paterson*, *The Bridge*, and *Four Quartets*—but does not, for Duncan, "complete" it. Duncan publicly plays out his ambivalence because this is not the ending-without-end that he (Duncan) would have sought and that he thought, given "Projective Verse," Olson should have forcefully declared. This drama of interpretive positions particularly reveals the poetics of Duncan's own non-long poem "Passages" within his whole non-long poem oeuvre.

Duncan more interestingly declares that Olson had constructed the ending of *Maximus* "so the close is both close and not-close."[97] I want to explore this notion of structure—for the statement (whether true or not about *Maximus*—endless debates might ensue) reveals the poetics that, exactly because of "ending," made Duncan refuse the entity "a long poem"—resulting in the imaginary, unwritten long poem that haunts his oeuvre.

Their long-poem differences had gone back many years. Duncan's non-long poem vocation gets indicated in response to an Olson query about "Passages," as those poems began to be published in journals in the early 1960s. Olson had assumed that these works, given such a unifying title, constituted one serial poem, called *Passages*. Tersely (in May 1964) Duncan tells Olson: "Correction: Passages *are*, not *is* [my emphasis]." That is, they take a plural verb because they are many poems; not a singular verb because it is one poem. They are "a number of passages; not parts of a thing calld [*sic*] passages." Each is "an instance of itself," and, even if revisited by the poet, they "do not have to do with sequence." In a further consideration, he notes (in June 1964) that although these are "now numbered *as if* in a sequence" (my emphasis), they might better be titled "individually, to lift them as free as I can from the idea of consequence, the consecutive, that numbering gives," raising the question why he *did* number them.[98]

Duncan makes clear: "Of my own poems, 'Passages' and 'The Structure of Rime,' [another intermittent series] it's impossible to have a leftover." That is, they are endless in concept—it's just a poetry of continuation, continuance, a going on and on under a suggestive rubric. In another definition: If the poems "belong in a volume," this "already tells you you're not in a long poem," because a long poem is not any finished poem that you can "measure from one end to another."[99]

Hence, Duncan refused Peter Quartermain's interest in publishing these works in a separate book, for when Quartermain suggested to Duncan in 1970 that "Passages" be published as a long serial poem, he got a nonnegotiable and absolute refusal. Duncan even refused the option of allowing these works together in a course-pack for classroom use; Duncan's choice not to do so has great symbolic weight. For Duncan this would not have been a harmless act of distribution but an undermining of his poetics.[100] And this remains true *despite* the fact that a chapbook of five "Passages" had in fact been published in early 1970 by Black Sparrow Press.[101]

Not only Quartermain was "wrong"—Robert Creeley was also. Creeley was so certain that "Passages" belonged among American long poems that, in a blurb for *Ark* by Ronald Johnson, he notes Duncan's work with other contemporary long poems, listing "Robert Duncan's PASSAGES" among Pound's, Zukofsky's, and Olson's long poems.[102] These ambiguities concerning the status of "Passages" are a challenge to consider.

How does one achieve a structure that is simultaneously "close and not-close"? The intermittent modular works called "Passages" (and presumably "Structure of Rime") taken as through-lines distributed here and there within his later poetic oeuvre—and overlapping through-lines at that—created a structure for the oeuvre, not developmental or teleological, but of activity vibrating around recurrences (the word and concept "passages" and the physical presence of these works in the wholeness of an ongoing collected writing). This is a structure Duncan used through his whole career. By through-lines, I do not necessarily mean thematic lines, but rather just the existence of a named entity ("Passages"), pulsing intermittently through his poetry, appearing and disappearing chronologically through the collected oeuvre.

What does the word "passages mean"? All these definitions are germane to *poesis* as forward and reflective pulsing: A movement from one place to another, a transit. Transit includes transitions from one state to another, life stages. Death is called a passage. Passages may be a journey—and the right to travel, by unimpeded passage, booking passage. It is the structure of a corridor, a channel, or a duct inside a structure. And it is a selection or segment for focus—the passage of a musical or literary work. As in the passage of legislation, it is the enactment of a measure, a definition that has a punning resonance in poetry. The enactment of a measure in Duncan's passages is not a law but precisely the enactment of an irregular measure (his passages are not spaced in any predictable periodicity), the perpetual availability of a transitional movement, a channel to define the "inside" space of something.

Duncan's title occurs by virtue precisely of the idea of passages in which things "become *in passage*: a poetic field of what is in passage"—in constant motion, not settled.[103] This mysterious reiteration of a title of poems ("Passages") and the activities of being "in passage" put an exorbitant stress on that single word, one that indicates motion and no rest, works of all middle. This word indicates the motor of a Grand Collage: "a series having no beginning and no end as its condition of form."[104] This violates our commonplace idea of structure (beginning-middle-end, and a held stasis at resolution) but plays in the ideal zone of form (designating an Ur-form) that inspires more and more writing. The "passage" is totally "middle" and always incipient motion.

When the term Grand Collage gets used—a good deal, and sometimes with capital letters—it may appear as though Duncan is declaring the existence of a large object, a thing in the world (like a visual collage or sculptural assemblage). But it is more. What Duncan comes to (in 1981) is a declaration of his work defined by motion, by passage, by continuous metamorphic creations of structures and statements without terminus.

Hence, at the time when Olson solidified his long-poem vocation and had published some completed sections of *Maximus*, Duncan rejected (in correspondence with Olson) two of the most characteristic and dynamic modes in which contemporary poets claim length—and specific structures: on one hand, field composition—inclusive, ranging, and infused with sociohistorical materials—and, on the other hand, any version of the serial poem. He resists both the documentary build from citation and discourse-rich collage-based work (one way of characterizing *Maximus*). And despite using the term "series" in *Maps* 6, he resists the serial sequenced work, linear but vectoring. Could he be clearer on his total rejection? Yet he has, in a synthesizing urgency, put these long-poem modes together while denying them, along with denying the designation "long poem." How and why does this tour de force occur?

The term "serial" concurs with the application to "Passages" of Joseph Conte's elegant typology of contemporary poetic structures. For Conte, this work exemplifies "infinite serial form," but there's something quite uncanny in Duncan's use.[105] Even the anodyne word "series" puts almost too much pressure of intention on the title term "passages." In a very hermetic notation,[106] Duncan seems to reject any teleological sense of the word "passage," for example by noting that the "A," his example of this thought, "is not Alpha"—a way of saying that any observation stated has no further status as either beginning or culmination.

This complex thought (written 1974) proposes that *series* is an instance of contingency, or chance, the chance of any individual seeking resonances and understanding by putting sections together to track thought. A throw of Duncan's dice never annuls the chances set out in another new throw. And the two most indexical kinds of series (numbers and the alphabet as particular primary enumerations) have no extra value or meaning. "A" is not "Alpha"—the first; it just is.

Further, "Passages" is/are inside another poetic structure—his oeuvre—and each poem in "Passages" is produced only intermittently with no repeatable periodicity in that structure. It is a wayward embedding of a named set emerging at (random) moments in a whole overwhelming oeuvre. How does one think about such a structure? The only parallel to Duncan's that I know of (except for Mallarmé's topic sentence in capital letters embedded in his nanorific poem) would be inside *The Holy Forest* by Robin Blaser—for two serial works ("Image-Nations" and "The Truth Is Laughter") "come and go throughout" in Blaser's oeuvre in the same way that "Passages" and "The Structure of Rime" do in Duncan's.[107] Evoking Blaser's work offers a kind of proof (even if his is done as an homage to Duncan) that this intermittent recurrent mode of serial poem appearance is a useful repeatable instance of this structure of similar items (separately named) "inside" an overarching oeuvre—a serial assemblage inside an album assemblage, perhaps.

For his lifework, Duncan inhabited a structure and specific traits characteristic of the long poem (sheer scale, an absorption of "everything" magnetically into the poems, an infinity of networks and correspondences, themes and allusions woven, recurrent), using this mode without naming it "long poem" as such. Everything he did was played out on the cosmic scale of metamorphosis, process, and affirming of creation. To assign the genre name of "long poem" to this energy or drive to make was inadequate to the overweening sense of *poesis* that motivated Duncan. Yet he achieved a simulacrum of the long poem by refusing an encirclement of even that voracious genre (the encyclopedic/epic poem "containing history" in Pound's influential phrase, or the vast quest) and by refusing the penetrating arrow of a notational genre (the serial poem) by affirmation of an even larger and more extreme or outlandish vision of the metagenre in which he worked. This is the poem of pure middle: "a further becoming" or "a further, a further, a further nature."[108] His *poesis* is therefore dangerous, unstoppable. It is close to cosmic drama. Scale itself demands excess. And excess has no limits.

Hence, the gigantic, endless—often that means quasi-endless, aspirationally endless, endless until you die (etc.)—long poems of modernism, these life-works by Pound and Olson, are too small for Duncan, and yet he never ceased to flirt with long-poem allure, that "accretion of disregarded splendors," a structure of totality (without totalization) and everything potentially included without filter.[109] Although being "beyond" the name of "long poem," he is still able to articulate some of its terms in Grand Collage—an endless assemblage.

His goal (and mine here) is also to articulate what (nonstructured) "form" means in this system of thinking. It indicates "the complexities of the field," "a design that is larger than the poem," a "great story that [. . .] will never be completed"—how many ways can Duncan say an endless additive totality, an infinite assemblage infused with eros itself as a drive to *poesis*? He is evoking the principles of creation belonging to the universe itself. It is at this dramatic juncture that his goal is announced as all things coming into existence through the "poetry of all poetries, *grand collage*."[110]

Duncan foresees a collective of meanings and a collective "building of form."[111] Such a work surpasses the boundaries of an individual author, is in part the responsibility of the reader, extends beyond individual languages, or beyond any specific poetic career, where any named individual is only one entity responsible for what can no longer be called an individual "work of art" but is a joining of poetries (by others and through time) as a force in a global sense.[112]

Grand Collage is not to be imagined as a unified theory or any theorized poetic practice that explains the known and unknown world by "one principle" fundamental to everything. Instead, Duncan imagines a continuous mutual creation of both connections and understanding, like the cosmos itself. Grand Collage "appears as a mobile structure in which events may move in time in ever-changing constellations." This Grand Collage entity (this changing system in motion) is characterized by a mix of times, places, and nations,[113] acknowledging not the "oneness" of everything (that would be unified thinking) but its relatedness and entanglement.

Grand Collage is a coinage with multiple functions and usages, as Stephen Fredman also has elaborated, seeing it, fundamentally, as a "contextual practice" among elements demanding boundless continuation, not mastery, "resolutely incomplete," and continuously "in process."[114] For Duncan it means no separation of nonetheless apparently separate items—meaning all the poems together as offering a context for each; an acknowledgment that all of the elements in Duncan's oeuvre are related and part of the "creative process"—there is not a separate titled item that would be its "goal," but the whole oeuvre is part of that process, a totality of drives to *poesis*.[115]

Grand Collage is a worldview more than only a poetics: liberatory, universalizing, and perpetually creative. Instead of positing the structure of the cosmos in his oeuvre (the structure as, say, Dante would have it), Duncan postulated the processes of the cosmos in his oeuvre. Formalist and categorizing thinking decontextualizes and deracinates an item (say, any natural specimen from its field) and refuses to see how this thing is dialectically (and ecologically) shaped by and shaping of its context. In contrast, Duncan always wants to affirm widening contexts, relations, affiliations, and networks among everything he perceives and to construct these by a vatically associative use of hypotactic and paratactic syntax. The "symposium of the whole" as a synthesizing idea must, for the sake of an aesthetic ethics, infuse the segmentivities of poetry.

Grand Collage is not made so much by specific juxtapositions (as in a visual collage) as made in one gigantic metonymic linkage of everything in continuous creation. A collage (as a visual item) stands as one single object. Grand Collage is as if a hovering system of metamorphic inclusions, almost like a moving collage, but really something like a continuously changing system. This is perhaps another version of the constantly "emerging system" that Paul Jaussen identifies as a characteristic of the contemporary long poem.[116]

Duncan's "Introduction" to *Bending the Bow* (1968) is not only where the idea of "grand collage" first emerges but also where the first group of poems called "Passages" appears.[117] We then have not only this Grand Collage as an expanse but a couple of separate entities defining that extent by interior, intermittent in-folded poems and prose poems, linked only by name, as passages through a larger text. In Steve McCaffery's succinct and accurate description, individual "Passages" appear "as textual nomads in serial plications upon a plenum."[118] The plenum is the whole of Duncan's poetry, the plications are infolded recurrences; their nomadism suggests the unpredictability of the appearance of "Passages" throughout. Yet that long serial poem "Passages" does not exist as a separate book because it has been surrounded and absorbed, swallowed into the idea of his whole oeuvre as a Grand Collage. We understand that this exorbitant structure with its poetics can include "passages" because all elements are seen as part of each, passages between and among each other, making together one grand (large) collage (items joined to each other variously)—but not joined by any declared goal, ending, or terminus.

However, if they are absorbed into this vast totality, then why name and distinguish these "passages"? Why are they necessary to Duncan's poetics? And how do they rearticulate the debate on ending that Duncan staged, claiming a contradiction between Olson's poetics and his poem? That is, once this endless grandeur is enunciated, why even think of "ending" as a concept to consider? Why bother with taking a stance toward conclusions, endings, termini, or any kind of closure?

Given that every poem that Duncan wrote is part of that Grand Collage, having one or two cross-book threads of series poems pulsing intermittently or in-folded during the other works is what helps make this long entity a structural departure, negotiating two solutions thought to be opposite (closure, no-closure), where both are plausible within the absorptive and metamorphic "grandeur" of such a "collage." That is, the two series poems, distinct, named but also palpable, are crucial to Duncan's teasing simulacrum of a long poem, one that is not a long poem at all but an entity in which "the formlessness of the work then is a significant form."[119] With the inclusion of the series poems, he has made a structure that doesn't either close or not close. Hence, Duncan's oeuvre in multiple poems exists as pure "middle" (neither any beginning nor any ending to what has been set in process). Duncan's choices embody a structural innovation not only *as* two long series poems but as a distinctive mode further characterizing such a grand-scale unstoppable work as his whole poetic output. It is important that those long endless chains of works (like "Passages") stand incorporated inside and are not separable from his whole oeuvre.

One test of this space of *poesis* for Duncan is that the poem and the oeuvre of *poesis* cannot end. It can have no external boundary. But—and this is a fantastic visualization—it could "close and not-close" by putting some defining boundary *inside* the work, not *outside* it. And Duncan marked this unusual structural decision by sending a pipeline or two through the work, not a boundary outside or closure, but a mark within, an intermittent recurrence as a structure of named extras, maybe meditations, maybe glosses, maybe notes, maybe elaborations, maybe parallels (they are not going to conform to one mode, certainly): in short, by passages and examinations of poetry itself.

The "form" or mode within which Duncan mimics the moves of a long poem is not an endless oeuvre with an external boundary, because there will always be "something left over" for Duncan, so you can never achieve this external boundary (a.k.a. an ending). But an oeuvre with an internal mark of making, a set of works with the same title ("Passages," and another with another title, "Structure of Rime") that thread or pulse within the oeuvre could establish a "close" that is simultaneously "not-close." These works are all within and define not an external line (boundary) but an internal string or act of interior marking, an inside-out shape. There is no exterior boundary—but there is an intestinal, invaginated, or conceptual tubing moving within this space that defines it from the inside, as a mark of form or a mark of shape within a boundless (if knowing, informed) shapelessness. You need an inner boundary, perhaps particularly an intermittent one, to express or allow boundlessness. This space is the tubular carrier of pure permission. Thus this "close and not-close" formulation of Duncan becomes the summary essence of endless *poesis* for the very long poem in modernity.

SOME SUMMARIES

Why are these long poems so long, such an obsessive practice, and sometimes so difficult? Even these questions are difficult—to face. Clearly long-poem writers want more from poetry than, for many people, poetry is reputed to give. Most want both an expanded overview and a grounded, granular view—a difficult maneuver, to say nothing of the difficulty linking the small to the large in compelling structures. In both moves, a social vision is marked, an attempt to see a world or a society or a history in its parts and its implications. In its *moving* parts, emotion and change are both palpable. As if this were not enough, this desire gets mixed and mingled with ethical and aesthetic attitudes—curiosity, grief, anger, mourning, resolve, compassion, and those in many dictions, tones, poetic craftiness, and ministructures.

The long poem is a uniquely positioned book of affects and effects. It is a kind of research, inhabiting poetry as a mode of inquiry. It is a literary attempt to organize a multitude (an "encyclopedia," a library, archives of several cultures) of materials, giving rise to an endless and generally unresolved network of realizations that intersect with and fold against and with each other. These are perceptions and realizations made as continuous discoveries in the acts of poetic thinking. We readers are often set among these materials and discoveries (as if we are somehow inside the poem). Sometimes this design has a linear arc, but sometimes we are saturated in the environment of the poem. This means inhabiting panoplies of poetic languages.

Because genres are social agreements (and involve many trajectories and outcomes), these became collection points for this book. I see any one poet take on large-scale descriptions and analyses of emotionally laden social, historical, and cosmological benchmarks through interpretation(s) and uses of one or several genres. Using the intricacies and delights of syntax and diction from which poetry is constituted, a long poem underscores the "is-ness" of a certain history, with its sense of being and solidity, its presence, and contradictions, and acknowledges a tragic vision with the tragic utopianism of the long poem's mental fight. Just face what is, Williams says about the destruction of plenitude and beauty that *Paterson* depicts, and then watch the growth spurt of refertilized ground. Just face what has been on this ground, Brathwaite says of a society intricate with colonial residues in a postcolonial time, and see bravery, rage, and creative answers to the mix of affirmations and destructions. Just face the plethora of struggles, says Waldman within that totality of relations (ecological, spiritual, daily social wrongs) that elude many attempts at rectification but provoke the courage of response. Sheer plethora—suffering it? mastering it? describing it? singing it? enjoying it? patterning it? interpreting it?—is at work in the poet of long poems, provoking attempts to try to give that plethora various shapes. All of these—and more—are responsibilities and longings claimed by a long-poem writer.

There might then be an answer to Pound's originating long-poem question in *Gaudier-Brzeska*—what is the relation of "haiku" to a "vorticist" long poem? The absolute implacability and irreducibility of haiku poems—their baseline of microfindings and shock of juxtapositions confront a reader with the paradoxes of irreducible being itself. In a long poem, these confrontations are scaled and expanded to a length by the images and commentaries of investigation (in history, in society, in the cosmos). These, compounded in a secular world without particularly dogmatic explanations for the shape of things, become the findings of the long poem—with unbound experiences of extensive confrontation with that implacability as a condition of reading the long poem.

This book is pragmatic in its analytic descriptions of works and pragmatic in its theorizing practices. By examining oversaturated and immersive long poems and their poetics, not close reading each of them (impossible here except in small bits), and probably intuitively choosing ones that would lead to this general socio-cosmological argument; by thereby leaving some important works out of consideration and creating other flaws and analytic lacunae, I did nonetheless make some interpretive lines for the long poem, based on genre and poetics with a background acknowledgment of the obsessive writing necessary for the poems as felt by their poets.

Unless a reader takes each nanorific, longish, or very long poem one by one and studies their particularities, there have to be some elements that join at least some of these poems. I have tried to organize this book to highlight those elements—meaning specific issues or problems—worked on by various poets-of-the-long-poem in our centuries. This involves a selection for comparison of both issues and poems, and a tendency in all these types of reading toward overgeneralization.

Some of these discussions—of segmentivity, of torquing or "rewriting" known texts, of the antithetical meanings of fundamental words, of nexus, and of the serial poem could be useful thoughts for poetry in general. Discussions of the shocks of scale and of poetics, genre polysemy, a definition of assemblage as a genre, the renewed interest in the *Gesamtkunstwerk*, the astonishingly frequent uses of the word "everything" to describe the goals of these works, the roles of numbers and numerology, the debates about endings, the trace of "the Book," the extensive role of heteroglossia and page space, and the "doubling" of a poet's lifetime by a long poem are specific observations offering some lexicon for long works.

But precisely what is the meaning of all those very long poems in the twentieth and twenty-first centuries? Not, what do they mean? But why did people feel the urgency to write them? What is the meaning of (translation: what do *we* think was going on with) those overwhelming acts of writing chosen by a number of poets? What was the longing they evinced, and how did each work this out? It is the longing to name a collective socio-cosmological and sometimes political shape—the shape of "everything" affecting our lives and driving our histories, filled with contradictions and cross pressures. This book centered on long poems as a praxis—a real practice within culture but beyond the literary. It's a study of different poets' drives to write poems of great and very great length, what it feels like in relation to language and one's time, what motivates the poet within the mechanisms of poetry, in the traditions of poetry, in the world issues—secular and spiritual, historical, and ontological—that each poet chooses to confront.

All may speak of the unspeakable, or the accumulation of unspeakable events on which our known—even unknown—social and cosmological spaces are built. The three genres are focused to postulate various diagnoses (if not suggested rectifications) of something largely social and spiritual at one and the same time. This makes poets who attempt long poems also be public intellectuals—poetic intellectuals, really, using the mechanisms and structures of poetic traditions to represent the forces and relations of "everything" in the world.

This book is based on three broad genres, with poems read not as how well they "fit" into fixed genres but as how they interpret some tasks to be taken up via those genres in our time. These involve findings in any poet's relationship with any chosen past ("tradition") of writing. The three inner chapters are based on studies in that zone. These are organized by genre, and by avatar figures (Dante and Mallarmé, sometimes Whitman).

These three chapters also set out to group issues in the genres that they loosely define. For the epic, this is the question of women's authorship (authority, really) and the representation of all gendered figures in the genre. It is the question being answered by various writers taking up a deep address to a gigantic cultural heritage of gender (among other prime social locations). Their various works consider what an epic is for women—that is, fundamentally, where to put women as agents while depicting societies indifferent to (even distrustful of) the question of female agency (or paying it lip service only). So where women can be in an epic is a question symbolic of that larger issue of representation and rectification, and some self-conscious uses of a monumental cluster of "epic" themes, plots, characters, and cultural ideas in both some women writers and in Olson, among others. This section concerns mainly women writers using the designation "epic" to define and affirm their vocations as poets, by the ways they interpret and use the epic modes that they have deliberately chosen.

This "epic" chapter is motivated both by my feminist suspicion of that institutional construction called literary history and by my interest in presenting a constantly changing terrain of interpretation where one seeks to have multiple voices and multiple themes not only listened to but compared, respected, and debated.

For quest narratives, poets today ask what can be a persuasive telos in a secular or mixed, nontheological world. This is expressed by several Anglophone poets who use Dante directly (if variously) in their poems. The power of Dante's *Commedia* and its culturally saturating presence are presented here in the ways Dante has been used and examined but then extended oddly, stretched, revamped, or even completely reversed in meaning by contemporary writers. The quest poems that contemporaries will write become worldly, often secular yet with redefined spiritual and investigative ethics.

This chapter answers to the postulate of "influence" of one writer on another—taking the case of Dante as a magisterial figure. Of course, writers read, use, love, hate, respond to, and make all sorts of complex moves with and on each other. A few close-ups of biographical challenges are also visible here, as Pound faces Eliot with ambivalence, or Duncan tries to debate (and criticize) Olson posthumously. How do poets establish literary relations that affect—that charge up—their own works? Rather than positing a hierarchic or genealogical relationship when one chooses to face a master poet or any poet, I emphasize a nexus of mutual, perhaps staged involvements, lateral connections over time that do not overlook issues of genders, races, differing/similar cultures, or social abrasions but discuss these, as needed.

Critics also construct various nexus-like arrangements; always an interpretive act of investigation is proposed in connecting one writer to another. That is, culture is built on a *nexus* of concerns and debates, not on models of any poet pouring literary powers into chosen followers, or younger critics gaining access to authority through a single figure, or active, if staged, literary parricides, matricides, sororicides, and fratricides. (Although these last four might just be part of "biography.") These models are generally obsolete but not ideologically superseded in the construction of critical interpretations; a substitution of nexus thinking can usefully help visualize as plural, historical, transnational, and continuous the struggles and adhesions in which writers engage with one another and with literary history (itself always, constantly under construction).

For the faceted genre "assemblage," poets may have different versions of that structure of collection that will emphasize paratactic album and seriality and also access the ideal that Mallarmé described: a rather exemplary, culturally summarizing capital-B Book with the possibility of allusive *Gesamtkunstwerk* elements, assembling "all" the arts under the rubric of activated Book or performative poem. ("All" the arts as a claim parallels that imagined "everything" put in one summary poem.) In the twentieth-century long poem, the Book becomes a metaphor and a drive, an object, and an imagined goal involving processes toward poetic vocation and cultural meanings—as realized in a very long poem. The temptation inherent in long-poem ambitions of culturally encompassing works is the idea of making (one) total Book—of everything. The continuing dream of writing these long poems as an aesthetic-intellectual experience or Book-Performance—postulated only (mainly unrealized) by Mallarmé—was, in my view, picked up, reinvented, or refound by several contemporaries. This mix of synthesizing Book and total artwork (*Gesamtkunstwerk*) that Mallarmé's poetics proposed is, perhaps coincidentally, at the root of many long poems discussed in the whole book.

A long poem may develop by rethinking its strategies and rationales as it is written. What those processes of choice entail is a repeated topic. If a poet chooses great length, one question (taken up in the fifth chapter) will concern ending such a poem—or not. This chapter offers some options and discusses how these choices work, and what, for each poet, motivated kinds of stopping or closures, their strategies and poetics, their persistence or suspension, and individual poet's struggles and debates with the structural concept of ending. This discussion ends with a peculiar summary phrase of Robert Duncan: "close and not-close."

At this point the critical findings become somewhat vatic and allegorical. If one writes a poem excessively long in time and in cultural space (not to speak of its generally challenging and self-complicating findings), certain features of the author have metamorphosed. Poets are displaced as single subjectivity, dispersed into subject matters themselves in their array, found in their choices of citations, or becoming a speaking internal ear, or dissolved into the heteroglossic dictions assumed in authorship. Authors may become sounds and claims that the poem is making through them. Here, I speak about the agency of the poem, as an idea or feeling in an authorial head, producing the committed poet who will continue into that poem with the drive toward the activities of making (*poesis*) itself.

I have found, in several writers, the sense (and claim) that the poem is speaking itself or that the language is speaking through them as author—all these stances, or findings, are characteristic of the long poem. If this is so, such a position of authorship is a gigantic assumption of responsibility along with the strange ego that manifests a gluttonous loss of ego. Waldman says it this way: "All the world fits in my mouth."[120] One might also say the inverse: my mouth speaks through the unfitting/unfit world. In trying to make a statement about how "everything" is, how to mourn it, analyze its ethical bearing, and how to refabricate it (a harder task), one does, as George Oppen said, "come here" [to] "the outer / Limits of the ego."[121] It is here that the long poem and its poetics seem to merge on an edge, and the author becomes possessed by language and longing on the scale of a polygeneric, panoramic making. This is a bardic manifestation of socio-cosmic stun, a poet's desire both to encompass and to improve the world. One tries to explore, keep pace, and indicate that knotted complexity in languages and structures. The poem finally chooses you. You must essay to be worthy of its trust and of the insights you fabricate with it.

How many ways and in how many tones can this book say "*poesis*"?

Postlude from bpNichol.

> I think that given the length of the work, *The Martyrology* [the long poem by bpNichol (1944–88)] ceases to be a reading experience, at least in the way we have come to think of it. Its very duration means that you must [. . .] inhabit it in some sense. Particularly since there is no "plot" to hang on to, only ideas, and the ideas relate to the terms used in the text and the very way the text is functioning. My thinking about it is still evolving. In that sense I probably treat the text more as a reader than a writer, i.e., when the text closes it continues to evolve in the mind of the reader tho it is over for the writer. This text has not closed.
>
> bpNichol, in *Tracing the Paths: Reading ≠ Writing the Martyrology*

Notes

Chapter 1

1. Including Peter Baker, M. A. Bernstein, Matthew Carbery, Joseph Conte, Anne Day Dewey, Margaret Dickie, Norman Finkelstein, Susan Stanford Friedman, Paul Jaussen, Smaro Kamboureli, Lynn Keller, John Lowney, Brian McHale, Peter Middleton, Roy Harvey Pearce, Bob Perelman, and hosts of intelligent author-based studies. Poets also comment on the long poem; their remarks are quite important here.

2. Given that I take Dante and Mallarmé as long-poem avatars (or provocateurs), any mention of their writings will come via translations, although I checked both languages a bit for myself.

3. "Nexus" emerged as a term for a literary formation when Peter Quartermain and I tried to define the relationships among objectivist writers, barely (and temporarily) joined, never constituted as a group but adhering loosely to a poetics.

4. Some losses are long-poem work of Allen Fisher (UK) and bpNichol (Canada).

5. Frank O'Hara, *Second Avenue* (New York: Totem Press, 1960), sec. 5.

6. Ronald Johnson, "Ronald Johnson—An Interview" [1974], by Barry Alpert, in *Ronald Johnson: Life and Works*, ed. Joel Bettridge and Eric Murphy Selinger (Orono, ME: National Poetry Foundation, 2008), 555.

7. Edgar Allan Poe, *Poetry, Tales, and Selected Essays* (New York: Library of America, 1996), 1431, 1433.

8. Nothing wrong with both experiencing emotions and thinking about them. Poe presented his cosmological work *Eureka* (1848) as a long prose poem essentially defending "the Beauty that abounds in its Truth" so that the work will be judged only as "a Poem"; in those criteria he neatly echoes Keats. Edgar Allan Poe, preface to *Eureka: A Prose Poem* (New York: Geo. P. Putnam, 1848).

9. "'What we term a long poem is, in fact, merely a succession of brief ones,' Poe says." Lyn Hejinian, *My Life in the Nineties* (New York: Shark Books, 2003), 9.

10. Meaning visually produced word-based statements like ASL or other signage, often almost danced. Also meaning semidecodable alphabetic shapes or glyphs, perhaps rebus.

11. Rachel Blau DuPlessis, "Statement on Poetics: Pleasures, Polemics, Practices, Stakes," in *Inciting Poetics: Thinking and Writing Poetry*, ed. Jeanne Heuving and Tyrone Williams (Albuquerque: University of New Mexico Press, 2019), 15.

12. In 1995, while trying to define the fundamental nature of poetry, I proposed "segmentivity" on the model of the then-assured terms "narrativity" and "performativity."

13. M. M. Bakhtin, "Discourse in Poetry and Discourse in the Novel," in *The Dialogic Imagination: Four Essays*, ed. Michael Holquist, trans. Caryl Emerson and Michael Holquist, (Austin: University of Texas Press, 1981), 275, 282, 291.

14. Bakhtin, "Discourse in Poetry," 285–86.

15. Roman Jakobson, "What Is Poetry?" in *Language in Literature*, by Roman Jakobson, ed. Krystyna Pomorska and Stephen Rudy (Cambridge, MA: Harvard University Press, 1987), 378.

16. W. B. Yeats, *Essays and Introductions* (New York: Macmillan, 1961), 499.

17. Bob Perelman, *The Trouble with Genius: Reading Pound, Joyce, Stein and Zukofsky* (Berkeley: University of California Press, 1994), 56.

18. Clark Coolidge, *A Book Beginning What and Ending Away* (New York: Fence Books, 2012), 577. This is cited as an efficient encapsulation of attitudes.

19. Louis Zukofsky, "Louis Zukofsky Interviewed by L. S. Dembo (1968)," *Contemporary Literature* 10, no. 2 (Spring 1969): 218.

20. A discussion *might* ensue about the role of characters in long poems. It won't happen here.

21. This is probably also an excluded question here, as many long-poem writers attend to general audience only in intermittent bursts of attention.

22. Here, I'll insert *The American Heritage Dictionary* definition of length: "the measurement of the extent of something along its greatest dimension." But is there any agreement about what the greatest dimensions of a poem would be? I mean this as a meta-question. It might be temporal: "staying power."

23. One might even say that, in this quip, Zukofsky is not facing the reading problems his work presents.

24. Jeffrey Twitchell-Waas curates the Zukofsky Z-site (https://z-site.net) with its necessary and devoted commentary.

25. Zukofsky, "Louis Zukofsky Interviewed by L. S. Dembo (1968)," 218.

26. Louis Zukofsky, *Complete Short Poetry* (Baltimore: Johns Hopkins University Press, 1991), 18 (see lines 256–57 of "Poem Beginning 'The'").

27. In an essay considering her work, Notley states that she has two methods of writing, one more deliberate and controlled, the other allowing a more unconscious language to burgeon "for a deeper veracity." Alice Notley, *Coming After: Essays on Poetry* (Ann Arbor: University of Michigan Press, 2005), 160.

28. Alice Notley, "Iovis Omnia Plena," *Chicago Review* 44 (1998): 126.

29. Ronald Bush, *The Genesis of Ezra Pound's "Cantos"* (Princeton: Princeton University Press, 1976), 53.

30. Allen Fisher, *Imperfect Fit: Aesthetic Function, Facture, and Perception in Art and Writing since 1950* (Tuscaloosa: University of Alabama Press, 2016), 16, 31–32.

31. Fisher, *Imperfect Fit*, 16.

32. Ezra Pound, *Gaudier-Brzeska, a Memoir* [1916; 2nd ed., 1918; with additions, 1934, 1960] (New York: New Directions, 1970), 94.

33. Bush, *Genesis of Ezra*, 56. The Pound is from 1917, from the original *Three Cantos* published in June, July, and August of *Poetry*, and reprinted in Bush, *Genesis of Ezra*, 53–73, as noted in Bush, *Genesis of Ezra*, 301.

34. Pound, in Bush, *Genesis of Ezra*, 57.

35. Ezra Pound, *Guide to Kulchur* [1938] (London: Peter Owen, 1966), 135.

36. Ezra Pound, *The Cantos* (1971; repr., New York: New Directions, 1996), 17.

37. Daniel Albright, "Early Cantos I–XLI," in *The Cambridge Companion to Ezra Pound*, ed. Ira B. Nadel (Cambridge: Cambridge University Press 1999), 60.

38. Roland Barthes, *Preparation of the Novel: Lecture Courses and Seminars at the Collège de France (1978–1979 and 1979–1980)*, trans. Kate Briggs (New York: Columbia University Press, 2011), 73, 90.

39. Charles Olson, *The Maximus Poems*, ed. George F. Butterick (Berkeley: University of California Press, 1983), 604.

40. Nathaniel Mackey, *Paracritical Hinge: Essays, Talks, Notes, Interviews* (Madison: University of Wisconsin Press, 2005), 309.

41. William Carlos Williams, *The Autobiography of William Carlos Williams* [1951] (New York: New Directions, 1967), 391. This everything is, on principle, local, particular—and diagnostic: "Not to talk in vague categories but to write particularly, as a physician works, upon a patient, upon the thing before him, in the particular to discover the universal" (391).

42. Ezra Pound to James Joyce, March 17, 1917, in *Pound/Joyce: The Letters of Ezra Pound to James Joyce, with Pound's Critical Essays and Articles about Joyce*, ed. Forrest Read (New York: New Directions, 1967), 102.

43. On September 21, 1915, Pound wrote to literary journalist Milton Bronner that he was "at work on a chryselephantine poem of immeasurable length which will occupy me for the next four decades unless it becomes a bore." This letter, in the Alice Corbin Henderson Archive, Harry Ransom Research Center, is cited from Robert M. Crunden, *American Salons: Encounters with European Modernism, 1885–1917* (New York: Oxford University Press, 1993), 472.

44. "Ezra Pound," interview by Donald Hall, 1962, in *Writers at Work: The Paris Review Interviews*, 2nd ser., ed. George Plimpton (New York: Penguin Books, 1979), 38.

45. Bernadette Mayer, *Midwinter Day* (Berkeley, CA: Turtle Island Foundation, 1982), 107; William Carlos Williams, *Paterson* [1946–51; 1958], ed. Christopher MacGowan (New York: New Directions, 1992), 231.

46. Mayer, *Midwinter Day*, found on 90–92, 72–75, 47, 44–45, and 111.

47. Anne Waldman, "An Interview with Anne Waldman," by Lee Christopher, *AWP Chronicle* 28, no. 3 (December 1995): 6.

48. Ron Silliman, "I Wanted to Write Sentences: Decision Making in the American Longpoem," *Sagetrieb* 11, no. 1 & 2 (Spring & Fall 1992): 14. Silliman deliberately closes the space between the words "long" and "poem" as his generic marker—it has the effect

of holding those concepts together as a single noun, almost giving this practice a further genre name. The Williams allusion in Silliman's title "I wanted to . . ." occurs in the final stanza of "January Morning: Suite"—"I wanted to write a poem / that you would understand." William Carlos Williams, *The Collected Poems of William Carlos Williams*, vol. 1, *1909–1939*, ed. A. Walton Litz and Christopher MacGowan (New York: New Directions, 1986), 103.

49. This recalls a fundamental stance in lyric poetry: the apostrophe—a calling out to an often-absent other, a natural force, that will act or inspire. Hence, both kinds of poems are different intensifications and scales of naming and calling (cf. Jonathan Culler, "Apostrophe," in *The Pursuit of Signs: Semiotics, Literature, Deconstruction* [New York: Cornell University Press, 1981]).

50. Mackey, *Paracritical Hinge*, 320.

51. Mackey, *Paracritical Hinge*, 320.

52. Paul Jaussen, *Writing in Real Time: Emergent Poetics from Whitman to the Digital* (Cambridge: Cambridge University Press, 2017), 33. Jaussen's findings around feedback parallel Matthew Carbery's discussion of "extension" as a trait central to long poems—one is driven to extend such a poem by reasons of its endless feedback provoking you as writer. Both Jaussen and Carbery treat DuPlessis, *Drafts*, a multibook work of six separate sets (over five volumes; see the bibliography for particulars). Matthew Carbery, *Phenomenology and the Late Twentieth-Century American Long Poem* (Cham, Switzerland: Palgrave Macmillan, 2019).

53. Williams, *Paterson*, 185.

54. Peter Middleton, *Expanding Authorship: Transformations in American Poetry since 1950* (Albuquerque: University of New Mexico Press, 2021), 265.

55. Not only a text that needs a library; indeed, it is a text that *is* a library—a text itself indebted to, synthetic of, and burrowing through a pile of archival and literary materials, often ones self-declared as vital. This is as true of Eliot's *The Waste Land* and Zukofsky's *"A"* as it is of later works like Ronald Johnson's *Ark* and Susan Howe's *The Liberties*.

56. Jacob Edmond, "Long, Wide, Deep, Heavy," paper presented at Short Takes on the Long Poem, Aotearoa conference, Auckland, NZ, March 2012, photocopy in the author's possession. His graduate assistant was Orchid Tierney, now a professor at Kenyon College.

57. Middleton, *Expanding Authorship*, 275, 279.

58. Middleton, *Expanding Authorship*, 258, 274, 275, 275.

59. The critical work of Bradly Fest occurs in this arena, often treating works of megaprose.

60. The argument of Adalaide Morris and Stephen Voyce, "Precarity, Poetics, and the Practice of Countermapping," in *Poetics and Precarity*, ed. Myung Mi Kim and Cristanne Miller (Albany: State University of New York Press, 2018), 117–43.

61. Alderman has less enthusiasm for "the grandiose projects of high modernism" but identifies a particular British local negotiation ("pocket epic") against the sprawl. Nigel Alderman, "Introduction: Pocket Epics: British Poetry after Modernism," *Yale Journal of Criticism* 13, no. 1 (2000): 1.

62. Silliman draws a definitional distinction here that is quite firm. For him, the only really "longpoems" consist of a very small, actual bibliography. That's in part why he invents the term "longpoem" for this group; it tightens the two words together. Despite being included in his exclusive summa because of *Drafts*, I am being relatively inclusive about the categories (as Middleton is, too), noting writers of both the long and the very long.

63. A side note: Similarly, I "folded up" or "closed" *Drafts* after twenty-five years of writing, at a precise point of numerological ambiguity (114/115 sections), this at over 1,000 pages. However, I deliberately never said that I was ending it, since that word implies a conclusion to its findings.

64. Alderman, "Pocket Epics," 1.

65. This complete poem, published in 1965 after eleven years' work, was intended to be the portal poem to a five-book work. The remaining four books were to offer a history of the Black *man*, said just that way. Tolson died in 1966, with the projected four works unwritten. A real loss.

66. The oddly repackaged *Book of Ephraim* by James Merrill (2018) claims that this portal text to *Changing Light* will adequately represent that longer work, a marketing idea hardly giving a real sense of Merrill's actual poem. Early Pound *Cantos* also do not give a sense of later ones.

67. There are also challenges inside this category. David Antin's "talk poems" as project verge on the very long poem (though this is not his chosen term) because of their absorptive boundlessness and sense of endless engagements, always ready to begin again. Similarly, Larry Eigner's oeuvre, in four large volumes of very short works, read as serial or constellated, could appear as a very long notational poem (this is not his intention, either). I say this not to make more trouble than I can handle but to indicate how certain works and oeuvres might be recentered in a critical zone defined by the existence and goals of the very long poem.

68. Middleton, *Expanding Authorship*, 262.

69. My typographical error when typing "honorific" led me to the typo "nonorific" and then by etymology to "nanorific." That seems definitionally appropriate—"nano" meaning "mini"—small but lots packed in. For this small group, Brian McHale takes hold of Nigel Alderman's "pocket epic" as a term in *The Obligation toward the Difficult Whole: Postmodernist Long Poems* (Tuscaloosa: University of Alabama Press, 2004), 101. Because of the cultural baggage of the term "epic," I had hoped to avoid that allusion in Alderman's terminology, and so invented mine.

70. Middleton, *Expanding Authorship*, 262.

71. Barthes, *Preparation of the Novel*, 262; also, on seeing the book, 251.

72. "I was very quickly—and I mean literally a matter of hours—in the midst of composing a longpoem, a poem that I am in fact still writing." Silliman, "I Wanted to Write Sentences," 14.

73. In Rachel Blau DuPlessis, *Drafts 1–38, Toll* (Middletown, CT: Wesleyan University Press, 2001), there is explicit wind, odic, and blowing imagery in many poems; an example would be at the end of "Draft 14: Conjunctions," 99.

74. In the *American Heritage* dictionary, the noun "form" is defined immediately with the word "structure," but "structure" (noun) is not defined by the word "form." The verb "to form" implies making; the verb "to structure" does use "to form" as a synonym. The words apparently come from two different proto-Indo-European roots.

75. Basil Bunting, "On the Fly-Leaf of Pound's *Cantos*," in *The Complete Poems*, ed. Richard Caddel (Oxford: Oxford University Press, 1994), 114. The city analogy is one often used in long-poem thinking, that sense of all the different stimuli, contacts, randomized events, comedies and tragedies happening "simultaneously" in an urban setting, various emotions in all the little rooms and spaces—this was a large motivator for T. S. Eliot, who spoke in fascinated ways in an early essay on the feeling of the urban. Brian McHale's analogy of the ruin for the long poem adds a pessimistic temporal dimension to the assemblage of the city as long poem analogy.

76. Rachel Blau DuPlessis, *Purple Passages: Pound, Eliot, Zukofsky, Olson, Creeley and the Ends of Patriarchal Poetry* (Iowa City: University of Iowa Press, 2012), 32–37, 46–57.

77. One sees this in the serious responses that this poem provoked, mainly in the form of answers to what was taken as pessimism. Poetic discussants of *The Waste Land* abound, and a whole book might be written on them, many proposing resistances to and critiques of its (apparent) findings and sometimes its methods. Among only the moderns: Hope Mirrlees's 1919 *Paris* prefigured its "sampling" fragmentations and sense of a collaged city and may have influenced Eliot. Williams discussed *The Waste Land* several times, at least in *Spring and All* (with direct allusions and rewritings), and also in *Paterson* with the scurrilous, cheap-shot masque (*Paterson* IV, i). Nancy Cunard's 1925 *Parallax* was so tonally close to Eliot as to be an act of identification. Pound's *Cantos* quickly acknowledges that work, in the "slut"/"bitch," astonishingly exposed moment opening Canto 8, and tries to "better" Eliot. Hart Crane's *The Bridge* was a direct "American" response; so too, Zukofsky's immigrant-identified "Poem beginning 'The'" along with Olson's midcentury "The Kingfishers." The erudite Yiddish poem of Mikhl Likht called "Protsesiye dray" (Procession Three, 1925) is an echo of its elegiac tone for a lost tradition—the tradition being Yiddish and a question about the forbidden but creative creolizing mixtures possible to make a new culture. (With thanks to Ariel Resnikoff and Jerome Rothenberg.) In 1937 the Singapore poet Francis P. Ng (aka Paul Teo Poh Leng) published *F.M.S.R. A Poem*. The initials refer to the Federated Malay States Railway, for his *Waste Land*–influenced poem takes shape as a meditation on a trip by the poet between Singapore and Kuala Lumpur, helping to found Malay modernism with this work. Eriko Ogihara-Schuck and Anne Teo, eds., *Finding Francis: A Poetic Adventure* (Singapore: Ethos Books, 2015), with thanks for the reference to Alvin Pang. Among several contemporary poets who respond to *The Waste Land*, Kamau Brathwaite makes a notable challenge in *The Arrivants* to the Eliotic reading of natural cycles. Brathwaite recontextualizes them within a Caribbean natural and national setting, proposing an alternate interpretation and uplifted reading of "dust" and generativity, and offering his propulsive, important "riddim" as a response to unfused "fragments." Both Matthew Hart and Jacob Edmond, noting Hart, discuss this; Matthew Hart, *Nations of Nothing but Poetry: Modernism, Transnationalism, and Synthetic Vernacular Writing* (New York:

Oxford University Press, 2010), 131–32; and Jacob Edmond, *Make It the Same: Poetry in the Age of Global Media* (New York: Columbia University Press, 2019), 48.

78. Pound to Eliot, December 24, An 1 [Fascist year (*sic*), 1921], in *The Letters of Ezra Pound, 1907–1941*, ed. D. D. Paige (New York: Harcourt, Brace & World, 1950), 169; DuPlessis, *Purple Passages*, 53–56.

79. Pound to Eliot, December 24, An 1 [Fascist year (*sic*), 1921], in *Letters*, 170. Pound cut Eliot's poem strategically to emphasize modernist newness. One issue was precisely the establishment of modernist "originality"—nothing similar to the work of any other literary figure would be allowed at length; thus (inter alia), the Joycean "He Do the Police" beginning and the Popean "Fresca" section were cut. This last despite the character Fresca's corresponding to all the canards concerning Perfectly Awful Woman Writers and Editors about whom these young men endlessly bitched—the women's boldness, their sexuality, their very presence, their challenge to *themselves*. Their male entitlement, incomes, and literary ambitions were, they felt, undercut by this horrible Type of rival professional. Leaving this passage in the poem would have been characteristic of their thinking at the time, yet, following his principles, Pound cut it as formally old-fashioned—just imitative.

80. The Williams 1923 *haibun* with euphoric Deweyan theorizing—*Spring and All*—and Moore's 1923 heteroglossic citational, meditative and shorter "Marriage" and "An Octopus," not to speak of Loy's acerbic Jewish and Anglican sociology of the self in *Anglo-Mongrels and the Rose*, were not in print in 1921; however, Pound's premature canonization effectively kept them out of the "modern long poem" loop for decades, even though all practice sociocultural naming and critique.

81. Pound to Joyce, *Pound/Joyce*, 102.

82. T. S. Eliot, *The Waste Land. A Facsimile and Transcript of the Original Drafts Including the Annotations of Ezra Pound*, ed. Valerie Eliot (New York: Harcourt Brace Jovanovich, 1971), 1.

83. T. S. Eliot, *Selected Essays* [1951] (London: Faber and Faber, 1963), 368; emphasis mine.

84. As early as 1922 (in a November 15 letter to Richard Aldington), he declares he will not write another poem in this mode. "As for 'The Waste Land', that is a thing of the past so far as I am concerned"; he wants "a new form and style." *Exhibition of Mss and First Editions*, June 1961, University of Texas, 8. This catalog item (my sole information) was in a library exhibit in a locked case.

85. Edward W. Said, *On Late Style: Music and Literature against the Grain* (New York: Pantheon Books, 2006), 8, xiii.

86. Said, *On Late Style*, 14.

87. Margaret Dickie, *On the Modernist Long Poem* (Iowa City: University of Iowa Press, 1986), 4.

88. Dickie, *On the Modernist*, 15.

89. Mackey, *Paracritical Hinge*, 316, 317.

90. Williams, *Autobiography*, 391.

91. Mackey, *Paracritical Hinge*, 317.

92. Joan Retallack, *The Poethical Wager* (Berkeley: University of California Press, 2003), 21.

93. Retallack, *Poethical Wager*, 28, 46.

94. "Ezra Pound," interview by Donald Hall, 38.

95. Perelman, *Trouble with Genius*; Alan Golding, "From Pound to Olson: The Avant-Garde Poet as Pedagogue," *Journal of Modern Literature* 34, no. 1 (Fall 2010): 86–106.

96. Rachel Blau DuPlessis, *Blue Studios: Poetry and Its Cultural Work* (Tuscaloosa: University of Alabama Press, 2006), 84–88, 92–95.

97. Bob Perelman, *Modernism the Morning After* (Tuscaloosa: University of Alabama Press, 2017), 92, 243, n. 4.

98. Not to forget, however, Mackey's pedagogic playlists throughout both his long works.

99. Theodor Adorno, "Commitment," in *Notes to Literature*, vol. 2, ed. Rolf Tiedemann, trans. by Shierry Weber Nicholsen (New York: Columbia University Press, 1992), 76–94.

100. DuPlessis, *Blue Studios*, 240.

101. William Kentridge, "Let Us Try for Once: 15 ½ Thoughts in the Library," message from the Brooklyn Public Library, December 9, 2018, https://www.bklynlibrary.org.

102. Williams, *Paterson*, 2.

103. Kentridge, "Let Us Try for Once."

104. Gerald L. Bruns, *What Are Poets For? An Anthropology of Contemporary Poetry and Poetics* (Iowa City: University of Iowa Press, 2012), 58.

Chapter 2

1. M. A. Bernstein, *The Tale of the Tribe: Ezra Pound and the Modern Verse Epic* (Princeton: Princeton University Press, 1980), 13.

2. Lyn Hejinian, *A Border Comedy* (New York: Granary Books, 2001), 54.

3. Kamboureli proposes that a "resistance to generic definitions" will "characterize [any individual] long poem as a 'new' genre," despite tempting readers with "lyric, epic, or documentary reading[s]." She does not privilege long poems as fundamentally epics, or serial lyric, or documentary, or narratives; she makes the operational claim that any modern and contemporary long poem draws on many genres, yet is "on the edge" among them, restlessly appropriating and contesting genres. Keller offers a range of examples illustrating the genre tendencies that emerge from specific allegiances in poetics; she tries to hold these poems to a named genre, but they escape her argument, since even defining a genre remains a "project" that is forever "in process." Smaro Kamboureli, *On the Edge of Genre: The Contemporary Canadian Long Poem* (Toronto: University of Toronto Press, 1991), xiv; Lynn Keller, *Forms of Expansion: Recent Long Poems by Women* (Chicago: University of Chicago Press, 1997), 8.

4. Ann Day Dewey, "The Modern American Long Poem," in *The Cambridge Companion to Modern American Poetry*, ed. Walter Kaladjian (New York: Cambridge University Press, 2015), 65, 67.

5. A. R. Ammons, *Tape for the Turn of the Year* (New York: W. W. Norton, 1965), 7. During the writing Ammons is waiting for his potential appointment to Cornell Univer-

sity; this real-life *nostos* achieving a home in Ithaca has amused a number of readers.

6. Raymond Williams uses these suggestive terms for cultural processes and ideologies clustered and in dialogue at any given moment—"dominant," "residual," and "emergent." Raymond Williams, *Marxism and Literature* (Oxford: Oxford University Press, 1977), 121–27.

7. That is the special fascination of the double "bards" of Books 8 and 9 of the *Odyssey* in which, after Demodocus sings a Trojan War episode involving Odysseus and Achilles, Homer has many-talented Odysseus narrate some of his own "epic."

8. Nathaniel Mackey, *Splay Anthem* (New York: New Directions, 2006), 78, 115.

9. Nathaniel Mackey, "Epic World," interview by Joseph Donahue, May 6, 2014, Poetry Foundation, https://www.poetryfoundation.org.

10. Remember Dewey's "genre in crisis and transformation." And Kamboureli's argument. My phrase resembles what Williams said about the rhetoric and diction of Moore's collaged longish works: that she wrote "an anthology of transit," "moving rapidly from one thing to the next." William Carlos Williams, "Marianne Moore" [1925], in *Selected Essays of William Carlos Williams* (New York: Random House, 1954), 123. These are tactics similar to, but much earlier than, Olson's "Projective Verse" announces.

11. Alastair Fowler gives a good summary of such respectful attitudes, as well as naming a witty and accurate panoply of shims for adjusting genres fixed by too much respect. See Fowler, "Transformations of Genre" [1982], in *Modern Genre Theory*, ed. David Duff (Oxfordshire: Routledge, 2014), 232–49.

12. Robert Creeley, *The Collected Poems of Robert Creeley, 1975–2005* (Berkeley: University of California Press, 2006), 82.

13. Jacques Derrida, "The Law of Genre [1979, trans. Avital Ronell, 1980]," in *Acts of Literature*, ed. Derek Attridge (New York: Routledge, 1992), 230.

14. I confess that this charming phrase does remain in one chapter. I also think of it as describing *Drafts*.

15. Ezra Pound, *Literary Essays of Ezra Pound* (London: Faber and Faber, 1954), 86.

16. I try to use "female figures" for poetic inventions and "women" when the poets depict historical persons.

17. Charles Olson, *The Collected Poems of Charles Olson, Excluding the Maximus Poems*, ed. George F. Butterick (Berkeley: University of California Press, 1987), 384–87.

18. I have made some of those critiques. However, I have no doubt about the seriousness and investments with which gender was considered and addressed by these poets.

19. I draw on Emily Wilson's remarks on Penelope and what we surmise about female figures and the depiction of gender in *The Odyssey*. Homer, *The Odyssey*, trans. and introduction by Emily Wilson (New York: W. W. Norton, 2018), 1–79.

20. Taking another tack, Jeanne Heuving proposes that erotic love, as a motivator of the propulsive stream of the "projective," and the "libidinized field poetics" that it generates, suffuse the epics of Olson, Pound, and Mackey, influencing both page space and the ecstatic energies of the verse. Social gender is therefore not an issue in her readings. Jeanne Heuving, *The Transmutation of Love and Avant-Garde Poetics* (Tuscaloosa: University of Alabama Press, 2016), ix, and passim.

21. William Carlos Williams, *Paterson* [1946–51; 1958], ed. Christopher MacGowan (New York: New Directions, 1992), xiv. He also resurrects the dog in the *Odyssey*, which greets and then follows the man.

22. Williams, *Paterson*, 253 and xii (both for "long poem"), 267, xiii. Perhaps "epic" came from an early commentator, James Thirlwall, who used that genre term in a subtitle to his 1961 study "The Search for the Redeeming Language—A Personal *Epic* in Five Parts." Williams, *Paterson*, 251; my emphasis.

23. William Carlos Williams, "Letter to an Australian Editor," *William Carlos Williams Review* 17, no. 2 (Fall 1991): 12.

24. Bernstein, *Tale of the Tribe*, 14.

25. The pattern: women are mythologized; men are historical agents *and* mythologized. Olson's *Maximus* deploys myths in which female figures are singularly dangerous or capricious or have a special aura—the woman who "fucked a serpent" or "the spirit of / that mountain," or other mythic figures, including "Our Lady of Good Voyage," the statue of the Virgin over the city. Charles Olson, *The Maximus Poems*, ed. George F. Butterick (Berkeley: University of California Press, 1983), 192–93, 309. Historical women are briefly mentioned as fruitful wives (229) or women simply part of the growth of Gloucester, present as property owner Widow Babson (110, 230), or as silly young ladies (252). There is also a brief tender mention of Olson's toddler daughter (92).

26. Olson, *Maximus*, 327.

27. Generally, the places where femaleness most richly occurs are in landscape features of the earth: "Kent Circle (aka 'Kunt Circle')" (Olson, *Maximus*, 299) showing the mythic necessity of sexual intercourse for social grounding.

28. Olson, *Maximus*, 77, 105, 78, 47, 48.

29. An exception: one of three formerly suppressed "Italian" cantos (Canto 73) speaks of a Fascist farm woman tricking Canadian soldiers into a minefield—she is one of the few female figures of action in the whole poem. She dies as do they; Pound eulogizes her bravery (Cantos 438–41 [in Italian only]). Ezra Pound, *The Cantos* (1971; repr., New York: New Directions, 1996).

30. Here I do not mean the inspiration and hoped-for guidance of goddesses to characters in epic or the invocation of a female "Muse" by the poet. I have already noted the lack of most female figures in Olson's depiction of the economy of the new society in David Herd, ed. *Contemporary Olson* (Manchester: Manchester University Press, 2015), 138. Here, I mean the reduction of historical women as depicted in artworks to transcendent inspirations or mockable annoyances (Fresca), not as historical actors inside art practices (Florence Farr vs. "Portrait d'une Femme"), and the rewriting of near chronologies to conceal indebtedness (Pound editing Loy, then also deploying her innovations). Rachel Blau DuPlessis, *Blue Studios: Poetry and Its Cultural Work* (Tuscaloosa: University of Alabama Press, 2006), 122–36; Rachel Blau DuPlessis, *Purple Passages: Pound, Eliot, Zukofsky, Olson, Creeley and the Ends of Patriarchal Poetry* (Iowa City: University of Iowa Press, 2012), 37–44.

31. Susan Stanford Friedman's articles in the early 1990s make valiant arguments. She observes that a weighting of importance in volume, space, time, scope, and authority is conventionally linked to hierarchies of genre and needs to be faced or consciously

addressed by women writers who are facing a patriarchal challenge in the epic.

32. Olson from a 1956 lecture, in Ann Charters, *Olson/Melville: A Study in Affinity* (Berkeley: Oyez, 1968), 88, cited in Robert von Hallberg, *Charles Olson: The Scholar's Art* (Cambridge, MA: Harvard University Press, 1978), 66.

33. Olson, *Maximus*, 138–39, 133–34.

34. Bernstein, *Tale of the Tribe*, 265, 238, 240, 244, 246, 251.

35. Bernstein, *Tale of the Tribe*, 258.

36. Olson, *Maximus*, 185.

37. Olson, *Maximus*, 307.

38. Accounts such as Michael Boughn's of Olson's impact on Buffalo poetics emphasize his focus on "epic" and the archaic, because "epic" answered the "lyric impasse." Michael Boughn, "Olson's Buffalo," in *The World in Time and Space: Towards a History of Innovative American Poetry in Our Time*, ed. Edward Foster and Joseph Donahue (Jersey City, NJ: Talisman House, 2001), 34.

39. This important critique of "lyrical interference" (not the lyric ego, as it sometimes is cited) is not my topic here, but the citation is Charles Olson, *Collected Prose*, ed. Donald Allen and Benjamin Friedlander (Berkeley: University of California Press, 1997), 247.

40. Olson, *Collected Prose*, 261–62, 242, 247.

41. I am borrowing language from the mathematical theorist Fernando Zalamea, who describes a "fluid universe," "mobile, unstable, contextual, in transit," similar enough to the modern long poem to be briefly evoked here. Fernando Zalamea, *Synthetic Philosophy of Contemporary Mathematics*, trans. Zachary Luke Fraser (Falmouth, UK: Urbanomic, 2012), 272, 271.

42. Olson, *Maximus*, 158.

43. Olson, *Collected Prose*, 348.

44. Olson, *Collected Prose*, 246–47, 117.

45. Olson, *Collected Prose*, 348.

46. Olson, *Maximus*, 8.

47. Olson, *Collected Prose*, 104, 118–19.

48. Alice Notley, *Coming After: Essays on Poetry*. Ann Arbor: University of Michigan Press, 2005, 84.

49. Royal rhyme has a tight seven-line decasyllabic stanza generally based on the rhyme scheme ababbcc, tightened even further by Brooks into a tetrameter (four-beat), not five-beat (ten-syllable) line, generally moving at seven syllables per line, along with some repeated lines in stanza-linking moves. Extreme tightness is allegorical of social containment. Her use varies the rhyme scheme but certainly makes its point about her defiant poetic skill.

50. Gwendolyn Brooks, *Annie Allen* (New York: Harper & Brothers, 1949), 32. The complete text of *Annie Allen* is found also in Gwendolyn Brooks, *Blacks* (Chicago: David, 1987). The text in Gwendolyn Brooks, *Selected Poems* from 1963, is not complete. Hortense Spillers, "Gwendolyn the Terrible: Propositions on Eleven Poems," in *Shakespeare's Sisters: Feminist Essays on Women Poets*, ed. Sandra Gilbert and Susan Gubar, 233–44 (Bloomington: University of Indiana Press, 1979).

51. Brooks, *Annie Allen*, 59.

52. Brooks, *Annie Allen*, 60, final lines of the book.

53. Gwendolyn Brooks, *Report from Part One* (Detroit: Broadside Press, 1972), 258.

54. Brooks, *Report from Part One*, 258.

55. Later (in a brief exhortation to Black students on writing poetry), Brooks is dismissive of "Negro"—not as color or ethnicity—but as an ideological marker: "The great 'Negro' dream was 'Hand in hand toge-ether!" Any dependence on white vision, judgment, or seeking empathy is thoroughly resisted in that cultural moment. There's some mocking pronunciation in "toge-ether"; if not a proofreading accident with the split of the syllables, it produces the judgment that Black affirmation would be anesthetized by any appeal to white sensibilities and the unity of the races. Gwendolyn Brooks, Keorapetse Kgositsile, Haki R. Madhubuti, and Dudley Randall, *A Capsule Course in Black Poetry Writing* (Detroit: Broadside Press, 1975), 6. This was a vital moment, but not her only position on many matters joining and separating Black and white citizens in poetry and the social and literary worlds. Her word "his," insistent, could be a holdover from the time this was originally written, or obedience to a grammatical rule.

56. Brooks, *Report from Part One*, 149.

57. I agree almost entirely with Evie Shockley's point—that, by alluding to the *Iliad*, Brooks intends her poem to appear in an epic context to claim that prestige. My argument wants to show that the multigeneric long poem incorporates many genres; Shockley's wants the claim of epic for Brooks as part of her poetic stature. Our perspectives depend on our differing arguments, not on differing opinions on the importance of Brooks. Eve Shockley, *Renegade Poetics: Black Aesthetics and Formal Innovation in African American Poetry* (Iowa City: University of Iowa Press, 2011), 41–44, 53.

58. Brooks, *Primer for Blacks* (Chicago: Third World Press, 1980), 10, 15.

59. Brooks was conscious of her hermetic surface—"it's labored," "a poem that's very interested in the mysteries and magic of technique," and (also from an interview, with Paul Angle in 1967) "the concentration, the crush" of language as a medium. "I was just very conscious of every word; I wanted every phrase to be beautiful and yet to contribute sanely to the whole." She later notes that it was so "tenderly cared for" that it might not be a "wild success," "but it was enjoyable [to write]." These comments suggest that such display was necessary in a world in which the motives and pressures on these characters —not to speak of on their author—were not generally acknowledged. Brooks, *Report from Part One*, 158, 146, 159.

60. Boughn, "Olson's Buffalo," 35.

61. The bibliographic account of a postmortem sorting of *The Maximus Poems* occurs in George F. Butterick, ed., *A Guide to the Maximus Poems of Charles Olson* [1978] (Berkeley: University of California Press, 1980), xliv–lv, and makes the mass of manuscript precisely a midden; Friedlander's 2006 essay on Olson argues that the "archive" of and around the poem constitutes his relevant oeuvre (and not the poem as limited site for scrutiny). The "epic" sails beyond a literary genre and gets to be bibliographic accumulations of its process studied with genetic scholarship. Ben Friedlander, "Charles Olson Now," *Olson Now* (blog), May 27, 2006, http://olsonnow.blogspot.com.

62. Olson, *Collected Prose*, 308. In Melville, Olson notes, "there is [. . .] an absence of

palpable woman in his works." Olson, *Call Me Ishmael* [1947] (Baltimore: Johns Hopkins University Press, 1997), 94.

63. For more information and comments about this project, see A Curriculum of the Soul, https://sites.google.com/view/notesonacurriculumofsoul/home.

64. See the discussion of John Weiners's "WOMAN" in DuPlessis, *Purple Passages*, 169–73. The other late completed works besides Notley's were Joanne Kyger's *Phenomenological* (1989), Robin Blaser's *Bach's Belief* (1995), Michael Boughn's *Mind* (1999), and Lisa Jarnot's *One's Own Language* (2002).

65. In the summer of 1970, Ted Berrigan and Notley lived in Buffalo, where Berrigan taught a course on modern mythology; Jack Clarke's library was available to them. In 1985 (Berrigan had died in 1983), Notley taught *The Maximus Poems* at a St. Mark's Poetry Project Workshop and also used the "fascicle/pamphlet" model of the *Curriculum of the Soul* booklets as an illustration of a community self-publishing project. This backstory is from a March 2020 email from Notley to the author.

66. Notley, *Coming After*, 234.

67. "White Phosphorus," treating the post-Vietnam traumas of her brother, is now best accessible in Alice Notley, *Grave of Light: New and Selected Poems* (Middletown, CT: Wesleyan University Press, 2006), 190–98.

68. In an email discussion from 2002 to 2003 with Claudia Keelen, Notley said she chose epic because she felt that "nothing in the world, not one object, not one practice or habit had been invented, as far as I could tell, by a woman"—a striking thought, leading to anger and its corollary, ambition. Alice Notley and Claudia Keelan, "A Conversation, September 2002–December 2003," *APR* [*American Poetry Review*] 33, no. 3 (May–June 2004): 16.

69. The back jacket of the Penguin edition (presumably from information by Notley) uses the term "a feminist epic." She also identifies this poem as her "epic poem," in the author's biography in *Alma, or The Dead Women* (New York: Granary Books, 2006), [347].

70. Alice Notley, *Homer's Art* (Canton, NY: Glover, 1990), 6, 7.

71. Alice Notley, "Epic and Women Poets," in *Disembodied Poetics: Annals of the Jack Kerouac School*, ed. Anne Waldman and Andrew Schelling. 103–9 (Albuquerque: University of New Mexico Press, 1994), 106; see also Alice Notley, "What Can Be Learned from Dreams?" *Scarlet* 5 [a pamphlet magazine] (September 1991), n.p. [18–21].

72. Notley, *Homer's Art*, 7.

73. Notley, *Homer's Art*, 7, 6.

74. This stark vision differs from the female plenitude and creative powers that Anne Waldman will depict in her epic.

75. Notley, *Homer's Art*, 6.

76. The Sumerian epic work *Inanna,* based on the groundbreaking and career-long scholarship and translations of Samuel Noah Kramer, had been given a transposed paraphrase and shaping by the folklorist Diane Wolkstein and became an influential text for feminists and classicists. Diane Wolkstein and Samuel Noah Kramer, *Inanna, Queen of Heaven and Earth: Her Stories and Hymns from Sumer* (New York: Harper & Row, 1983).

77. Notley, "Epic and Women Poets," 105.

78. DuPlessis, *Purple Passages*, 117–41.

79. Charles Olson and Frances Boldereff, *Charles Olson and Frances Boldereff: A Modern Correspondence*, ed. Ralph Maud and Sharon Thesen (Middletown, CT: Wesleyan University Press, 1999), 417.

80. *Charles Olson and Frances Boldereff*, xiii, 422.

81. About gender, Olson often talked the talk but could not walk the walk. See DuPlessis, *Purple Passages*.

82. H.D., *Helen in Egypt* (New York: New Directions, 1961), 34, 157.

83. Notley, *Grave of Light*, 195. Not epic as "lies" but the reconfigured epic becomes her goal. All quotation marks are Notley's; they are her tactic marking segmentivity.

84. Notley, *Grave of Light*, 194.

85. Alice Notley, "An Interview with Shawn Walker and Heather Starr," *COMBO: A Journal of Poetry and Poetics* 3 (Spring 1999): 42.

86. This ethical decision about depicted violence involved her narrative embodiment of sociopolitical control in one dictator figure and a storyline in which that single strategic murder changes society.

87. Alice Notley, *The Descent of Alette* (New York: Penguin Books, 1996), 136.

88. Notley, *Descent of Alette*, 128, 142, 145.

89. Notley, *Descent of Alette*, 147.

90. Notley, *Homer's Art*, 7.

91. Alice Notley, "Alice Notley" [January 1997], *Contemporary Authors Autobiography Series*, vol. 27 (Detroit: Gale, 1997), 229.

92. Anne Waldman to the author, personal communication, August 8, 2014.

93. Notley, *Coming After*, 84. It is unclear without further research whether these two women and perhaps Bernadette Mayer, all in complicated relationships with each other, knew of the epic concerns of the other (more than likely) and what impact this had on their work. All three did something critical with epic; that is my interest here.

94. Notley, *Coming After*, 85.

95. Notley, *Coming After*, 84, 91, 92.

96. Anne Waldman, *The Iovis Trilogy: Colors in the Mechanism of Concealment* (Minneapolis: Coffee House Press, 2011), 370–71.

97. The whole letter is a datum about the gender relations in one of the important US poetry worlds.

98. My appeal for information to the poetry community around SUNY-Buffalo led to these two possible dates. No one asked could resolve the year of Creeley's class.

99. One might then predict contradictory counterclaims of female "opportunism" or "stubborn intransigence."

100. Notley, *Coming After*, 168.

101. Denise Riley, *"Am I That Name?": Feminism and the Category of "Women" in History* (Minneapolis: University of Minnesota Press, 1988), 113.

102. Waldman, *Iovis*, 1.

103. Every canto's italicized headnote, in a tactic usefully borrowed from H.D.'s *Helen*

in Egypt, gives a prose summary and analytic or emotionally rich comments functioning as miniessays on each section of the work.

104. Waldman, *Iovis*, 656.

105. Waldman, *Iovis*, 298.

106. Anne Waldman, "An Interview with Anne Waldman," by Edward Foster, *Talisman* 13 (Fall 1994/Winter 1995): 70.

107. Anne Waldman, *Kill or Cure* (New York: Penguin Books, 1994), 144.

108. Waldman, *Iovis*, 187.

109. Waldman, *Iovis*, 657.

110. Waldman, *Iovis*, 883, 901.

111. Anne Waldman, *Vow to Poetry: Essays, Interviews, & Manifestos* (Minneapolis: Coffee House Press, 2001), 290.

112. Waldman saw Olson's lecture-performance at the Berkeley Poetry Conference in 1965 as an inspiration to a personal epic. She responded with astonished joy to his substance-fueled performative excess. Waldman, *Vow to Poetry*, 27, 108, 290.

113. Waldman, *Kill or Cure*, 145.

114. Waldman, *Iovis*, 7, 296.

115. In a brave move and a plausible homage to Williams, Waldman even incorporates into her poem the critique of the poem by A. H. (Anselm Hollo), as with Williams and the letters of Marcia Nardi ("Cress"), the fuel that *Paterson* Book II runs on. Waldman, *Iovis*, 473–75.

116. Waldman, *Iovis*, 946.

117. As in Waldman, *Vow to Poetry*, 286.

118. Waldman, *Vow to Poetry*, 287, 286.

119. Anne Waldman, *Outrider: Essays, Poems, Interviews* (Albuquerque, NM: La Alameda Press, 2006), 90.

120. Waldman, *Iovis*, 685.

Chapter 3

1. As an example, the first lines of the *Commedia* are so powerful in literature that Caroline Bergvall's conceptual homage "VIA" in *Fig* repeats the opening tercet in forty-seven Anglophone translations.

2. Robert Duncan, *Collected Later Poems and Plays*, ed. Peter Quartermain (Berkeley: University of California Press, 2014), xxxii.

3. When Blaser discusses his Dante, he is clear that "Purgatory is our condition," the place in which both personally and culturally you purge yourself of error, crime, lack of love. "John Sakkis Interviews Robin Blaser" [2004], in *The Poker* 5 (Winter 2005): 63.

4. The *American Heritage Dictionary* waxes biblical in its definition of "cosmos": "All existing things, including the earth, the heavens, the galaxies, and all therein, regarded as a whole; the cosmos; macrocosm." The words "therein" and "heavens" do it.

5. Roman Jakobson, "What Is Poetry?," in *Language in Literature*, by Roman Jakobson, ed. Krystyna Pomorska and Stephen Rudy (Cambridge, MA: Harvard University Press, 1987), 378.

6. This incisive article by Alastair Fowler and Roland Greene is my source for numerology in poetry: "Numerology," in *Princeton Encyclopedia of Poetry and Poetics*, 4th ed., ed. Roland Greene (Princeton: Princeton University Press, 2012), 959.

7. Tone and diction bolstering conviction? As for nonvatic, satiric, comic poetries—perhaps in compensation, an exaggerated sense of number is used to propel those poems' intense wit, as in *Don Juan* by Byron. There is also a response to theistic fullness, by exaggerating language and poetic sound, and intensifying poetic numbers with supersaturated richness as a form of worship (in Gerard Manley Hopkins).

8. *Contrapasso* is the compensatory appropriateness of any particular punishment/ or penitential suffering to a particular sin or crime. There are also sub rosa traces of payback time.

9. Duncan, *Collected Later Poems*, xxxii.

10. In Eliot's review of Joyce's *Ulysses*, "Ulysses, Order, and Myth," in *The Waste Land*, ed. Michael North (New York: W. W. Norton, 2001), 130.

11. Eliot, "Ulysses," 130.

12. Dante was interested in reconciling findings of science with faith; the journey is astronomically, temporally, and "geographically" exact if also metaphysical. He also makes special efforts to allude to three culturally vital mythic systems—pagan-classical, Hebrew scriptural, and New Testament whenever he needs examples of traits and choices, of exemplary or flawed acts; within this triplex his notes on Mary always stand first, and the other systems are very gradually subsumed into Christian triumph.

13. Norman Finkelstein's study of some US contemporary poets overlaps with this study, particularly in the topic of this chapter, although Dante is not the link, nor is the category long poem: *On Mt. Vision: Forms of the Sacred in Contemporary American Poetry* (Iowa City: University of Iowa Press, 2010). Finkelstein's subtitle makes clear that his chosen task is clarifying the "sacred." There is a distinct difference between the two key words in our investigations: "the sacred" and "socio-cosmological," one a noun and the other an adjective. For Finkelstein, "the sacred" and the long-standing relationships of poetry to that category are investigated but also assumed as a solution. Finkelstein wants to see the "heterodox, syncretic, and revisionary" modern and contemporary poems sharing something fundamental, at root—a "foundational relationship to the sacred, to a source of life that is both apart from and within us" (7, 26). I tend to be more agnostic; "the sacred" for Finkelstein is a fixed category that is only sometimes confluent with my term "socio-cosmological," concerning ontological questions about our place in the universe. Neither of us denies traces of visionary and cosmological thought in poetry; we differ in what these traces indicate. For me, these poems treating the cosmological seem often to emerge from respectful critique, reframing, and contestation, sometimes even taking the Dantean poems in directions quite contrary to his.

14. John Ashbery, *Three Poems* (New York: Viking Press, 1972).

15. T. S. Eliot, *Collected Poems, 1909–1962* (London: Faber and Faber, 1963), 222, citing "Little Gidding."

16. Eliot, *Collected Poems*, 217.

17. T. S. Eliot, "What Dante Means to Me," in *The Poets' Dante: Twentieth-Century Responses*, ed. Peter S. Hawkins and Rachel Jacoff (New York: Farrar Straus, 2001), 32.

18. This word does not appear in this particular passage in Italian, but Beatrice's criticism of his gesture is a key event. There is a later use in *Paradiso* applied to Dante—after he asks a question proven to be dangerously near heresy. And see his "doctoral/doctrinal exam" supervised by three saints in turn. When awaiting St. Peter's question, he lifts his face up, now in readiness.

19. Eliot, *Collected Poems*, 217.

20. Eliot, *Collected Poems*, 218.

21. Eliot, *Collected Poems*, 218, 219.

22. Eliot, *Collected Poems*, 214.

23. *Paradiso* I.76; also XII.19 for "eternal roses" and XIX.59 for "eternal justice."

24. Louis Zukofsky, *Prepositions+: The Collected Critical Essays* [1967], ed. with additional prose by Mark Scroggins (Middletown, CT: Wesleyan University Press, 2000), 10, 9.

25. Louis Zukofsky, *Complete Short Poetry* (Baltimore: Johns Hopkins University Press, 1991), 18, line 262.

26. Dante, "Al poco giorno," in *Dante's Lyric Poetry*, ed. and trans. Kenelm Foster and Patrick Boyde (Oxford: Clarendon Press, 1967), 162–65.

27. Zukofsky, *Complete Short Poetry*, includes *80 Flowers* (pp. 321–51). "Number-tumbling is usually near the heart of Zukofsky's poetry." Michele Leggott, *Reading Zukofsky's "80 Flowers"* (Baltimore: Johns Hopkins University Press, 1989, 14). I am deeply indebted to Leggott's intensive book-length study of this key poem.

28. The poem emphasized here is either the fourth or the fifth if you count the introductory poem—note that 4 + 5 = 9.

29. David Levi Strauss, "Approaching *80 Flowers*," in *Code of Signals: Recent Writings in Poetics*, ed. Michael Palmer (Berkeley: North Atlantic Books, 1983), 84.

30. For Zukofsky's earlier proof of aggressive mastery, he tests the contemporary viability of formalism, using Dante's "Al poco giorno" and concluding that an *almost* perfect sestina is possible in modernism but only as a mode of de-idealized procedural poetry.

31. He had made a decade's schema for his poetic production and an intricate plan for *80 Flowers* that referred to his own past work and both "old Testament" numbers (like forty), Pythagorean numbers (number 8 as sign of Love and of infinity), and other distinctive dialogues between his life, his already written works, and certain culturally august numbers. Leggott, *Reading "80 Flowers,"* 13–19.

32. Leggott, *Reading "80 Flowers,"* 3–33 et passim.

33. See Zukofsky, *Prepositions+*, 10.

34. Maria Damon, *Postliterary America: From Bagel Shop Jazz to Micropoetries* (Iowa City: University of Iowa Press, 2011), 25.

35. Zukofsky, *Complete Short Poetry*, 326. See the full text on page 326.

36. Leggott, *Reading "80 Flowers,"* 148.

37. Louis Zukofsky, *"A"* (Berkeley: University of California Press, 1978), 7; Leggott, *Reading "80 Flowers,"* 145. In the version of "A"-2 in *An "Objectivists" Anthology*, ed. Zukofsky (Le Beausset, Var, France: To, 1932), the Dantean word "pearl-clean" is added for this rose, a possible allusion to *Paradiso* III and XXII. Mark Scroggins, *The Poem of a Life: A Biography of Louis Zukofsky* (Emeryville, CA: Shoemaker, Hoard, 2007), 98.

38. Leggott, *Reading "80 Flowers,"* 356; Scroggins, *Poem of a Life*, 96–102.

39. He includes a second succulent in his *80 Flowers* as well, the one called *Telephus sedum*. This occurs because in 1975 he discovered that he had mixed up poem #4's *Sedum* with #68's *Sedum*. In correcting this error of identification, Zukofsky ends up (neatly, insistently) with two "liveforever" succulents in this work. He uses the Dantean/Eliotic word for one of those two—"sempiternal." Zukofsky, *Complete Short Poetry*, 347.

40. With many thanks for clarifications to Norman Finkelstein.

41. The discussion of Ashbery's *Three Poems* continues later.

42. H.D., "Dante and His Circle," manuscript at Beinecke Library, Yale University, YCAL MSS 24, box 43, folder 1103.

43. His heterodoxy (information based on Robert Hollander's annotations): in his drawing on various theologians in contradictory combinations; in his use of a suicide (Cato) as doorkeeper to *Purgatorio*, and in his placement of some proto-Christian pagans and mysteriously redeemed Jews in *Paradiso*.

44. H.D., *Helen in Egypt* (New York: New Directions, 1961), 185. This discussion continues the observations on this work and on *Trilogy* from the prior section.

45. Rachel Blau DuPlessis, *H.D.: The Career of That Struggle* (Bloomington: Indiana University Press, 1986), 90–95.

46. Ashbery, *Three Poems*, 61, 65. Ashbery says his model was Traherne's *Centuries of Meditation*. He schematically narrates this work for interviewer Piotr Sommer as a "pseudo-platonic stage of love going from [. . .] the physical up to the spiritual" (this is Dantean) and a journey in which at the end there is "peace, pleasure, an earthly paradise sort of thing" based in part on meeting someone new, the last a definite litotes after the Dantean rhetoric of love-transcendence but similar to Blaser's erotic-social vision. "An Interview in Warsaw with Piotr Sommer" [1980], in *Code of Signals: Recent Writings in Poetics*, ed. Michael Palmer (Berkeley: North Atlantic Books, 1983), 304.

47. Ashbery, *Three Poems*, 114, 116.

48. Ashbery, *Three Poems*, 90.

49. Dante, *The Divine Comedy of Dante Alighieri: Inferno* [1980], trans. Allen Mandelbaum (New York: Bantam Books, Random House, 1982), XXV.46–93 and XXV.100–102.

50. Dante, *Inferno*, 379.

51. Dante, *Inferno* XXV.103–36 or 139.

52. James Merrill, *The Changing Light at Sandover* [1982], with a new coda (New York: Alfred A. Knopf, 1992), 80–82, 255–56, 502–6 (quotation at 506).

53. A particularly lively overview of the Merrill is Brian McHale's, also insistent on its masque poetics as indicating the plurality of its worlds, its prosthetic Ouija proceduralism, and its postmodern ontological poetics (interested in plethoras of being—and in death). Brian McHale, *The Obligation toward the Difficult Whole: Postmodernist Long Poems* (Tuscaloosa: University of Alabama Press, 2004).

54. Merrill, *Changing Light*, 269, 149.

55. A whole critical literature worries this; I see those notes as helpful prematerials on a page so horror vacui does not trouble Merrill, and he can thereby write even from sketchy suggestions. Merrill's structure and style generally abhor a vacuum.

56. Timothy Materer's book on Merrill is devoted to the serious issue of apocalypse

in the whole of his oeuvre, but particularly in *Changing Light*. The impact of plutonium waste is on Merrill's mind as well. Timothy Materer, *James Merrill's Apocalypse* (Ithaca, NY: Cornell University Press, 2000).

57. I have always read "Little Gidding," Section IV, with scandalized shock. Eliot, *Collected Poems*, 221.

58. Robin Blaser, *The Fire: Collected Essays of Robin Blaser*, ed. Miriam Nichols (Berkeley: University of California Press, 2006), 97.

59. Actually, there is another part—the "Good-Bye" at the bottom of the board.

60. Merrill, *Changing Light*, 530.

61. Merrill, *Changing Light*, 350.

62. Some souls (Chester Kallman) bitch about their new "assignment"; he will be born Black in Africa. This is pretty snide—one of the really dubious moments, if honest in a calling-out of a racist moment, even in an imagined scene.

63. Merrill, *Changing Light*, 327–31.

64. Merrill, *Changing Light*, 154.

65. There are two maternal-female figures of great centrality, but Merrill is clear: there will be no "Ewig-Weibliche" in his work for the role that Beatrice plays in Dante's—more like "AN EWIG SHALL WE SAY HERMAPHRODITE" (Merrill, *Changing Light*, 305). Both Maya Deren and Maria Mitsotaki are queered females.

66. Merrill, *Changing Light*, 216.

67. Merrill, *Changing Light*, 154, 157–61.

68. Dante fondly acknowledges his teacher Brunetto Latini (although he is placed among the damned—with the sodomites). All this means only that—rare for his own time, as Robert Hollander points out in his gloss of those specific lines of the poem in the Princeton Dante Project—Dante seems to have understood homosexual attraction and acknowledged homosexual acts, even if he knew where to place them in his cosmological scheme.

69. Merrill, *Changing Light*, 455.

70. The intertwining of the two worlds (living and dead) occurs when the two sides not only complete each other's sentences but complete each other's rhymes. Rhyme is the mechanism of dialogic concordance through which the porous veil between living and dead messengers and informants is penetrated at every turn. Merrill here makes rhyme (a tactic of segmentivity) solidify his dialogue with cosmic otherness. And incidentally he is one of the best users of rhyme in English in the long twentieth century: my list is Yeats, Tolson, Brooks, Merrill.

71. John Kinsella, *Divine Comedy: Journeys through a Regional Geography, Three New Works* (New York: W. W. Norton, 2008).

72. Kinsella, *Divine Comedy*, 270, 272.

73. Philip Mead, "Connectivity, Community and the Question of Literary Universality: Reading Kim Scott's *Chronotope* and John Kinsella's *Commedia*," in *Republics of Letters: Literary Communities in Australia*, ed. Peter Kirkpatrick and Robert Dixon (Sydney: Sydney University Press, 2012), 154.

74. Kinsella, *Divine Comedy*, 269.

75. Dante, *The Divine Comedy of Dante Alighieri: Purgatorio* [1981], trans. Allen Mandelbaum (New York: Bantam Books, Random House, 1984), 20–27.

76. Kinsella, *Divine Comedy*, 272.

77. Kinsella, *Divine Comedy*, 269.

78. Kinsella, *Divine Comedy*, 163, 4, 162, 5.

79. *Purgatorio* XV; Kinsella, *Divine Comedy*, 76, 322.

80. Kinsella, *Divine Comedy*, 366.

81. Kinsella, *Divine Comedy*, 267.

82. Kinsella, *Divine Comedy*, 90, 100, 113, 155.

83. John Kinsella, "Ali Alizadeh Interviews John Kinsella," *Cordite Poetry Review*, December 1, 2009.

84. "Templating" is creating "a dialogic structure between a foundational [classic] work" and his own "convers[ing]" with it and "writ[ing] away from it," a method of serious critique. John Kinsella, *Activist Poetics: Anarchy in the Avon Valley*, ed. with an introduction by Niall Lucy (Liverpool: Liverpool University Press, 2010), 18.

85. This twenty-page essay-poem was commissioned by Professor Annalisa Goldoni as the plenary address at a conference in Pescara, "Dante in North America." Three times in his career, Blaser invoked intellectual and cosmological mentors, called "the great companions": the first was Pindar (1971); the second Robert Duncan (1988); the third is Dante (1997). Robin Blaser, *The Holy Forest: Collected Poems of Robin Blaser*, ed. Miriam Nichols (Berkeley: University of California Press, 2006), 139, 333, 435.

86. Blaser, *Holy Forest*, 456.

87. Blaser, "John Sakkis Interviews Robin Blaser," 72.

88. Blaser, *Holy Forest*, 4, 444.

89. Dante, *Inferno*, XXVI.98 and 120.

90. Blaser, "Summary and Explanation of the Final Section of 'Great Companions: Dante Alighieri,'" Università d'Annuzio, April 22, 1997, http://writing.upenn.edu/.

91. Dante, *The Divine Comedy of Dante Alighieri: Paradiso* [1982], trans. Allen Mandelbaum (New York: Bantam Books, Random House, 1986), XXV.2; Blaser, *Holy Forest*, 438.

92. Blaser, *Holy Forest*, 440.

93. Blaser, *Holy Forest*, 447.

94. Blaser, *The Astonishment Tapes: Talks on Poetry and Autobiography with Robin Blaser and Friends* [1974], ed. Miriam Nichols (Tuscaloosa: University of Alabama Press, 2015), 74.

95. Blaser, *The Fire*, 198–99; the epigraph to this book is from the same source.

96. This is a method for experiencing a forceful "synchronicity" out of "nonsynchronous materials" and is the fundamental Poundean leap, leading to both his power and his waywardness. Julien Murphet, "'Events Listening to Their Own Tremors': Zukofsky and Objective Anachrony," *Textual Practice* 26, no. 4 (August 2012): 714.

97. Blaser, *Holy Forest*, 454.

98. Blaser, *Holy Forest*, 449, 448, 451, 457.

99. Blaser, *Holy Forest*, 442, 443, 453.

100. Blaser, *The Fire*, 97.

101. Blaser, *Holy Forest*, 441.

102. Blaser, *The Fire*, 97.

103. Blaser, *Holy Forest*, 453; Blaser, *The Fire*, 97.

Chapter 4

1. Narrative bits, flurries and fragments of partial stories, distributed narrative pockets, discontinuous, unsutured but suggestive narratives make the term "anarrative" more apt than "nonnarrative" for these poems.

2. The titles of the overarching text and then the essay variously translated are *Quant au Livre*, meaning "On the Question of the Book," "Concerning the Book." Stéphane Mallarmé, *Divigations* [1897], trans. Barbara Johnson (Cambridge, MA: Belknap Press of Harvard University Press, 2007), 226; Stéphane Mallarmé, *Mallarmé*, trans. Anthony Hartley (Harmondsworth, England: Penguin Books, 1965), 189.

3. Authors, whose "death" (once much discussed by Barthes and Michel Foucault), Barthes here attributes to his own "Lack of Curiosity," a welcome about-face, worth examining in detail, but not my topic now. Roland Barthes, *Preparation of the Novel: Lecture Courses and Seminars at the Collège de France (1978–1979 and 1979–1980)*, trans. Kate Briggs (New York: Columbia University Press, 2011), 208 and 208–11ff.

4. With a typology drawn from biographies and other texts, Barthes enumerates attitudes necessary for one's writing vocation (Barthes, *Preparation of the Novel*, 131 passim). However, Barthes was injured in an accident in February 1980 and died about a month later, at age sixty-four. His new work was not accomplished.

5. Barthes, *Preparation of the Novel*, 182, 437n21.

6. Barthes, *Preparation of the Novel*, 177, 262, 251, 260.

7. Barthes, *Preparation of the Novel*, 224, 189.

8. Barthes: "It's possible to feel the other way [from Mallarmé] and to exalt the Album as the equal of the Book." Barthes, *Preparation of the Novel*, 186.

9. Barthes, *Preparation of the Novel*, 189.

10. Barthes, *Preparation of the Novel*, 186, citing Sherer, editor of "Le Livre," the first presentation of the sketchy notes in Stéphane Mallarmé, *Le "Livre" de Mallarmé* (Paris: Gallimard, 1957).

11. Barthes, *Preparation of the Novel*, 186–87.

12. And Zukofsky (with his family helper figures) produced a *Gesamtkunstwerk* as "A"-24, collated in four voices by his wife from his own writings and scored by his son from Handel.

13. Hart Crane, *The Collected Poems of Hart Crane*, ed. Waldo Frank (New York: Liveright, 1933), 45.

14. Fredric Jameson then lists assemblages, including *The Arcades Project* and Pascal's *Pensées*, that he calls "cousins" to the (to me) always oddly named "Menippean satires." These are compendia (assemblages) in their structure; the satiric is one attitude of the shifting stances of dialogism and plurality of patchwork genres as seen from a fixed norm. Fredric Jameson, *The Benjamin Files* (London: Verso, 2020), 13, 9.

15. Ben Friedlander, "Charles Olson Now," *Olson Now* (blog), May 27, 2006. http://olsonnow.blogspot.com.

16. Hart Crane, *The Bridge*, in *The Collected Poems of Hart Crane*, 39.

17. Walt Whitman, *Leaves of Grass. Authoritative Texts, Prefaces*, ed. Sculley Bradley and Harold W. Blodgett (New York: W. W. Norton, 1973), 354, 713.

18. Walt Whitman, "A Backward Glance O'er Traveled Roads" [1889], in *Leaves of Grass*, 564. His broad critique of normative poetry, involving genders, genres, imagery, rhyme, mythology, and aesthetic goals involves a sweeping away of any but the robust "masculine voice" for a national-historical poetry. For instance, the *Drum-Taps* poem "Eighteen Sixty-One" (a Civil War poem) is contemptuous of "dainty rhymes or sentimental love verses" written by "some pale poetling seated at a desk lisping cadenzas piano [softly]." Walt Whitman, *Leaves of Grass*, 282.

19. Whitman, *Leaves of Grass*, 713, 714.

20. Whitman, *Leaves of Grass*, 714, 119, 713.

21. Lately affirmed by Nathaniel Mackey, *Tej Bet*, vol. 1 of *Double Trio* (New York: New Directions, 2021), xvi.

22. There even seems (impossibly) to be no lag between event and writing—as in his writing about sex.

23. Ron Silliman, *Ketjak* [written 1974], in *The Age of Huts (compleat)* (Berkeley: University of California Press, 2007), 89.

24. Ron Silliman, *The Alphabet* (Tuscaloosa: University of Alabama Press, 2008), 1062, 1060.

25. Ron Silliman, *Tjanting* [1981] (Great Barrington: MA: The Figures, 1986), 161; Silliman, *Ketjak*, 29.

26. Silliman, *Ketjak*, 73.

27. In 1999, discussing his work for my Temple University class on the long poem, Silliman stated, "Stein died [nine days] before I was born." The Lord giveth and the Lord taketh away was the implication.

28. Silliman, *Alphabet*, 835.

29. Silliman, *Tjanting*, 20.

30. Silliman, *Tjanting*, 20.

31. The first *Ketjak* in *Age of Huts*, the second in *The Alphabet*.

32. Ron Silliman, "The New Sentence," in *The New Sentence* (New York: Roof Books, 1987), 63–93.

33. Ron Silliman, "'As to Violin Music': Time in the Longpoem," *Jacket Magazine* 27 (April 2005). On his "longpoem" as one word, it indicates the very long poem (see chapter 1).

34. Silliman, *Tjanting*, 22.

35. Silliman, *Tjanting*, 59.

36. Silliman, *Tjanting*, 130.

37. Mallarmé, *Divigations*, 3. This passage continues with Mallarmé's evocations of this imagined Book balancing the sacred with nature to offer "the orphic explanation of earth."

38. World-scope is a metaphor for the omnivorous very long poem, sometimes acknowledging globalizing forces in exchanges of ideas and art, by trade, travel, and reading (or listening). It may also be imperialist as well as omnivorous.

39. Mallarmé, *Divigations*, 228.

40. Mallarmé, *Divigations*, 229.

41. Lutz Koepnick, "Gesamtkunstwerk," in *The Cambridge History of Modernism*, ed. Vincent Sherry (New York: Cambridge University Press, 2016), 273, 277.

42. Without Sylvia Gorelick's edition and translation (Stéphane Mallarmé, *The Book*, trans. Sylvia Gorelick [Cambridge, MA: Exact Change, 2018]), my readings would not have been possible. *All* descriptions of this missing work are critical extrapolations by myself and others.

43. Stéphane Mallarmé, "Crisis of Verse," in *Divigations*, 204.

44. Mallarmé, "Crisis of Verse," *Divigations*, 210 (my clarifications in brackets).

45. This is validated by "The Only One Would Have to Be as Fluid," in which Mallarmé notes the inadequacy of mere theater to this *Gesamtkunstwerk*: "Theater always alters, from a special or literary point of view, the arts it appropriates: music cannot participate without losing some of its depth and darkness; neither can song, which ceases to be a solitary lightning-bolt; and, strictly speaking, neither can one recognize in Ballet the name of Dance—which is, if you will, a hieroglyphic language" (Mallarmé, *Divigations,* 139). It rests to poetry (not opera/theater) to gather ideal essences of various media toward the Total Artwork.

46. Danielle Follett, "Tout et n'importe quoi: The Total Artwork and the Aesthetics of Chance," in *The Aesthetics of the Total Artwork: On Borders and Fragments*, ed. Ake Finger and Danielle Follett (Baltimore: Johns Hopkins University Press, 2011), 97, 98, 99, 98, 100.

47. Trevor Stark, *Total Expansion of the Letter. Avant-Garde Art and Language after Mallarmé* (Cambridge, MA: MIT Press, 2020), 233–37.

48. Mallarmé, "Crisis of Verse," 209.

49. Emphasis on "Euro"; some Asian cultures have different visual traditions for poem presentation, possibly an influence on Mallarmé.

50. Arthur Symons, *The Symbolist Movement in Literature* [1899] (New York: E. P. Dutton, 1919), 181, 202, 9.

51. Richard Ellmann, *Yeats: The Man and the Masks* (London: Faber & Faber, 1961), 216–17. However, my scan of James Longenbach's richly biographical and circumstantial study of their interaction reveals almost no references to Mallarmé or to Symons.

52. Symons, *Symbolist Movement*, 202, 203. To underline here—Symons's "symbolist" interpretation is his contemporaneous extrapolation from the mystique-filled buzz around Mallarmé's thought. Current critics like Stark extrapolate, with more access to Mallarmé's texts and other insights, a "civic ritual appropriate for the emergence of a future secular and democratic collectivity emptied of [traditional religion- and nation-based] myth" (Stark, *Total Expansion*, 186). "Democratic" is debatable to me; "secular-spiritual assemblage" (with all paradoxes) seems right.

53. Ezra Pound to John Drummond, February 18, 1932, in *The Letters of Ezra Pound, 1907–1941*, ed. D. D. Paige (New York: Harcourt, Brace & World, 1950), 240.

54. Ezra Pound, *Polite Essays* [1937] (Freeport, NY: Books for Libraries Press, 1966), 144.

55. M. M. Bakhtin, "Discourse in Poetry and Discourse in the Novel," in *Dialogic Imagination: Four Essays*, ed. Michael Holquist, trans. Caryl Emerson and Michael Holquist (Austin: University of Texas Press 1981), 285, 287.

56. Bakhtin, "Discourse in Poetry," 262–63.

57. Ezra Pound to James Joyce, March 17, 1917, in *Pound/Joyce: The Letters of Ezra Pound to James Joyce, with Pound's Critical Essays and Articles about Joyce*, ed. Forrest Read (New York: New Directions, 1967), 102. Constructing his long poem began (circa) 1915, soon after he had made his famously brief, comically arrogant "pact" with Walt Whitman. Pound says Whitman "broke the wood" with Pound ready to do the "carving," to take Whitman's assembled pile of logs (his paratactic segmentivity) and turn that raw material into art. Ezra Pound, *Personae: The Collected Shorter Poems of Ezra Pound* [1926] (New York: New Directions, 1950), 89; Ezra Pound, *Lustra, with Earlier Poems* (New York: Alfred A. Knopf, 1917).

58. Pound to Harriet Monroe, August 18, 1912, in *Letters*, 10.

59. Ezra Pound, "Desideria," *The Exile*, no. 3 (Spring 1928): 108.

60. Ezra Pound, *Guide to Kulchur* [1938] (London: Peter Owen, 1966), 95.

61. Ezra Pound, *Impact: Essays on Ignorance and the Decline of American Civilization*, ed. Noel Stock (Chicago: Henry Regnery, 1960), 50, 74.

62. Pound to Homer L. Pound, April 11, 1927, in *Letters*, 210.

63. Pound to John Drummond, February 18, 1932, in *Letters*, 239. William Cookson compiled "An Anthology of Statements by Ezra Pound on the Cantos," in Cookson, *A Guide to the Cantos of Ezra Pound* (London: Croon Helm, 1985), xxiii–xxx.

64. "Ezra Pound," interview by Donald Hall, 1962, in *Writers at Work: The Paris Review Interviews*, 2nd ser., ed. George Plimpton (New York: Penguin Books, 1979), 57.

65. Charles Bernstein, in a summary overview, affirms that "Pound's [poetry] contradicts his fascism." Charles Bernstein, *My Way: Speeches and Poems* (Chicago: University of Chicago Press, 1999), 158. The two may exist in an unstable contradiction, but Pound willingly put his poetry and rhetoric at the service of the "new civilization" that he foresaw from fascism.

66. With his encouragements to US white supremacists in the St. Elizabeths salons. With his (still illegal) fascist salute upon landing back in Italy. Many Poundeans, Peter Stoicheff points out, presented Pound, in the return-to-Italy period, as a "tragic hero," a position he criticizes. Peter Stoicheff, *The Hall of Mirrors: "Drafts & Fragments" and the End of Ezra Pound's "Cantos"* (Ann Arbor: University of Michigan Press, 1995), 135. It appears, from Robin Blaser's quite presentational late Pound anecdote, that Blaser held a version of the "tragic hero" position interwoven with (and necessary to) Blaser's critique of authoritarianism.

67. Ezra Pound, *ABC of Reading* (New York: New Directions, 1934), 46. See also Pound, *Impact*, 142.

68. In Pound, *ABC*, 43.

69. "Ezra Pound," interview by Donald Hall, 39.

70. Bob Perelman, *Trouble with Genius: Reading Pound, Joyce, Stein and Zukofsky* (Berkeley: University of California Press, 1994), 50–54, 60–68.

71. Pound, *Guide to Kulchur*, 31.

72. These are familiar and dangerous tropes; their banality does not make them harmless.

73. Pound, *Impact*, 55.

74. Pound, *Guide to Kulchur*, 30.

75. Anderson Araujo, "Italian Fascism," in *The New Ezra Pound Studies*, ed. Mark Byron (Cambridge: Cambridge University Press, 2020), 216, 213, 214.

76. Historical note: Mussolini practiced coup thuggery unto outright political assassination against his elected political and social opponents. Pound explicitly shakes off his clear knowledge of fascist violence with the excuse that he did not see it with his very own eyes. Ezra Pound, *Jefferson and/or Mussolini: L'idea Statale, Fascism as I Have Seen It* [1935] (New York: Liveright, 1970), 51.

77. Lawrence Rainey, "Between Mussolini and Me," *London Review of Books* 21, no. 6 (March 18, 1999).

78. Pound, *Jefferson and/or Mussolini*, 34, 113.

79. Ezra Pound, "Murder by Capital" [1933], in *Selected Prose, 1909–1965*, ed. William Cookson (New York: New Directions, 1973), 228.

80. "Ezra Pound," interview by Donald Hall, 39.

81. His cracker-barrel, folk-dialect broadcasts had enough understandable substance to support a charge of treason in wartime (he stated that Allied troops were fighting the wrong enemy); perhaps ironically this charge took no account of Pound's own polemical contexts for his statements and slogans. Further, his many articles for both British fascist periodicals (like *British Union Quarterly*) and Italian ones (*Meridiano di Roma*) made no secret of his allegiances as opinion.

82. Ezra Pound, *The Pisan Cantos* [1948], ed. Richard Sieburth (New York: New Directions, 2003). Sieburth's introduction is clear on ambiguities and sub rosa allegiance.

83. Pound, *Guide to Kulchur*, 55. The context surrounding this affirmation contains angry rhetoric about siloed scholarship that prevents "correlation of learning" (55, 54). Pound is the scholar-warrior: he "has struggled in vain for corrections" to useless assumptions. He has "howled in vain for odd bits of supplementary knowledge." He has wanted to make knowledge public; he is a martyr to "reading," described it as a form of suffering. A remarkable passage of pain (54, 54, 55).

84. Ezra Pound, *The Cantos* (1971; repr., New York: New Directions, 1996), 775, 82.

85. Pound, *The Cantos*, 784.

86. Pound, *The Cantos*, 816.

87. Pound, *The Cantos*, 817.

88. Pound, *Guide to Kulchur*, 295.

89. The preface to *Blue Fasa* identifies the "unending" claim of these poems beyond ego: "To pull the long song, the long poem, particularly the serial poem, the extended lyric, is to be taken over and to be taken afar." Nathaniel Mackey, *Blue Fasa* (New York: New Directions, 2015), xiv, xiii.

90. Nathaniel Mackey, *Paracritical Hinge: Essays, Talks, Notes, Interviews* (Madison: University of Wisconsin Press, 2005), 308, 309.

91. Mackey, *Blue Fasa*, xv, 144.

92. Mackey, *Tej Bet*, xvi, 324.

93. Mackey, *Tej Bet*, 156, 190.

94. Nathaniel Mackey, *Splay Anthem* (New York: New Directions, 2006), x; replayed and recollected by Mackey, in *Blue Fasa* and *Paracritical Hinge*. In *Blue Fasa* we are told it is 1971, "where the Andoumboulou / first / beckoned," when Mackey is randomly "spin-/ning discs" (99). He extended his founding story in the late 1980s by reading ethnographers Griaule and Dieterlen.

95. Mackey, *Splay Anthem*, xi.

96. Mackey, *Blue Fasa*, xi.

97. Mackey, *Splay Anthem*, xvi.

98. The first phase of the "long song," before *Double Trio*, is not called *Song of the Andoumboulou*, and Mackey has not sanctioned this or any general title. That set consists of book-length serial instances or chapbook articulations, individually titled (e.g., *Nod House*, *Blue Fasa*). Readers who confer any general title onto the works before *Double Trio* (possibly for convenience of handling) filter out the struggle or swing between the two section titles, and the bifurcated sounds (unsummarizable—but plausibly rasp and sublimity) that are part of the history and meanings of Mackey's long poem.

99. See Mackey, *Splay Anthem*, 18.

100. Mackey, *Blue Fasa*, xiii.

101. Mackey, *Splay Anthem*, 125.

102. Mackey, *Splay Anthem*, 78, 115.

103. Mackey, *Tej Bet*, 165; Nathaniel Mackey, *Nerve Church*, vol. 3 of *Double Trio* (New York: New Directions, 2021), 344.

104. Norman Finkelstein uses a differently inflected "logbook," arguing that Mackey's allusions to anthropological knowledge and spiritual rituals/initiation rites reveal the poet's "shamanic" subjectivity. Norman Finkelstein, *On Mt. Vision: Forms of the Sacred in Contemporary American Poetry* (Iowa City: University of Iowa Press, 2010).

105. See Mackey, *Paracritical Hinge*, 335ff.

106. Mackey, *Blue Fasa*, xv, xii.

107. Mackey, *Splay Anthem*, xi.

108. Mackey, *Blue Fasa*, 149.

109. Mackey, *Splay Anthem*, xiv.

110. Mackey, *Paracritical Hinge*, 125.

111. Nathaniel Mackey, *So's Notice*, vol. 2 of *Double Trio* (New York: New Directions, 2021), 46.

112. In "Projective Verse" Olson talks of Frances Boldereff as his sister-ear.

113. The serif also alludes to a fine line completing a letter in many typefaces (an extra, a small supplement); it also enriches the letters decoratively, as one sees from the contrasting *moderne* typefaces "sans serif." It is a defining "extra" or "surplus."

114. Mackey, *Blue Fasa*, 88.

115. Citations respectively from Nathaniel Mackey, *Nod House* (New York: New Directions, 2011), 3; and Nathaniel Mackey, *School of Udhra* (San Francisco: City Lights Books, 1993), 73 and 72.

116. Nathaniel Mackey, *Whatsaid Serif* (San Francisco: City Lights Books, 1998), 104.

117. Mackey, *Splay Anthem*, xi–xii.

118. Mackey, *Whatsaid Serif*, 107, 105.

119. Mackey, *Blue Fasa*, 14.

120. Mackey, *Blue Fasa*, 7.

121. Mackey, *Nod House*, 147.

122. Mackey, *Blue Fasa*, 63.

123. Mackey, *Tej Bet*, xv.

124. Mackey, *Eroding Witness* (Urbana: University of Illinois Press, 1985), 91–92, evoking Olivier Messiaen's end of time.

125. Mackey, *School of Udhra*, 67.

126. Mackey, *Nerve Church*, 337, 338.

127. H.D., *Trilogy*, in *Collected Poems, 1912–1944*, ed. Louis L. Martz (New York: New Directions, 1983), 570; Mackey, *Nerve Church*, 286.

128. Mackey, *Splay Anthem*, 26.

129. Mackey, *Tej Bet*, 93, 196, 278.

130. Mackey, *Tej Bet*, 282.

131. Mackey, *Tej Bet*, xvi.

132. Mackey, *Nerve Church*, 344.

133. Rachel Blau DuPlessis, "Statement on Poetics: Pleasures, Polemics, Practices, Stakes," in *Inciting Poetics: Thinking and Writing Poetry*, ed. Jeanne Heuving and Tyrone Williams (Albuquerque: University of New Mexico Press, 2019), 33.

134. Mackey, *Tej Bet*, xiv.

135. Mackey, *Tej Bet*, xvi.

136. Mackey, *Nerve Church*, 325.

137. Mackey, *Nerve Church*, 317ff. Sharing this information, Nathaniel Mackey noted "as in math, the 'i' makes it imaginary" (email to the author, September 2021).

138. "I played with an awkwardness they said was / true." Mackey, *Nerve Church*, 320.

139. Mackey, *Nerve Church*, 344, 337, 338.

140. Mackey, *Nerve Church*, 340.

141. This phrase is from Johanna Drucker's elegant typology of artist's books, books that have a special fascination for the emotional energy invested in them. Although neither Philip nor Brathwaite made their books as small-batch rarities (like artist's books), both bring the psychological—and political—commitment of the artist's book's aura into their long poem Books. Johanna Drucker, *The Century of Artists' Books* [1994]. (New York: Granary Books, 2004), 94ff.

142. M. NourbeSe Philip, *Zong! As Told to the Author by Setaey Adamu Boateng* (Middletown, CT: Wesleyan University Press, 2008), 210–11.

143. Philip, *Zong!*, 204, 205.

144. Philip, *Zong!*, 205.

145. Philip, a lawyer, practiced law for seven years in Canada. She was born in Trinidad and Tobago and has been in Canada since about 1970.

146. Philip, *Zong!*, 185–86, 186.

147. This book is thematically congruent with Philip's work in *She Tries Her Tongue, Her Silence Softly Breaks* (1989), including an emphasis on Greek myths of rape and abuse of female figures, the resetting of language as an answer to power, the rescuing of lost or obliterated voices, and a particular emphasis on the colonial destructions in the Caribbean.

148. M. NourbeSe Philip, "Sycorax, Spirit, and 'Zong!,'" interview by Jordon Scott, 2016, *Jacket2*, May 14, 2019.

149. Philip, *Zong!*, 57–182.

150. This is Philip's statement about her procedure of dissolution—to decode "a story locked in this text," a survey of the ethical rationale for rhetorical tactics that also critically negate sense and the so-called rational uses of language. Philip, *Zong!*, 191–201.

151. "In more than 60 readings/performances of Zong! that NourbeSe has presented in nine countries." "Zong!," M. NourbeSe Philip (website), nourbese.com.

152. Kamau Brathwaite, *Ancestors: A Reinvention of "Mother Poem," "Sun Poem" and "X/Self"* (New York: New Directions, 2001). Brathwaite's home island was Barbados; he had worked and lived in St. Lucia (at the University of the West Indies), in Jamaica, and also in Ghana, New York, and the UK. He had a Pan-Caribbean and internationalist sensibility.

153. Joseph Donahue's shorthand for a font (and attitude) that rejects "the regulatory function of conventional typography" within a postcolonial analysis of British prosody and university cultural residues of enslavement. Joseph Donahue, "Kamau Brathwaite's Videolect: Spirit and Letter," in *Ngugi wa Thiong'o: Texts and Contexts*, ed. Charles Cantalupo (Trenton, NJ: Africa World Press, 1995), 272.

154. Brathwaite, *Ancestors*, title page.

155. Brathwaite, *Ancestors*, copyright page.

156. Charles Pollard is keen to make the "Sycorax video-style" be a more complete and intense vision of nation-language "as distinct from 'Western' poetic and written conventions." Charles W. Pollard, *New World Modernisms: T. S. Eliot, Derek Walcott, and Kamau Brathwaite* (Charlottesville: University of Virginia Press, 2004), 121. Here, I argue further that Brathwaite comes to this intense visual text via the modernist vision of the political-cultural Book and via *Gesamtkunstwerk* claims of "carpenter," "dancer," computer-sculpture, these modes and practices expressing a long-poem poetics.

157. Brathwaite, *Ancestors* 119, 109, 105 in poster-font.

158. Paul Naylor offers an account of Brathwaite's prosodic shifts and discusses the problematic of the iambic pentameter line in a Caribbean context. Naylor, *Poetic Investigations: Singing the Holes in History* (Evanston, IL: Northwestern University Press, 1999), 143–45.

159. Edward Kamau Brathwaite, *Mother Poem* (Oxford: Oxford University Press, 1977), 38, compared to Brathwaite, *Ancestors*, 51. Note also the author's name on the Oxford publication.

160. Brathwaite, *Ancestors*, 72.

161. Brathwaite, *Mother Poem*, 56–64; Brathwaite, *Ancestors*, 86–95.

162. Brathwaite, *Mother Poem*, 121, 122.

163. Pollard, *New World Modernisms*, 31–33.

164. Pollard, *New World Modernisms*, 111–21.

165. Kamau Brathwaite, *ConVERSations (with Nathaniel Mackey)* (Staten Island, NY: We Press, 1999), 35.

166. I am aware that *ConVERSations* (1999) occurs before *Ancestors* is published (2001)—but clearly not before it was written; sheer vagaries of presses might explain this. The large-form book (8½ × 11 inches, or 21½ × 28 centimeters) was designed by Brathwaite.

167. Brathwaite, *ConVERSations*, 222.

168. As a preposition, *vers* is pluralist, meaning to, towards, about, around. As a noun it is mainly verse, poetry, line.

169. Brathwaite, *ConVERSations*, copyright page.

170. Brathwaite, *ConVERSations*, 86–87.

171. Brathwaite, *ConVERSations*, 38, 44, 45, 47, 117.

172. Brathwaite's is not the only "transgressive appropriation" evoking that play and its characters by postcolonial writers. Roberto Fernández Retamar presents Caliban as a figure of identification, used to explore the sign of marginality and resistance; Aimé Césaire has also retold that play, so too other novelists and theorists, including Sylvia Wynter. Rob Nixon, "Caribbean and African Appropriations of *The Tempest*," *Critical Inquiry* 13, no. 3 (Spring 1987): 557–78.

173. Drucker 1998, 139; Brathwaite *ConVERSations*, 207, 208.

174. Brathwaite *ConVERSations*, 214.

175. An archive is another kind of assemblage that undergirds some long poems, another cultural repository like the analogy of library or museum.

Chapter 5

1. Peter Middleton, *Expanding Authorship: Transformations in American Poetry since 1950* (Albuquerque: University of New Mexico Press, 2021), 258.

2. Charles Olson, *The Maximus Poems*, ed. George F. Butterick (Berkeley: University of California Press, 1983), 635; George F. Butterick, *A Guide to the Maximus Poems of Charles Olson* [1978] (Berkeley: University of California Press, 1980), xlvii. I assume "my color" alludes to the changes in his skin color with liver cancer. His wife, Betty Olson, was already dead. "My car" might be the one with "fetish status" that had to be replaced exactly. Tom Clark, *Charles Olson: The Allegory of a Poet's Life* (New York: W. W. Norton, 1991), 326.

3. "E-mail Interview with Ron Silliman, conducted by Thomas C. Marshall and Thomas A. Vogler, 1995–1997," in "Ron Silliman and the ALPHABET," special issue, *Quarry West* 34 (1998): 14.

4. Ron Silliman, "The Middle," email to the author, 2014.

5. Rachel Blau DuPlessis, *Surge: Drafts 96–114* (Cromer, UK: Salt, 2013), 160.

6. William Carlos Williams, *Paterson* [1946–51; 1958], ed. Christopher MacGowan (New York: New Directions, 1992), 202.

7. Williams, *Paterson*, xii, xiii.

8. Williams, *Paterson*, xiii, xiv. The titled *Paterson* VI, a handful of notations, was found among his papers at his death in 1963.

9. One curious demurral about the effectiveness of *Paterson* V comes from Ronald Johnson, whose desire for stasis and balance made him think that this fifth section "set [*Paterson*] off-kilter." Ronald Johnson, "An Interview with Ronald Johnson," by Peter O'Leary, in *Ronald Johnson: Life and Works*, ed. Joel Bettridge and Eric Murphy Selinger (Orono, ME: National Poetry Foundation, 2008), 561.

10. Williams, *Paterson*, xiv, 236.

11. Williams, *Paterson*, xiii.

12. It is difficult to date her work; she will often note places at the end or in the course of the cantos but rarely dates. Book I was published in 1993; Book II in 1997; Book III within the *Iovis Trilogy* in 2011.

13. Anne Waldman, *The Iovis Trilogy: Colors in the Mechanism of Concealment* (Minneapolis: Coffee House Press, 2011), 1004. It is unclear what this means—"identity" of a person who declared she was writing a "feminist epic"; identity of promising to end a threefold structure; or pressure from the publisher?

14. Waldman, *Iovis*, 1008.

15. Stéphane Mallarmé, "Dice Thrown" ["Un coup de dés"], trans. Brian Coffey, in *Selected Poetry and Prose*, ed. Mary Ann Caws (New York: New Directions, 1982), 107, 109, 115, 123, 127.

16. Kamau Brathwaite, *Ancestors: A Reinvention of "Mother Poem," "Sun Poem" and "X/Self"* (New York: New Directions, 2001), 466, 465.

17. From a 1976 Helen Frankenthaler talk, in Helen Frankenthaler, *Giving Up One's Mark: Helen Frankenthaler in the 1960s and 1970s*, curated by Douglas Dreishpoon (Buffalo: Albright-Knox Art Gallery, 2014), 7. Of course a poem may "tell you" to revise. Often they do.

18. Nathaniel Mackey, interview by A. L. Nielsen on his radio show *Incognito Lounge*, July 18, 1991, PennSound, https://writing.upenn.edu/pennsound/. With thanks to Matthew Carbery.

19. Yet if this poem is tending toward a lifelong work, it might be aversive to stop, given that necessity for continuing that we find with Scheherazade. Does keeping your poem going mean keeping yourself alive to continue to write it?

20. Robert Duncan, "The World Felt as Presence" [established text of the lecture on Olson, March 29, 1979], in *Imagining Persons: Robert Duncan's Lectures on Charles Olson*, ed. Robert J. Bertholf and Dale M. Smith (Albuquerque: University of New Mexico Press, 2017), 143.

21. We have arrived at Samuel Beckett as mantra.

22. David Antin, *John Cage Uncaged Is Still Cagey* (San Diego: Singing Horse Press, 2005), 69.

23. Ron Silliman, *Ketjak* [1974], in *The Age of Huts (compleat)* (Berkeley: University of California Press, 2007), 14.

24. As chapter 2 argues, in cosmological long poems, like Dante's, numbers become a serious argument proving, in the poem's allusions, structures, idea system, and structure itself, the poem's Ur-form (original apprehension) mirroring the cosmological universe.

25. Hélène Aji, "'Life' 'Drafts': Towards Two Non-Dogmatic Poetic Archives," in *Revue française d'études américaines*, no. 147 (2016): 80.

26. Ron Silliman, email correspondence with the author, April 9–10, 2010.

27. This is exactly an eclectic set of poems. Among other methodological elements that emerge from advancing this array (poems different in tone, subjectivity, goals, traditions, poetics) is that in the long-poem field as I see it, anything can be compared fruitfully to anything else because that comparative act helps to define the long poem in general.

28. Ammons's *Tape for the Turn of the Year* (in its first edition, 1965) is a 205-page mid-length long poem. Johnson's *ARK*, in its 1996 first edition, had no page numbers at all, but the 2013 Flood Edition book is 307 pages. The length for Hejinian's *My Life* depends on the edition, but circa 203 pages is accurate to the books in my library. The 2013 Wesleyan edition has 143 pages.

29. There are other ways to talk about this work, notably the daily life discussions, and ideas about representation and life-writing. See Andrew Epstein, *Attention Equals Life: The Pursuit of the Everyday in Contemporary Poetry and Culture* (Oxford: Oxford University Press, 2016), 110–55.

30. There is a striking picture of the roll on the cover of the 2012 *Chicago Review* issue (57, nos. 1/2) devoted to Ammons.

31. A. R. Ammons, "Correspondence with Denise Levertov," *Chicago Review* 57, nos. 1/2 (2012): 209.

32. A. R. Ammons, *Tape for the Turn* (New York: W. W. Norton, 1965), 14, 144, 16.

33. Ammons, *Tape for the Turn*, 66.

34. Ammons, *Tape for the Turn*, 192–197.

35. Ammons, *Tape for the Turn*, 205, 206, 204.

36. Ammons, *Tape for the Turn*, 188, 189.

37. Ammons, *Tape for the Turn*, 95–98.

38. A. R. Ammons, "The Art of Poetry: LXXIII," interview by David Lehman, *Paris Review* 38, no. 139 (Summer 1996), accessed January 21, 2019, from Literature Online, without original pagination.

39. "Interview with Ronald Johnson," by Peter O'Leary, 570.

40. Ronald Johnson, *Ark*, ed. Peter O'Leary (Chicago: Flood Editions, 2013), 53.

41. "Interview with Ronald Johnson," by Peter O'Leary, 564.

42. Incidentally, Johnson was quite annoyed at the popularity (*after* he had first used it) of Leonardo's Vitruvian Man, a nude form stretching out in his now-familiar circle, so that Johnson's evocation eventually had the unfortunate look of a cliché.

43. "Interview with Ronald Johnson," by Peter O'Leary, 565.

44. Johnson, *Ark*, 49.

45. Ronald Johnson, "Ark 38: Ariel's Songs to Prospero" [the birdsong canto], http://www.luxhominem.com. The matching Ark 37 is a *verbal* "quilt" describing and imitating Western birds, built of citations from Peterson's *Field Guide to the Birds*.

46. Johnson considered but rejected the idea that this Milton-based erasure work would serve as a "roof" over the rest of the poem and become the hundredth section. Such a roof would have had to open to allow the rocket launch, not technologically impossible. Johnson seriously debated the numerical choice between 99 and 100 sections.

47. Johnson, *Ark*, 23.

48. The work draws on the objectivist essays of the 1930s by Zukofsky where that taut poetics of sight-sound-intellection is enunciated.

49. A photo of spires of some of the Watts Towers is on the cover of the 1996 Living Batch edition of Ronald Johnson's *Ark*, the book incidentally unpaginated.

50. Johnson, *Ark*, 76–77, 181. He speaks of Charles Ives similarly, a knowledgeable musician, but "he was like me"; "he wanted to appear a naïf," as if to take the art back to a beginning "and then start all over again." "Interview with Ronald Johnson," by Peter O'Leary, 580.

51. "Interview with Ronald Johnson," by Peter O'Leary, 564, 565. "Endings—how does one know? I think that's part of becoming a poet" (565). In general, the frankness and charm of this interview are a tribute to the skill and commitment of interlocutor O'Leary.

52. Johnson: "I had all those big poems in front of me, *A*, and *The Cantos* and *Maximus* to look at. And I said, can I do this any differently? And as Robert Duncan pointed out [. . .] [I] was the only one to make it an architecture." "Interview with Ronald Johnson," by Peter O'Leary, 565.

53. It is possible that Johnson knew that Zukofsky's 1972 ending to his long poem, the canto "A"-24 was entirely selected from Zukofsky's prior works and arranged by Celia Zukofsky as a birthday gift to the poet; it is seriatim coauthorship.

54. "Interview with Ronald Johnson," by Peter O'Leary, 561.

55. Johnson, *Ark*, 311.

56. "Interview with Ronald Johnson," by Peter O'Leary, 561–62. You'd have to overlook Eliot's *Four Quartets* and Crane's *The Bridge*—evidently not confrères—fully to appreciate this point. He does acknowledge H.D.'s *Trilogy* (562).

57. "Interview with Ronald Johnson," by Peter O'Leary, 563.

58. Johnson, *Ark*, 311; see "Interview with Ronald Johnson," by Peter O'Leary, 561–63.

59. "Interview with Ronald Johnson," by Peter O'Leary, 563.

60. From a historian's point of view, the overgeneralized readings from dramatic but possibly random documents mix antiquarian scrambling of interesting tidbits and historicist overgeneralizations to make allegories of, and claims for historical tendencies from, too few sources, too little data.

61. In 1974, however, interviewed by Barry Alpert for *Vort*, Johnson said his inspiration then was Wordsworth's *The Prelude*, "a personal epic," "a spontaneous growth of mind." This poem, like many long poems, will always claim plural sources of poetic inspiration. "Ronald Johnson—An Interview" [1974], by Barry Alpert, in *Ronald Johnson: Life and Works*, ed. Joel Bettridge and Eric Murphy Selinger (Orono, ME: National Poetry Foundation, 2008), 550.

62. "Interview with Ronald Johnson," by Peter O'Leary, 563.

63. Johnson, *Ark*, 312.

64. "Interview with Ronald Johnson," by Peter O'Leary, 566.

65. "Interview with Ronald Johnson," by Peter O'Leary, 567.

66. In the first of the "Lives," she used 37 sections of 37 sentences arbitrarily, not "representing" each year of 37 years of her life but loosely suggesting she might; the second version, 45 sections with 45 sentences, necessitated 8 new sentences per year to be distributed within every section (that is, not tacked to the ends of any).

67. Lyn Hejinian, *The Language of Inquiry* (Berkeley: University of California Press, 2000), 159.

68. One does find things out, for example, circa age twenty-three, her being pregnant, then again about age twenty-six: "I couldn't join the demonstration because I was pregnant, and so I had revolutionary experience without taking revolutionary action," and about six years later, "A child is a real person, very lively." But unveiling a life is not the point. Nor is a "diary"—"the very word [. . .] depresses me." Lyn Hejinian, *My Life* (Los Angeles: Sun & Moon Press) [hereafter referred to as *My Life* II], respectively 60, 65, 77, 46.

69. Hejinian, *My Life* (Providence: Burning Deck, 1980) [hereafter referred to as *My Life* I], 87, 87, 87–88, 88.

70. Hejinian, *My Life* II, 92, 93. In section 41, in *My Life* II, those key sentences in 37 (*My Life* I) are alluded to, closing that section: "Such is the rhythm of cognition, and the obvious analogy is with music" (103).

71. Other genres—pastoral, diary (explicitly rejected), essay, adventures, prose poem, epigram, sketch, aphorism. The self-conscious *My Life in the Nineties* offers a further array of allusions to genres (melodrama, long poem, encyclopedia, scrapbook). Lyn Hejinian, *My Life in the Nineties* (New York: Shark Books, 2003), 7, 9, 8.

72. In an extraordinary extension or apologia, Hejinian spoke in 2004 about "what's missing from *My Life*." The paper is a social history of California and US issues suffusing her childhood, suggesting that the "family romance" veiled, obscured, and also walled off the materials of the 1940s—early 1960s—Japanese internment, xenophobia, loyalty oaths, anticommunism, polio. Lyn Hejinian, "What's Missing from *My Life*," paper presented at "Experimental Writing and Social Location," panel at Diasporic Avant-Gardes, conference at University of California, Irvine, November 19, 2004, photocopy in the author's possession.

73. None of these is required, but it remains interesting that almost all are skirted. The sense of writer singularity is strong—and compelling.

74. Hejinian, *My Life* II, 83.

75. Hejinian, *My Life* I, 81.

76. Hejinian, *My Life* II, 92–93.

77. Hejinian, *My Life* II, 93.

78. A reader might note with pleasure that there are, as if titled by Stein, three Lives.

79. Hejinian, *Language of Inquiry*, 44.

80. Hejinian, *Language of Inquiry*, 46.

81. Hejinian, *Language of Inquiry*, 47.

82. Robert Duncan, *Collected Later Poems and Plays*, ed. Peter Quartermain (Berkeley: University of California Press, 2014), xxxii.

83. Robert Duncan, *Collected Essays and Other Prose*, ed. James Maynard (Berkeley: University of California Press, 2014), 33.

84. Robert Duncan, "Charles Olson Memorial Lecture" [March 29, 1979], ed. Ammiel Alcalay et al., *Lost and Found: The CUNY Poetics Document Initiative*, ser. 2, no. 4 (Spring 2011): 35.

85. Duncan, "The World Felt as Presence," 149. Slightly different specific formulations provoked me to use both versions—lecture and essay—although they are not that different overall.

86. Duncan, "Charles Olson," 31.

87. Robert Duncan, *A Selected Prose*, ed. Robert J. Bertholf (New York: New Directions, 1995), 97.

88. Duncan *Collected Later Poems*, 301, 298; Duncan, *Selected Prose*, 98.

89. Stéphane Mallarmé, *Mallarmé*, trans. Anthony Hartley (Harmondsworth, England: Penguin Books, 1965), 189.

90. Duncan, "The World Felt as Presence," 144. "Finished his work" might refer exactly to *The Maximus Poems* themselves, or it may refer to an affirmation of poetic adequacy that Olson felt on his deathbed.

91. Olson, *Maximus*, 635.

92. Butterick, *Guide to Maximus*, xlvi, xlvii.

93. Duncan, "Charles Olson," 23; Duncan, "The World Felt as Presence," 144.

94. Duncan, "The World Felt as Presence," 144.

95. Duncan, "Charles Olson," 24; Duncan, "The World Felt as Presence," 144.

96. Duncan, "The World Felt as Presence," 144.

97. Duncan, "The World Felt as Presence," 144.

98. Robert Duncan and Charles Olson, *An Open Map: The Correspondence of Robert Duncan and Charles Olson*, ed. Robert J. Bertholf and Dale M. Smith (Albuquerque: University of New Mexico Press, 2017), 199, 200, 204.

99. Duncan, "The World Felt as Presence," 144.

100. Duncan, *Collected Later Poems*, xliii, 799–800.

101. Thanks to Peter Middleton for this revelation. Whatever were Duncan's motives in allowing the chapbook *Tribunals* ("Passages 31–35") into print with Black Sparrow Press—as visible on WorldCat (softcover edition of 1,000, hardcover of 250, along with a single-pamphlet enticement of "Passages 34"), he must have subsequently changed his position on any book publication of the title *Passages*.

102. Back cover of the 1996 Living Batch Press edition of *Ark*.

103. Duncan, *Collected Later Poems*, 800.

104. Duncan, *Collected Later Poems*, 800, from an essay in *Maps* 6 (1974).

105. Joseph Conte, *Unending Design: The Forms of Postmodern Poetry* (Ithaca, NY: Cornell University Press, 1991).

106. Duncan, *Collected Later Poems*, 581.

107. Robin Blaser, *The Holy Forest: Collected Poems of Robin Blaser*, ed. Miriam Nichols (Berkeley: University of California Press, 2006), xxv.

108. Duncan, "Charles Olson," 39.

109. Duncan, *Collected Later Poems*, 119.

110. Duncan, *Collected Later Poems*, 298.

111. Duncan, *Collected Later Poems*, 299.

112. This utopian totalizing resembles Wagner's conception of a *Gesamtkunstwerk*.

113. Robert Duncan, *H.D. Book*, ed. Michael Boughn and Victor Coleman (Berkeley: University of California Press, 2011), 173, 187.

114. Stephen Fredman, *Contextual Practice: Assemblage and the Erotic in Postwar Poetry and Art* (Stanford: Stanford University Press, 2010), 84. Fredman's central contribution studying "contextual practice" involves the literary-historical identifications of the social and cultural surround for Jess and Duncan, among other California artists, notably the Semina group with its aesthetic and liberatory positions.

115. Duncan, *Collected Essays*, 80.

116. Duncan, *H.D. Book*, 173; Paul Jaussen, *Writing in Real Time: Emergent Poetics from Whitman to the Digital* (Cambridge: Cambridge University Press, 2017), 22–27.

117. Duncan, *Collected Later Poems*, 293–300.

118. Steve McCaffery, "Blaser's Deleuzian Folds," in *Prior to Meaning: The Protosemantic and Poetics* (Evanston, IL: Northwestern University Press, 2001), 41.

119. Duncan, *Collected Essays*, 305.

120. Waldman, *Iovis*, 34.

121. George Oppen, *New Collected Poems*, ed. Michael Davidson (New York: New Directions, 2002), 211.

Bibliography

Adorno, Theodor. "Commitment." In *Notes to Literature*, vol. 2, edited by Rolf Tiedemann, translated by Shierry Weber Nicholsen, 76–94. New York: Columbia University Press, 1992.

Aji, Hélène. "'Life' 'Drafts': Towards Two Non-dogmatic Poetic Archives." *Revue française d'études américaines*, no. 147 (2016): 78–92.

Albright, Daniel. "Early Cantos I–XLI." In *The Cambridge Companion to Ezra Pound*, edited by Ira B. Nadel, 59–91. Cambridge: Cambridge University Press, 1999.

Alderman, Nigel. "Introduction: Pocket Epics: British Poetry after Modernism." *Yale Journal of Criticism* 13, no. 1 (2000): 1–2.

Ammons, A. R. "Correspondence with Denise Levertov." *Chicago Review* 57, nos. 1/2 (2012): 173–211.

———. "The Art of Poetry: LXXIII." Interview by David Lehman. *Paris Review* 38, no. 139 (Summer 1996): 62–91.

———. *Tape for the Turn of the Year*. New York: W. W. Norton, 1965.

Antin, David. *John Cage Uncaged Is Still Cagey*. San Diego: Singing Horse Press, 2005.

Araujo, Anderson. "Italian Fascism." In *The New Ezra Pound Studies*, edited by Mark Byron, 208–26. Cambridge: Cambridge University Press, 2020.

Ashbery, John. *Flow Chart*. New York: Alfred A. Knopf, 1991.

———. "An Interview in Warsaw with Piotr Sommer" [1980]. *Code of Signals: Recent Writings in Poetics*, edited by Michael Palmer, 294–314. Berkeley, CA: North Atlantic Books, 1983.

———. *Three Poems*. New York: Viking Press, 1972.

Bakhtin, M. M. "Discourse in Poetry and Discourse in the Novel." In *The Dialogic Imagination: Four Essays*, edited by Michael Holquist, translated by Caryl Emerson and Michael Holquist, 275–300. Austin: University of Texas Press 1981.

Barthes, Roland. *Preparation of the Novel: Lecture Courses and Seminars at the Collège de France (1978–1979 and 1979–1980)*. Translated by Kate Briggs. New York: Columbia University Press, 2011.

Bergvall, Caroline. *Alisoun Sings*. New York: Nightboat Books, 2019.

———. *Drift*. Brooklyn, NY: Nightboat Books, 2014.

———. *Meddle English*. Callicoon, NY: Nightboat Books, 2011.

———. "VIA: 48 Dante Variations" [final version 47]. In *Fig: goan atom 2*, 63–71. Cambridge: Salt, 2005.

Bernstein, Charles. *Content's Dream: Essays, 1975–1984*. Los Angeles: Sun & Moon Press, 1986.

———. *My Way: Speeches and Poems*. Chicago: University of Chicago Press, 1999.

Bernstein, M. A. *The Tale of the Tribe: Ezra Pound and the Modern Verse Epic*. Princeton: Princeton University Press, 1980.

Blaser, Robin. *The Astonishment Tapes: Talks on Poetry and Autobiography with Robin Blaser and Friends* [1974]. Edited by Miriam Nichols. Tuscaloosa: University of Alabama Press, 2015.

———. *The Fire: Collected Essays of Robin Blaser*. Edited by Miriam Nichols. Berkeley: University of California Press, 2006.

———. *The Holy Forest: Collected Poems of Robin Blaser*. Edited by Miriam Nichols. Berkeley: University of California Press, 2006.

———. "John Sakkis Interviews Robin Blaser" [2004]. *The Poker* 5 (Winter 2005): 61–73.

———. "Summary and Explanation of the Final Section of 'Great Companions: Dante Alighieri.'" Università d'Annuzio, April 22, 1997. http://writing.upenn.edu.

Boughn, Michael. "Olson's Buffalo." In *The World in Time and Space: Towards a History of Innovative American Poetry in Our Time*, edited by Edward Foster and Joseph Donahue, 34–48. Jersey City, NJ: Talisman House, 2001.

Brathwaite, Kamau. *Ancestors: A Reinvention of "Mother Poem," "Sun Poem," and "X/Self."* New York: New Directions, 2001.

———. *ConVERSations (with Nathaniel Mackey)*. Staten Island, NY: We Press, 1999.

———. *Mother Poem*. Oxford: Oxford University Press, 1977.

Brooks, Gwendolyn. *Annie Allen*. New York: Harper & Brothers. 1949.

———. *Blacks*. Chicago: David, 1987.

———. *Primer for Blacks*. Chicago: Third World Press, 1980.

———. *Report from Part One*. Detroit: Broadside Press, 1972.

———. *Selected Poems*. New York: Harper and Row, 1963.

Brooks, Gwendolyn, Keorapetse Kgositsile, Haki R. Madhubuti, and Dudley Randall. *A Capsule Course in Black Poetry Writing*. Detroit: Broadside Press, 1975.

Bruns, Gerald L. *What Are Poets For? An Anthropology of Contemporary Poetry and Poetics*. Iowa City: University of Iowa Press, 2012.

Bunting, Basil. *The Complete Poems*. Edited by Richard Caddel. Oxford: Oxford University Press, 1994.

Bush, Ronald. *The Genesis of Ezra Pound's "Cantos."* Princeton: Princeton University Press, 1976.

Butterick, George F. *A Guide to the Maximus Poems of Charles Olson* [1978]. Berkeley: University of California Press, 1980.

Byron, Mark, ed. *The New Ezra Pound Studies*. Cambridge: Cambridge University Press, 2020.

Carbery, Matthew. *Phenomenology and the Late Twentieth-Century American Long Poem*. Cham, Switzerland: Palgrave Macmillan, 2019.

Charters, Ann. *Olson/Melville: A Study in Affinity*. Berkeley, CA: Oyez, 1968.

Clark, Tom. *Charles Olson: The Allegory of a Poet's Life*. New York: W. W. Norton, 1991.

Cookson, William. *A Guide to the Cantos of Ezra Pound*. London: Croon Helm, 1985.

Coolidge, Clark. *A Book Beginning What and Ending Away*. New York: Fence Books, 2012.

Conte, Joseph. *Unending Design: The Forms of Postmodern Poetry*. Ithaca, NY: Cornell University Press, 1991.

Crane, Hart. *The Collected Poems of Hart Crane*. Edited by Waldo Frank. New York: Liveright, 1933.

Creeley, Robert. *The Collected Poems of Robert Creeley, 1975–2005*. Berkeley: University of California Press, 2006.

Crunden, Robert M. *American Salons: Encounters with European Modernism, 1885–1917*. New York: Oxford University Press, 1993.

Culler, Jonathan. "Apostrophe." In *The Pursuit of Signs: Semiotics, Literature, Deconstruction*, 135–54. New York: Cornell University Press, 1981.

———. *Theory of the Lyric*. Cambridge, MA: Harvard University Press, 2015.

Damon, Maria. *Postliterary America: From Bagel Shop Jazz to Micropoetries*. Iowa City: University of Iowa Press, 2011.

Dante. "Al poco giorno." In *Dante's Lyric Poetry*, edited and translated by Kenelm Foster and Patrick Boyde, 162–65. Oxford: Clarendon Press, 1967.

———. *Dante's Lyric Poetry*. Edited and translated by Kenelm Foster and Patrick Boyde. Oxford: Clarendon Press, 1967.

———. Dartmouth Dante Project. https://dante.dartmouth.edu.

———. *The Divine Comedy of Dante Alighieri: Inferno* [1980]. Translated by Allen Mandelbaum. New York: Bantam Books, Random House, 1982.

———. *The Divine Comedy of Dante Alighieri: Paradiso* [1982]. Translated by Allen Mandelbaum. New York: Bantam Books, Random House, 1986.

———. *The Divine Comedy of Dante Alighieri: Purgatorio* [1981]. Translated by Allen Mandelbaum. New York: Bantam Books, Random House, 1984.

———. Princeton Dante Project. Translated by Robert Hollander and Jean Hollander, 2000–2007. https://dante.princeton.edu.

Derrida, Jacques. "The Law of Genre" [1979, translated by Avital Ronell, 1980]. In *Acts of Literature*, edited by Derek Attridge, 221–52. New York: Routledge, 1992.

Dewey, Anne Day. "The Modern American Long Poem." In *The Cambridge Companion to Modern American Poetry*, edited by Walter Kaladjian, 65–76. New York: Cambridge University Press, 2015.

Dickie, Margaret. *On the Modernist Long Poem*. Iowa City: University of Iowa Press, 1986.

Donahue, Joseph. "Kamau Brathwaite's Videolect: Spirit and Letter." In *Ngugi wa Thiong'o: Texts and Contexts*, edited by Charles Cantalupo, 271–82. Trenton, NJ: Africa World Press, 1995.

Drucker, Johanna. *The Century of Artists' Books* [1994]. New York: Granary Books, 2004.

Duncan, Robert. "Charles Olson Memorial Lecture" [March 29, 1979]. Edited by Ammiel Alcalay et al. *Lost and Found: The CUNY Poetics Document Initiative*, ser. 2, no. 4 (Spring 2011).

———. *Collected Essays and Other Prose*. Edited by James Maynard. Berkeley: University of California Press, 2014.

———. *Collected Later Poems and Plays*. Edited by Peter Quartermain. Berkeley: University of California Press, 2014.

———. *The H.D. Book*. Edited by Michael Boughn and Victor Coleman. Berkeley: University of California Press, 2011.

———. *A Selected Prose*. Edited by Robert J. Bertholf. New York: New Directions, 1995.

———. "The World Felt as Presence" [established text of the lecture on Olson, March 29, 1979]. In *Imagining Persons: Robert Duncan's Lectures on Charles Olson*, edited by Robert J. Bertholf and Dale M. Smith, 141–55. Albuquerque: University of New Mexico Press, 2017.

Duncan, Robert, and Charles Olson. *An Open Map: The Correspondence of Robert Duncan and Charles Olson*. Edited by Robert J. Bertholf and Dale M. Smith. Albuquerque: University of New Mexico Press, 2017.

DuPlessis, Rachel Blau. "After the Long Poem." *Dibur*, no. 4. Summer 2017.

———. *Blue Studios: Poetry and Its Cultural Work*. Tuscaloosa: University of Alabama Press, 2006.

———. *Drafts 1–38, Toll*. Middletown, CT: Wesleyan University Press, 2001.

———. *DRAFTS: Drafts 39–57, Pledge, with Draft, unnumbered: Précis*. Cambridge: Salt, 2004.

———. *H.D.: The Career of That Struggle*. Bloomington: Indiana University Press, 1986.

———. *Pitch: Drafts 77–95*. London: Salt, 2010.

———. *Purple Passages: Pound, Eliot, Zukofsky, Olson, Creeley, and the Ends of Patriarchal Poetry*. Iowa City: University of Iowa Press, 2012.

———. "Statement on Poetics: Pleasures, Polemics, Practices, Stakes." In *Inciting Poetics: Thinking and Writing Poetry*, edited by Jeanne Heuving and Tyrone Williams, 13–37. Albuquerque: University of New Mexico Press, 2019.

———. *Surge: Drafts 96–114*. Cromer, UK: Salt, 2013.

———. *Torques: Drafts 58–76*. Cambridge: Salt, 2007.

Edmond, Jacob. "Long, Wide, Deep, Heavy." Paper presented at Short Takes on the Long Poem, Aotearoa conference, Auckland, NZ, March 2012.

———. *Make It the Same: Poetry in the Age of Global Media*. New York: Columbia University Press, 2019.

Eliot, T. S. *Collected Poems, 1909–1962*. London: Faber and Faber, 1963.

———. *Selected Essays* [1951]. London: Faber and Faber, 1963.

———. "Ulysses, Order, and Myth." In *The Waste Land*, edited by Michael North, 128–30. New York: W. W. Norton, 2001.

———. *The Waste Land. A Facsimile and Transcript of the Original Drafts Including the Annotations of Ezra Pound*. Edited by Valerie Eliot. New York: Harcourt Brace Jovanovich, 1971.

———. "What Dante Means to Me." In *The Poets' Dante: Twentieth-Century Responses*, edited by Peter S. Hawkins and Rachel Jacoff, 28–39. New York: Farrar Straus, 2001.

Ellmann, Richard. *Yeats: The Man and the Masks*. London: Faber and Faber, 1961.

Epstein, Andrew. *Attention Equals Life: The Pursuit of the Everyday in Contemporary Poetry and Culture*. Oxford: Oxford University Press, 2016.

Finkelstein, Norman. *On Mt. Vision: Forms of the Sacred in Contemporary American Poetry*. Iowa City: University of Iowa Press, 2010.

Fisher, Allen. *Imperfect Fit: Aesthetic Function, Facture, and Perception in Art and Writing since 1950*. Tuscaloosa: University of Alabama Press, 2016.

Follett, Danielle. "Tout et n'importe quoi: The Total Artwork and the Aesthetics of Chance." In *The Aesthetics of the Total Artwork: On Borders and Fragments*, edited by Ake Finger and Danielle Follett, 86–109. Baltimore: Johns Hopkins University Press, 2011.

Fowler, Alastair. "Transformations of Genre" [1982]. In *Modern Genre Theory*, edited by David Duff, 232–49. Oxfordshire: Routledge, 2014.

Fowler, Alastair, and Roland Greene. "Numerology." In *Princeton Encyclopedia of Poetry and Poetics*, 4th ed., edited by Roland Greene. Princeton: Princeton University Press, 2012.

Frankenthaler, Helen. *Giving Up One's Mark: Helen Frankenthaler in the 1960s and 1970s*. Curated by Douglas Dreishpoon. Buffalo, NY: Albright-Knox Art Gallery, 2014.

Fredman, Stephen. *Contextual Practice: Assemblage and the Erotic in Postwar Poetry and Art*. Stanford: Stanford University Press, 2010.

Friedlander, Ben. "Charles Olson Now." *Olson Now* (blog), May 27, 2006. http://olsonnow.blogspot.com.

Friedman, Susan Stanford. "When a 'Long' Poem Is a 'Big' Poem: Self-Authorizing Strategies in Women's Twentieth-Century 'Long Poems.'" *LIT* 2, no. 1 (1990): 9–25.

Golding, Alan. "From Pound to Olson: The Avant-Garde Poet as Pedagogue." *Journal of Modern Literature* 34, no. 1 (Fall 2010): 86–106.

Hart, Matthew. *Nations of Nothing but Poetry: Modernism, Transnationalism, and Synthetic Vernacular Writing*. New York: Oxford University Press, 2010.

Hawkins, Peter S., and Rachel Jacoff. *The Poets' Dante: Twentieth-Century Responses*. New York: Farrar, Straus and Giroux, 2001.

H.D. "Dante and His Circle." Manuscript at Beinecke Library, Yale University, YCAL MSS 24, box 43, folder 1103.

———. *Helen in Egypt*. New York: New Directions, 1961.

———. *Trilogy*. In *Collected Poems, 1912–1944*, edited by Louis L. Martz. New York: New Directions, 1983.

Hejinian, Lyn. *A Border Comedy*. New York: Granary Books, 2001.

———. *The Language of Inquiry*. Berkeley: University of California Press, 2000.

———. *My Life*. Providence, RI: Burning Deck, 1980.

———. *My Life*. Los Angeles: Sun & Moon Classics, 1987.

———. *"My Life" and "My Life in the Nineties."* Middletown, CT: Wesleyan University Press, 2013.

———. *My Life in the Nineties*. New York: Shark Books, 2003.

———. "What's Missing from *My Life*." Paper presented at "Experimental Writing and Social Location," panel at Diasporic Avant-Gardes, conference at University of California, Irvine, November 19, 2004.

Hentoff, Nat. "John Coltrane" [1976]. In *Reading Jazz: A Gathering of Autobiography, Reportage, and Criticism from 1919 to Now*, edited by Robert Gottlieb, 620–28. New York: Pantheon, 1996.

Herd, David, ed. *Contemporary Olson*. Manchester: Manchester University Press, 2015.

Heuving, Jeanne, ed. *Nathaniel Mackey "Destination Out": Essays on His Work*. Iowa City: University of Iowa Press, 2021.

———. *The Transmutation of Love and Avant-Garde Poetics*. Tuscaloosa: University of Alabama Press, 2016.

Heuving, Jeanne, and Tyrone Williams, eds. *Inciting Poetics: Thinking and Writing Poetry*. Albuquerque: University of New Mexico Press, 2019.

Homer. *The Odyssey*. Translated with an introduction by Emily Wilson. New York: W. W. Norton, 2018.

Howe, Susan. *The Liberties*. Guilford, CT: loon books, 1980.

Jabès, Edmond. "Providence" [Interview by Paul Auster, 1978]. In *The Art of Hunger: Essays, Prefaces, Interviews and "The Red Notebook,"* 144–69. New York: Penguin Books, 1997.

Jakobson, Roman. "What Is Poetry?" In *Language in Literature*, by Roman Jakobson, edited by Krystyna Pomorska and Stephen Rudy, 368–78. Cambridge, MA: Harvard University Press, 1987.

Jameson, Fredric. *The Benjamin Files*. London: Verso, 2020.

Jaussen, Paul. *Writing in Real Time. Emergent Poetics from Whitman to the Digital*. Cambridge: Cambridge University Press, 2017.

Johnson, Ronald. *ARK*. Albuquerque, NM: Living Batch Press, 1996.

———. *ARK*. Edited by Peter O'Leary. Chicago: Flood Editions, 2013.

———. "Ark 38: Ariel's Songs to Prospero" [the birdsong canto]. http://www.luxhominem.com.

———. "An Interview with Ronald Johnson." By Peter O'Leary. In *Ronald Johnson: Life and Works*, edited by Joel Bettridge and Eric Murphy Selinger, 561–85. Orono, ME: National Poetry Foundation, 2008.

———. *RADI OS*. Berkeley, CA: Sand Dollar Press, 1977.

———. "Ronald Johnson—An Interview" [1974]. By Barry Alpert. In *Ronald Johnson: Life and Works*, edited by Joel Bettridge and Eric Murphy Selinger, 545–59. Orono, ME: National Poetry Foundation, 2008.

———. "Take a Chisel to Write: Key to Briggflatts." *Sagetrieb* 14, no. 3 (Winter 1995): 7–17.

Kamboureli, Smaro. *On the Edge of Genre: The Contemporary Canadian Long Poem*. Toronto: University of Toronto Press, 1991.

Keller, Lynn. *Forms of Expansion: Recent Long Poems by Women*. Chicago: University of Chicago Press, 1997.

Kentridge, William. "Let Us Try for Once: 15 ½ Thoughts in the Library." Message from

the Brooklyn Public Library, December 9, 2018. https://www.bklynlibrary.org.
Kinsella, John. *Activist Poetics: Anarchy in the Avon Valley*. Edited with an introduction by Niall Lucy. Liverpool: Liverpool University Press, 2010.
———. "Ali Alizadeh Interviews John Kinsella." *Cordite Poetry Review*, December 1, 2009.
———. *Divine Comedy: Journeys through a Regional Geography: Three New Works*. New York: W. W. Norton, 2008.
Koepnick, Lutz. "Gesamtkunstwerk." In *The Cambridge History of Modernism*, edited by Vincent Sherry, 273–88. New York: Cambridge University Press, 2016.
Leggott, Michele. *Reading Zukofsky's "80 Flowers."* Baltimore: Johns Hopkins University Press, 1989.
Likht, Mikhl. "Procession Three." Translated by Merle Bachman. In *Recovering "Yiddishland": Threshold Moments in American Literature*, by Merle Bachman, 226–47. New York: Syracuse University Press, 2008.
Mackey, Nathaniel. *Blue Fasa*. New York: New Directions, 2015.
———. *Double Trio* [comprising *Tej Bet* (vol. 1), *So's Notice* (vol. 2), and *Nerve Church* (vol. 3)]. New York: New Directions, 2021.
———. *Eroding Witness*. Urbana: University of Illinois Press, 1985.
———. Interview by A. L. Nielsen. July 18, 1991. PennSound. https://writing.upenn.edu/pennsound/.
———. "Epic World." Interview by Joseph Donahue. May 6, 2014. Poetry Foundation. https://www.poetryfoundation.org.
———. *Nerve Church*. Vol. 3 of *Double Trio*. New York: New Directions, 2021.
———. *Nod House*. New York: New Directions, 2011.
———. *Paracritical Hinge: Essays, Talks, Notes, Interviews*. Madison: University of Wisconsin Press, 2005.
———. *School of Udhra*. San Francisco: City Lights Books, 1993.
———. *So's Notice*. Vol. 2 of *Double Trio*. New York: New Directions, 2021.
———. *Splay Anthem*. New York: New Directions, 2006.
———. *Tej Bet*. Vol. 1 of *Double Trio*. New York: New Directions, 2021.
———. *Whatsaid Serif*. San Francisco: City Lights Books, 1998.
Mallarmé, Stéphane. *The Book*. Translated by Sylvia Gorelick. Cambridge, MA: Exact Change, 2018.
———. "Dice Thrown" ["Un coup de dés"]. Translated by Brian Coffey. In *Selected Poetry and Prose*, edited by Mary Ann Caws, 103–27 New York: New Directions, 1982.
———. *Divigations* [1897]. Translated by Barbara Johnson. Cambridge, MA: Belknap Press of Harvard University Press, 2007.
———. *Le "Livre" de Mallarmé*. Edited by Jacques Sherer. Paris: Gallimard, 1957.
———. *Mallarmé*. Translated by Anthony Hartley. Harmondsworth, UK: Penguin Books, 1965.
———. *Selected Poetry and Prose*. Edited by Mary Ann Caws. New York: New Directions, 1982.
Materer, Timothy. *James Merrill's Apocalypse*. Ithaca, NY: Cornell University Press, 2000.
Mayer, Bernadette. *Midwinter Day*. Berkeley, CA: Turtle Island Foundation, 1982.

McCaffery, Steve. "Blaser's Deleuzian Folds." In *Prior to Meaning: The Protosemantic and Poetics*, 31–44. Evanston, IL: Northwestern University Press, 2001.

McHale, Brian. *The Obligation toward the Difficult Whole: Postmodernist Long Poems*. Tuscaloosa: University of Alabama Press, 2004.

Mead, Philip. "Connectivity, Community and the Question of Literary Universality: Reading Kim Scott's *Chronotope* and John Kinsella's *Commedia*." In *Republics of Letters: Literary Communities in Australia*, edited by Peter Kirkpatrick and Robert Dixon, 137–55. Sydney: Sydney University Press, 2012.

Meillassoux, Quentin. *The Number and the Siren: A Decipherment of Mallarmé's "Coup de Dés"* [2011]. Translated by Robin Mackay. New York: Urbanomic and Sequence Press, 2013.

Merrill, James. *The Book of Ephraim*. Annotated and introduced by Stephen Yenser. New York: Alfred A. Knopf, 2018.

———. *The Changing Light at Sandover* [1982]. With a new coda. New York: Alfred A. Knopf, 1992.

Middleton, Peter. *Expanding Authorship: Transformations in American Poetry since 1950*. Albuquerque: University of New Mexico Press, 2021.

———. "The Longing of the Long Poem." *Jacket Magazine* 40 (July 2010).

Morris, Adalaide. *How to Live/What to Do: H.D.'s Cultural Poetics*. Urbana: University of Illinois Press, 2003.

Morris, Adelaide, and Stephen Voyce. "Precarity, Poetics, and the Practice of Counter-mapping." In *Poetics and Precarity*, edited by Myung Mi Kim and Cristanne Miller, 117–43. Albany: State University of New York Press, 2018.

Mullen, Harryette. *Muse & Drudge*. Philadelphia: Singing Horse Press, 1995.

Murphet, Julien. "'Events Listening to Their Own Tremors': Zukofsky and Objective Anachrony." *Textual Practice* 26, no. 4 (2012): 707–27.

Nadel, Ira, ed. *The Cambridge Companion to Ezra Pound*. Cambridge: Cambridge University Press, 1999.

Naylor, Paul. *Poetic Investigations: Singing the Holes in History*. Evanston, IL: Northwestern University Press, 1999.

Nichol, bp. *Gifts, The Martyrology Book(s) 7&*. Toronto: Coach House Press, 1990–2003.

———. *The Martyrology, Book 5* [1982]. Facsimile ed. Toronto: Coach House Press, 1994.

Nichol, bp, and Steve McCaffery. "In Tens/tion: Dialoguing with bp." In *Tracing the Path: Reading≠Writing the Martyrology*, edited by Roy Miki, 72–94. Vancouver: Talonbooks, 1988.

Nixon, Rob. "Caribbean and African Appropriations of *The Tempest*." *Critical Inquiry* 13, no. 3 (Spring 1987): 557–78.

Notley, Alice. "Alice Notley" [January 1997]. In *Contemporary Authors Autobiography Series*, vol. 27, 221–40. Detroit: Gale, 1997.

———. *Alma, or The Dead Women*. New York: Granary Books, 2006.

———. *"Close to Me & Closer . . . (The Language of Heaven)" and "Désamère."* San Francisco: O Books, 1995.

———. *Coming After: Essays on Poetry*. Ann Arbor: University of Michigan Press, 2005.

———. *The Descent of Alette*. New York: Penguin Books, 1996.

———. "Epic and Women Poets." In *Disembodied Poetics: Annals of the Jack Kerouac School*, ed. Anne Waldman and Andrew Schelling, 103–9. Albuquerque: University of New Mexico Press, 1994.

———. *Grave of Light: New and Selected Poems*. Middletown, CT: Wesleyan University Press, 2006.

———. *Homer's Art*. Canton, NY: Institute of Further Studies, 1990.

———. "An Interview with Shawn Walker and Heather Starr." *COMBO: A Journal of Poetry and Poetics* 3 (Spring 1999): 40–49.

———. "Iovis Omnia Plena." *Chicago Review* 44 (1998): 117–29.

———. "What Can Be Learned from Dreams?" *Scarlet* 5 (September 1991): n.p. [18–21].

Notley, Alice, and Claudia Keelan. "A Conversation, September 2002–December 2003." *APR* [*American Poetry Review*] 33, no. 3 (May–June 2004): 15–19.

Notley, Alice, and Douglas Oliver, eds. *The Scarlet Cabinet. A Compendium of Books by Alice Notley & Douglas Oliver*. New York: Scarlet Editions, 1992.

Ogihara-Schuck, Eriko, and Anne Teo, eds. *Finding Francis: A Poetic Adventure*. Singapore: Ethos Books, 2015.

O'Hara, Frank. *Second Avenue*. New York: Totem Press, 1960.

Olson, Charles. *Call Me Ishmael* [1947]. With an introduction by Merton M. Sealts Jr. Baltimore: Johns Hopkins University Press, 1997.

———. *The Collected Poems of Charles Olson, Excluding the Maximus Poems*. Edited by George F. Butterick. Berkeley: University of California Press, 1987.

———. *The Maximus Poems*. Edited by George F. Butterick. Berkeley: University of California Press, 1983.

———. *Collected Prose*. Edited by Donald Allen and Benjamin Friedlander, with an introduction by Robert Creeley. Berkeley: University of California Press, 1997.

Olson, Charles, and Frances Boldereff. *Charles Olson and Frances Boldereff: A Modern Correspondence*. Edited by Ralph Maud and Sharon Thesen. With an introduction by Sharon Thesen. Middletown, CT: Wesleyan University Press, 1999.

Oppen, George. *New Collected Poems*. Edited by Michael Davidson. With a preface by Eliot Weinberger. New York: New Directions, 2002.

Perelman, Bob. *Modernism the Morning After*. Tuscaloosa: University of Alabama Press, 2017.

———. *The Trouble with Genius: Reading Pound, Joyce, Stein and Zukofsky*. Berkeley: University of California Press, 1994.

Philip, M. NourbeSe. *Looking for Livingstone: An Odyssey of Silence*. Stratford, ON: Mercury Press, 1991.

———. *She Tries Her Tongue: Her Silence Softly Breaks*. Charlottetown, PE: Ragweed Press, 1989.

———. "Sycorax, Spirit, and 'Zong!'" Interview by Jordon Scott. 2016. *Jacket2*, May 14, 2019.

———. *Zong! As Told to the Author by Setaey Adamu Boateng*. Middletown, CT: Wesleyan University Press, 2008.

Plimpton, George, ed. *Writers at Work: The Paris Review Interviews.* 2nd ser. New York: Penguin Books, 1979.

Poe, Edgar Allan. "The Poetic Principle" [1850]. In *Poetry, Tales, and Selected Essays,* 1431–54. New York: Library of America, 1996.

———. Preface to *Eureka: A Prose Poem.* New York: Geo. P. Putnam, 1848.

Pollard, Charles W. *New World Modernisms: T. S. Eliot, Derek Walcott, and Kamau Brathwaite.* Charlottesville: University of Virginia Press, 2004.

Pound, Ezra. *ABC of Reading.* New York: New Directions, 1934.

———. "An Anthology of Statements by Ezra Pound on the Cantos." In *A Guide to the Cantos of Ezra Pound,* ed. William Cookson, xvi–xxiii. London: Croon Helm, 1985.

———. *The Cantos.* 1971. Reprint, New York: New Directions, 1996.

———. [E.P.] "Desideria." *The Exile,* no. 3 (Spring 1928): 108.

———. "Ezra Pound." Interview by Donald Hall. 1962. In *Writers at Work: The Paris Review Interviews,* 2nd ser., ed. George Plimpton, 38–59. New York: Penguin Books, 1979.

———. *Gaudier-Brzeska, a Memoir* [1916; 2nd ed., 1918; with additions, 1934, 1960]. New York: New Directions, 1970.

———. *Guide to Kulchur* [1938]. London: Peter Owen, 1966.

———. *Impact: Essays on Ignorance and the Decline of American Civilization.* Edited by Noel Stock. Chicago: Henry Regnery, 1960.

———. *Jefferson and/or Mussolini: L'idea Statale, Fascism as I Have Seen It* [1935]. New York: Liveright, 1970.

———. *The Letters of Ezra Pound, 1907–1941.* Edited by D. D. Paige. New York: Harcourt, Brace & World, 1950.

———. *Literary Essays of Ezra Pound.* London: Faber and Faber, 1954.

———. *Lustra, with Earlier Poems.* New York: Alfred A. Knopf, 1917.

———. *Personae: The Collected Shorter Poems of Ezra Pound* [1926]. New York: New Directions, 1950.

———. *The Pisan Cantos* [1948]. Edited by Richard Sieburth. New York: New Directions, 2003.

———. *Polite Essays* [1937]. Freeport, NY: Books for Libraries Press, 1966.

———. *Pound/Joyce. The Letters of Ezra Pound to James Joyce, with Pound's Critical Essays and Articles about Joyce.* Edited by Forrest Read. New York: New Directions, 1967.

———. *Selected Prose, 1909–1965.* Edited with an introduction by William Cookson. New York: New Directions, 1973.

Rainey, Lawrence. "Between Mussolini and Me." *London Review of Books* 21, no. 6 (March 18, 1999).

Resnikoff, Ariel. "Louis Zukofsky and Mikhl Licht, 'A Test of Jewish American Modernist Poetics,' Part Two." *Jacket2,* September 19, 2013.

Retallack, Joan. *The Poethical Wager.* Berkeley: University of California Press, 2003.

Reznikoff, Charles. *Testimony: The United States, 1885–1890, Recitative.* New York: New Directions (with San Francisco Review), 1965.

Riley, Denise. *"Am I That Name?": Feminism and the Category of "Women" in History.* Minneapolis: University of Minnesota Press, 1988.

Said, Edward W. *On Late Style: Music and Literature against the Grain*. New York: Pantheon Books, 2006.

Shockley, Eve. *Renegade Poetics: Black Aesthetics and Formal Innovation in African American Poetry*. Iowa City: University of Iowa Press, 2011.

Scroggins, Mark. *The Poem of a Life: A Biography of Louis Zukofsky*. Emeryville, CA: Shoemaker, Hoard, 2007.

Silliman, Ron. *The Alphabet*. Tuscaloosa: University of Alabama Press, 2008.

———. "'As to Violin Music': Time in the Longpoem." *Jacket Magazine* 27 (April 2005).

———. "E-mail Interview with Ron Silliman, conducted by Thomas C. Marshall and Thomas A. Vogler, 1995–1997." In "Ron Silliman and the ALPHABET," special issue, *Quarry West* 34 (1998): 10–44.

———. "I Wanted to Write Sentences: Decision Making in the American Longpoem." *Sagetrieb* 11, no. 1 & 2 (Spring & Fall 1992): 11–20.

———. *Ketjak* [1974]. In *The Age of Huts (compleat)*. Berkeley: University of California Press, 2007.

———. "The New Sentence." In *The New Sentence*, 63–93. New York: Roof Books, 1987.

———. *Tjanting* [1981]. Great Barrington, MA: Figures, 1986.

———. "Un-seen, Ur-new: The History of the Longpoem and 'The Collage Poems of *Drafts*.'" *Jacket2*, December 14, 2011.

Spillers, Hortense. "Gwendolyn the Terrible: Propositions on Eleven Poems." In *Shakespeare's Sisters: Feminist Essays on Women Poets*, edited by Sandra Gilbert and Susan Gubar, 233–44. Bloomington: Indiana University Press, 1979.

Stark, Trevor. *Total Expansion of the Letter: Avant-Garde Art and Language after Mallarmé*. Cambridge, MA: MIT Press, 2020.

Stein, Gertrude. "Composition as Explanation" [1926]. In *Selected Writings of Gertrude Stein* [1946], edited by Carl Van Vechten, 513–23. New York: Modern Library, 1962.

Stoicheff, Peter. *The Hall of Mirrors: "Drafts & Fragments" and the End of Ezra Pound's "Cantos."* Ann Arbor: University of Michigan Press, 1995.

Strauss, David Levi. "Approaching *80 Flowers*." In *Code of Signals: Recent Writings in Poetics*, edited by Michael Palmer, 79–102. Berkeley, CA: North Atlantic Books, 1983.

Symons, Arthur. *The Symbolist Movement in Literature* [1899]. New York: E. P. Dutton, 1919.

von Hallberg, Robert. *Charles Olson: The Scholar's Art*. Cambridge, MA: Harvard University Press, 1978.

Waldman, Anne. "An Interview with Anne Waldman." By Edward Foster. *Talisman* 13 (Fall 1994/Winter 1995): 62–78.

———. "An Interview with Anne Waldman." By Lee Christopher. *AWP Chronicle* 28, no. 3 (December 1995): 1–6.

———. *The Iovis Trilogy: Colors in the Mechanism of Concealment*. Minneapolis: Coffee House Press, 2011.

———. *Kill or Cure*. New York: Penguin Books, 1994.

———. *Outrider: Essays, Poems, Interviews*. Albuquerque, NM: La Alameda Press, 2006.

———. *Trickster Feminism*. New York: Penguin Books, 2018.

———. *Vow to Poetry: Essays, Interviews, & Manifestos*. Minneapolis: Coffee House Press, 2001.

Whitman, Walt. *Leaves of Grass: Authoritative Texts, Prefaces*. Edited by Sculley Bradley and Harold W. Blodgett. New York: W. W. Norton, 1973.

Wieners, John. *WOMAN*. Vol. 3 of *A Curriculum of the Soul*. Canton, NY: Institute of Further Studies, 1972.

Williams, Raymond. *Marxism and Literature*. Oxford: Oxford University Press, 1977.

Williams, William Carlos. *The Autobiography of William Carlos Williams* [1951]. New York: New Directions, 1967.

———. *The Collected Poems of William Carlos Williams*. Vol. 1, *1909–1939*. Edited by A. Walton Litz and Christopher MacGowan. New York: New Directions, 1986.

———"Letter to an Australian Editor." *William Carlos Williams Review* 17, no. 2 (Fall 1991): 8–12.

———. "Marianne Moore" [1925]. In *Selected Essays of William Carlos Williams*, 121–31. New York: Random House, 1954.

———. *Paterson* [1946–51; 1958]. Edited by Christopher MacGowan. New York: New Directions, 1992.

Wolkstein, Diane, and Samuel Noah Kramer. *Inanna, Queen of Heaven and Earth: Her Stories and Hymns from Sumer*. New York: Harper & Row, 1983.

Yeats, W. B. *Essays and Introductions*. New York: Macmillan, 1961.

Zalamea, Fernando. *Synthetic Philosophy of Contemporary Mathematics*. Translated by Zachary Luke Fraser. Falmouth, UK: Urbanomic, 2012.

Z-site: A Companion to the Work of Louis Zukofsky. Curated by Jeffrey Twitchell-Waas. https://z-site.net.

Zukofsky, Louis. "A." Berkeley: University of California Press, 1978.

———. *Complete Short Poetry*. Baltimore: Johns Hopkins University Press, 1991.

———. "Louis Zukofsky Interviewed by L. S. Dembo (1968)." *Contemporary Literature* 10, no. 2 (Spring 1969): 203–19.

———, ed. *An "Objectivists" Anthology*. Le Beausset, Var, France: To, 1932.

———. *Prepositions+: The Collected Critical Essays* [1967]. Edited and with additional prose by Mark Scroggins. Middletown, CT: Wesleyan University Press, 2000.

Index